W9-CAE-900

JUL X X 2015

WITHDRAWN

CUMBERLAND COUNTY COLLEGE LIBRARY
P.O. BOX 517
CUMBERLAND, N.J. 08360

Twentieth-Century
Short Story Explication

Supplement V to the Third Edition

With Checklists of Books
and Journals Used

WARREN S. WALKER
Horn Professor Emeritus of English
Texas Tech University

THE SHOE STRING PRESS, INC.
1991

REFERENCE
NOT TO BE TAKEN FROM
THIS ROOM

ReF
Z
5917
S5
W33
1991
Supp.5

93-318

Third Edition, Supplement V
© 1991 The Shoe String Press, Inc.
Hamden, Connecticut 06514

All rights reserved

Printed in the United States of America

First edition published 1961
Supplement I to first edition published 1963
Supplement II to first edition published 1965
Second edition published 1967
Supplement I to second edition published 1970
Supplement II to second edition published 1973
Third edition published 1977
Supplement I to third edition published 1980
Supplement II to third edition published 1984
Supplement III to third edition published 1987
Supplement IV to third edition published 1989

The paper in this book meets the minimum requirements
of American National Standard for Information Sciences—Permanence
of Paper for Printed Library Materials, ANSI Z39.48–1984. ∞

Library of Congress Cataloging-in-Publication Data
(Revised for vol. 5)

Walker, Warren S.
Twentieth-century short story explication.
Includes indexes.
1. Short stories—Indexes.   2. Short story—
Bibliography.   I. Title.
Z5917.S5W33   1977, Suppl.   016.8093   80–16175
[PN3373]
ISBN 0–208–02299–6 (3rd Ed. S. V)
ISBN 0–208–01813–1 (v. 1)

For
Barbara K. Walker
Storyteller, Folklorist, and Scholar

CONTENTS

PREFACE

More than 5,400 entries are included in this twelfth volume of *Twentieth-Century Short Story Explication*. Of the 827 short story authors represented, 288 appear here for the first time, bringing to 2,304 the total number of authors covered in the Third Edition and its five Supplements. Notable among the newcomers are Hispanic and Japanese writers. Many of the former were lifted to prominence by the "Boom" in Latin-American literature which began in the third quarter of this century and continues apace. Only 4.8% of the fiction writers listed in the Third Edition (1977) were Hispanic, as opposed to 16.7% in this volume. Recent translation of Japanese literature into various Western languages invited a commensurate increase in criticism, with the result that 4.6% of the storytellers cited here are Japanese, compared with .8% in 1977.

Whatever the original language of the stories themselves, the explications are here limited to those published in the major languages of Western Europe. Although these parameters seem unduly restrictive, the fact of the matter is that they encompass the vast majority of critical studies on the genre. The growing numbers of competent Indian writers, for example, are far more frequently discussed in English than they are in Hindi or Bengali or Tamil. Similarly, despite the emphasis on indigenous languages among African states that were once colonies, their literary journals are usually printed in French or English.

Twentieth-Century Short Story Explication is a bibliography of interpretations that have appeared since 1900 of short stories published since 1800. The term *short story* here has the same meaning it carries in the Wilson Company's *Short Story Index*: "A brief narrative of not more than 150 average-sized pages." By *explication* I suggest simply interpretation or explanation of the meaning of the story, including observations on theme, symbol, and sometimes structure. This excludes from the bibliography what are essentially studies of sources, biographical data, and background materials. Occasionally there are explicatory passages cited in works otherwise devoted to these external considerations. All page numbers refer strictly to interpretive passages, not to the longer works in which they occur.

The profusion of interpretations generated in the "knowledge explosion" of recent decades required that, beginning with the Third Edition, we adopt a system of coding and consequently a format different from that used in the first two editions and their Supplements. Each book is cited by author or editor and a short title; the full title and publication data are provided in "A Checklist of Books Used"—and 625 were used in the compilation of this Supplement. For an article in a journal or an essay in a critical collection, the full publication information is provided in the text the first time the study is cited. In subsequent entries, only the critic's or scholar's name and a short title are used as long as these entries appear under the name of the same short story author; if an article or essay explicates stories of two or more authors, a complete initial entry is made for each author. As in previous volumes, we have again included a "Checklist of Journals Used"—and this time 364 were used. This should be especially helpful to students who may not be familiar with titles of professional journals, much less the abbreviations for such titles.

Supplement V extends the coverage of interpretations through December 31, 1988. Although most of its entries were published during 1987 and 1988, there are also included (1) earlier interpretations that were unavailable or had been overlooked previously, and (2) new reprintings of earlier studies. An asterisk preceding an entry indicates that the item is a reprinting of an explication listed in the Third Edition.

In the preparation of this book I have been indebted to the editors of such journals as *PMLA, Modern Fiction Studies, Studies in Short Fiction,* and *Journal of Modern Literature.* I wish to extend thanks to the Interlibrary Loan Department of Texas Tech University Library, especially to its chairperson, Amy Chang, and her industrious assistant, Carol Roberts. As usual, I am most grateful to my wife, Barbara K. Walker, for her blue pencil and her gimlet-eyed scrutiny of my text.

Warren S. Walker
Texas Tech University

LEE K. ABBOTT

"Time and Fear and Somehow Love"
Pope, Dan. "The Post-Minimalist American Story; or, What Comes after
Carver?" *Gettysburg R,* 1 (1988), 338–339.

YAHYA TAHER ABDULLAH

"Granddad Hasan"
Harlow, Barbara. "*Mismar Goha*: The Arab Challenge to Cultural Dependency,"
So Atlantic Q, 87 (1988), 122.

ABE KŌBŌ

"Red Cocoon"
Currie, William. "Abe Kōbō," in Swann, Thomas E., and Kinya Tsuruta, Eds.
. . . *Modern Japanese Short Story,* 1–4.

"Stick"
Currie, William. "Abe Kōbō," 5–8.

WALTER ABISH

"The Second Leg"
Varsava, Jerry A. "Walter Abish and the Topographies of Desire," *Thought,* 62
(1987), 301–302.

"This Is Not a Film This Is a Precise Act of Disbelief"
Varsava, Jerry A. "Walter Abish . . . ," 299–301.

ALICE ADAMS

"Barcelona"
Cassill, R. V. . . . *Instructor's Handbook,* 1.

"The Swastika on Our Door"
Charters, Ann, William E. Sheidley, and Martha Ramsey. *Instructor's Manual . . . ,* 2nd ed., 175.

BILL ADAMS

"God Rest You Merry, Gentlemen"
Perrine, Laurence, and Thomas R. Arp. *Instructor's Manual . . . ,* 7th ed., 33–
35.

EDWARD C. L. ADAMS

"The Animal Court"
O'Meally, Robert G. "Introduction," *Tales of the Congaree,* li.

"Big Charleston"
O'Meally, Robert G. "Introduction," 1.

"The Big Swamp of the Congaree"
O'Meally, Robert G. "Introduction," xlvi–xlviii.

"A Damn Nigger"
O'Meally, Robert G. "Introduction," lix–lx.

"A Freshet on the Congaree"
O'Meally, Robert G. "Introduction," xliv–xlv.

"Jonas"
O'Meally, Robert G. "Introduction," xlii–xliii.

"Thirteen Years"
O'Meally, Robert G. "Introduction," lx–lxi.

"Tournament in Heaven"
O'Meally, Robert G. "Introduction," xli–xlii.

ADALET AĞAOĞLU

"Come On, Let's Go"
Ervin, Ellen W. "Narrative Technique in the Fiction of Adalet Ağaoğlu," *Ede-biyat: J Middle Eastern Lit,* 1 N.S. (1987), 140–144.

SHMUEL [SHAY] YOSEF AGNON
[SHMUEL YOSEF CZACZKES]

"Another Face"
Hakak, Lev. "Sexual Symbols in 'Another Face' by S. Y. Agnon," *Hebrew Annual R,* 10 (1986), 95–108.

"Linen Man"
Wineman, Aryeh. "Agnon's 'Linen Man': Abraham and Satan in the Land of Ambiguity," *Prooftexts,* 7, i (1987), 65–71.

"The Sign"
Wineman, Aryeh. "Agnon: The Writer and His Town," *Jewish Book Annual,* 45 (1987–1988), 59.

JOSÉ AGUSTÍN

"Cual es la onda"
Menton, Seymour. *El Cuento Hispanoamericano,* II, 3rd ed., 311–313.

ILSE AICHINGER

"Eliza, Eliza"
Ratych, Joanne M. "Ilse Aichinger," in Daviau, Donald G., Ed. *Major Figures . . .*, 33–34.

CONRAD AIKEN

"Silent Snow, Secret Snow"
Harris, E. Lynn. "Snow as a Literary Image for a Schizophrenic State," *J Mental Imagery*, 10, ii (1986), 69–77.

AJÑEYA [SACCIDANANDA HIRANAND VATSYAYAN]

"Cursed"
Damsteegt, Theo. "Violence in the Age of Gandhi—Ajñeya's Early Short Stories," *Studien zum Indologie und Iranistik*, 11–12 (1986), 337–339.

"Hili-bon's Ducks"
Damsteegt, Th. "Ajñeya's 1947 Stories," *Brahmayidya*, 50 (1986), 228–230.

"Home Abandoned"
Damsteegt, Theo. "Violence in the Age of Gandhi . . . ," 343–344.

"An Incident in the Naga Mountains"
Damsteegt, Th. "Ajñeya's 1947 Stories," 232–234.

"Letterbox"
Damsteegt, Th. "Ajñeya's 1947 Stories," 223–224.

"Links"
Damsteegt, Theo. "Violence in the Age of Gandhi . . . ," 342–343.

"Major Chaudhri's Return"
Damsteegt, Th. "Ajñeya's 1947 Stories," 230–232.

"A Meeting"
Damsteegt, Theo. "Violence in the Age of Gandhi . . . ," 326–327.

"More Important Than Reason"
Damsteegt, Theo. "Violence in the Age of Gandhi . . . ," 335–337.

"Muslims Are Brothers"
Damsteegt, Th. "Ajñeya's 1947 Stories," 226–228.

"The Pagoda Tree"
Damsteegt, Theo. "Violence in the Age of Gandhi . . . ," 339–342.

"Providing a Refuge"
Damsteegt, Th. "Ajñeya's 1947 Stories," 221–223.

"Revenge"
Damsteegt, Th. "Ajñeya's 1947 Stories," 224–226.

"Shadow"
Damsteegt, Theo. "Violence in the Age of Gandhi . . . ," 333–335.

"There the Gods Live"
Damsteegt, Th. "Ajñeya's 1947 Stories," 219–221.

"The Traitor"
Damsteegt, Theo. "Violence in the Age of Gandhi . . . ," 327–333.

"Unblemished"
Damsteegt, Theo. "Violence in the Age of Gandhi . . . ," 324–326.

"The Words of a Cell"
Damsteegt, Theo. "Violence in the Age of Gandhi . . . ," 344–346.

AKUTAGAWA RYŪNOSUKE

"Autumn"
Yu, Beongcheon. *Akutagawa* . . . , 57–58.

"A Clod of Soil"
Yu, Beongcheon. *Akutagawa* . . . , 60–61.

"Cogwheels"
Yu, Beongcheon. *Akutagawa* . . . , 93–99.

"Creative Frenzy"
Yu, Beongcheon. *Akutagawa* . . . , 36–39.

"Death of a Convert"
Yu, Beongcheon. *Akutagawa* . . . , 104–105.

"Dialogue in Darkness"
Yu, Beongcheon. *Akutagawa* . . . , 99–100.

"The Flatcar"
Yu, Beongcheon. *Akutagawa* . . . , 55–56.

"The Garden"
Yu, Beongcheon. *Akutagawa* . . . , 58–60.

"The Hell Screen"
Kinya, Tsuruta. "Akutagawa Ryūnosuke," in Swann, Thomas E., and Kinya
    Tsuruta, Eds. . . . *Modern Japanese Short Story*, 11–19.
Yu, Beongcheon. *Akutagawa* . . . , 39–42.

"The House of Genkaku"
Yu, Beongcheon. *Akutagawa* . . . , 84–86.

"In the Grove"
Kinya, Tsuruta. "Akutagawa's 'In the Grove,'" in Takeda, Katsuhiko, Ed.
 . . . *Japanese Literature*, 95–104.
————. "Akutagawa Ryūnosuke," 20–36.
Yu, Beongcheon. *Akutagawa* . . . , 35–36.

"Kappa"
Kinya, Tsuruta. "Akutagawa Ryūnosuke," 37–44.
Yu, Beongcheon. *Akutagawa* . . . , 86–90.

"Kesa and Morito"
Yu, Beongcheon. *Akutagawa* . . . , 34–35.

"The Life of a Fool"
Yu, Beongcheon. *Akutagawa* . . . , 101–104.

"The Mirage"
Yu, Beongcheon. *Akutagawa* . . . , 90–93.

"Momotaro"
Yu, Beongcheon. *Akutagawa* . . . , 52–53.

"The Nose"
Yu, Beongcheon. *Akutagawa* . . . , 15–17.

"One Day of the Year's End"
Yu, Beongcheon. *Akutagawa* . . . , 73–74.

"Rashōmon"
Yu, Beongcheon. *Akutagawa* . . . , 27–28.

"Spiderthread"
Yu, Beongcheon. *Akutagawa* . . . , 22–26.

PEDRO ANTONIO DE ALARCÓN

"The Nail"
Hart, Patricia. *The Spanish Sleuth* . . . , 17–18.

LOUISA MAY ALCOTT

"Cupid and Chow-Chow"
Elbert, Sarah. *A Hunger for Home* . . . , 237–239.

"The Fate of the Forest"
Stern, Madeleine B. *A Double Life* . . . , 20–23.

"An Hour"
Elbert, Sarah. *A Hunger for Home* . . . , 159–160.

"M. L."
Elbert, Sarah. *A Hunger for Home* . . . , 148–149.

"The Marble Woman"
Elbert, Sarah. *A Hunger for Home* . . . , 177–178.

"Mountain Laurel and Maiden Hair"
Elbert, Sarah. *A Hunger for Home* . . . , 274–275.

"My Contraband" [same as "My Brothers"]
Elbert, Sarah. *A Hunger for Home* . . . , 134–135.

"Pauline's Passion and Punishment"
Elbert, Sarah. *A Hunger for Home* . . . , 171–172.

"Taming a Tartar"
Stern, Madeleine B. *A Double Life* . . . , 25–27.

"Transcendental Wild Oats"
Elbert, Sarah. *A Hunger for Home* . . . , 73–74.

IGNACIO ALDECOA

"Balada del Manzanares"
Brandenberger, Erna. *Estudios* . . . , 188–190.

BRIAN W. ALDISS

"Backwater"
Smith, Philip E. "*Last Orders* and First Principles for the Interpretation of Aldiss's Enigmas," in Collings, Michael R., Ed. *Reflections on the Fantastic* . . . , 76–77.

"Brothers of the Head"
Collings, Michael R. " 'Brothers of the Head': Brian W. Aldiss's Psychological Landscape," in Palumbo, Donald, Ed. *Spectrum of the Fantastic,* 119–126.

"Creatures of Apogee"
Smith, Philip E. "*Last Orders* . . . ," 72–73.

"Hothouse"
Silverberg, Robert. "Three Worlds of Wonder," *Foundation,* 38 (1987), 12–16.

"Last Orders"
Smith, Philip E. "*Last Orders* . . . ," 71–72.

CIRO ALEGRÍA

"Calixto Garmendia"
Early, Eileen. *Joy in Exile* . . . , 66–69.

"The Mother"
Early, Eileen. *Joy in Exile* . . . , 71–74.

"The Piece of Quartz"
Early, Eileen. *Joy in Exile* . . . , 69–71.

"The Stone Offering" [originally titled "The Stone and the Cross"]
Early, Eileen. *Joy in Exile* . . . , 62–66.

SHOLEM ALEICHEM [SHOLOM RABINOWITZ]

"Station Baranovich"
Boyarin, Jonathan. "Sholem-Aleykhem's 'Stantsye Baranovitsh,'" in Gelber, Mark H., Ed. *Identity and Ethos* . . . , 89–99.

EDWARD AL-KHARRAT

"Inside the Wall"
Al-Sharuni, Yusuf. "Edward Al-Kharrat," trans. Roger Allen, in Allen, Roger, Ed. *Modern Arabic Literature*, 184.

WOODY ALLEN

"The Kugelmass Episode"
Cassill, R. V. . . . *Instructor's Handbook*, 2–4.
Charters, Ann, William E. Sheidley, and Martha Ramsey. *Instructor's Manual* . . . , 2nd ed., 199–201.
Harty, John. "Allen's 'The Kugelmass Episode,'" *Explicator*, 46, iii (1988), 50–51.

CONCHA ALÓS

"La coraza"
Talbot, Lynn K. "La mujer y lo fantástico: *Rey de gatos* de Concha Alós," *Hispanic J*, 10, i (1988), 112–114.

"Cosmos"
Talbot, Lynn K. "La mujer y lo fantástico . . . ," 107–109.

"El legroso"
Talbot, Lynn K. "La mujer y lo fantástico . . . ," 109–110.

"Mariposas"
Talbot, Lynn K. "La mujer y lo fantástico . . . ," 110–112.

"La otra bestia"
Talbot, Lynn K. "La mujer y lo fantástico . . . ," 106–107.

FUAD AL-TIKIRLI

"The Other Face"
Al-Talib, Umar. "Fuad Al-Tikirli," trans. Roger Allen, in Allen, Roger, Ed.
   Modern Arabic Literature, 323–324.

RUDOLFO ANAYA

"The Silence of the Llano"
Schiavones, James D. "Distinct Voices in the Chicano Short Story: Anaya's Out-
   reach, Portillo Trambley's Outcry, Rosaura Sánchez's Outrage," *Americas*,
   16, ii (1988), 69–73.

"El Velorio"
Schiavones, James D. "Distinct Voices . . . ," 73.

HANS CHRISTIAN ANDERSEN

"The Shadow"
Koelb, Clayton. *Invention of Reading* . . . , 202–220.

"The Snow Queen"
Blum, Joanne. *Transcending Gender* . . . , ix–xi.

POUL ANDERSON

"Call Me Joe"
McGregor, Gaile. *The Noble Savage* . . . , 236–237.

"Captive of the Centaurianess"
Bogert, Judith. "From Barsoom to Giffard: Sexual Comedy in Science Fiction
   and Fantasy," in Palumbo, Donald, Ed. *Erotic Universe* . . . , 92–93.

"Duel on Syrtis"
McGregor, Gaile. *The Noble Savage* . . . , 255–256.

"Sister Planet"
McGregor, Gaile. *The Noble Savage* . . . , 257–258.

SHERWOOD ANDERSON

"The Book of the Grotesque"
Fischer, Andreas. "Context-Free and Context-Sensitive Literature: Sherwood
   Anderson's *Winesburg, Ohio* and James Joyce's *Dubliners*," in Forsyth, Neil,
   Ed. *Reading Contexts*, 24–25.

"Brother Death"
Townsend, Kim. *Sherwood Anderson*, 282.

"Death in the Woods"
Kennedy, Thomas E. "Fiction as Its Own Subject: An Essay and Two Examples: Anderson's 'Death in the Woods' and Weaver's 'The Parts of Speech,'" *Kenyon R,* 9, iii (1987), 65–67.
Sheidley, William E., and Ann Charters. *Instructor's Manual . . . ,* 65–66; Charters, Ann, William E. Sheidley, and Martha Ramsey. *Instructor's Manual . . . ,* 2nd ed., 67–68.

"Hands"
Fischer, Andreas. "Context-Free . . . ," 13–18.
Sheidley, William E., and Ann Charters. *Instructor's Manual . . . ,* 63; Charters, Ann, William E. Sheidley, and Martha Ramsey. *Instructor's Manual . . . ,* 2nd ed., 65.
Townsend, Kim. *Sherwood Anderson,* 104–108.
White, Ray L. "Socrates in *Winesburg,*" *Notes Mod Am Lit,* 10, i (1986), Item 2.

"I'm a Fool"
*Perrine, Laurence, and Thomas R. Arp. *Instructor's Manual . . . ,* 7th ed., 7–8.

"The Man Who Became a Woman"
Townsend, Kim. *Sherwood Anderson,* 195–197.

"The Mother"
Nims, Margaret. "Sherwood Anderson's Use of Setting and Sexual Symbolism in 'The Mother,'" *J Evolutionary Psych,* 8, iii–iv (1987), 219–222.

"Paper Pills"
Cowan, James C. "The *Pharmakos* Figure in Modern American Stories of Physicians and Patients," *Lit & Med,* 6 (1987), 98–100.

"The Philosopher"
Cowan, James C. "The *Pharmakos* Figure . . . ," 97–98.

"The Rabbit Pen"
Townsend, Kim. *Sherwood Anderson,* 85–86.

"Seeds"
Townsend, Kim. *Sherwood Anderson,* 139–140.

"Tandy"
Arcana, Judith. "'Tandy': At the Core of *Winesburg,*" *Stud Short Fiction,* 24 (1987), 66–70.
Bidney, Martin. "Anderson and the Androgyne: 'Something More Than Man or Woman,'" *Stud Short Fiction,* 25 (1988), 263–264.

RENOS APOSTOLIDIS

"The John of My Life"
Lambropoulos, Vassilis. *Literature as National Institution . . . ,* 133–139.

AHARON APPELFELD

"To the Isle of St. George"
Shaked, Gershon. *The Shadow Within* . . . , 18.

MAX APPLE

"Eskimo Love"
Wilde, Alan. *Middle Grounds* . . . , 146–155.

"Pizza Time"
Wilde, Alan. *Middle Grounds* . . . , 149–150.

"Small Island Republics"
Wilde, Alan. *Middle Grounds* . . . , 28–30.

"Vegetable Love"
Wilde, Alan. *Middle Grounds* . . . , 138–140.

DEMETRIO AQUILERA MALTA

"En cholo que se vengó"
Menton, Seymour. *El Cuento Hispanoamericano,* II, 69–70; 2nd ed., 69–70; 3rd
    ed., 283–284.

FRANCISCO ARCELLANA

"Benediction"
Nudas, Alfeo G. *Telic Contemplation* . . . , 67–74.

"Christmas Gift"
Nudas, Alfeo G. *Telic Contemplation* . . . , 41–53.

"The Flowers of May"
Nudas, Alfeo G. *Telic Contemplation* . . . , 61–67.

"The Mats"
Nudas, Alfeo G. *Telic Contemplation* . . . , 53–61.

"Thy Kingdom Come"
Nudas, Alfeo G. *Telic Contemplation* . . . , 82–88.

"The Wing of Madness"
Nudas, Alfeo G. *Telic Contemplation* . . . , 74–82.

HUMBERTO ARENAL

"El caballero Charles"
Menton, Seymour. *El Cuento Hispanoamericano,* II, 3rd ed., 259–261.

REINALDO ARENAS

"El hijo y la madre"
Bush, Andrew. "The Riddled Text: Borges and Arenas," *Mod Lang Notes,* 103
    (1988), 374–397.

RAFAEL ARÉVALO MARTÍNEZ

"Galatea"
Klein, Dennis A. "The Supernatural Elements in Selected Short Stories of Ra-
    fael Arévalo Martínez," *Monographic R,* 4 (1988), 63.

"Las glándulas endocrinas"
Klein, Dennis A. "The Supernatural Elements . . . ," 62–63.

"El hombre que parecía un caballo"
Herszenhorn, Jaime. "Modernismo, surrealismo y expresionismo en 'El hombre
    que parecía un caballo,'" in Jiménez, José O., Ed. *Estudios críticos . . . ,* 269–
    280.
Klein, Dennis A. "The Supernatural Elements . . . ," 60–62.

"La signatura de la esfinge"
Menton, Seymour. *El Cuento Hispanoamericano,* I, 210–211; 2nd ed., 210–211;
    3rd ed., 210–212.

"El trovador colombiano"
Klein, Dennis A. "The Supernatural Elements . . . ," 63–64.

GUILLERMO ARGUEDAS

"Quico"
Menton, Seymour. *El Cuento Costarricense,* 30–31.

JOSÉ MARÍA ARGUEDAS

"The Agony of Rasu-Niti"
Columbus, Claudette K. *Mythological Consciousness . . . ,* 113–114.

"Los escoleros"
Columbus, Claudette K. *Mythological Consciousness . . . ,* 111.

"Orovilca"
Columbus, Claudette K. *Mythological Consciousness . . . ,* 131.

ANTONIO ARGÜELLO

"Yo y la negra histérico-musical"
Menton, Seymour. *El Cuento Costarricense,* 25.

MANUEL ARGÜELLO MORA

"Margarita"
Menton, Seymour. *El Cuento Costarricense,* 13–14.

AYI KWEI ARMAH

"An African Fable"
Amaizo, Eliane. "La Femme, la terre et la nouvelle: Une Lecture de 'An African Fable,'" *Commonwealth Essays,* 8, i (1985), 102–106.

ACHIM VON ARNIM

"Die Majoratsherren"
Oesterle, Günter. "'Illegitimate Kreuzungen': Zur Ikonität und Temporalität des Grotesken in Achim von Arnim's 'Die Majoratsherren,'" *Études Germaniques,* 43, i (1988), 25–51.

JUAN JOSÉ ARREOLA

"The Switchman"
Bruce-Novoa, Juan D. "Rulfo y Arreola: Dos vias hacia lo mismo," *Monographic R,* 4 (1988), 25–32.
Burt, John R. "This Is No Way To Run a Railroad: Arreola's Allegorical Railroad and a Possible Source," *Hispania,* 71 (1988), 806–811.
Knapp, Bettina. "Arreola's 'The Switchman'—The Train and the Desert Experience," *Confluencia,* 3, i (1987), 85–94.
Menton, Seymour. *El Cuento Hispanoamericano,* II, 230–232; 2nd ed., 230–232; 3rd ed., 124–126.

IGNACIO ARRIOLA HARO

"Cuarto menguante"
Beverido Duhalt, Francisco. "El verdadero tiempo de agonía," *Texto Crítico,* 13 (1987), 164–184.

ISAAC ASIMOV

"Dreaming Is a Private Thing"
Blish, James. "The Arts in Science Fiction," in Chauvin, Cy, Ed. *A Multitude . . . ,* 61–62.

"The Evitable Conflict"
Hassler, Donald M. "Some Asimov Resonances from the Enlightenment," *Sci-Fiction Stud,* 15 (1988), 38–40.

"Liar"
Allen, Virginia, and Terri Paul. "Science and Fiction: Ways of Theorizing about
    Women," in Palumbo, Donald, Ed. *Erotic Universe* . . . , 171–172.

"Nightfall"
Berger, Albert I. "Theories of History and Social Order in *Astounding Science
    Fiction*, 1934–1955," *Sci-Fiction Stud*, 15 (1988), 19–20.

"Trends"
Berger, Albert I. "Theories of History . . . ," 17–18.

MARGARET ATWOOD

"Betty"
Davey, Frank. *Margaret Atwood* . . . , 147–148.

"Bluebeard's Egg"
Davey, Frank. *Margaret Atwood* . . . , 146–147.

"Dancing Girls"
Davey, Frank. *Margaret Atwood* . . . , 141–142.
Thompson, Lee B. "Minuets and Madness: Margaret Atwood's *Dancing Girls*,"
    in Davidson, Arnold, and Cathy Davidson, Eds. *The Art of Margaret At-
    wood* . . . , 112–113.

"Giving Birth"
Brown, Russell. "Atwood's Sacred Wells," *Essays Canadian Writing*, 17 (Spring,
    1980), 39–41; rpt. McCombs, Judith, Ed. *Critical Essays* . . . , 226–227.
Davey, Frank. *Margaret Atwood* . . . , 142–143.
Thompson, Lee B. "Minuets and Madness . . . ," 117–119.

"The Grave of the Famous Poet"
Thompson, Lee B. "Minuets and Madness . . . ," 113–114.

"Hair Jewellery"
Davey, Frank. *Margaret Atwood* . . . , 134–135.

"Hurricane"
Davey, Frank. *Margaret Atwood* . . . , 146.

"The Lives of Poets"
Thompson, Lee B. "Minuets and Madness . . . ," 115.

"Loulou; or, The Domestic Life of the Language"
Davey, Frank. *Margaret Atwood* . . . , 143–144.

"The Man from Mars"
Davey, Frank. *Margaret Atwood* . . . , 130–131.
Thompson, Lee B. "Minuets and Madness . . . ," 111–112.

"Polarities"
Davey, Frank. *Margaret Atwood* . . . , 131–132.

Thompson, Lee B. "Minuets and Madness . . . ," 121.

"Rape Fantasies"
Cassill, R. V. . . . *Instructor's Handbook,* 4–6.
Davey, Frank. *Margaret Atwood . . . ,* 133–134.
Perrine, Laurence, and Thomas R. Arp. *Instructor's Manual . . . ,* 6th ed., 69–71; 7th ed., 84–87.
Thompson, Lee B. "Minuets and Madness . . . ," 115–116.

"The Resplendent Quetzal"
Brown, Russell. "Atwood's Sacred Wells," 17–21, 33, 37, 38–39; rpt., revised, McCombs, Judith, Ed. *Critical Essays . . . ,* 217–221, 224–226.
Thompson, Lee B. "Minuets and Madness . . . ," 114–115.

"Scarlet Ibis"
Davey, Frank. *Margaret Atwood . . . ,* 150–151.

"Significant Moments in the Life of My Mother"
Davey, Frank. *Margaret Atwood . . . ,* 144–146.

"The Sin Eater"
Davey, Frank. *Margaret Atwood . . . ,* 148–149.

"Spring Song of the Frogs"
Davey, Frank. *Margaret Atwood . . . ,* 150.

"Training"
Davey, Frank. *Margaret Atwood . . . ,* 140–141.
Thompson, Lee B. "Minuets and Madness . . . ," 117.

"A Travel Piece"
Davey, Frank. *Margaret Atwood . . . ,* 137–140.
Rigney, Barbara H. *Margaret Atwood,* 108–109.
Thompson, Lee B. "Minuets and Madness . . . ," 116–117.

"Uglypuss"
Davey, Frank. *Margaret Atwood . . . ,* 150.

"Under Glass"
Davey, Frank. *Margaret Atwood . . . ,* 132–133.
Thompson, Lee B. "Minuets and Madness . . . ," 119–120.

"Unearthing Suite"
Davey, Frank. *Margaret Atwood . . . ,* 151–152.

"The War in the Bathroom"
Davey, Frank. *Margaret Atwood . . . ,* 130.
Thompson, Lee B. "Minuets and Madness . . . ," 110–111.

"When It Happens"
Charters, Ann, William E. Sheidley, and Martha Ramsey. *Instructor's Manual . . . ,* 2nd ed., 218–219.

Davey, Frank. *Margaret Atwood* . . . , 135–136.
Thompson, Lee B. "Minuets and Madness . . . ," 119.

MAX AUB

"Juan Luis Cisniega"
Brandenberger, Erna. *Estudios* . . . , 213–216.

NAPOLÉON AUBIN

"My Voyage to the Moon"
Gouanvic, Jean-Marc. "Rational Speculation in French Canada, 1839–1947,"
    trans. Martin Gauthier and Renée Lallier, *Sci-Fiction Stud,* 15 (1988), 72–
    73.

LOUIS AUCHINCLOSS

"The Arbiter"
O'Sullivan, M. "Postlapsarians: Louis Auchincloss's *The Winthrop Covenant,*"
    Dutch Q R, 18, i (1988), 41–43.

"The Covenant"
O'Sullivan, M. "Postlapsarians . . . ," 38–39.

"The Diplomat"
O'Sullivan, M. "Postlapsarians . . . ," 40–41.

"The Fall"
O'Sullivan, M. "Postlapsarians . . . ," 39–40.

"In the Beauty of the Lilies Christ Was Born Across the Sea"
O'Sullivan, M. "Postlapsarians . . . ," 41.

"The Martyr"
O'Sullivan, M. "Postlapsarians . . . ," 40.

"The Penultimate Puritan"
O'Sullivan, M. "Postlapsarians . . . ," 44–45.

"The Triplets"
O'Sullivan, M. "Postlapsarians . . . ," 43–44.

WILLIAM AUSTIN

"Martha Gardner, or Moral Reaction"
Thomas, Brook. *Cross-Examinations* . . . , 51–52.

FRANCISCO AYALA

"El ángel de Bernini, mi ángel"
Brandenberger, Erna. *Estudios . . .* , 349–350.

CHINGIZ AYTMATOV

"The Early Cranes"
Lowe, David. *Russian Writing Since 1953 . . .* , 68–69.

AZORÍN [JOSÉ MARTÍNEZ RUIZ]

"El secreto oriental"
Joiner, Lawrence D., and Joseph W. Zdenek. "Two Neglected Stories of Azorín,"
    Stud Short Fiction, 15 (1978), 284–287; rpt. Joiner, Lawrence D. *Studies in
    Azorín,* ed. Joseph W. Zdenek, 66–67.

"El topacio"
Joiner, Lawrence D., and Joseph W. Zdenek. "Two Neglected Stories . . . ," 287–
    288; rpt. Joiner, Lawrence D. *Studies in Azorín,* ed. Joseph W. Zdenek, 67–
    69.

MARIANO AZUELA

"Domitilo Aspires to Congress"
Spell, Jefferson R. . . . *Spanish-American Fiction,* 80–81.

"Flies"
Spell, Jefferson R. . . . *Spanish-American Fiction,* 79–80.

SAMIRA AZZAM

"Because He Loved Them"
Piselli, Kathyanne. "Samira Azzam: Author's Works and Vision," *Int'l J Middle
    East Stud,* 20 (1988), 98.

"Bread of Sacrifice"
Piselli, Kathyanne. "Samira Azzam . . . , " 98–99.

"Cries of Joy"
Piselli, Kathyanne. "Samira Azzam . . . , " 96–97.

"The Feast Day from the Western Window"
Piselli, Kathyanne. "Samira Azzam . . . , " 100–101.

"Hajj Muhammad Sold His Hajj"
Piselli, Kathyanne. "Samira Azzam . . . , " 99–100.

"On the Road to Solomon's Pools"
Piselli, Kathyanne. "Samira Azzam . . . , " 97–98.

"Palestinian"
Piselli, Kathyanne. "Samira Azzam . . . , " 98.

ISAAC BABEL

"Alfonka Bida"
Luplow, Carol. . . . *Red Cavalry*, 37.

"The Church at Novograd"
Luplow, Carol. . . . *Red Cavalry*, 47–48.

"Crossing into Poland" [same as "Crossing the Zbruch"]
Luplow, Carol. . . . *Red Cavalry*, 47.

"Di Grasso"
Frieden, Gregory. "Fat Tuesday in Odessa: Isaac Babel's 'Di Grasso' as Testa-
    ment and Manifesto," *Russian R*, 40 (1981), 101–121; rpt. Bloom, Harold,
    Ed. *Isaac Babel*, 199–214.

"Gedali"
Friedberg, Maurice. "Yiddish Folklore Motifs in Isaac Babel's *Konarmija*," in
    Terras, Victor, Ed. *American Contributions . . .* , II, 198–199.
Luplow, Carol. . . . *Red Cavalry*, 32.

"Italian Sunshine"
Luplow, Carol. . . . *Red Cavalry*, 21.

"Kolyvushka"
Ziolkowski, Margaret. "The Reversal of Stalinist Literary Motifs: The Image of
    the Wounded Bird in Recent Russian Literature," *Mod Lang R*, 83, i (1988),
    111–112.

"My First Goose"
Sheidley, William E., and Ann Charters. *Instructor's Manual . . .* , 98–99; Char-
    ters, Ann, William E. Sheidley, and Martha Ramsey. *Instructor's Man-
    ual . . .* , 2nd ed., 100.

"Pan Apolek"
*Carden, Patricia. "*Red Cavalry*: Art Renders Justice," in Bloom, Harold, Ed.
    Isaac Babel, 123–124.
Luplow, Carol. . . . *Red Cavalry*, 54–57.

"The Rabbi"
Friedberg, Maurice. "Yiddish Folklore . . . ," 193–196.
Luplow, Carol. . . . *Red Cavalry*, 32.

"The Rabbi's Son"
Friedberg, Maurice. "Yiddish Folklore . . . ," 196–198.
Luplow, Carol. . . . *Red Cavalry*, 33.

INGEBORG BACHMANN

"A Step Toward Gomorrah"
Achberger, Karen. "Bachmann und die Bibel: 'Ein Schritt nach Gomorrah' als
    weibliche Schöpfungsgeschichte," in Höller, Hans, Ed. *Die dunkle Schat-
    ten . . .* , 97–110.
Vansant, Jacqueline. *Against the Horizon . . .* , 64–65.

MURRAY BAIL

"The Drover's Wife"
Bowering, George. *Imaginary Hand . . .* , I, 53–54.

RAY STANNARD BAKER [DAVID GRAYSON]

"Pippins"
Good, Howard. *Acquainted with the Night . . .* , 26–28.

W. BAKER-EVANS

"The Children"
Büssing, Sabine. *Aliens in the Home . . .* , 35–37.

JAMES BALDWIN

"Going to Meet the Man"
Freese, Peter. *Die amerikanische Kurzgeschichte . . .* , 313–318.

"The Man Child"
Freese, Peter. *Die amerikanische Kurzgeschichte . . .* , 308–310.

"The Outing"
Freese, Peter. *Die amerikanische Kurzgeschichte . . .* , 301–302.

"Previous Condition"
Freese, Peter. *Die amerikanische Kurzgeschichte . . .* , 264–301.

"Sonny's Blues"
Bieganowski, Ronald. "James Baldwin's Vision of Otherness: 'Sonny's Blues'
    and *Giovanni's Room*," *Coll Lang Assoc J*, 32 (1988), 69–80.
Byerman, Keith E. "Words and Music: Narrative Ambiguity in 'Sonny's Blues,' "
    Stud Short Fiction, 19 (1982), 367–372; rpt. Standley, Fred L., and Nancy V.
    Burt, Eds. *Critical Essays . . .* , 198–204.

Dixon, Melvin. *Ride Out the Wilderness . . .* , 136–137.
Freese, Peter. *Die amerikanische Kurzgeschichte . . .* , 303–308.

"This Morning, This Evening, So Soon"
Freese, Peter. *Die amerikanische Kurzgeschichte . . .* , 312–313.

LILIA S. BALISNOS

"The Box"
Lucero, Rosario Cruz. "Notes on the Contemporary Hiligaynon Short Story," *Solitary,* 108–109 (1986), 167–168.

HONORÉ BALZAC

"Gambara"
Knapp, Bettina L. *Music, Archetype . . .* , 32–44.

"The Girl with the Golden Eyes"
Kadish, Doris Y. "Hybrids in Balzac's 'La Fille aux yeux d'or,'" *Nineteenth-Century French Stud,* 16 (1988), 270–278.

"Gobseck"
Pasco, Allan H. *Novel Configurations . . .* , 51–71.

"The House of the Cat and the Racket"
Festa, Diana. "Linguistic Intricacies in Balzac's 'La Maison du Chat qui Pelote,'" *Nineteenth-Century French Stud,* 17 (1988), 30–43.

"The Succubus"
Nesci, Catherine. "Balzac et l'incontinence de l'histoire: À propos des *Contes drolatiques,*" *French Forum,* 13 (1988), 358–359.

TONI CADE BAMBARA

"The Hammer Man"
Charters, Ann, William E. Sheidley, and Martha Ramsey. *Instructor's Manual . . .* , 2nd ed., 216.
Hargrove, Nancy D. "The Comic Sense in the Short Stories of Toni Bambara," *Revista Canaria,* 11 (1985), 133, 136–137.

"The Lesson"
Hargrove, Nancy D. "The Comic Sense . . . ," 134–135.

"Maggie of the Green Bottles"
Hargrove, Nancy D. "The Comic Sense . . . ," 135–136.

"Mississippi Ham Rider"
Hargrove, Nancy D. "The Comic Sense . . . ," 137–138.

"My Man Bovanne"
Hargrove, Nancy D. "The Comic Sense . . . ," 134.

"Raymond's Run"
Hargrove, Nancy D. "The Comic Sense . . . ," 137.

"Sweet Town"
Hargrove, Nancy D. "The Comic Sense . . . ," 135.

IMAMU AMIRI BARAKA [formerly LE ROI JONES]

"The Alternative"
Fox, Robert E. *Conscientious Sorcerers* . . . , 23–24.

"Answers in Progress"
Fox, Robert E. *Conscientious Sorcerers* . . . , 26–27.

"Blank"
Fox, Robert E. *Conscientious Sorcerers* . . . , 28–29.

"Heroes"
Fox, Robert E. *Conscientious Sorcerers* . . . , 22–23.

JULES-AMÉDÉE BARBEY D'AUREVILLY

"Le Dessous de cartes d'une partie de whist"
Brooks, Peter. "The Storyteller," *Yale J Criticism*, 1, i (1987), 21–38.

BERNARDO M. BARCEBAL

"Ma'am Weds a Farmer"
Lucero, Rosario Cruz. "Notes on the Contemporary Hiligaynon Short Story," *Solitary*, 108–109, 168.

RUBÉN BAREIRO SAGUIER

"Diente por diente"
Andreu, Jean. "L'Île secrete de Rubén Bareiro Saguier," *Co-textes*, 14 (December, 1987), 67–78.

HÉCTOR BARRERA

"El Judas"
Melendez, Concha. *El arte del cuento* . . . , 250–251.

EDUARDO BARRIOS

"Antipathy"
Spell, Jefferson R. . . . *Spanish-American Fiction,* 150–151.

JOHN BARTH

"Ambrose His Mark"
Freese, Peter. *Die amerikanische Kurzgeschichte* . . . , 362–364.

"Anonymiad"
Freese, Peter. *Die amerikanische Kurzgeschichte* . . . , 376–379.
Gorak, Jan. *God the Artist* . . . , 165–166.
Ziegler, Heide. *John Barth,* 54–55.

"Bellerophoniad"
Levitt, Morton P. *Modernist Survivors* . . . , 119–120.
Ziegler, Heide. *John Barth,* 56–61.

"Dunyazadiad"
Bedetti, Gabriella. "Women's Sense of the Ludicrous in Barth's 'Dunyazadiad,' "
    Stud Am Humor, 4 N.S., i–ii (1985), 74–81.
Levitt, Morton P. *Modernist Survivors* . . . , 118–119.
Ziegler, Heide. *John Barth,* 61–62.

"Echo"
Freese, Peter. *Die amerikanische Kurzgeschichte* . . . , 384–385.

"Life-Story"
Cassill, R. V. . . . *Instructor's Handbook,* 6–7.
Olsen, Lance. "Neorealism, Postmodern Fantasy, and the American Short
    Story," in Logsdon, Loren, and Charles W. Mayes, Eds. *Since Flannery
    O'Connor* . . . , 127–128.

"Lost in the Funhouse"
Freese, Peter. *Die amerikanische Kurzgeschichte* . . . , 368–376.
Gorak, Jan. *God the Artist* . . . , 164.
Sheidley, William E., and Ann Charters. *Instructor's Manual* . . . , 170–172;
    Charters, Ann, William E. Sheidley, and Martha Ramsey. *Instructor's Man-
    ual* . . . , 2nd ed., 185–187.

"Menelaiad"
Freese, Peter. *Die amerikanische Kurzgeschichte* . . . , 379–384.
Ziegler, Heide. *John Barth,* 53–54.

"Night-Sea Journey"
Freese, Peter. *Die amerikanische Kurzgeschichte* . . . , 386–387.
Gorak, Jan. *God the Artist* . . . , 161–162.
Mistri, Zenobia. "Absurdist Contemplations of a Sperm in John Barth's 'Night-
    Sea Journey,' " *Stud Short Fiction,* 25 (1988), 151–152.

"Perseid"
Levitt, Morton P. *Modernist Survivors* . . . , 120–123.
Ziegler, Heide. *John Barth,* 56–61.

"Petition"
Freese, Peter. *Die amerikanische Kurzgeschichte* . . . , 385–386.

"Water Message"
Freese, Peter. *Die amerikanische Kurzgeschichte* . . . , 364–367.

DONALD BARTHELME

"The Balloon"
Owens, Clarke. "Donald Barthelme's Existential Acts of Art," in Logsdon, Loren, and Charles W. Mayes, Eds. *Since Flannery O'Connor* . . . , 76–78.

"Basil from Her Garden"
Wilde, Alan. *Middle Grounds* . . . , 162–166.

"The Emerald"
Wilde, Alan. *Middle Grounds* . . . , 234–238.

"The Indian Uprising"
Cassill, R. V. . . . *Instructor's Handbook,* 7–9.
McHale, Brian. *Postmodern Fiction,* 162–164.
Olsen, Lance. "Neorealism, Postmodern Fantasy, and the American Short Story," in Logsdon, Loren, and Charles W. Mayes, Eds. *Since Flannery O'Connor* . . . , 128–130.
Owens, Clarke. "Donald Barthelme's Existential Acts . . . ," 79–80.

"The Leaf"
Wilde, Alan. *Middle Grounds* . . . , 161–162.

"Me and Miss Mandible"
Herrscher, Walter. "Names in Donald Barthelme's Short Stories," *Names,* 34, ii (1986), 131–132.

"The President"
Charters, Ann, William E. Sheidley, and Martha Ramsey. *Instructor's Manual* . . . , 2nd ed., 189–190.

"A Shower of Gold"
Engler, Bernd. "Entwürfe der Wirklichkeit: Donald Barthelmes 'A Shower of Gold,'" in Halemann, Ulrich, Kurt Müller, and Klaus Weiss, Eds. *Wirklichkeit und Dichtung* . . . , 387–402.

"Some of Us Had Been Threatening Our Friend Colby"
Perrine, Laurence, and Thomas R. Arp. *Instructor's Manual* . . . , 6th ed., 62–64; 7th ed., 79–82.

HARRY BATES and DESMOND WINTER HALL

"A Scientist Rises"
Bartter, Martha A. *The Way to Ground Zero . . .* , 58–59.

CHARLES BAUDELAIRE

"La Fanfarlo"
Hannoosh, Michele. "The Function of Literature in Baudelaire's 'La Fanfarlo,'"
L'Esprit Createur, 28, i (1988), 42–55.

BARBARA BAYNTON

"Billy Skywokie"
Krimmer, Sally, and Alan Lawson, Eds. "Introduction," *The Portable Barbara
Baynton,* xx–xxii.

"Bush Church"
Krimmer, Sally, and Alan Lawson, Eds. "Introduction," xxiv–xxv.

"A Dreamer"
Krimmer, Sally, and Alan Lawson, Eds. "Introduction," xiv–xv.

PETER BEAGLE

"Come Lady Death"
Zahorski, Kenneth J. *Peter Beagle,* 80–85.

"Lila the Werewolf"
Zahorski, Kenneth J. *Peter Beagle,* 85–89.

"My Daughter's Name Is Sarah"
Zahorski, Kenneth J. *Peter Beagle,* 79–80.

"Telephone Call"
Zahorski, Kenneth J. *Peter Beagle,* 76–77.

"Thirty-Day Stretch"
Zahorski, Kenneth J. *Peter Beagle,* 77–78.

ANN BEATTIE

"The Burning House"
Cassill, R. V. . . . *Instructor's Handbook,* 10–12.

"Gravity"
McKinstry, Susan J. "The Speaking Silence of Ann Beattie's Voice," *Stud Short
Fiction,* 24 (1987), 112–113.

"In the White Night"
McKinstry, Susan J. "The Speaking Silence . . . ," 115–117.

"Janus"
Miller, Philip. "Beattie's 'Janus,'" *Explicator,* 46, i (1987), 48–49.

"Waiting"
Sheidley, William E., and Ann Charters. *Instructor's Manual . . . ,* 191; Charters,
    Ann, William E. Sheidley, and Martha Ramsey. *Instructor's Manual . . . ,* 2nd
    ed., 226–227.

SIMONE DE BEAUVOIR

"The Age of Discretion"
Fallaize, Elizabeth. *Simone de Beauvoir,* 155–160.

"Anne"
Keefe, Terry. *Simone de Beauvoir . . . ,* 143–144.

"Chantal"
Keefe, Terry. *Simone de Beauvoir . . . ,* 141–142.

"Lisa"
Keefe, Terry. *Simone de Beauvoir . . . ,* 142–143.

"Marcelle"
Keefe, Terry. *Simone de Beauvoir . . . ,* 140–141.

"Marguerite"
Keefe, Terry. *Simone de Beauvoir . . . ,* 144–145.

"Monologue"
Fallaize, Elizabeth. *Simone de Beauvoir,* 160–165.

"A Very Easy Death"
Cottrell, Robert. *Simone de Beauvoir,* 134–137.
Keefe, Terry. *Simone de Beauvoir . . . ,* 56–61.
Marks, Elaine. *Simone de Beauvoir . . . ,* 100–112.

"The Woman Destroyed"
Cottrell, Robert. *Simone de Beauvoir,* 142.
Fallaize, Elizabeth. *Simone de Beauvoir,* 165–171.

SAMUEL BECKETT

"All Strange Away"
Pilling, John. "Shards of Ends and Odds in Prose: From 'Fizzles' to 'The Lost
    One,'" in Gontarski, S. E., Ed. *On Beckett . . . ,* 172–173.

"The Calmative"
Hale, Jane A. *The Broken Window* . . . , 84–85.

"Enough"
Brienza, Susan D. *Samuel Beckett's New Worlds* . . . , 70–87.
Pilling, John. "Shards . . . ," 177–178.

"First Love"
Walton, S. Jean. "Extorting Love's Tale from the Banished Son: Origins of
    Narratability in Samuel Beckett's 'First Love,'" *Contemp Lit,* 29 (1988), 549–
    563.

"He Is Barehead"
Pilling, John. "Shards . . . ," 171.

"How It Is"
Brienza, Susan D. *Samuel Beckett's New Worlds* . . . , 88–120.

"Imagination Dead Imagine"
Brienza, Susan D. *Samuel Beckett's New Worlds* . . . , 120–138.
Pilling, John. "Shards . . . ," 173–174.

"The Lost Ones"
Brienza, Susan D. *Samuel Beckett's New Worlds* . . . , 139–159.
Pilling, John. "Shards . . . ," 178–179.

"Old Earth"
Pilling, John. "Shards . . . ," 171–172.

GUSTAVO ADOLFO BÉCQUER

"Los ojos verdes"
Rodríguez, Alfred, and Shirley Mangini González. "El amor y la muerte en
    'Los ojos verdes' de Bécquer," *Hispanofilia,* 29, ii (1986), 69–73.

MAX BEERBOHM

"The Crime"
Gilbert, Sandra M., and Susan Gubar. *No Man's Land* . . . , 126–129.

EMILIO S. BELAVAL

"Nuestra Cruz Menchaca"
Melendez, Concha. *El arte del cuento* . . . , 91–93.

SAUL BELLOW

"Cousins"
Weinstein, Ann. "Ijah, 'our cousins' keeper': Bellow's Paradigm of Man," *Saul
    Bellow J,* 7, ii (1988), 58–70.

"Dora"
McCadden, Joseph F. *The Flight from Women . . .* , 239–242.

"A Father-to-Be"
McCadden, Joseph F. *The Flight from Women . . .* , 231–235.

"The Gonzaga Manuscript"
McCadden, Joseph F. *The Flight from Women . . .* , 227–231.

"Him with His Foot in His Mouth"
Knight, Karl F. "Bellow's Shawmut: Rationalizations and Redemption," *Stud Short Fiction,* 24 (1987), 375–380.

"Leaving the Yellow House"
Gutierrez, Donald. *The Dark and the Light Gods . . .* , 91–102.
McCadden, Joseph F. *The Flight from Women . . .* , 213–218.
Marovitz, Sanford E. "Images of America in American-Jewish Fiction," in Fried, Lewis, Ed. *Handbook of American-Jewish Literature . . .* , 344–345.
Shear, Walter. "'Leaving the Yellow House': Hattie's Will," *Saul Bellow J,* 7, i (1988), 51–56.

"The Mexican General"
Marovitz, Sanford E. "Images of America . . . ," 345–346.

"Mosby's Memoirs"
McCadden, Joseph F. *The Flight from Women . . .* , 236–239.

"The Old System"
McCadden, Joseph F. *The Flight from Women . . .* , 218–222.

"Seize the Day"
Birindelli, Roberto. "Tamkin's Folly: Myths Old and New in 'Seize the Day' by Saul Bellow," *Saul Bellow J,* 7, ii (1988), 35–48.
Bowman, Diane K. "This Man Will Self-Destruct: Kafkaesque Ambiguity in Saul Bellow's 'Seize the Day,'" *McNeese R,* 28 (1981–1982), 34–43.
Clayton, John J. "Saul Bellow's 'Seize the Day': A Study of Midlife Transition," in Debusscher, Gilbert, and Marc Maufort, Eds. *American Literature . . .* , 135–147.
Costello, Patrick. "Tradition in 'Seize the Day,'" *Essays Lit,* 14, i (1987), 117–131.
Harap, Louis. *In the Mainstream . . .* , 107–109.
Loe, Thomas. "Modern Allegory and the Form of 'Seize the Day,'" *Saul Bellow J,* 7, i (1988), 57–66.
McCadden, Joseph F. *The Flight from Women . . .* , 89–108.
Scrafford, B. L. "Water and Stone: The Confluence of Textual Imagery in 'Seize the Day,'" *Saul Bellow J,* 6, ii (1987), 64–70.
Shechner, Mark. *After the Revolution . . .* , 132–134.
Stout, Janice P. "Suffering as Meaning in Saul Bellow's 'Seize the Day,'" *Renascence,* 39 (1987), 365–373.

"A Silver Dish"
Clayton, John. "A Rich Reworking," *Saul Bellow J,* 6, ii (1987), 19–25.

Ikeda, Chōko. "Narrative Devices in Saul Bellow's 'A Silver Dish,'" *Kyushu Am Lit*, 29 (1988), 31–39.

"What Kind of Day Did You Have?"
Knight, Karl F. "Bellow's Victor Wulpy: The Failure of Intellect," *Saul Bellow J*, 6, ii (1987), 26–35.
———. "Sexual Irony in Bellow's 'What Kind of Day Did You Have?'" *Notes Contemp Lit*, 17, ii (1987), 10–11.

JUAN BENET

"An Incomplete Line"
Compitello, Malcolm A. "Juan Benet and the New Spanish *Novela Negra*," *Monographic R*, 3 (1987), 213–214.

GREGORY BENFORD

"In Alien Flesh"
Benford, Gregory. "Effing the Ineffable," in Slusser, George E., and Eric S. Rabkin, Eds. *Alien . . .* , 24–25.

YITZHAK BEN NERO

"Nicole"
Fuchs, Esther. *Israeli Mythologies . . .* , 28–29.

ARNOLD BENNETT

"The Death of Simon Fuge"
Anderson, Linda R. *Bennett, Wells, and Conrad . . .* , 59–62.

HERMAN BERNSTEIN

"A Ghetto Romance"
Marovitz, Sanford E. "Images of America in American-Jewish Fiction," in Fried, Lewis, Ed. *Handbook of American-Jewish Literature . . .* , 318–319.

AMBROSE BIERCE

"A Baby Tramp"
Büssing, Sabine. *Aliens in the Home . . .* , 15–16.

"Chickamauga"
Büssing, Sabine. *Aliens in the Home . . .* , 98–99.

"Moxon's Master"
Bleiler, Everett F. "More on 'Moxon's Master,'" *Sci-Fiction Stud*, 15 (1988), 386–388.
Rottensteiner, Franz. "More on 'Moxon's Master,'" *Sci-Fiction Stud*, 15 (1988), 388–390.

"An Occurrence at Owl Creek Bridge"
Ames, Clifford R. "Do I Wake or Sleep?: Technique as Content in Ambrose Bierce's Short Story 'An Occurrence at Owl Creek Bridge,'" *Am Lit Realism*, 19, iii (1987), 52–67.
Linklin, Harriet K. "Narrative Technique in 'An Occurrence at Owl Creek Bridge,'" *J Narrative Technique*, 18 (1988), 137–152.
Sheidley, William E., and Ann Charters. *Instructor's Manual* . . . , 20–21; Charters, Ann, William E. Sheidley, and Martha Ramsey. *Instructor's Manual* . . . , 2nd ed., 23–24.

ADOLFO BIOY CASARES

"Mosca y Arañas"
Snook, Margaret L. "The Power Struggle: Gender and Voices in 'Mosca y Arañas' by Bioy Casares," *Monographic R*, 4 (1988), 268–277.

"La trama celeste"
Mignolo, Walter D. "Ficción fantástica y mundos posibles (Borges, Bioy y Blanqui)," in Schwartz Lerner, Lía, and Isaías Lerner, Eds. *Homenaje a Ana María Barrenechea*, 484–485.

MICHAEL BISHOP

"Blooded on Arachne"
McGregor, Gaile. *The Noble Savage* . . . , 276.

"Dogs' Lives"
Hassler, Donald M. "Enlightenment Genres and Science Fiction: Belief and *Animated Nature* (1774)," *Extrapolation*, 29 (1988), 326–327.

JEROME BIXBY

"It's a *Good* Life"
Büssing, Sabine. *Aliens in the Home* . . . , 107–108.

ALGERNON BLACKWOOD

"The Willows"
Varnado, S. L. *Haunted Presence* . . . , 121–123.

CLARK BLAISE

"The Salesman's Son Grows Older"
Darling, Michael. "The Psychology of Alienation: Clark Blaise's 'The Salesman's Son Grows Older,'" in Struthers, J. R. (Tim), Ed. *The Montreal Story Tellers* . . . , 140–147.
Ricou, Laurie. *Everyday Magic* . . . , 42–47.

WILLIAM H. BLAKE

"A Tale of the Grand Jardin"
Atwood, Margaret. "Canadian Monsters: Some Aspects of the Supernatural in Canadian Fiction," in Staines, David, Ed. *The Canadian Imagination* . . . , 101–103.

TOMÁS BLANCO

"Los aguinaldos del Infante: Glosa de Epifania"
Melendez, Concha. *El arte del cuento* . . . , 58–59.

"Cultura: Tres pasos y un encuentro"
Melendez, Concha. *El arte del cuento* . . . , 55–57.

"La Dragontea: Cuento de Semana Santa"
Melendez, Concha. *El arte del cuento* . . . , 59–60.

VICENTE BLASCO IBÁÑEZ

"The Last Lion"
Di Salvo, Thomas J. "El costumbrismo bajo una nueva luz: análisis de 'El último león' de Blasco Ibáñez," *Revista Canadiense*, 12 (1988), 317–326.

JAMES BLISH

"Against the Stone Beasts"
Ketterer, David. *Imprisoned* . . . , 40.

"Beep"
Ketterer, David. *Imprisoned* . . . , 227–232.

"Bindlestiff"
Ketterer, David. *Imprisoned* . . . , 179–180.

"Citadel of Thought"
Ketterer, David. *Imprisoned* . . . , 34–36.

"The City That Was the World"
Ketterer, David. *Imprisoned* . . . , 233–235.

"Common Time"
Ketterer, David. *Imprisoned . . .* , 222–227.
Silverberg, Robert. "Three Worlds of Wonder," *Foundation,* 38 (1987), 5–12.

"Darkside Crossing"
Ketterer, David. *Imprisoned . . .* , 235.

"A Dusk of Idols"
Ketterer, David. *Imprisoned . . .* , 138–139.

"First Strike"
Ketterer, David. *Imprisoned . . .* , 111.

"Get Out of My Sky"
Ketterer, David. *Imprisoned . . .* , 116–117.

"Let the Finder Beware"
Ketterer, David. *Imprisoned . . .* , 48–52.

"Mistake Inside"
Ketterer, David. *Imprisoned . . .* , 38–40.

"More Light"
Ketterer, David. *Imprisoned . . .* , 154–155.

"No Jokes on Mars"
Ketterer, David. *Imprisoned . . .* , 145–146.

"Okie"
Ketterer, David. *Imprisoned . . .* , 177–178.

"Our Binary Brothers"
Ketterer, David. *Imprisoned . . .* , 235–236.

"Sargasso of Lost Cities"
Ketterer, David. *Imprisoned . . .* , 180–182.

"Seeding Program"
Ketterer, David. *Imprisoned . . .* , 57–60.

"Skysign"
Ketterer, David. *Imprisoned . . .* , 148–149.

"Statistician's Day"
Ketterer, David. *Imprisoned . . .* , 236–237.

"Surface Tension"
Ketterer, David. *Imprisoned . . .* , 66–69.

"There Shall Be No Darkness"
Ketterer, David. *Imprisoned . . .* , 42–43.

"The Thing in the Attic"
Ketterer, David. *Imprisoned* . . . , 61–63.

"This Earth of Hours"
Ketterer, David. *Imprisoned* . . . , 260.

"To Pay the Piper"
Ketterer, David. *Imprisoned* . . . , 113–114.

"Tomb Tapper"
Ketterer, David. *Imprisoned* . . . , 115–116.

"Watershed"
Ketterer, David. *Imprisoned* . . . , 60–61.

"We All Die Naked"
Ketterer, David. *Imprisoned* . . . , 149–151.
McGregor, Gaile. *The Noble Savage* . . . , 238–239.

"The Writing of the Rat"
Ketterer, David. *Imprisoned* . . . , 114–115.

JAMES BLISH and JUDITH ANN BLISH

"Getting Along"
Ketterer, David. *Imprisoned* . . . , 156.

JAMES BLISH and DAMON KNIGHT

"The Weakness of RVOG"
Ketterer, David. *Imprisoned* . . . , 124–125.

HEINRICH BÖLL

"Arise, Please Arise"
Rosensprung, Ingrid. " 'Steh auf, steh doch auf,' " in Rosensprung, Ingrid, et al. [8]. *Interpretationen zu Heinrich Böll*, II, 9–16.

"The Balek Scales"
Burns, Robert A. *The Theme of Non-Conformity* . . . , 18–20.
Frank, Brigitte. " 'Die Waage der Baleks,' " in Rosensprung, Ingrid, et al. [8]. *Interpretationen zu Heinrich Böll*, II, 57–65.

"Business Is Business"
Kitzing, Elfriede. " 'Geschäft ist Geschäft,' " in Doderer, Klaus, et al. [5]. *Interpretationen zu Heinrich Böll*, I, 92–101.

"Daniel the Just"
Renken, Ute. "'Daniel der Gerechte,'" in Rosensprung, Ingrid, et al. [8]. *Interpretationen zu Heinrich Böll*, II, 66–80.

"The Death of Elsa Baskoleit"
Schäfer, Rudolf H. "'Der Tod der Elsa Baskoleit,'" in Rosensprung, Ingrid, et al. [8]. *Interpretationen zu Heinrich Böll*, II, 44–56.

"The Discarder"
Burns, Robert A. *The Theme of Non-Conformity . . .* , 16.
Macpherson, Enid. *A Student's Guide . . .* , 80–82.

"Dr. Murke's Collected Silences"
Macpherson, Enid. *A Student's Guide . . .* , 68.

"The Foragers"
Görk, Brigitte. "'Die Essenholer,'" in Doderer, Klaus, et al. [5]. *Interpretationen zu Heinrich Böll*, I, 23–32.

"In the Valley of the Thundering Hooves"
Macpherson, Enid. *A Student's Guide . . .* , 62–63.

"Like a Bad Dream"
Charters, Ann, William E. Sheidley, and Martha Ramsey. *Instructor's Manual . . .* , 2nd ed., 150–151.

"The Man with the Knives"
Abela, Elisabeth. "'Der Mann mit dem Messern,'" in Rosensprung, Ingrid, et al. [8]. *Interpretationen zu Heinrich Böll*, II, 17–31.
Reid, J. H. *Heinrich Böll . . .* , 66.

"Mate with the Long Hair"
Macpherson, Enid. *A Student's Guide . . .* , 53–54.

"The Message"
Macpherson, Enid. *A Student's Guide . . .* , 47–48.

"My Melancholy Face"
Reid, J. H. *Heinrich Böll . . .* , 68–69.

"Not Just at Christmas Time"
Burns, Robert A. *The Theme of Non-Conformity . . .* , 15–16.
Macpherson, Enid. *A Student's Guide . . .* , 67–68.
Reid, J. H. *Heinrich Böll . . .* , 78–80.

"On the Hook"
Beerheide, Hannelore. "'An der Angel,'" in Rosensprung, Ingrid, et al. [8]. *Interpretationen zu Heinrich Böll*, II, 32–43.

"Reunion in the Avenue"
Krödel, Angela. "'Wiedersehen in der Allee,'" in Doderer, Klaus, et al. [5]. *Interpretationen zu Heinrich Böll*, I, 33–41.
Macpherson, Enid. *A Student's Guide . . .* , 52, 56.

"Reunion with Drüng"
Macpherson, Enid. *A Student's Guide . . .* , 54–55.
Webert, Theo. "'Wiedersehen mit Drüng,'" in Doderer, Klaus, et al. [5]. *Interpretationen zu Heinrich Böll*, I, 66–91.

"Something Is Going to Happen"
Egger, Fritz. "'Es wird etwas geschehen,'" in Rosensprung, Ingrid, et al. [8]. *Interpretationen zu Heinrich Böll*, II, 94–101.
Macpherson, Enid. *A Student's Guide . . .* , 76–77.

"That Time in Odessa"
Macpherson, Enid. *A Student's Guide . . .* , 49–50.

"Traveler, You Will Come to a Spa"
Macpherson, Enid. *A Student's Guide . . .* , 51.
Weber, Albrecht. "'Wanderer, kommst du nach Spa,'" in Doderer, Klaus, et al. [5]. *Interpretationen zu Heinrich Böll*, I, 42–65.

"When War Broke Out"
Doderer, Klaus. "'Als der Krieg ausbrach,'" in Doderer, Klaus, et al. [5]. *Interpretationen zu Heinrich Böll*, I, 9–22.
Macpherson, Enid. *A Student's Guide . . .* , 48–49.

"Zimpren Railroad Station"
Seifried, Ulrike. "'Der Bahnhof von Zimpren,'" in Rosensprung, Ingrid, et al. [8]. *Interpretationen zu Heinrich Böll*, II, 81–93.

MARÍA LUISA BOMBAL

"The Tree"
Agosín, Marjorie. "La mímesis de la interioridad: 'Soledad de la sangre' de Marta Brunet y 'El árbol' de María Luisa Bombal," *Neophilologus*, 68 (1984), 380–388.
Menton, Seymour. *El Cuento Hispanoamericano*, II, 146–147; 2nd ed., 146–147.
Scott, Nina M. "Verbal and Nonverbal Messages in María Luisa Bombal's 'El árbol,'" *Mod Lang Stud*, 17, iii (1987), 3–9.

NAPOLEON BONAPARTE

"Le Masque prophète"
Martin, Andrew. "The Mask of the Prophet: Napoleon, Borges, Verne," *Comp Lit*, 40 (1988), 318–334.

NELSON BOND

"The Priestess Who Rebelled"
Spector, Judith. "The Functions of Sexuality in the Science Fiction of Russ, Piercy, and Le Guin," in Palumbo, Donald, Ed. *Erotic Universe . . .* , 199–200.

MARITA BONNER

"High Stepper"
Roses, Lorraine E., and Ruth E. Randolph. "Marita Bonner: In Search of Other
    Mothers' Gardens," *Black Am Lit Forum*, 21, i–ii (1987), 173–176.

"On the Altar"
Roses, Lorraine E., and Ruth E. Randolph. "Marita Bonner . . . ," 171–173.

"One True Love"
Roses, Lorraine E., and Ruth E. Randolph. "Marita Bonner . . . ," 177–178.

"Reap It as You Sow"
Roses, Lorraine E., and Ruth E. Randolph. "Marita Bonner . . . ," 178–179.

JORGE LUIS BORGES

"Abenjacán the Bojarí, Dead in His Labyrinth"
Rio, Carmen M. del. *Jorge Luis Borges . . .* , 153–155.

"The Aleph"
Holloway, James E. "Borges' Early Conscious Mythicization of Buenos Aires,"
    Symposium, 42, i (1988), 17–36.
Magnarelli, Sharon. "Literature and Desire: Women in the Fiction of Jorge
    Luis Borges," *Revista/Review Interamericana*, 13 (1983), 140–142.
Rio, Carmen M. del. *Jorge Luis Borges . . .* , 143–146.
Siganos, André. "Animalité et passion du non-sens chez Jorge Luis Borges,
    Clarice Lispector et J. M. G. Le Clézio," *Recherches et Études*, 6 (1984), 127–
    133.
Thiem, Jon. "Borges, Dante, and the Poetics of Total Vision," *Comp Lit*, 40
    (1988), 97–121.

"The Approach to Almotásim"
Holloway, James E. ". . . Mythicization of Bueno Aires," 17–36.

"Averroes' Search"
McHale, Brian. *Postmodern Fiction*, 103–104.
Stavans, Ilan. "Borges, Averroes y la imposibilidad del teatro," *Latin Am Theatre
    R*, 22, i (1988), 13–22.

"The Babylonian Lottery"
Boegeman, Margaret. "From Amhoretz to Exegete: The Swerve from Kafka
    to Borges," in Alazraki, Jaime, Ed. *Critical Essays . . .* , 182–183.

"The Circular Ruins"
McMurray, George R. *Spanish American Writing . . .* , 17–18.
Rabell, Carmen R. "'Las ruinas circulares': Una reflexión sobre la literatura,"
    Revista Chilena Literatura, 31 (April, 1988), 95–104.

"El condenado"
Carullo, Sylvia G. "Honor Among *Malevos* and *Compadritos* in Some Short Sto-
    ries by Borges," *Hispanic J*, 10, i (1988), 98.

"The Congress"
Rio, Carmen M. del. *Jorge Luis Borges . . .* , 172–177.
Standish, Peter. " 'El Congreso' in the Works of J. L. Borges," *Hispanic R*, 55
    (1987), 347–359.

"The Dead Man"
Magnarelli, Sharon. "Literature and Desire . . . ," 142–144.

"Death"
Carullo, Sylvia G. "Honor Among *Malevos . . .* ," 97–98.

"Death and the Compass"
Alazraki, Jaime. *Borges and the Kabbalah*, 16–17.
Alonso M., María de las Nieves. "El desplazamiento en 'La muerte y la brújula,' "
    Las Palabra y el Hombre, 61 (January–March, 1987), 27–34.
Cave, Terence. *Recognitions . . .* , 234–235.
Echavarría, Arturo. "Los arlequines y 'el mundo al revés' en 'La muerte y la
    brújula' de Jorge Luis Borges," *Nueva Revista de Filología Hispánica*, 34
    (1985–1986), 610–630.
Miller, J. Hillis. "Figure in Borges' 'Death and the Compass': Rod Scharlach as
    Hermeneut," *Dieciocho*, 10, i (1987), 53–61.
Prieto Inzunza, Angélica. " 'La muerte y la brújula': Una lectura paródica del
    relato political," *Texto Crítico*, 13 (1987), 79–91.

"Deutsches Requiem"
Weinstein, Arnold. *The Fiction of Relationship*, 204–206.

"Emma Zunz"
Fishburn, Evelyn. " 'Algebra y fuego' in the Fiction of Borges," *Revista Cana-
    diense*, 12, iii (1988), 390–391.
Magnarelli, Sharon. "Literature and Desire . . . ," 145–146.
Sotomayor, Aurea M. " 'Emma Zunz' y los azares de la causalidad: Lectura y
    elaboración de lo verosímil jurídico," *Escritura*, 11 (1986), 257–271.

"The End of the Duel"
Sheidley, William E., and Ann Charters. *Instructor's Manual . . .* , 115–116;
    Charters, Ann, William E. Sheidley, and Martha Ramsey. *Instructor's Man-
    ual . . .* , 2nd ed., 114–115.

"Examination of the Work of Herbert Quain"
Rio, Carmen M. del. *Jorges Luis Borges . . .* , 161–165.

"Funes the Memorious"
Olaso, Ezequiel de. "Borges y filosofía," *La Nación (Lit Supp)*, [n.v.] (August 7,
    1988), 1.
Weinstein, Arnold. *The Fiction of Relationship*, 206–207.

"The Garden of Forking Paths"

Balderston, Daniel. " 'El Jardín de senderos que se bifurcan': Un cuento de la guerra," *Perspectives Contemp Lit,* 14 (1988), 90–96.
Bush, Andrew. "The Riddled Text: Borges and Arenas," *Mod Lang Notes,* 103 (1988), 374–397.
Ezquerro, Milagros. "Borges, Oedipe et Schéherazade," *Les Langues Néo-Latines,* 80, ii (1986), 35–52.
Frank, Roslyn M., and Nancy Vosburg. "Textos y contra-textos en 'El jardín de senderos que se bifurcan,'" *Revista Iberoamericana,* 100–101 (1977), 517–534.
Friedman, Mary L. *The Emperor's Kites . . . ,* 17–26.
McHale, Brian. *Postmodern Fiction,* 106–107.
Menton, Seymour. *El Cuento Hispanoamericano,* II, 130–132; 2nd ed., 130–132.
Rimmon-Kenan, Shlomith. "Doubles and Counterparts: Patterns of Interchangeability in Borges' 'The Garden of Forking Paths,'" *Critical Inquiry,* 6 (1980), 639–647.
Weinstein, Arnold. *The Fiction of Relationship,* 212–218.
Yarrow, Ralph. "Irony Grows in My Garden: Generative Processes in Borges's 'The Garden of Forking Paths,'" in Morse, Donald E., Ed. *The Fantastic . . . ,* 73–86.

"The Gospel According to Mark"

Rodríguez F., Mario. "Tres versiones de Cristo, según Borges: O n versiones de un texto según . . . ," *Acta Literaria,* 12 (1987), 5–19.

"The Immortal"

Aguinis, Marcos. "Muerte, immortalidad y un cuento de Borges: 'El immortal,'" *Hispamerica,* 17 (August, 1988), 27–40.
Rio, Carmen M. del. *Jorge Luis Borges . . . ,* 146–151.

"Juan Muraña"

Friedman, Mary L. *The Emperor's Kites . . . ,* 189–193.

"The Life of Tadeo Isidoro Cruz"

Alazraki, Jaime. *Borges and the Kabbalah,* 82–86.
Rio, Carmen M. del. *Jorge Luis Borges . . . ,* 151–153.

"The Maker"

Fernández, Theodosio. " 'El hacedor': Sobre los poderes y el fracaso de la literatura," *Revista de Occidente,* 86–87 (July–August, 1988), 82–94.

"The Masked Dyer, Hakim of Merv"

Martin, Andrew. "The Mask of the Prophet: Napoleon, Borges, Verne," *Comp Lit,* 40 (1988), 318–334.

"The Other"

Rio, Carmen M. del. *Jorges Luis Borges . . . ,* 169–171.

"The Other Death"

Friedman, Mary L. *The Emperor's Kites . . . ,* 193–197.
Rio, Carmen M. del. *Jorge Luis Borges . . . ,* 155–158.

"Pierre Menard, Author of *Quixote*"
Levitt, Morton P. *Modernist Survivors . . .* , 109–110.
Medina, Dante. "El arte borgiano de hacer lectura," *Káñina*, 10, ii (1986), 25–27.
Rio, Carmen M. del. *Jorge Luis Borges . . .* , 158–161.

"The Secret Miracle"
Quackenbush, L. Howard. "Borges's Tragedy," *Hispanófila*, 31 (January, 1988), 77–86.
Weinstein, Arnold. *The Fiction of Relationship*, 210–212.

"The Shape of the Sword"
Balderston, Daniel. "The Mark of the Knife: Scars as Signs in Borges," *Mod Lang R*, 83, i (1988), 71–75.
McGrady, Donald. "Prefiguration, Narrative Transgression and Eternal Return in Borges' 'La forma de la espada,'" *Revista Canadiense*, 11 (1987), 141–149.

"The South"
Alazraki, Jaime. *Borges and the Kabbalah*, 65–76.
Christ, Ronald. "Forking Narrative," *Latin Am Lit R*, 7 (Spring–Summer, 1979), 57–59.

"The Story of Rosendo Juárez"
Carullo, Sylvia G. "Honor Among *Malevos . . .* ," 96–97.

"Theme of the Traitor and the Hero"
Prieto, René. "Mimetic Stratagems: The Unreliable Narrator in Latin American Literature," *Revista Estudios Hispánicos*, 19, iii (1985), 61–73.
Weinstein, Arnold. *The Fiction of Relationship*, 202–203.

"The Theologians"
Echavarría Ferrari, Arturo. "Tiempo, lenguaje e identidad personal: 'Los teólogos' de Jorge Luis Borges," in McDuffie, Keith, and Alfredo Roggiano, Eds. *Texto/Contexto . . .* , 79–87.

"Tlön, Uqbar, Orbis Tertius"
Flury, Victor J. "Fenómeno y enigma," *Revista de Filosofía*, 24 (1986), 257–260.
Friedman, Mary L. *The Emperor's Kites . . .* , 183–188.
Levitt, Morton P. *Modernist Survivors . . .* , 110–111.
MacAdam, Alfred J. *Textual Confrontations . . .* , 135–136.
McHale, Brian. *Postmodern Fiction*, 77–78.
Rio, Carmen M. del. *Jorge Luis Borges . . .* , 165–169.
Tanner, Tony. "Borges and American Fiction . . . ," in Alazraki, Jaime, Ed. *Critical Essays . . .* , 168–170.

"The Uncivil Master of Ceremonies Kotsuké no Suké"
Balderston, Daniel. "The Mark . . ." 70.

"The Unworthy One"
Carullo, Sylvia G. "Honor Among *Malevos . . .* ," 97.
Fishburn, Evelyn. "'Algebra y fuego' . . . ," 391–392.

"The Widow Ching"
Ghassemi, Ruth L. "Borges y la metahistoria," *Romance Notes,* 29, ii (1988), 139–
147.

"The Zahir"
Alazraki, Jaime. *Borges and the Kabbalah,* 45–46.
Rio, Carmen M. del. *Jorge Luis Borges . . . ,* 139–143.

JUAN BOSCH

"In a Hut"
Barradas, Efraín. "La seducción de las máscaras: José Alcantara Almánzar,
Juan Bosch y la joven narrativa dominicana," *Revista Iberoamericana,* 54
(1988), 11–25.

"The Woman"
Menton, Seymour. *El Cuento Hispanoamericano,* II, 98–100; 2nd ed., 98–100;
3rd ed., 312–314.

HERMAN CHARLES BOSMAN

"Dopper"
Zeiss, Cecelia. "Aspects of the Short Story: A Consideration of Selected Works
of Frank O'Connor and Herman Charles Bosman," in Zach, Wolfgang,
and Heinz Kosak, Eds. *Literary Interrelations . . . ,* II, 126–127.

"Mafeking Road"
Zeiss, Cecelia. "Aspects of the Short Story . . . ," 123–124.

ELIZABETH BOWEN

"The Cat Jumps"
Bates, Judith. "Undertones of Horror in Elizabeth Bowen's 'Look at All Those
Roses' and 'The Cat Jumps,'" in *J Short Story Engl,* 8 (Spring, 1987), 83–
86.

"Dead Mabelle"
Jarrett, Mary. "Ambiguous Ghosts: The Short Stories of Elizabeth Bowen," *J
Short Story Engl,* 8 (Spring, 1987), 73.

"The Demon Lover"
Charters, Ann, William E. Sheidley, and Martha Ramsey. *Instructor's Man-
ual . . . ,* 2nd ed., 112–113.
Gilbert, Sandra M., and Susan Gubar. *No Man's Land . . . ,* 112–113.

"Human Habitation"
Jarrett, Mary. "Ambiguous Ghosts . . . ," 75–76.

"Look at All Those Roses"
Bates, Judith. "Undertones of Horror . . . ," 86–89.
Jarrett, Mary. "Ambiguous Ghosts . . . ," 76–77.

"Mysterious Kôr"
Bayley, John. *The Short Story . . .* , 165–178.

"Tears, Idle Tears"
*Perrine, Laurence, and Thomas R. Arp. *Instructor's Manual . . .* , 7th ed., 10–11.

JANE BOWLES

"Camp Cataract"
Lougy, Robert E. "The World and Art of Jane Bowles," *Coll Engl Assoc Critic,* 49, ii–iv (1987), 164–165, 169.

"A Stick of Green Candy"
Bassett, Mark T. "Imagination, Control and Betrayal in Jane Bowles' 'A Stick of Green Candy,'" *Stud Short Fiction,* 24 (1987), 25–29.

PAUL BOWLES

"At Paso Rojo"
Patterson, Richard F. *A World Outside . . .* , 66–68.

"Call at Corazón"
Patterson, Richard F. *A World Outside . . .* , 24–26.

"The Delicate Prey"
Patterson, Richard F. *A World Outside . . .* , 4–6.

"A Distant Episode"
Patterson, Richard F. *A World Outside . . .* , 62–64.

"The Echo"
Patterson, Richard F. *A World Outside . . .* , 19–20.

"The Frozen Fields"
Patterson, Richard F. *A World Outside . . .* , 11–13.

"The Garden"
Patterson, Richard F. *A World Outside . . .* , 98–99.

"He of the Assembly"
Patterson, Richard F. *A World Outside . . .* , 123–126.

"Here to Learn"
Patterson, Richard F. *A World Outside . . .* , 71–74.

"The Hours after Noon"

Patterson, Richard F. *A World Outside . . .* , 26–30.

"How Many Midnights"
Patterson, Richard F. *A World Outside . . .* , 20–22.

"The Hyena"
Charters, Ann, William E. Sheidley, and Martha Ramsey. *Instructor's Manual . . .* , 2nd ed., 136.
Patterson, Richard F. *A World Outside . . .* , 126–129.

"If I Should Open My Mouth"
Patterson, Richard F. *A World Outside . . .* , 120–122.

"Kitty"
Patterson, Richard F. *A World Outside . . .* , 13—14.

"Pages from Cold Point"
Patterson, Richard F. *A World Outside . . .* , 8–11.

"Pastor Dowe at Tacaté"
Patterson, Richard F. *A World Outside . . .* , 60–62.
St. Louis, Ralph. "The Affirming Silence: Paul Bowles's 'Pastor Dowe at Tacaté,'" *Stud Short Fiction,* 24 (1987), 381–386.

"Tea on the Mountain"
Patterson, Richard F. *A World Outside . . .* , 78–80.

"The Time of Friendship"
Patterson, Richard F. *A World Outside . . .* , 77–78.

"You Are Not I"
Patterson, Richard F. *A World Outside . . .* , 118–120.

"You Have Left Your Lotus Pods on the Bus"
Patterson, Richard F. *A World Outside . . .* , 74–75.

KAY BOYLE

"Army of Occupation"
Uehling, Edward M. "Tails, You Lose: Kay Boyle's War Fiction," *Twentieth Century Lit,* 34 (1988), 379–382.

"The Astronomer's Wife"
Gronnin, Robyn M. "Boyle's 'Astronomer's Wife,'" *Explicator,* 46, iii (1988), 51–53.

"Episode in the Life of an Ancestor"
Clark, Suzanne. "Revolution, the Woman, and the Works: Kay Boyle," *Twentieth Century Lit,* 34 (1988), 324–326.

"The Lost"
Uehling, Edward M. "Tails, You Lose . . . ," 375–376.

"On the Run"
Clark, Suzanne. "Revolution . . . ," 329–332.

"Wedding Day"
Clark, Suzanne. "Revolution . . . ," 326–328.

T. CORAGHESSAN BOYLE

"Descent of Man"
Cassill, R. V. . . . *Instructor's Handbook,* 12–13.

RAY BRADBURY

"August 2026: Then Will Come Soft Rains"
Charters, Ann, William E. Sheidley, and Martha Ramsey. *Instructor's Manual . . . ,* 2nd ed., 158.

"Jack-in-the-Box"
Büssing, Sabine. *Aliens in the Home . . . ,* 90–91.

"The Night"
Büssing, Sabine. *Aliens in the Home . . . ,* 11–12.

"The October Game"
Büssing, Sabine. *Aliens in the Home . . . ,* 92–93.

"The Veld"
Büssing, Sabine. *Aliens in the Home . . . ,* 32–33.

FORBES BRAMBLE

"Holiday"
Büssing, Sabine. *Aliens in the Home . . . ,* 68–69.

JOHANNA and GÜNTHER BRAUN

"The Mistake Factor"
Suvin, Darko. *Positions and Presuppositions . . . ,* 176–177.

GREGORIO BRILLANTES

"The Distance to Andromeda"
Nudas, Alfeo G. *Telic Contemplation . . . ,* 88–97.

"Faith, Love, Time and Dr. Lazaro"
Nudas, Alfeo G. *Telic Contemplation . . . ,* 97–105.

ALICE BROWN

"Dooryards"
Fisken, Beth W. "Within the Limits of Alice Brown's 'Dooryards': Introspective
Powers in *Tiverton Tales*," *Legacy*, 5, i (1988), 17–18.

"The Flat Iron Lot"
Fisken, Beth W. "Within the Limits . . . ," 23.

"Honey and Myrrh"
Fisken, Beth W. "Within the Limits . . . ," 19–20.

"Horn o' the Moon"
Fisken, Beth W. "Within the Limits . . . ," 20.

"A Last Assembling"
Fisken, Beth W. "Within the Limits . . . ," 21–23.

"A Second Marriage"
Fisken, Beth W. "Within the Limits . . . ," 21–23.

MARTA BRUNET

"Aguas abajo"
Berg, Mary G. "The Short Stories of Marta Brunet," *Monographic R*, 4 (1988),
198–199.

"Encrucijada de ausencias"
Berg, Mary G. "The Short Stories . . . ," 200.

"Una mañana cualquiera"
Berg, Mary G. "The Short Stories . . . ," 200.

"La niña que quiso ser estampa"
Berg, Mary G. "The Short Stories . . . ," 201.

"La otra voz"
Berg, Mary G. "The Short Stories . . . ," 200.

"Piedra callada"
Berg, Mary G. "The Short Stories . . . ," 198.

"Soledad de la sangre"
Angosín, Marjorie. "La mímesis de la interioridad: 'Soledad de la sangre' de
Marta Brunet y 'El árbol' de Maria Luisa Bombal," *Neophilologus*, 68 (1984),
380–388.
Berg, Mary G. "The Short Stories . . . ," 199.

"Un trapo de piso"
Berg, Mary G. "The Short Stories . . . ," 201.

EDWARD BRYANT

"2.46593"
Broege, Valerie. "Technology and Sexuality in Science Fiction: Creating New
Erotic Interfaces," in Palumbo, Donald, Ed. *Erotic Universe . . . ,* 111–112.

ALFREDO BRYCE ECHENIQUE

"El Papa Guido Sin Número"
Gutiérrez Mouat, Ricardo. "Lector y narratario en dos relatos de Bryce Eche-
nique," *Inti,* 24–25 (Fall–Spring, 1986–1987), 118–121.

"Pepi Monkey y la Educatión de su hermana"
Gutiérrez Mouat, Ricardo. "Lector . . . ," 114–117.

"With Jimmy in Paracas"
Higgins, James. . . . *Peruvian Literature,* 312.

PEARL S. BUCK

"The Enemy"
Dagi, Teo F. "Medical Ethics and the Problem of Role Ambiguity in Mikhail
Bulgakov's 'The Murderer' and Pearl S. Buck's 'The Enemy,'" *Lit & Med,*
7 (1988), 114–115.

MIKHAIL BULGAKOV

"The Murderer"
Dagi, Teo F. "Medical Ethics and the Problem of Role Ambiguity in Mikhail
Bulgakov's 'The Murderer' and Pearl S. Buck's 'The Enemy,'" *Lit & Med,*
7 (1988), 113–114.

SILVINA BULLRICH

"The Lover"
Brunton, Rosanne. "A Note on Contemporary Argentine Women's Writing: A
Discussion of *The Web,*" *Int'l Fiction R,* 15 (1988), 11–12.

CARLOS BULOSAN

"The Capitalism of My Father"
Tolentino, Delfin L. "Satire in Carlos Bulosan's *The Laughter of My Father,*" *Philippine Stud,* 34 (1986), 457–458.

"The Gift of My Father"
Tolentino, Delfin L. "Satire . . . ," 456–457.

"The Laughter of My Father"
Tolentino, Delfin L. "Satire . . . ," 460.

"My Father Goes to Church"
Tolentino, Delfin L. "Satire . . . ," 459.

"My Father Goes to Court"
Tolentino, Delfin L. "Satire . . . ," 454–455.

"My Mother's Boarders"
Tolentino, Delfin L. "Satire . . . ," 456–457.

"The Politics of My Father"
Tolentino, Delfin L. "Satire . . . ," 458.

"The Soldiers Came Marching"
Tolentino, Delfin L. "Satire . . . ," 455–456.

"The Tree of My Father"
Tolentino, Delfin L. "Satire . . . ," 457.

IVAN BUNIN

"Aleksey Alekseevich"
Zweers, A. F. "The Function of the Theme of Death in the Works of Ivan
    Bunin," *Russian Lit*, 8 (1980), 161–162.

"The Devouring Fire"
Zweers, A. F. "The Function of the Theme of Death . . . ," 159–160.

"The Father"
Mendelson, Danuta. *Metaphor . . . ,* 56–79.

"Gedali"
Mendelson, Danuta. *Metaphor . . . ,* 40–42.

"Ida"
Isenberg, Charles. "Variations on a Theme: Bunin's 'Ida,'" *Slavic & East Eu-
    ropean J,* 31 (1987), 490–502.

"Justice in Parentheses"
Mendelson, Danuta. *Metaphor . . . ,* 92–93.

"The King"
Mendelson, Danuta. *Metaphor . . . ,* 100–105.

"A Letter"
Mendelson, Danuta. *Metaphor . . . ,* 117–118.

"Light Breathing"
Bowie, Robert, Ed. "Introduction," *In a Far Country* . . . [by Ivan Bunin], xiv–
   xvi.

"Line and Color"
Mendelson, Danuta. *Metaphor* . . . , 106–112.

"The Mad Artist"
Bowie, Robert, Ed. "Introduction," x.

"Mitya's Love"
Zweers, A. F. "The Function of the Theme of Death . . . ," 152–154.

"Old Shloime"
Mendelson, Danuta. *Metaphor* . . . , 34–36.

"On the Field of Honor"
Mendelson, Danuta. *Metaphor* . . . , 92.

"The Passing"
Zweers, A. F. "The Function of the Theme of Death . . . ," 158–159.

"The Pines"
Fetzer, Leland. "Man and Nature in Bunin's 'The Pines,'" in Flier, Michael S.,
   and Simon Karlinsky, Eds. *Language, Literature, Linguistics* . . . , 21–28.

"The Son"
Zweers, A. F. "The Function of the Theme of Death . . . ," 155–156.

"An Unknown Friend"
Bowie, Robert, Ed. "Introduction," x.

"The Yelagin Affair"
Zweers, A. F. "The Function of the Theme of Death . . . ," 154–155.

WILHELM BUSCH

"Edward's Dream"
Schnell, Ralf. "Kulturpessimismus und Ironie: Wilhelm Buschs Erzählung 'Edwards Traum,'" in Vogt, Michael, Ed. *Die boshafte Heiterkeit* . . . , 50–78.

DINO BUZZATI

"Fear at La Scala"
Biasin, Gian-Paolo. "The Secret Fears of Men: Dino Buzzati," *Italian Q,* 6 (1962),
   83–85.

"The Seven-Storied Hospital"
Biasin, Gian-Paolo, "The Secret Fears . . . ," 82–83.

GEORGE WASHINGTON CABLE

"Belles Demoiselles Plantation"
Petry, Alice H. *A Genius* . . . , 59–74.

"Café des Exilés"
Petry, Alice H. *A Genius* . . . , 49–58.

"Jean-ah Poquelin"
Petry, Alice H. *A Genius* . . . , 90–99.

"Madame Délicieuse"
Petry, Alice H. *A Genius* . . . , 131–137.

"Posson Jone'"
Petry, Alice H. *A Genius* . . . , 75–89.

"'Sieur George"
Petry, Alice H. *A Genius* . . . , 75–89.

"'Tite Poulette"
Petry, Alice H. *A Genius* . . . , 100–117.

GUILLERMO CABRERA INFANTE

"Undertow"
MacAdam, Alfred J. "Seeing Double: Cabrera Infante and Cain," *World Lit Today,* 61 (1987), 546.

"Water of Memory"
MacAdam, Alfred J. "Seeing Double: Cabrera Infante and Cain," 545.

VÍCTOR CÁCERES LARA

"Paludismo"
Menton, Seymour. *El Cuento Hispanoamericano,* II, 93–94; 2nd ed., 93–94; 3rd ed., 307–308.
Scott, Wilder P. "An Existentialist Analysis of Víctor Cáceres Lara's 'Paludismo,'" in Zayas-Bazán, Eduardo, and M. Laurentino Suárez, Eds. *Selected Proceedings* . . . , 218–224.

HORTENSE CALISHER

"The Old Stock"
Harap, Louis. *In the Mainstream* . . . , 26–27.

MORLEY CALLAGHAN

"Ancient Lineage"
New, W. H. *Dreams of Speech . . .* , 74–75.

"Last Spring They Came Over"
MacCulloch, Clare. *The Neglected Genre . . .* , 51–52.

"Sick Call"
MacCulloch, Clare. *The Neglected Genre . . .* , 52–53.
New, W. H. *Dreams of Speech . . .* , 73–74.

ITALO CALVINO

"Adventure of a Photographer"
Watson, David S. "Calvino and the Problem of Textual Referentiality," *Italianist*,
    8 (1988), 67–73.

"All at One Point"
Gery, John. "Love and Annihilation in Calvino's Qfwfq Tales," *Critique S*, 30
    (1988), 61.

"The Argentina Ant"
Carter, Albert H. *Italo Calvino . . .* , 62–64.

"The Baron in the Trees"
Carter, Albert H. *Italo Calvino . . .* , 37–47.

"Blood, Sea"
Gery, John. "Love and Annihilation . . . ," 63–64.

"The Cloven Viscount"
Carter, Albert H. *Italo Calvino . . .* , 25–36.

"The Contemplation of the Stars"
Hannay, John. "Description as Science and Art: Calvino's Narrative of Obser-
    vation," *Mosaic*, 21, iv (1988), 82–83.

"Crystals"
Gery, John. "Love and Annihilation . . . ," 63.

"The Dinosaurs"
Koelb, Clayton. *Invention of Reading . . .* , 140–149.

"The Distance of the Moon"
Gery, John. "Love and Annihilation . . . ," 60–61.

"Last Comes the Crow"
Carter, Albert H. *Italo Calvino . . .* , 16–23.

"My Aquatic Uncle"
Gery, John. "Love and Annihilation . . . ," 61.

"The Nonexistent Knight"
Carter, Albert H. *Italo Calvino* . . . , 49–60.

"Priscilla"
Gery, John. "Love and Annihilation . . . ," 64–67.

"Reading a Wave"
Hannay, John. "Description as Science . . . ," 77–78.

"Smog"
Carter, Albert H. *Italo Calvino* . . . , 64–67.

"The Watcher"
Carter, Albert H. *Italo Calvino* . . . , 67–72.

"Without Colors"
Gery, John. "Love and Annihilation . . . ," 59–60.

ANNE CAMERON

"Copper Woman"
Mumford, Marilyn R. "Woman-Centered Myth in Anne Cameron's *Daughters of Copper Woman* and *Dzelarhons*," *Coll Engl Assoc Critic*, 50, i (1987), 87–88.

"Old Magic"
Mumford, Marilyn R. "Woman-Centered Myth . . . ," 86–87.

JOHN W. CAMPBELL

"When the Atoms Failed"
Bartter, Martha A. *The Way to Ground Zero* . . . , 60–61.

RAMSEY CAMPBELL

"Before the Storm"
Crawford, Gary W. *Ramsey Campbell*, 12–13.

"The Cellars"
Crawford, Gary W. *Ramsey Campbell*, 20–21.

"The End of a Summer Day"
Crawford, Gary W. *Ramsey Campbell*, 17–18.

DAVID CAMPTON

"At the Bottom of the Garden"
Büssing, Sabine. *Aliens in the Home* . . . , 86–87.

ALBERT CAMUS

"The Adulterous Woman"
Barnes, Hazel E. *Humanistic Existentialism* . . . , 190–192.
Festa-McCormick, Diana. "Existential Exile and a Glimpse of the Kingdom," in Knapp, Bettina L., Ed. *Critical Essays* . . . , 109–110.

"The Fall"
Axthelm, Peter M. . . . *Confessional Novel,* 90–96.
Barnes, Hazel E. *Humanistic Existentialism* . . . , 142–151.
Gorak, Jan. *God the Artist* . . . , 81–83.
McGrath, Susan M. "Albert Camus Witness to Modern Man's Moral Duality: Jean-Baptiste Clamence, Comedian-Artist," *Michigan Academician,* 19, i (1987), 125–132.
Reilly, Patrick. *The Literature of Guilt* . . . , 114–137.

"The Growing Stone"
Barnes, Hazel E. *Humanistic Existentialism* . . . , 240–242.
Festa-McCormick, Diana. "Existential Exile . . . ," 114–115.

"The Guest"
Barnes, Hazel E. *Humanistic Existentialism* . . . , 254–255.
Festa-McCormick, Diana. "Existential Exile . . . ," 112–113.
*Perrine, Laurence, and Thomas R. Arp. *Instructor's Manual* . . . , 7th ed., 22–24.

"Jonas, or The Artist at Work"
Festa-McCormick, Diana. "Existential Exile . . . ," 113–114.
Knabe, Peter-Eckhard. "Essai de interprétation de la 'polémique interne' dans l'*Exil et le royaume* d'Albert Camus," in Roellenbleck, Georg, Ed. *Le Discours polémiques* . . . , 75–84.

"The Renegade"
Barnes, Hazel E. *Humanistic Existentialism* . . . , 107–110.
Blythe, Hal, and Charlie Sweet. "Speaking in 'Tongues': Psychoses in 'The Renegade,'" *Stud Short Fiction,* 25 (1988), 129–134.
Festa-McCormick, Diana. "Existential Exile . . . ," 110–111.

"The Silent Men"
Barnes, Hazel E. *Humanistic Existentialism* . . . , 254.
Festa-McCormick, Diana. "Existential Exile . . . ," 111–112.

"The Stranger"
Barnes, Hazel E. *Humanistic Existentialism* . . . , 176–187.
Bryson, Dorothy. "Plot and Counter-Plot in 'L'Étranger,'" *Forum Mod Lang Stud,* 24 (1988), 272–279.
Erickson, John. "Albert Camus and North Africa: A Discourse of Exteriority," in Knapp, Bettina L., Ed. *Critical Essays* . . . , 74–78.
Longstaffe, M. R. A. "Camus et la sagesse humaine: A Reading of Camus' 'L'Étranger,'" *Mod Langs,* 69, ii (1988), 91–96.
Lutwack, Leonard. *The Role of Place* . . . , 93–94.
McCarthy, Patrick. *Albert Camus* . . . , 15–78.

McConnell, Winder. "Sado-Masochism and Punishment Instincts in Two Works of Camus," *J Evolutionary Psych,* 9, i–ii (1988), 100–106.

TRUMAN CAPOTE

"A Christmas Memory"
Perrine, Laurence, and Thomas R. Arp. *Instructor's Manual . . . ,* 6th ed., 31–32; 7th ed., 31–32.

"Miriam"
Büssing, Sabine. *Aliens in the Home . . . ,* 131–132.

"My Side of the Matter"
Allmendinger, Blake. "The Room Was Locked, with the Key on the Inside: Female Influence in Truman Capote's 'My Side of the Matter,'" *Stud Short Fiction,* 24 (1987), 279–288.

PETER CAREY

"Peeling"
Tate, Trudi. "Unravelling the Feminine: Peter Carey's 'Peeling,'" *Meanjin,* 46 (1987), 394–399.

WILLIAM CARLETON

"Dinner at Helen's"
Broege, Valerie. "Technology and Sexuality in Science Fiction: Creating New Erotic Interfaces," in Palumbo, Donald, Ed. *Erotic Universe . . . ,* 123–124.

"The Hedge School"
Krans, Horatio S. *Irish Life . . . ,* 171–176.

"The Poor Scholar"
Krans, Horatio S. *Irish Life . . . ,* 176–179.

EDWARD CARPENTER

"Narayan"
Rahman, Tariq. "The Literary Treatment of Indian Themes in the Works of Edward Carpenter," *Durham Univ J,* 80, i (1987), 77–81.

ALEJO CARPENTIER

"The Fugitives"
Díaz, Nancy G. *The Radical Self . . . ,* 16–18.
Janney, Frank. "Apuntes sobre un cuento de Alejo Carpentier: 'Los fugitivos,'" in Müller-Bergh, Klaus, Ed. *Asedios a Carpentier . . . ,* 89–100.

Müller-Bergh, Klaus. "Alejo Carpentier: Autor y obra un su época," in Mazzioti, Nora, Ed. *Historia y Mito* . . . , 29–30.

"The High Road of St. James"
Alegría, Fernando. "Alejo Carpentier: Realismo Magico," in Giacoman, Helmy F., Ed. *Homenaje a Alejo Carpentier* . . . , 66.
Ariza González, Julio. "Alejo Carpentier en el contexto histórico y estilístico," in Kossoff, A. David, et al. [3], Eds. *Actas del VIII Congreso* . . . , I, 164–166.
Foster, David W. "The 'Everyman' Theme in Carpentier's 'El camino de Santiago,'" *Symposium,* 18 (1964), 229–240.
Magnarelli, Sharon. "'El camino de Santiago' de Alejo Carpentier y la picaresca," *Revista Iberoamericana,* 40 (1974), 65–86.
Mocega-González, Esther P. *La narrativa* . . . , 26–39.
———. *Alejo Carpentier* . . . , 55–62.
Müller-Bergh, Klaus. "Alejo Carpentier . . . ," 37–39.
Rodríguez-Alcalá, Hugo. *Narrativa Hispanoamericana,* 22–35.
———. "Sobre 'El camino de Santiago' de Alejo Carpentier," in Giacoman, Helmy F., Ed. *Homenaje a Alejo Carpentier* . . . , 245–259.
———. "Sentido de 'El camino de Santiago,'" in Müller-Bergh, Klaus, Ed. *Asedios a Carpentier* . . . , 165–176.
Sorel, Andrés. "El mundo novelístico de Alejo Carpentier," in Giacoman, Helmy F., Ed. *Homenaje a Alejo Carpentier* . . . , 85.
Verzasconi, Ray. "Juan and Sisyphus in Carpentier's 'El camino de Santiago,'" *Hispania,* 48 (1965), 70–75; rpt. Mazzioti, Nora, Ed. *Historia y Mito* . . . , 45–52.

"Journey to the Source" [same as "Journey to the Seed"]
Durán, Manuel. "'Viaje a la semilla': El cómo y el porqué de una pequeña obra maestra," in Müller-Bergh, Klaus, Ed. *Asedios a Carpentier* . . . , 63–87.
Eiríksdóttir, Sigrún A. "Some Examples of Irony in Carpentier's Early Fiction," *Chasqui,* 16, ii–iii (1987), 6–7.
Mocega-González, Esther P. *La narrativa* . . . , 40–51.
Sorel, Andrés. "El mundo novelístico . . . ," 84.

"Like the Night"
Ariza González, Julio. "Alejo Carpentier en el contexto . . . ," 166–167.
Assardo, M. Roberto. "'Semejante a la noche' o la contemporaneidad del hombre," in Giacoman, Helmy F., Ed. *Homenaje a Alejo Carpentier* . . . , 211–225.
González Echevarría, Roberto. "'Semejante a la noche' de Alejo Carpentier: historia/ficcion," in Müller-Bergh, Klaus, Ed. *Asedios a Carpentier* . . . , 178–190.
Mocega-González, Esther P. *La narrativa* . . . , 51–62.
Quesada, Luis M. "'Semejante a la noche': Análisis evaluativo," in Giacoman, Helmy F., Ed. *Homenaje a Alejo Carpentier* . . . , 229–241.
Sorel, Andrés. "El mundo novelístico . . . ," 85–86.

"Manhunt"
Alegría, Fernando. "Alejo Carpentier . . . ," 66–68.
Carlos, Alberto J. "'El anti-héroe en 'El acoso,'" in Giacoman, Helmy F., Ed. *Homenaje a Alejo Carpentier* . . . , 367–384.

Mocega-González, Esther P. "La simbología religiosa en 'El acoso,'" *Anales de la Universidad Complutense,* 2–3 (1973–1974), 521–532.
——. *La narrativa . . . ,* 63–88.
——. *Alejo Carpentier . . . ,* 19–34.
Serra, Edelweis. "Estructura y estilo de 'El acoso,'" in Mazzioti, Nora, Ed. *Historia y Mito . . . ,* 153–179.
Sorel, Andrés. "El mundo novelístico . . . ," 86–89.
Volek, Emil. "Análisis del sistema de estructuras musicales e interpretación de 'El acoso' de Alejo Carpentier," in Giacoman, Helmy F., Ed. *Homenaje a Alejo Carpentier . . . ,* 387–438.
Weber, Frances W. "'El acoso': Alejo Carpentier's War on Time," *PMLA,* 78 (1963), 440–448; rpt. Müller-Bergh, Klaus, Ed. *Asedios a Carpentier . . . ,* 147–164.

"Morning Service"
Eiríksdóttir, Sigrún A. "Some Examples . . . ," 6.
Müller-Bergh, Klaus. "'Oficio de tinieblas': Un cuento escasamente conocido," in Müller-Bergh, Klaus, Ed. *Asedios a Carpentier . . . ,* 53–61.

TOMÁS CARRASQUILLA

"San Antoñito"
Menton, Seymour. *El Cuento Hispanoamericano,* I, 107–109; 2nd ed., 107–109; 3rd ed., 107–109.

LEONORA CARRINGTON

"The Debutante"
Knapp, Bettina L. "Leonora Carrington's Whimsical Dreamworld: Animals Talk, Children Are Gods, a Black Swan Lays an Orphic Egg," *World Lit Today,* 51 (1977), 527–529.

MIGUEL DE CARRÓN

"Astros y besos"
González, Mirza L. *La novela y el cuento . . . ,* 134–135.

"Un contraste"
González, Mirza L. *La novela y el cuento . . . ,* 129–130.

"De la guerra"
González, Mirza L. *La novela y el cuento . . . ,* 131–133.

"En familia"
González, Mirza L. *La novela y el cuento . . . ,* 139–141.

"El error"
González, Mirza L. *La novela y el cuento* . . . , 142.

"Inocencia"
González, Mirza L. *La novela y el cuento* . . . , 143–145.

"La noche virtuosa"
González, Mirza L. *La novela y el cuento* . . . , 142–143.

"El rebaño"
González, Mirza L. *La novela y el cuento* . . . , 133–134.

"La última voluntad"
González, Mirza L. *La novela y el cuento* . . . , 128–129.

"El viudo"
González, Mirza L. *La novela y el cuento* . . . , 135–139.

ANGELA CARTER

"Black Venus"
Hanson, Clare. "Each Other: Images of Otherness in the Short Fiction of Doris
    Lessing, Jean Rhys, and Angela Carter," *J Short Story Engl,* 10 (Spring,
    1988), 78–79.

"The Cabinet of Edgar Allan Poe"
Hanson, Clare. "Each Other . . . ," 80–81.

"Our Lady of the Massacre"
Hanson, Clare. "Each Other . . . ," 79–80.

CLEVE CARTMILL

"Deadline"
Franklin, H. Bruce. *War Stars* . . . , 147–148.

RAYMOND CARVER

"After the Denim"
Saltzman, Arthur M. *Understanding Raymond Carver,* 113–114.

"Are You a Doctor?"
Saltzman, Arthur M. *Understanding Raymond Carver,* 30–32.

"The Bath"
Saltzman, Arthur M. *Understanding Raymond Carver,* 109–111.

"Bicycles, Muscles, Cigarettes"
Saltzman, Arthur M. *Understanding Raymond Carver,* 62–65.

"Boxes"
Saltzman, Arthur M. *Understanding Raymond Carver,* 170–171.

"The Bridle"
Perrine, Laurence, and Thomas R. Arp. *Instructor's Manual . . . ,* 7th ed., 88–
    89.
Saltzman, Arthur M. *Understanding Raymond Carver,* 140–142.

"The Calm"
Saltzman, Arthur M. *Understanding Raymond Carver,* 115–116.

"Careful"
Saltzman, Arthur M. *Understanding Raymond Carver,* 136–137.

"Cathedral"
Saltzman, Arthur M. *Understanding Raymond Carver,* 151–154.

"Chef's House"
Saltzman, Arthur M. *Understanding Raymond Carver,* 129–130.
Wilde, Alan. *Middle Grounds . . . ,* 111–112.

"Collectors"
Saltzman, Arthur M. *Understanding Raymond Carver,* 45–47.

"The Compartment"
Saltzman, Arthur M. *Understanding Raymond Carver,* 131–134.

"Distance"
Saltzman, Arthur M. *Understanding Raymond Carver,* 80–83.

"The Ducks"
Saltzman, Arthur M. *Understanding Raymond Carver,* 59–60.

"Dummy"
Saltzman, Arthur M. *Understanding Raymond Carver,* 79–80.

"Elephant"
Saltzman, Arthur M. *Understanding Raymond Carver,* 171–172.

"Fat"
Saltzman, Arthur M. *Understanding Raymond Carver,* 23–24.

"The Father"
Saltzman, Arthur M. *Understanding Raymond Carver,* 32–33.

"Feathers"
Saltzman, Arthur M. *Understanding Raymond Carver,* 125–129.

"Fever"
Saltzman, Arthur M. *Understanding Raymond Carver,* 149–151.

"The Fling"
Saltzman, Arthur M. *Understanding Raymond Carver*, 91–93.

"Furious Seasons"
Saltzman, Arthur M. *Understanding Raymond Carver*, 96–98.

"Gazebo"
Saltzman, Arthur M. *Understanding Raymond Carver*, 107–108.

"Harry's Death"
Saltzman, Arthur M. *Understanding Raymond Carver*, 59–60.

"How About This?"
Saltzman, Arthur M. *Understanding Raymond Carver*, 60–62.

"I Could See the Smallest Things"
Saltzman, Arthur M. *Understanding Raymond Carver*, 108–109.

"The Idea"
Saltzman, Arthur M. *Understanding Raymond Carver*, 26–27.

"Jerry and Molly and Sam"
Saltzman, Arthur M. *Understanding Raymond Carver*, 55–58.

"The Lie"
Saltzman, Arthur M. *Understanding Raymond Carver*, 83–84.

"Mine"
Saltzman, Arthur M. *Understanding Raymond Carver*, 95–96.

"Mr. Coffee and Mr. Fixit"
Saltzman, Arthur M. *Understanding Raymond Carver*, 105–107.

"Neighbors"
Saltzman, Arthur M. *Understanding Raymond Carver*, 24–25.

"Night School"
Saltzman, Arthur M. *Understanding Raymond Carver*, 43–45.

"Nobody Said Anything"
Saltzman, Arthur M. *Understanding Raymond Carver*, 34–37.

"One More Thing"
Saltzman, Arthur M. *Understanding Raymond Carver*, 120–121.

"Pastoral"
Saltzman, Arthur M. *Understanding Raymond Carver*, 93–95.

"Popular Mechanics"
German, Norman, and Jack Bedell. "Physical and Social Laws in Ray Carver's
    'Popular Mechanics,'" *Criticism*, 29 (1988), 257–260.

"Preservation"
Saltzman, Arthur M. *Understanding Raymond Carver,* 130–131.

"Put Yourself in My Shoes"
Saltzman, Arthur M. *Understanding Raymond Carver,* 52–55.

"Sacks"
Vander Weele, Michael. "Raymond Carver and the Language of Desire," *Denver Q,* 22, i (1987), 112–116.

"A Serious Talk"
Saltzman, Arthur M. *Understanding Raymond Carver,* 114–115.

"Signals"
Saltzman, Arthur M. *Understanding Raymond Carver,* 67–68.

"Sixty Acres"
Saltzman, Arthur M. *Understanding Raymond Carver,* 37–40.

"A Small, Good Thing"
Saltzman, Arthur M. *Understanding Raymond Carver,* 143–147.
Vander Weele, Michael. "Raymond Carver . . . ," 118–120.

"So Much Water So Close to Home"
Saltzman, Arthur M. *Understanding Raymond Carver,* 85–91.

"The Student's Wife"
Saltzman, Arthur M. *Understanding Raymond Carver,* 49–52.

"Tell the Women We're Going"
Saltzman, Arthur M. *Understanding Raymond Carver,* 111–112.

"They're Not Your Husband"
Saltzman, Arthur M. *Understanding Raymond Carver,* 28–30.

"The Train"
Saltzman, Arthur M. *Understanding Raymond Carver,* 137–140.

"Vitamins"
Saltzman, Arthur M. *Understanding Raymond Carver,* 134–136.

"What Do You Do in San Francisco?"
Saltzman, Arthur M. *Understanding Raymond Carver,* 47–49.

"What Is It?"
Saltzman, Arthur M. *Understanding Raymond Carver,* 65–67.

"What's in Alaska?"
Saltzman, Arthur M. *Understanding Raymond Carver,* 40–43.

"What We Talk About When We Talk About Love"
Charters, Ann, William E. Sheidley, and Martha Ramsey. *Instructor's Manual . . . ,* 2nd ed., 205–206.

Saltzman, Arthur M. *Understanding Raymond Carver*, 117–120.

"Where I'm Calling From"
Cassill, R. V. . . . *Instructor's Handbook*, 14–15.
Saltzman, Arthur M. *Understanding Raymond Carver*, 147–149.

"Why Don't You Dance?"
Charters, Ann, William E. Sheidley, and Martha Ramsey. *Instructor's Manual* . . . , 2nd ed., 207–208.
Saltzman, Arthur M. *Understanding Raymond Carver*, 101–104.
Vander Weele, Michael. "Raymond Carver . . . ," 111–112.

"Why, Honey?"
Saltzman, Arthur M. *Understanding Raymond Carver*, 58–59.

ROSARIO CASTELLANOS

"Aceite guapo"
Dorward, Frances R. "The Short Story as a Vehicle for Mexican Literary *Indigenismo*," *Letras Femeninas*, 13, i–ii (1987), 57–58.
Rosas, Yolanda. "Soledad y visión de mundo en la cuentística de Rosario Castellanos," *Monographic R*, 4 (1988), 231–232.

"The Caprice Waltz"
Miller, Beth. "Rosario Castellanos' *Guests in August*: Critical Realism and the Provincial Middle Class," *Latin Am Lit R*, 7 (Spring–Summer, 1979), 12–14.
Rosas, Yolanda. "Soledad y visión . . . ," 233–234.

"Cooking Lesson"
Ahern, Maureen. "Introduction," in Castellanos, Rosario. *A Rosario Castellanos Reader*, 36–38.

"Ephemeral Friendships"
Miller, Beth. "Rosario Castellanos' *Guests in August* . . . ," 10–11.

"Family Album"
Rosas, Yolanda. "Soledad y visión . . . ," 235.

"Fleeting Friends"
Ahern, Maureen. "Introduction," 33–34.

"Guests in August"
Miller, Beth. "Rosario Castellanos' *Guests in August* . . . ," 6–10.
Rosas, Yolanda. "Soledad y visión . . . ," 234.

"Lección de cocina"
Zeitz, Eileen M. "Técnica e ideología en un cuento de Rosario Castellanos," in Kossoff, A. David, et al. [3], Eds. *Actas del VIII Congreso* . . . , II, 765–771.

"A Man of Destiny"
Ahern, Maureen. "Introduction," 35–36.

"La muerte del tigre"
Dorward, Frances R. "The Short Story . . . ," 55–56.

"La rueda del hambriento"
Rosas, Yolanda. "Soledad y visión . . . ," 232–233.

"Sunday"
Rosas, Yolanda. "Soledad y visión . . . ," 235–239.

"La tregua"
Dorward, Frances R. "The Short Story . . . ," 56–57.

"The Widower Roman"
Ahern, Maureen. "Introduction," 34.
Miller, Beth. "Rosario Castellanos' *Guests in August* . . . ," 14–17.

WILLA CATHER

"Alexandra"
O'Brien, Sharon. *Willa Cather* . . . , 399–400.

"Before Breakfast"
Woodress, James. . . . *A Literary Life*, 498–499.

"Behind the Singer Tower"
O'Brien, Sharon. *Willa Cather* . . . , 383–385.
Woodress, James. . . . *A Literary Life*, 215–216.

"The Best Years"
Ambrose, Jamie. *Willa Cather* . . . , 145–146.
Nelson, Robert J. *Willa Cather* . . . , 127–129.
Woodress, James. . . . *A Literary Life*, 500–501.

"The Bohemian Girl"
Ambrose, Jamie. *Willa Cather* . . . , 78–80.
O'Brien, Sharon. *Willa Cather* . . . , 394–399.
Woodress, James. . . . *A Literary Life*, 227–229.

"The Burglar's Christmas"
O'Brien, Sharon. *Willa Cather* . . . , 51–54.

"The Clemency of the Court"
O'Brien, Sharon. *Willa Cather* . . . , 207–208.

"Coming, Aphrodite!" [same as "Coming, Eden Bower"]
Woodress, James. . . . *A Literary Life*, 312–316.

"The Count of Crow's Nest"
Nelson, Robert J. *Willa Cather* . . . , 55–56.

Woodress, James. . . . *A Literary Life,* 121.

"A Death in the Desert"
Woodress, James. . . . *A Literary Life,* 175–176.

"Double Birthday"
Woodress, James. . . . *A Literary Life,* 417–419.

"Eleanor's House"
Nelson, Robert J. *Willa Cather. . . ,* 59–61.
O'Brien, Sharon. *Willa Cather. . . ,* 302–303.
Woodress, James. . . . *A Literary Life,* 192.

"The Elopement of Allen Poole"
O'Brien, Sharon. *Willa Cather. . . ,* 203–204.

"Eric Hermannson's Soul"
Ambrose, Jamie. *Willa Cather. . . ,* 53–55.
Woodress, James. . . . *A Literary Life,* 144–146.

"Flavia and Her Artists"
Nelson, Robert J. *Willa Cather. . . ,* 57–59.
Woodress, James. . . . *A Literary Life,* 173–174.

"The Garden Lodge"
O'Brien, Sharon. *Willa Cather. . . ,* 275–276.

"A Gold Slipper"
Woodress, James. . . . *A Literary Life,* 283.

"Jack-a-Boy"
Woodress, James. . . . *A Literary Life,* 149.

"The Joy of Nellie Dean"
Woodress, James. . . . *A Literary Life,* 449–450.

"The Marriage of Phaedra"
Woodress, James. . . . *A Literary Life,* 178–179.

"The Namesake"
O'Brien, Sharon. *Willa Cather. . . ,* 328–332.

"Neighbour Rosicky"
Ambrose, Jamie. *Willa Cather. . . ,* 133–134.
Leddy, Michael. "Observation and Narration in Willa Cather's *Obscure Destinies,*"
	Stud Am Fiction, 16 (1988), 142–144.
Woodress, James. . . . *A Literary Life,* 438–441.

"The Old Beauty"
Nelson, Robert J. *Willa Cather. . . ,* 98–104.
Wasserman, Loretta. "Willa Cather's 'The Old Beauty' Reconsidered," *Stud Am
	Fiction,* 16 (1988), 217–227.
Woodress, James. . . . *A Literary Life,* 475–477.

"Old Mrs. Harris"
Leddy, Michael. "Observation and Narration . . . ," 144–148.
Woodress, James. . . . *A Literary Life,* 141–144.

"On the Gull's Road"
Ambrose, Jamie. *Willa Cather. . . ,* 69–70.
O'Brien, Sharon. *Willa Cather. . . ,* 367–370.

"Paul's Case"
O'Brien, Sharon. *Willa Cather. . . ,* 282–285.
*Perrine, Laurence, and Thomas R. Arp. *Instructor's Manual . . . ,* 7th ed., 18–19.
Sheidley, William E., and Ann Charters. *Instructor's Manual . . . ,* 54–56; Charters, Ann, William E. Sheidley, and Martha Ramsey. *Instructor's Manual . . . ,* 2nd ed., 60–61.
Woodress, James. . . . *A Literary Life,* 174–175.

"Peter"
Ambrose, Jamie. *Willa Cather. . . ,* 35–36.
Nelson, Robert J. *Willa Cather. . . ,* 54–56.
Woodress, James. . . . *A Literary Life,* 76–78.

"The Professor's Commencement"
Hall, Joan W. "Treacherous Texts: The Perils of Allusion in Cather's Early Stories," *Colby Lib Q,* 24 (1988), 144–150.
Woodress, James. . . . *A Literary Life,* 155–156.

"The Profile"
O'Brien, Sharon. *Willa Cather. . . ,* 49–51.
Woodress, James. . . . *A Literary Life,* 191.

"A Tale of the White Pyramid"
O'Brien, Sharon. *Willa Cather. . . ,* 198–200.

"Tommy, the Unsentimental"
O'Brien, Sharon. *Willa Cather. . . ,* 229–230.

"The Treasure of Far Island"
Hall, Joan W. "Teacherous Texts . . . ," 142–144.

"Two Friends"
Leddy, Michael. "Observation and Narration . . . ," 148–152.
Nelson, Robert J. *Willa Cather. . . ,* 145–148.

"Uncle Valentine"
Nelson, Robert J. *Willa Cather. . . ,* 84–88.
Woodress, James. . . . *A Literary Life,* 359–361.

"A Wagner Matinée"
O'Brien, Sharon. *Willa Cather* . . . , 280–282.
Woodress, James. . . . *A Literary Life,* 177.

"The Willing Muse"
Gilbert, Sandra M., and Susan Gubar. *No Man's Land* . . . , 174–176.
O'Brien, Sharon. *Willa Cather* . . . , 294–295.

CAMILO JOSÉ CELA

"La lata de galletas del Chirlerín Marcial, randa de parlos"
Brandenberger, Erna. *Estudios* . . . , 335–337.

ADELBERT VON CHAMISSO

"Peter Schlemihls Wundersame Geschichte"
Freund, Winfried. *Adelbert von Chamisso* . . . , 25–58.
Pracht-Fitzell, Illse. "'Peter Schlemihls wundersame Geschichte' von A. v. Chamisso in psychologischer Sicht," *Germ Notes,* 7, i (1976), 2–6.

JEFFERY PAUL CHAN

"The Chinese in Faifa"
Lim, Shirley G. "Twelve Asian American Writers: In Search of Self-Definition," *MELUS,* 13, i–ii (1986), 66–67.

"Jackrabbit"
Lim, Shirley G. "Twelve Asian American Writers . . . ," 67.

FRANÇOIS RENÉ DE CHATEAUBRIAND

"Atala"
Hamilton, James F. "Ritual Passage in Chateaubriand's 'Atala,'" *Nineteenth Century French Stud,* 15 (1987), 385–393.
Kadish, Doris Y. *The Literature of Images* . . . , 53–80.
Porter, Laurence M. "Writing Romantic Epiphany: 'Atala,' *Séraphîa, Aurélia, Dieu,*" *Romance Q,* 34 (1987), 435–442.

"René"
Call, Michael J. *Back to the Garden* . . . , 15–56.
Hamilton, James F. "The Anxious Hero in Chateaubriand's 'René,'" *Romance Q,* 34 (1987), 415–424.

JOHN CHEEVER

"The Country Husband"
Donaldson, Scott. *John Cheever* . . . , 141–143.
Waldeland, Lynne. "Isolation and Integration: John Cheever's 'The Country Husband,'" *Ball State Univ Forum,* 27, i (1986), 5–11.

"The Death of Justina"
Donaldson, Scott. *John Cheever . . .* , 180–181.

"The Enormous Radio"
Sheidley, William E., and Ann Charters. *Instructor's Manual . . .* , 136; Charters, Ann, William E. Sheidley, and Martha Ramsey. *Instructor's Manual . . .* , 2nd ed., 137–138.

"Expelled"
Donaldson, Scott. *John Cheever . . .* , 37–38.

"The Leaves, the Lion-Fish, and the Bear"
Gilmore, Thomas B. *Equivocal Spirits . . .* , 78–79.

"Reunion"
Gilmore, Thomas B. *Equivocal Spirits . . .* , 67–69.

"The Scarlet Moving Van"
Gilmore, Thomas B. *Equivocal Spirits . . .* , 75–78.

"The Seaside House"
Gilmore, Thomas B. *Equivocal Spirits . . .* , 69–70.

"The Season of Divorce"
Roberts, Edgar V., and Henry E. Jacobs. *Instructor's Manual . . .* , 70.

"The Sorrows of Gin"
Gilmore, Thomas B. *Equivocal Spirits . . .* , 64–65.

"The Swimmer"
Bell, Loren C. " 'The Swimmer': A Midsummer's Nightmare," *Stud Short Fiction,* 24 (1987), 433–436.
Blythe, Hal, and Charles Sweet. "De Havilland and 'The Swimmer,' " *Notes Contemp Lit,* 18, iv (1988), 7–8.
Gilmore, Thomas B. *Equivocal Spirits . . .* , 64–65, 72–75.
Kruse, Horst. "Parsing a Complex Structure: Literary Allusion and Mythic Evocation in John Cheever's Short Story 'The Swimmer,' " *Literatur in Wissenschaft,* 20 (1987), 217–231.
Perrine, Laurence, and Thomas R. Arp. *Instructor's Manual . . .* , 7th ed., 49–51.
Sheidley, William E., and Ann Charters. *Instructor's Manual . . .* , 138–139; Charters, Ann, William E. Sheidley, and Martha Ramsey. *Instructor's Manual . . .* , 2nd ed., 139–140.

"A Vision of the World"
Stengel, Wayne. "John Cheever's Surreal Vision and the Bridge of Language," *Twentieth Century Lit,* 33 (1987), 223–233.

ANTON CHEKHOV

"About Love"
De Maegd-Soëp, Caroline. *Chekhov and Women . . .* , 302–303.
Freedman, John. "Narrative Technique and the Art of Story-telling in Anton Chekhov's 'Little Trilogy,'" *So Atlantic R,* 53, i (1988), 9–14.
Pritchett, V. S. *Chekhov . . .* , 168–171.
Wilks, Ronald, Ed. "Introduction," *"The Kiss . . ."* [by Anton Chekhov], 22–23.

"Agafya"
Heldt, Barbara. *Terrible Perfection . . .* , 49–52.
Pritchett, V. S. *Chekhov . . .* , 38–39.

"Anna on the Neck"
Pritchett, V. S. *Chekhov . . .* , 137–138.
Wilks, Ronald, Ed. "Introduction," 28–29.

"An Anonymous Story"
Pritchett, V. S. *Chekhov . . .* , 129–130.

"Anyuta"
Pritchett, V. S. *Chekhov . . .* , 24–26.

"Ariadne"
Pritchett, V. S. *Chekhov . . .* , 127–128.

"Betrothed"
Busch, Ulrich. "Leser und Interpret von Čechovs 'Braut': Versuch einer literaturwissenschaftlichen Differenzierung," *Die Welt der Slaven,* 32 (1987), 225–229.
Schmid, Wolf. "Analysieren oder Deuten? Überlegungen zur Kontroverse zwischen Strukturalismus und Hermeneutik am Beispiel von Čechovs 'Nevesta,'" *Die Welt der Slaven,* 32, i (1987), 101–120.

"The Birthday Party"
Pritchett, V. S. *Chekhov . . .* , 71–72.

"The Bishop"
Klimenkov, Michael. "Problem of Communication in Chekhov's Story 'The Bishop': Question of Theme," in Hadlich, Roger L., and J. D. Ellsworthy, Eds. *East Meets West,* 176–192.
Pritchett, V. S. *Chekhov . . .* , 206–211.
Wilks, Ronald, Ed. "Introduction," 15–18.

"The Black Monk"
Lavrin, Janko, Ed. *Russian Short Stories . . .* , 18–19.
Ponomareff, Constantin V. *On the Dark Side . . .* , 189–190.
Pritchett, V. S. *Chekhov . . .* , 122–123.

"The Bride"
Pritchett, V. S. *Chekhov . . .* , 217–219.

"A Case History"
Wilks, Ronald, Ed. "Introduction," 23–24.

"Champagne"
De Maegd-Soëp, Caroline. *Chekhov and Women* . . . , 226.

"The Chorus Girl"
Pritchett, V. S. *Chekhov* . . . , 39–40.

"The Darling"
Bayley, John. *The Short Story* . . . , 185–186.
De Maegd-Soëp, Caroline. *Chekhov and Women* . . . , 244–247.
Heldt, Barbara. *Terrible Perfection* . . . , 52–55.
Pritchett, V. S. *Chekhov* . . . , 171–172.

"Difficult People"
Pritchett, V. S. *Chekhov* . . . , 10–12.

"A Doctor's Visit"
Pritchett, V. S. *Chekhov* . . . , 134–135.

"A Dreary Story" [same as "A Boring Story," "A Dull Story," or "A Tedious
    Story"]
De Maegd-Soëp, Caroline. *Chekhov and Women* . . . , 254–257.
Ponomareff, Constantin V. *On the Dark Side* . . . , 185–186.
Pritchett, V. S. *Chekhov* . . . , 74–83.
Wilks, Ronald, Ed. "Introduction," 18.

"The Duel"
De Maegd-Soëp, Caroline. *Chekhov and Women* . . . , 304–307.
Pritchett, V. S. *Chekhov* . . . , 103–110.

"Easter Eve"
Ponomareff, Constantin V. *On the Dark Side* . . . , 186–187.
Pritchett, V. S. *Chekhov* . . . , 40–41.

"The Fish"
Pritchett, V. S. *Chekhov* . . . , 29–30.

"Gooseberries"
Freedman, John. "Narrative Tehcnique . . . ," 7–9.
Perrine, Laurence, and Thomas R. Arp. *Instructor's Manual* . . . , 7th ed., 51–
    53.
Pritchett, V. S. *Chekhov* . . . , 167–168.
Wilks, Ronald, Ed. "Introduction," 21–22.

"The Grasshopper"
Pritchett, V. S. *Chekhov* . . . , 110–111.

"Gusev"
Pritchett, V. S. *Chekhov* . . . , 97–100.

"Happiness"
Pritchett, V. S. *Chekhov* . . . , 64–66.

"The House with the Mezzanine"
Pritchett, V. S. *Chekhov* . . . , 140–141.

"The Huntsman" [same as "The Gamekeeper"]
De Maegd-Soëp, Caroline. *Chekhov and Women* . . . , 217–218.
Pritchett, V. S. *Chekhov* . . . , 30–32.

"In the Cart"
De Maegd-Soëp, Caroline. *Chekhov and Women* . . . , 247–249.

"In the Gully"
Wilks, Ronald, Ed. "Introduction," 24–27.

"Ivanov"
Pritchett, V. S. *Chekhov* . . . , 46–51.

"The Kiss"
Pritchett, V. S. *Chekhov* . . . , 42–45.
Wilks, Ronald, Ed. "Introduction," 12.

"The Lady with the Dog" [same as "The Lady with the Lapdog," "The Lady
    with the Pet Dog," or "The Lady with the Small Dog"]
Bayley, John. *The Short Story* . . . , 111–122.
De Maegd-Soëp, Caroline. *Chekhov and Women* . . . , 314–321.
Pritchett, V. S. *Chekhov* . . . , 180–186.
Roberts, Edgar V., and Henry E. Jacobs. *Instructor's Manual* . . . , 71–72.
Sheidley, William E., and Ann Charters. *Instructor's Manual* . . . , 41–42; Char-
    ters, Ann, William E. Sheidley, and Martha Ramsey. *Instructor's Man-
    ual* . . . , 2nd ed., 45.

"The Man in a Case" [same as "The Man in a Shell"]
Freedman, John. "Narrative Technique . . . ," 2–7.
Ponomareff, Constantin V. *On the Dark Side* . . . , 188–189.
Wilks, Ronald, Ed. "Introduction," 20–21.

"My Life"
Pritchett, V. S. *Chekhov* . . . , 141–145.

"My Wife"
De Maegd-Soëp, Caroline. *Chekhov and Women* . . . , 277–278.

"The Name Day"
De Maegd-Soëp, Caroline. *Chekhov and Women* . . . , 276–277.

"On Official Duty"
Pritchett, V. S. *Chekhov* . . . , 186–187.

"On the Road"
De Maegd-Soëp, Caroline. *Chekhov and Women* . . . , 239–241.

Pritchett, V. S. *Chekhov* . . . , 46–48.

"The Order of St. Anne"
De Maegd-Soëp, Caroline. *Chekhov and Women* . . . , 288–289.

"Peasants"
Pritchett, V. S. *Chekhov* . . . , 152–155.
Wilks, Ronald, Ed. "Introduction," 12–14.

"The Princess"
Thiergen, Peter. "Fürstin und Braut: Zu A. P. Čechovs Erzählung 'Kniaginia,'"
    in Olesch, Reinhold, and Hans Rothe, Eds. *Festschrift für Herbert Bräuer* . . . ,
    585–608.

"The Russian Master"
Wilks, Ronald, Ed. "Introduction," 18–20.

"The Shooting Party"
Pritchett, V. S. *Chekhov* . . . , 22–23.

"Sleepy"
Harmat, Andrée-Marie. "Un très mansfieldien plagiat de Tchékov: 'L'Enfant-
    qui-était-fatiguée' de Katherine Mansfield," *Littératur,* 16 (Spring, 1987),
    49–68.
Ponomareff, Constantin V. *On the Dark Side* . . . , 188.

"The Steppe"
Ponomareff, Constantin V. *On the Dark Side* . . . , 190.
Pritchett, V. S. *Chekhov* . . . , 57–64.

"The Story of an Unknown Person"
De Maegd-Soëp, Caroline. *Chekhov and Women* . . . , 307–314.

"The Student"
Pritchett, V. S. *Chekhov* . . . , 130–132.

"Terror"
De Maegd-Soëp, Caroline. *Chekhov and Women* . . . , 303–304.

"The Three Sisters"
Pritchett, V. S. *Chekhov* . . . , 212–217.

"Three Years"
De Maegd-Soëp, Caroline. *Chekhov and Women* . . . , 242–243.
Pritchett, V. S. *Chekhov* . . . , 135–137.

"A Trifle from Real Life"
Sheidley, William E., and Ann Charters. *Instructor's Manual* . . . , 39–40; Char-
    ters, Ann, William E. Sheidley, and Martha Ramsey. *Instructor's Man-
    ual* . . . , 2nd ed., 43–44.

"Typhus"
Ponomareff, Constantin V. *On the Dark Side* . . . , 187.

"Verochka"
De Maegd-Soëp, Caroline. *Chekhov and Women* . . . , 250–252.

"Ward No. 6"
Ponomareff, Constantin V. *On the Dark Side* . . . , 190–191.
Pritchett, V. S. *Chekhov* . . . , 117–121.

"The Witch"
Pritchett, V. S. *Chekhov* . . . , 37–38.

"A Woman's Kingdom"
Jackson, Robert L. "Chekhov's 'A Woman's Kingdom': A Drama of Character
and Fate," *Russian Lang J,* 39 (1985), 1–11.

CH'EN YING-CHEN

"A Certain Afternoon"
Lau, Joseph S. M. "Death in the Void: Three Tales of Spiritual Atrophy in
Ch'en Ying-chen's Post-Incarceration Fiction," *Mod Chinese Lit,* 2, i (1986),
21–23.

"Forever Terra"
Lau, Joseph S. M. "Death in the Void . . . ," 23–24.

"Mountain Path"
Lau, Joseph S. M. "Death in the Void . . . ," 24–26.

MAXINE CHERNOFF

"Don't Send Poetry, Send Money"
Perloff, Marjorie. "Fiction as Language Game: The Hermeneutic Parables of
Lydia Davis and Maxine Chernoff," in Friedman, Ellen G., and Miriam
Fuchs, Eds. *Breaking the Sequence* . . . , 203–205.

CHARLES W. CHESNUTT

"The Conjurer's Revenge"
Baker, Houston A. *Modernism* . . . , 46–47.
Stepto, Robert B. "'The Simple but Intensely Human Inner Life of Slavery':
Storytelling, Fiction and the Revision of History in Charles W. Chesnutt's
'Uncle Julius Stories,'" in Lenz, Günter H., Ed. *History and Tradition* . . . ,
37–39.

"Dave's Neckliss"
Stepto, Robert B. ". . . Chesnutt's 'Uncle Julius Stories,'" 39–41.

"The Goophered Grapevine"
Callahan, John F. *In the African-American Grain . . .* , 45–47.
Stepto, Robert B. ". . . Chesnutt's 'Uncle Julius Stories,'" 34.

"The Gray Wolf's Ha'nt"
Baker, Houston A. *Modernism . . .* , 45–46.

"Hot-Foot Hannibal"
Callahan, John F. *In the African-American Grain . . .* , 54–56.
Condit, John H. "Pulling a Chesnutt Out of the Fire: 'Hot-Foot Hannibal,'"
    Coll Lang Assoc J, 30 (1987), 428–437.

"Mars Jeems's Nightmare"
Callahan, John F. *In the African-American Grain . . .* , 50–52.

"Po' Sandy"
Babb, Valerie. "Subversion and Repatriation in *The Conjure Woman,*" *Southern
    Q,* 25, ii (1987), 71–73.
Burnette, R. V. "Charles W. Chesnutt's *The Conjure Woman* Revisited," *Coll Lang
    Assoc J,* 30 (1987), 438–453.
Callahan, John F. *In the African-American Grain . . .* , 47–50.
Fienberg, Lorne. "Charles W. Chesnutt and Uncle Julius: Black Storyteller at
    the Crossroads," *Stud Am Fiction,* 15, ii (1987), 168–170.
Stepto, Robert B. ". . . Chesnutt's 'Uncle Julius Stories,'" 34–37.

"The Sheriff's Children"
Andrews, William L. "Charles Waddell Chesnutt," in Bain, Robert, and
    Joseph M. Flora, Eds. *Fifty Southern Writers Before 1900,* 112–113.

"Sis' Becky's Pickaninny"
Callahan, John F. *In the African-American Grain . . .* , 52–54.

RONALD CHETWYND-HAYES

"The Brats"
Büssing, Sabine. *Aliens in the Home . . .* , 45–46.

"My Mother Married a Vampire"
Büssing, Sabine. *Aliens in the Home . . .* , 111–112.

"Why?"
Büssing, Sabine. *Aliens in the Home . . .* , 114–115.

CHIKAMATSU SHŪKŌ

"A Snowy Day"
Fowler, Edward. *The Rhetoric of Confession . . .* , 158–160.

FRANK CHIN

"Food for All His Dead"
Lim, Shirley G. "Twelve Asian American Writers: In Search of Self-Definition,"
    MELUS, 13, i–ii (1986), 67–68.

KATE CHOPIN

"A Pair of Silk Stockings"
Valentine, Kristin B., and Janet L. Palmer. "The Rhetoric of Nineteenth-
    Century Feminism in Kate Chopin's 'A Pair of Silk Stockings,'" *Weber Stud,*
    4, ii (1987), 59–67.

"Regret"
Sheidley, William E., and Ann Charters. *Instructor's Manual . . .* , 32; Charters,
    Ann, William E. Sheidley, and Martha Ramsey. *Instructor's Manual . . .* , 2nd
    ed., 34–35.

SADEQ CHUBAK

"Flowers of Flesh"
Mostaghel, Deborah M. "The Second Sadeq: The Short Stories of Iranian
    Writer Sadeq Chubak," *World Lit Today,* 53 (1979), 229; rpt. Ricks,
    Thomas M., Ed. *Critical Perspectives . . .* , 314–315.

"The Glass Eye"
Mostaghel, Deborah M. "The Second Sadeq . . . ," 228; rpt. Ricks, Thomas M.,
    Ed. *Critical Perspectives . . .* , 312.

"Gravediggers"
Mostaghel, Deborah M. "The Second Sadeq . . . ," 230; rpt. Ricks, Thomas M.,
    Ed. *Critical Perspectives . . .* , 317.

"The Maroon Dress"
Mostaghel, Deborah M. "The Second Sadeq . . . ," 229; rpt. Ricks, Thomas M.,
    Ed. *Critical Perspectives . . .* , 314.

"The Monkey Whose Master Had Died"
Mostaghel, Deborah M. "The Second Sadeq . . . ," 228; rpt. Ricks, Thomas M.,
    Ed. *Critical Perspectives . . .* , 313–314.

"Monsieur Ilyas"
Mostaghel, Deborah M. "The Second Sadeq . . . ," 230; rpt. Ricks, Thomas M.,
    Ed. *Critical Perspectives . . .* , 319.

"Under the Red Light"
Mostaghel, Deborah M. "The Second Sadeq . . . ," 229; rpt. Ricks, Thomas M.,
    Ed. *Critical Perspectives . . .* , 316.

CLARÍN [LEOPOLDO ALAS]

"El caballero de la mesa redonda"
Thompson, Clifford R. "Egoism and Alienation in the Works of Leopoldo Alas," *Romanische Forschungen*, 81 (1969), 195–196.

"La conversion de Chirpa"
Griswold, Susan C. "Rhetorical Strategies and Didacticism in Clarín's Short Fiction," *Kentucky Romance Q*, 29 (1982), 426–427.
Thompson, Clifford R. "Egoism and Alienation . . . ," 198.

"Cuervo"
Thompson, Clifford R. "Egoism and Alienation . . . ," 194–195.

"El diablo en Semana Santa"
Richmond, Carolyn. "Gérmenes de *La Regenta* en tres cuentos de Clarín," in Kossoff, A. David, et al. [3], Eds. *Actas del VIII Congreso . . . ,* II, 499–502.

"El doctor Pértinax"
Richmond, Carolyn. "Gérmenes de *La Regenta . . . ,*" 504–505.

"Las dos cajas"
McBride, Charles A. "Alienation from Self in the Short Fiction of Leopoldo Alas, 'Clarín,'" in Pincus Sigele, Rizel, and Gonzalo Sobrejano, Eds. *Homenaje a Casalduero . . . ,* 382–383.

"El dúo de la tos"
McBride, Charles A. "Alienation from Self . . . ," 383–384.
Thompson, Clifford R. "Egoism and Alienation . . . ," 197–198.

"The Golden Rose"
Miller, Martha L. "Oppositions and Their Subversion in Clarín's 'La rosa de oro,'" *Mod Lang Stud,* 12, iii (1982), 99–109.

"Una medianía"
Valis, Noël M. "A Spanish Decadent Hero: Clarín's Reyes of 'Una medianía,'" *Mod Lang Stud,* 9, ii (1979), 53–60.

"Mi entierro"
Richmond, Carolyn. "Gérmenes de *La Regenta . . . ,*" 505–506.

"La mosca sabia"
Feeny, Thomas. "Burlesque Krausist Type in Pedera and Clarín," *Hispanic J,* 9, ii (1988), 50–51.

"Para vicios"
Griswold, Susan C. "Rhetorical Strategies . . . ," 429–430.

"Pipá"
Richmond, Carolyn. "Conexiones temáticas y estílisticas entre 'Pipá' y *La Regenta* de 'Clarín,'" in Vilanova, Antonio, Ed. *Clarín y su obra . . . ,* 229–250.

Valis, Noël M. "La 'Pipá' de Clarín y 'El incendio' de Ana María Matute: Una infancia traicionada," *Cuadernos del Norte*, 2 (May–June, 1981), 72–77.

"La Reina Margarita"
McBride, Charles A. "Alienation from Self . . . ," 384–385.

"Snob"
Griswold, Susan C. "Rhetorical Strategies . . . ," 428–429.

"Superchería"
McBride, Charles A. "Alienation from Self . . . ," 385–387.

"Zurita"
Feeny, Thomas. "Burlesque Krausist Type . . . ," 49–50.
McBride, Charles A. "Alienation from Self . . . ," 380–382.

WALTER VAN TILBURG CLARK

"Hook"
Ronald, Ann. "Walter Van Tilburg Clark's Brave Bird, 'Hook,'" *Stud Short Fiction*, 25 (1988), 433–439.

ARTHUR C. CLARKE

"The Star"
Ferrara, Patricia. "'Nature's Priest': Establishing Literary Criteria for Arthur C. Clarke's 'The Star,'" *Extrapolation*, 28 (1987), 148–158.

MARCUS CLARKE

"La Béguine"
Wilding, Michael. "The Short Stories of Marcus Clarke," in Cantrell, Leon, Ed. *Bards, Bohemians* . . . , 90–91.

"The Gypsies of the Sea"
Wilding, Michael. "'Weird Melancholy': Inner and Outer Landscapes in Marcus Clarke's Stories," in Eaden, P. R., and F. H. Mares, Eds. *Mapped But Unknown* . . . , 138–139.

"Holiday Peak"
Wilding, Michael. *Marcus Clarke*, 33.
———. "'Weird Melancholy' . . . ," 142–143.

"Human Repetends"
Wilding, Michael. "The Short Stories . . . ," 93–94.
———. *Marcus Clarke*, 34–35.

"Hunted Down"
Wilding, Michael. "'Weird Melancholy' . . . ," 132–133.

"A Mining Township"
Wilding, Michael. "'Weird Melancholy' . . . ," 130–131.

"The Mystery of Major Molineux"
Wilding, Michael. "The Short Stories . . . ," 94–95.

"Pretty Dick"
Wilding, Michael. "The Short Stories . . . ," 82–86.
————. *Marcus Clarke*, 32–33.

"An Up-Country Township"
Wilding, Michael. "The Short Stories . . . ," 76–78.

MILDRED CLINGERMAN

"A Red Heart and Blue Roses"
Büssing, Sabine. *Aliens in the Home* . . . , 135–136.

MANUEL COFRIÑO LÓPEZ

"Dania"
Salper, Roberta L. "Ideología y visión de la mujer en los cuentos de Manuel Cofriño," *Hispamerica*, 16 (April–August, 1987), 63–65.

"Magda, el mar, el aire"
Salper, Roberta L. "Ideología y visión . . . ," 64–66.

"El milagro de la lluvia"
Salper, Roberta L. "Ideología y visión . . . ," 61–62.

"Mirna"
Salper, Roberta L. "Ideología y visión . . . ," 67–69.

"Para leer mañana"
Salper, Roberta L. "Ideología y visión . . . ," 62–63.

"Tiempo de cambio"
Salper, Roberta L. "Ideología y visión . . . ," 60–61.

SIDONIE-GABRIELLE COLETTE

"Chéri"
Bal, Mieke. "Inconsciences de 'Chéri'—Chéri existe-i-ul?" in Bray, Bernard, Ed. *Colette* . . . , 15–25.
Kloepfer, R., V. Borso-Borgarello, J. Mecke, S. Kleinert, and E. Stern. "La Production du sens dans 'Chéri' de (1920)," in Bray, Bernard, Ed. *Colette* . . . , 117–129.
Massie, Allan. *Colette*, 91–94.

"Gigi"
Massie, Allan. *Colette*, 126–127.

"The Hidden Woman"
Holmes, Diana. "The Hidden Woman: Disguise and Paradox in Colette's 'La Femme cachée,'" *Essays French Lit,* 23 (November, 1986), 29–37.

"The Last of Chéri"
Massie, Allan. *Colette,* 135–136.

"The Tender Shoot"
Ketchum, Anne D. "Defining an Ethics from a Later Short Story by Colette," in Myers, Eunice, and Ginette Adamson, Eds. *Continental, Latin-American and Francophone Women Writers . . . ,* 71–77.

ALFREDO COLLADO MARTELL

"Guillo 'el Holandes'"
Melendez, Concha. *El arte del cuento . . . ,* 15–16.

"The Last Adventure of Patito Feo"
Melendez, Concha. *El arte del cuento . . . ,* 14–15.
Rosa, William. "'La última aventura del Papito Feo' o la posibilidades de un simbolo," *Revista de Estudios Hispánicos,* 22, ii (1988), 53–61.

[WILLIAM] WILKIE COLLINS

"A Terribly Strange Bed"
Rance, Nick. "'A Terribly Strange Bed': Self-Subverting Gothic," *Wilkie Collins Soc J,* 7 (1987), 5–12.

ENRIQUE CONGRAINS MARTÍN

"El niño de junto al cielo"
Menton, Seymour. *El Cuento Hispanoamericano,* II, 318–319; 2nd ed., 318–319; 3rd ed., 213–214.

RICHARD CONNELL

"The Most Dangerous Game"
*Perrine, Laurence, and Thomas R. Arp. *Instructor's Manual . . . ,* 7th ed., 1–2.

JOSEPH CONRAD

"Amy Foster"
Lester, John. *Conrad and Religion,* 83–84.
Wilson, Robert. *Conrad's Mythology,* 107–109.

"The Black Mate"
Lester, John. *Conrad and Religion,* 38–39.

Wilson, Robert. *Conrad's Mythology,* 100–101.

"The Brute"
Wilson, Robert. *Conrad's Mythology,* 99–100.

"The End of the Tether"
Lester, John. *Conrad and Religion,* 84–86.
Wilson, Robert. *Conrad's Mythology,* 54–56.

"Falk"
Anderson, Walter E. "'Falk': Conrad's Tale of Evolution," *Stud Short Fiction,* 25 (1988), 101–108.
Coates, Paul. *The Double and the Other...,* 79–80.
Lester, John. *Conrad and Religion,* 63–65.
Wilson, Robert. *Conrad's Mythology,* 64–67.

"Heart of Darkness"
Adelman, Gary. *Heart of Darkness...,* 61–88.
Anderson, Linda R. *Bennett, Wells, and Conrad...,* 181–190.
Baldick, Chris. *In Frankenstein's Shadow...,* 165–167.
Boyle, Ted. "Marlow's Choice in 'Heart of Darkness,'" in Gamache, Lawrence B., and Ian S. MacNiven, Eds. *The Modernists...,* 92–102.
Church, Andreas. "Conrad's 'Heart of Darkness,'" *Explicator,* 45, ii (1987), 35–37.
Clegg, Jerry S. "Conrad's Reply to Kierkegaard," *Philosophy & Lit,* 12 (1988), 280–289.
Coates, Paul. *The Double and the Other...,* 72–77.
*Cox, C. B. "'Heart of Darkness': A Choice of Nightmares?" in Bloom, Harold, Ed. *Joseph Conrad's "Heart of Darkness,"* 29–43.
Dilworth, Thomas. "Listeners and Lies in 'Heart of Darkness,'" *R Engl Stud,* 38 (1987), 510–522.
Echavarría, Arturo. "La confluencia de las aguas: La geografía como configuración del tiempo en *Los pasos perdidos* de Carpentier y 'Heart of Darkness' de Conrad," *Nueva Revista de Filología Hispánica,* 35, ii (1987), 531–541.
Fogle, Aaron. *Coercion...,* 18–21; rpt. Bloom, Harold, Ed. *Joseph Conrad's "Heart of Darkness,"* 131–134.
Fraser, Gail. *Interweaving Patterns...,* 85–97.
Geise, J. P., and L. A. Lange. "Deliberate Belief and Digging Holes: Joseph Conrad and the Problem of Restraint," *Interpretation,* 16, ii (1988–1989), 193–209.
Gekoski, R. A. *Conrad...,* 72–90; rpt. Bloom, Harold, Ed. *Joseph Conrad's "Heart of Darkness,"* 57–75.
Glenn, Ian. "Conrad's 'Heart of Darkness': A Sociological Reading," *Lit & Hist,* 13 (1987), 238–256.
Graham, Kenneth. *Indirections...,* 95–106.
*Guerard, Albert J. "The Journey Within," in Bloom, Harold, Ed. *Joseph Conrad's "Heart of Darkness,"* 5–16.
*Guetti, James. "'Heart of Darkness': The Failure of Imagination," in Bloom, Harold, Ed. *Joseph Conrad's "Heart of Darkness,"* 17–28.
Guth, Deborah. "Conrad's 'Heart of Darkness' as Creation Myth," *J European Stud,* 17 (1987), 155–166.
Hannson, Karin. "Two Journeys into the Country of the Mind: Joseph Conrad's

'Heart of Darkness' and Saul Bellow's *Henderson the Rain King*," in Jurak, Mirko, Ed. *Cross-Cultural Studies . . .* , 433–444.

Henricksen, Bruce. "'Heart of Darkness' and the Gnostic Myth," *Mosaic*, 11, iv (1978), 35–44; rpt. Bloom, Harold, Ed. *Joseph Conrad's "Heart of Darkness,"* 45–55.

Hewitt, Douglas. *English Fiction . . .* , 31–38.

Hoeppner, Edward H. "'Heart of Darkness': An Archeology of the Lie," *Conradiana*, 20 (1988), 137–146.

Hyland, Peter. "The Little Woman in the 'Heart of Darkness,'" *Conradiana*, 20 (1988), 3–11.

Kharbutli, Mahmoud K. "The Treatment of Women in 'Heart of Darkness,'" *Dutch Q R*, 17 (1987), 237–248.

Lester, John. *Conrad and Religion*, 94–97, 117–119, 146–148.

Levine, George. *The Realistic Imagination . . .* , 278–281.

Losey, Jay B. "'Moments of Awakening' in Conrad's Fiction," *Conradiana*, 20 (1988), 93–95, 101–102.

Meisel, Perry. *The Myth of the Modern . . .* , 229–232.

Milne, Fred L. "Marlow's Lie and the Intended: Civilization as the Lie in 'Heart of Darkness,'" *Arizona Q*, 44 (1988), 106–112.

Neilson, Renn G. "Conrad's 'Heart of Darkness,'" *Explicator*, 45, iii (1987), 41–42.

Reilly, Patrick. *The Literature of Guilt . . .* , 46–68.

Ressler, Steve. *Joseph Conrad . . .* , 7–23.

Rowe, Joyce A. *Equivocal Endings . . .* , 118–121.

Saha, P. K. "Conrad's 'Heart of Darkness,'" *Explicator*, 45, ii (1987), 34–35.

Sexton, Mark S. "Kurtz's Sketch in Oil: Its Significance to 'Heart of Darkness,'" *Stud Short Fiction*, 24 (1987), 387–392.

Sheidley, William E., and Ann Charters. *Instructor's Manual . . .* , 36–37; Charters, Ann, William E. Sheidley, and Martha Ramsey. *Instructor's Manual . . .* , 2nd ed., 40–41.

Sisk, John P. "The Doubtful Pleasures of the Higher *Agape*," *Southern R*, 24, i (1988), 134–144.

Skinner, John. "The Oral and the Written: Kurtz and Gatsby Revisited," *J Narrative Technique*, 17 (1987), 131–140.

Straus, Nina P. "The Exclusion of the Intended from Secret Sharing in Conrad's 'Heart of Darkness,'" *Novel*, 20 (1987), 123–137.

Tessitore, John. "Freud, Conrad, and 'Heart of Darkness,'" *Coll Lit*, 7 (1980), 30–40; rpt. Bloom, Harold, Ed. *Joseph Conrad's "Heart of Darkness,"* 91–103.

Trethewey, Eric. "Language, Experience, and Selfhood in Conrad's 'Heart of Darkness,'" *Southern Hum R*, 22, ii (1988), 101–111.

*Wasserman, Jerry. "Narrative Presence: The Illusion of Language in 'Heart of Darkness,'" in Billy, Ted, Ed. *Critical Essays . . .* , 102–113.

Wilson, Robert. *Conrad's Mythology*, 44–48.

Winners, Anthony. *Culture and Irony . . .* , 1–5.

"The Idiots"

Lester, John. *Conrad and Religion*, 70–72.

"The Inn of the Two Witches"

Wilson, Robert. *Conrad's Mythology*, 102–103.

"Karain"
Lester, John. *Conrad and Religion,* 56–57.
Wilson, Robert. *Conrad's Mythology,* 63–64.

"The Lagoon"
Fraser, Gail. *Interweaving Patterns . . . ,* 27–34.
Wilson, Robert. *Conrad's Mythology,* 98–99.

"An Outpost of Progress"
Gibert, Teresa. "'An Outpost of Progress': La ironía imperial de Joseph Con-
     rad," *Epos,* 4 (1988), 469–482.
Lester, John. *Conrad and Religion,* 148–149.

"The Return"
Kramer, Dale. "Conrad's Experiments with Language and Narrative in 'The
     Return,'" *Stud Short Fiction,* 25 (1988), 1–11.
Lester, John. *Conrad and Religion,* 149–152.
Wilson, Robert. *Conrad's Mythology,* 97–98.

"The Secret Sharer"
Adelman, Gary. *Heart of Darkness . . . ,* 50–53.
Bayley, John. *The Short Story . . . ,* 38–40.
Coates, Paul. *The Double and the Other . . . ,* 56–58.
Cohen, Michael. "Sailing through 'The Secret Sharer': The End of Conrad's
     Story," *Massachusetts Stud Engl,* 10 (1985), 102–109.
Facknitz, Mark A. R. "Cryptic Allusions and the Moral of the Story," *J Narrative
     Technique,* 17 (1987), 115–130.
Fraser, Gail. *Interweaving Patterns . . . ,* 112–133.
Johnson, Barbara, and Marjorie Garber. "Secret Sharing: Reading Conrad Psy-
     choanalytically," *Coll Engl,* 49 (1987), 628–640.
Lester, John. *Conrad and Religion,* 142–143.
Meisel, Perry. *The Myth of the Modern . . . ,* 232–236.
Paccaud, Josiane. "Under the Other's Eye: Conrad's 'The Secret Sharer,'" *Con-
     radiana,* 12 (1987), 59–73.
Ressler, Steve. *Joseph Conrad . . . ,* 80–97.
Wilson, Robert. *Conrad's Mythology,* 101–102.

"The Shadow Line"
Graham, Kenneth. *Indirections . . . ,* 142–153.
Lester, John. *Conrad and Religion,* 140–142.

"The Tale"
D'Elia, Gaetano. "Let Us Make Tales, Not Love: Conrad's 'The Tale,'" *Conra-
     diana,* 12 (1987), 50–58.

"Tomorrow"
Wilson, Robert. *Conrad's Mythology,* 57–58.

"Typhoon"
Kolupke, Joseph. "Elephants, Empires, and Blind Men: A Reading of the Fig-
     urative Language in Conrad's 'Typhoon,'" *Conradiana,* 20 (1988), 71–85.
Lester, John. *Conrad and Religion,* 124–128.

Piticari, Cornelia. "J. Conrad's 'Typhoon': Point of View and Characterization," *Analele Ştiinţifice ale Universităţii*, 33 (1987), 93–97.
Wilson, Robert. *Conrad's Mythology*, 53–54.

"Youth"
Fraser, Gail. *Interweaving Patterns . . .* , 51–83.
Hanford, James. "Reflection and Self-Consumption in 'Youth,'" *The Conradian*, 12 (1987), 150–165.
Lester, John. *Conrad and Religion*, 143–144.
Renner, Stanley. "'Youth' and the Sinking Ship of Faith: Conrad's Miniature Nineteenth-Century Epic," *Ball State Univ Forum*, 28, i (1987), 57–73.
Roberts, Edgar V., and Henry E. Jacobs. *Instructor's Manual . . .* , 72–73.
Wilson, Robert. *Conrad's Mythology*, 40–43.

BENJAMIN CONSTANT

"Adolphe"
Call, Michael J. *Back to the Garden . . .* , 95–124.
Dawson, Terence. "Victims of Their Own Contending Passions: Unexpected Death in 'Adolphe,' *Ivanhoe*, and *Wuthering Heights*," *New Comparison*, 6 (Autumn, 1988), 84–89.
Spencer, Michael. "'L'on se recontait mon histoire': Embedding, Narration and Judgment in 'Adolphe,'" *French Forum*, 12, ii (1987), 175–185.
Wood, Dennis, *Benjamin Constant . . .* , 32–51.

GONZALO CONTRERAS

"Naves quemadas"
Jorquera, Cecilia. "'Naves quemadas': La demitificación de un héroe histórico," *Revista Chilena Literatura*, 29 (April, 1987), 171–177.

ROBERT COOVER

"The Babysitter"
Cassill, R. V. . . . *Instructor's Handbook*, 16–18.

"The Brother"
Levitt, Morton P. *Modernist Survivors . . .* , 92–94.
Wilczynski, Marek. "The Game of Response in Robert Coover's Fiction," *Kwartalnik Neofilologiczny*, 33 (1986), 519.

"The Elevator"
Christ, Donald. "Forking Narrative," *Latin Am Lit R*, 7 (Spring–Summer, 1979), 55–56.

"In a Train Station"
Mackey, Louis. "Robert Coover's Dirty Stories: Allegories of Reading in 'Seven Exemplary Fictions,'" *Iowa R*, 17, ii (1987), 108–110.
Wilczynski, Marek. "The Game . . . ," 520–521.

"J's Marriage"
Wilczynski, Marek. "The Game . . . ," 520.

"Klee Dead"
Wilczynski, Marek. "The Game . . . ," 521–522.

"The Marker"
Mackey, Louis. "Robert Coover's Dirty Stories . . . ," 106–108.

"Panel Game"
Mackey, Louis. "Robert Coover's Dirty Stories . . . ," 103–106.
Wilczynski, Marek. "The Game . . . ," 517–518.

"Quenby and Ola, Swede and Carl"
McHale, Brian. *Postmodern Fiction,* 107–108.

"The Wayfarer"
Mackey, Louis. "Robert Coover's Dirty Stories . . . ," 110–113.
Wilczynski, Marek. "The Game . . . ," 522–523.

DANIEL CORKERY

"The Awakening"
Doherty, Francis. "Daniel Corkery and the Isolate," *J Short Story Engl,* 8 (1987),
    43–44.

"The Eyes of the Dead"
Doherty, Francis. "Daniel Corkery . . . ," 44–46.

"A Looter of the Hills"
Doherty, Francis. "Daniel Corkery . . . ," 38–39.

"The Serenade"
Doherty, Francis. "Daniel Corkery . . . ," 41–43.

"Vision"
Doherty, Francis. "Daniel Corkery . . . ," 40–41.

"The Wraith of the Kilronans"
Doherty, Francis. "Daniel Corkery . . . ," 47–48.

JULIO CORTÁZAR

"After Breakfast"
Mora Valcárcel, Carmen de. *Teoría y Práctica . . . ,* 214.
Standish, Peter. "Adolescence in the Stories of Julio Cortázar," *Mod Lang R,* 82
    (1987), 641–642.

"Ahí pero dónde, cómo"
Mora Valcárcel, Carmen de. *Teoría y Práctica . . . ,* 120–121.

"All Fires the Fire"
Mora Valcárcel, Carmen de. *Teoría y Práctica* . . . , 117, 218–219.
Saad, Gabriel. "El personaje y la producción de lo fantástico en 'Todos los fuegos el fuego,'" in *Coloquio internacional* . . . , II, 197–209.

"Apocalypse at Solentiname"
Tittler, Jonathan. "Los dos Solentinames de Cortázar," in *Coloquio internacional* . . . , II, 111–117.

"Around the Day in Eighty Worlds"
Hernández de López, Ana María. "Los ochenta mundos de la vuelta al día: El arte de Cortázar," in Burgos, Fernando, Ed. *Los ochenta mundos* . . . , 191–198.

"Axolotl"
Díaz, Nancy G. *The Radical Self* . . . , 76–82.
Fontmarty, Francis. "Xolotl, mexolotl, axolotl: Una metamorfosis recreativa," *Coloquio internacional* . . . , II, 79–88.
Leenhardt, Jacques. "La americanidad de Julio Cortázar: El otro y su mirada," *Inti*, 22–23 (Autumn–Spring, 1985–1986), 307–315.
Llanos, Bernardita. "'Axolotl': Fluidez existencial," *ULULA*, 2 (1986), 111–116.
Mora Valcárcel, Carmen de. *Teoría y Práctica* . . . , 123–124, 167.
Pérez Firmat, Gustavo. "Lecture de/en 'Axolotl,'" *Chasqui*, 17, ii (1988), 41–45.
Shivers, George R. "The Other Within and the Other Without: The Writer's Role and Personality in Works by Julio Cortázar and Gabriel García Márquez," in Rogers, Elizabeth S. and Timothy S., Eds. *In Retrospect* . . . , 141–142.
Smith, Kim. "Cortázar's Tragic Hero," *Hispanófila*, 93 (May, 1988), 79–84.
Wight, Doris F. "Cortázar's 'Axolotl,'" *Explicator*, 45, ii (1987), 59–63.

"The Band"
Mora Valcárcel, Carmen de. *Teoría y Práctica* . . . , 129, 169–170.
Morello-Frosch, Marta. "La Banda de los Otros: política fantástica en un cuento de Julio Cortázar," in Schwartz Lerner, Lía, and Isaías Lerner, Eds. *Homenaje de Ana María Barrenechea*, 497–503.
————. "El discurso de armas y letras en las narraciones de Julio Cortázar," in *Coloquio internacional* . . . , I, 151–162.
Wilson, Jason. "Julio Cortázar and the Drama of Reading," in King, John, Ed. *On Modern Latin American Fiction*, 180–181.

"Bestiary"
Díaz, Nancy G. *The Radical Self* . . . , 74–75.
Mora Valcárcel, Carmen de. *Teoría y Práctica* . . . , 104–105, 211–212.

"Blow-Up"
Esrock, Ellen J. "Visual Imagining and Reader Response," *Coll Engl Assoc Critic*, 51, i (1988), 30–38.
Gutiérrez Mouat, Ricardo. "'Las babas del diablo': Exorcismo traducción, voyeurismo," in Burgos, Fernando, Ed. *Los ochenta mundos* . . . , 37–46.
McMurray, George R. *Spanish American Writing* . . . , 57–58.
Mora Valcárcel, Carmen de. *Teoría y Práctica* . . . , 130–131, 175–178.

Muñoz, Willy O. "Julio Cortázar: Vertices de una figura comprometida," *Hispanic J*, 8, i (1986), 135–145.
Rabkin, Eric. "Fantastic Verbal Portraits of Fantastic Visual Portraits," *Mosaic*, 21, 4 (1988), 91–92.
Shivers, George R. "The Other Within . . . ," 143–144.
Volek, Emil. "'Las babas del diablo," la narración political y el relato conjetural borgeano: Esquizofrenia crítica y creación literaria," in Burgos, Fernando, Ed. *Los ochenta mundos* . . . , 27–35.

"La caricia más profunda"
Mora Valcárcel, Carmen de. *Teoría y Práctica* . . . , 127–128.

"Cefalea"
Mora Valcárcel, Carmen de. *Teoría y Práctica* . . . , 145–146, 201–202.

"Circe"
Mora Valcárcel, Carmen de. *Teoría y Práctica* . . . , 153–154, 203–204.

"The Condemned Door"
Mora Valcárcel, Carmen de. *Teoría y Práctica* . . . , 109–110.

"Continuity of Parks"
Greimas, Algirdas-Julien. "Una mano, una mejilla," *Revista de Occidente*, 85 (June, 1988), 31–37.
Lagmanovich, David. "Estrategias del cuento breve en Cortázar: Un paseo por 'Continuidad de los parques,'" *Explicación de Textos Literarios*, 17, i–ii (1988–1989), 177–185.
Smith, Kim. ". . . Tragic Hero," 79–84.

"Deshoras"
Abdala, Marisa. "Secuencia y temporalidad en 'Deshoras' de Julio Cortázar," *Hispanic J*, 7, ii (1986), 115–120.

"Diario para un cuento"
Barrera, Trinidad. "Los Mecanismos discursivos de 'Diario para un cuento,'" in *Coloquio internacional* . . . , II, 155–165.
Berg, Walter B. "De convergencias, confesiones y confesores: 'Diario para un cuento,'" *Inti*, 22–23 (Autumn–Spring, 1985–1986), 327–336.
Frölicher, Peter. "El sujeto y su relato: 'Argentinidad' y reflexión estética en 'Diario para un cuento,'" *Inti*, 22–23 (Autumn–Spring, 1985–1986), 337–344.

"The Distances"
Lavaud, Elaine. "Acercamiento a 'Lejana' de Julio Cortázar," *Coloquio internacional* . . . , II, 67–77.
Mora Valcárcel, Carmen de. *Teoría y Práctica* . . . , 124–126, 167–168.

"End of the Game"
Cavallari, Hector M. "Julio Cortázar: Todos los juegos el juego," in Burgos, Fernando, Ed. *Los ochenta mundos* . . . , 111–120.
Mora Valcárcel, Carmen de. *Teoría y Práctica* . . . , 159–160, 216.

"Estación de la mano"
Mora Valcárcel, Carmen de. *Teoría y Práctica* . . . , 111–112, 162–163.

"Footsteps in the Footprints"
Birkerts, Sven. *An Artificial Wilderness* . . . , 247–248.
Mora Valcárcel, Carmen de. *Teoría y Práctica* . . . , 115–116, 164–165, 206–207.

"The Gates of Heaven"
Mora Valcárcel, Carmen de. *Teoría y Práctica* . . . , 129–130, 172.

"Graffiti"
Cochran, Terry. "Critical Action and the 'Third World,'" *Critical Exchange*, 22 (Spring, 1987), 1–9.
Díaz-Navarro, Epicteto. "Estrategias narrativas en 'Graffiti' de Julio Cortázar," *Romance Notes*, 29, ii (1988), 99–106.
Morell-Frosch, Marta. "Espacios públicos y discurso clandestino en los cuentos de Julio Cortázar," in Burgos, Fernando, Ed. *Los ochenta mundos* . . . , 75–83.
Moreno, Fernando. "Cuento y politica, politica del cuento: Lectura de 'Graffiti' de Julio Cortázar," *Inti*, 22–23 (Autumn–Spring, 1985–1986), 239–245.

"The Health of the Sick Ones"
Dixon, Paul B. "Ficción sobre ficción: 'La salud de los enfermos' de Julio Cortázar," *Crítica Hispánica*, 8, ii (1986), 137–143.
Mora Valcárcel, Carmen de. *Teoría y Práctica* . . . , 154–155, 214–216.

"House Taken Over"
Cifuentes, Claudio. "Un personaje ausente en fantasticidad de dos relatos de Julio Cortázar: La let de la propiedad privada," in *Coloquio internacional* . . . , II, 89–95.
Mora Valcárcel, Carmen de. *Teoría y Práctica* . . . , 119–120, 146–147, 208–209.
Ramond, Michèle. "La casa de sus sueños: Sobre 'Casa tomada' de Julio Cortázar," in *Coloquio internacional* . . . , II, 97–109.
Rosenblat, María. "La nostalgia de la unidad en elcuento fantástico: 'The Fall of the House of Usher' y 'Casa tomada,'" in Burgos, Fernando, Ed. *Los ochenta mundos* . . . , 199–209.
Smith, Kim. ". . . Tragic Hero," 79–84.
Soifer, Miguelina. "Cortázar: 'Casa tomada': Casa desertada," *Revista Letras*, 35 (1986), 173–184.

"The Idol of the Cyclades"
Mora Valcárcel, Carmen de. *Teoría y Práctica* . . . , 102–103, 212–213.

"In the Name of Bobby"
Ezquerro, Milagros. "Alguien que habla por ahí: De los efectos fantásticos de la enunciación en dos cuentos de *Alguien que anda ahí*," *Coloquia internacional* . . . , I, 119–124.

"The Isle at Noon"
Mora Valcárcel, Carmen de. *Teoría y Práctica* . . . , 178–180.

Schulz, Bernhardt R. "'La señorita Cora' a la sombra del mito," *Tropos*, 4, i (1988), 1–8.

Standish, Peter. "Adolescence in the Stories . . . ," 639–641, 643–646.

"Omnibus"
Mora Valcárcel, Carmen de. *Teoría y Práctica* . . . , 106–107, 152, 209–211.

"Orientation of Cats"
Mora Valcárcel, Carmen de. "'Orientación de los gatos': Apuntes para una poetica," *Coloquio internacional* . . . , II, 167–180.

"The Other Heaven"
McGuirk, Bernard J. "La semi(er)ótica de la otredad: 'El otro cielo,'" *Inti*, 22–23 (Autumn–Spring, 1985–1986), 345–354.
Mora Valcárcel, Carmen de. *Teoría y Práctica* . . . , 131–132, 180–182.
Standish, Peter. "Adolescence in the Stories . . . ," 642.
Terramorsi, Bernard. "Lieux de l'irréel et place de l'idéologie dans les recits de Julio Cortázar," *Licorne*, 10 (1986), 56–60.

"Paseo entre las jaulas"
Galeota Cajeti, Adele. "Continuidad de los bestiarios: Consideraciones sobre 'Paseo entre las jaulas,'" *Coloquio internacional* . . . , I, 45–54.

"Pesadillas"
Kason, Nancy M. "Las 'pesadillas' metafóricas de Cortázar," in Burgos, Fernando, Ed. *Los ochenta mundos* . . . , 149–156.

"The Pursuer"
Gyurko, Lanin A. "Quest and Betrayal in Cortázar's 'El perseguidor,'" *Hispano*, 31, iii (1988), 59–78.
Hudde, Hinrich. "El negro Fausto del jazz," trans. Gabriela La Torre, in *Coloquio internacional* . . . , II, 37–47.
Mora Valcárcel, Carmen de. *Teoría y Práctica* . . . , 132–133, 191–193.
Shaw, Donald L. *Nueva narrativa* . . . , 2nd ed., 91–92.
Suárez-Galbán Guerra, Eugenio. "Cortázar como negro: 'El perseguidor,'" in *Coloquio internacional* . . . , II, 49–58.

"Recortes de prensa"
Alazraki, Jaime. "From *Bestiario* to *Glenda*: Pushing the Short Story to Its Utmost Limits," in Rogers, Elizabeth S. and Timothy S., Eds. *In Retrospect* . . . , 137–138.

"Relato con un fondo de agua"
Mora Valcárcel, Carmen de. *Teoría y Práctica* . . . , 101–102, 202–203.

"Reunion"
González, Aníbal. "Revolución y alegoría en 'Reunión' de Julio Cortázar," in Burgos, Fernando, Ed. *Los ochenta mundos* . . . , 93–109.
Mora Valcárcel, Carmen de. *Teoría y Práctica* . . . , 170–171.

"The River"
Mora Valcárcel, Carmen de. *Teoría y Práctica* . . . , 110–111.

Turner, John H. "Sexual Violence in Two Stories by Julio Cortázar: Reading as Psychotherapy," *Latin Am Lit R*, 15 (July–December, 1987), 43–56.

"Satarsa"
Sicard, Alain. "Satarsa: (M)atar a la rata," *Coloquio internacional* . . . , II, 191–195.

"Second Time Around"
Terramorsi, Bernard. "Acotaciones sobre lo fantástico y lo político: A propósito de 'Secunda vez' de Julio Cortázar," *Inti*, 22–23 (Autumn–Spring, 1985–1986), 231–237.

"Secret Weapons"
Dehennin, Elsa. "Estrategia discursiva al servicio de lo fantástico en 'Las armas secretas,'" in *Coloquio internacional* . . . , II, 21–36.
Mora Valcárcel, Carmen de. *Teoría y Práctica* . . . , 127, 172–174.
Solortorevsky, Myrna. "Contienda entre indicios y anti-indicios en una meta-lectura de 'Las armas secretas' de Julio Cortázar," *Anales de Literatura Hispanoamericana*, 13 (1984), 105–127.
Turner, John H. "Sexual Violence . . . ," 43–56.

"Siesta"
Mora Valcárcel, Carmen de. *Teoría y Práctica* . . . , 110, 161–162, 205–206.

"Silvia"
Mora Valcárcel, Carmen de. *Teoría y Práctica* . . . , 112, 165–166, 208.
Tyler, Joseph. "El elemento infantil en la ficción de Julio Cortázar," Burgos, Fernando, Ed. *Los ochenta mundos* . . . , 157–165.

"Someone Walks Around"
Vázquez, Carmen. "La functión de la música en 'Alguien que anda por ahí,'" in *Coloquio internacional* . . . , II, 125–133.

"The Southern Throughway"
Antonucci, Fausta. "Juego, rito y pasaje en 'La autopista del sur,'" *Coloquio internacional* . . . , II, 145–154.
McMurray, George R. *Spanish American Writing* . . . , 54–55.
Mora Valcárcel, Carmen de. *Teoría y Práctica* . . . , 114–115, 166–167.

"Torito"
Alegría, Fernando. "El 'Torito': Pasión y descanso," *Explicacíon de Textos Literarios*, 17, i–ii (1988–1989), 21–26.

"Usted se tendio a tu lado"
Ezquerro, Milagros. "Alguien que habla . . . ," 119–124.

"Los venenos"
Mora Valcárcel, Carmen de. *Teoría y Práctica* . . . , 155–156.

"Verano"
McMurray, George R. *Spanish American Writing* . . . , 55–56.
Mora Valcárcel, Carmen de. *Teoría y Práctica* . . . , 163–164, 206.

"We Love Glenda So Much"
Berg, Mary G. "Obsesionado con Glenda: Cortázar, Quiroga, Poe," in Burgos, Fernando, Ed. *Los ochenta mundos* . . . , 211–214.

"Witch"
Andreu, Jean. "La 'Bruja' nuclear de Julio Cortázar," in *Coloquio internacional* . . . , II, 59–66.

"With True Pride"
Mora Valcárcel, Carmen de. *Teoría y Práctica* . . . , 105–106, 142.

"A Yellow Flower"
Mora Valcárcel, Carmen de. *Teoría y Práctica* . . . , 169.

MARK COSTELLO

"Murphy's Xmas"
Cassill, R. V. . . . *Instructor's Handbook,* 18–20.

STEPHEN CRANE

"The Blue Hotel"
Knapp, Bettina L. *Stephen Crane,* 158–161.
Tanner, Tony. *Scenes of Nature* . . . , 145–146.

"The Bride Comes to Yellow Sky"
Knapp, Bettina L. *Stephen Crane,* 155–156.
Perrine, Laurence, and Thomas R. Arp. *Instructor's Manual* . . . , 6th ed., 52–53; 7th ed., 54–55.
Sheidley, William E., and Ann Charters. *Instructor's Manual* . . . , 52–53; Charters, Ann, William E. Sheidley, and Martha Ramsey. *Instructor's Manual* . . . , 2nd ed., 58–59.
Tanner, Tony. *Scenes of Nature* . . . , 144–145.

"The Clan of No-Name"
Knapp, Bettina L. *Stephen Crane,* 171–172.

"Death and the Child"
Fried, Michael. *Realism* . . . , 108–119.

"An Episode of War"
Knapp, Bettina L. *Stephen Crane,* 169–170.
*Trachtenberg, Alan. "Experiments in Another Country: Stephen Crane's City Sketches," in Bloom, Harold, Ed. *Stephen Crane,* 74–75.

"An Experiment in Misery"
Fried, Michael. *Realism* . . . , 101–104.

Knapp, Bettina L. *Stephen Crane,* 17–18.
*Trachtenberg, Alan. "Experiments in Another Country . . . ," 75–78.

"Five White Mice"
Knapp, Bettina L. *Stephen Crane,* 149–150.

"Four Men in a Cave"
Knapp, Bettina L. *Stephen Crane,* 13–14.

"George's Mother"
Green, Carol H. "Stephen Crane and the Fallen Woman," in Fleischmann, Fritz,
    Ed. *American Novelists Revisited . . . ,* 236–237; rpt. Bloom, Harold, Ed. *Stephen Crane,* 111–112.

"His New Mittens"
Knapp, Bettina L. *Stephen Crane,* 175–178.

"An Indian Campaign"
Knapp, Bettina L. *Stephen Crane,* 166–167.

"Killing His Bear"
Knapp, Bettina L. *Stephen Crane,* 14–15.

"The Little Regiment"
Aaron, Daniel. *The Unwritten War . . . ,* 218–219.

"Maggie: A Girl of the Streets"
Green, Carol H. ". . . Fallen Woman," 234–236; rpt. Bloom, Harold, Ed. *Stephen Crane,* 109–111.
Knapp, Bettina L. *Stephen Crane,* 39–58.

"A Man and Some Others"
Knapp, Bettina L. *Stephen Crane,* 150–151.

"The Monster"
Fried, Michael. "Stephen Crane's Upturned Faces," in Bloom, Harold, Ed. *Stephen Crane,* 146–148; rpt. Fried, Michael. *Realism . . . ,* 94–96.
Green, Carol H. ". . . Fallen Woman," 237–238; rpt. Bloom, Harold, Ed. *Stephen Crane,* 112–113.

"A Mystery of Heroism"
Knapp, Bettina L. *Stephen Crane,* 165–166.

"One Dash—Horses"
Knapp, Bettina L. *Stephen Crane,* 147–148.

"The Open Boat"
*LaFrance, Marston. "'The Open Boat,'" in Bloom, Harold, Ed. *Stephen Crane,* 55–63.
Muhlestein, Daniel K. "Crane's 'The Open Boat,'" *Explicator,* 45 (1987), 42–43.
Sheidley, William E., and Ann Charters. *Instructor's Manual . . . ,* 48–50; Char-

ters, Ann, William E. Sheidley, and Martha Ramsey. *Instructor's Manual . . .* , 2nd ed., 55–56.

"The Pace of Youth"
Knapp, Bettina L. *Stephen Crane,* 146–147.

"The Price of the Harness"
Knapp, Bettina L. *Stephen Crane,* 170–171.

"The Upturned Face"
Fried, Michael. "Stephen Crane's Upturned Faces," 148–152; rpt. Fried, Michael. *Realism . . .* , 96–101.
Knapp, Bettina L. *Stephen Crane,* 172–174.

"The Veteran"
Knapp, Bettina L. *Stephen Crane,* 167–168.

"When Man Falls, a Crowd Gathers"
Fried, Michael. *Realism . . .* , 104–108.

"The Wise Men"
Knapp, Bettina L. *Stephen Crane,* 148–149.

BERNARD DADIÉ

"The Black Loincloth"
MacGaffey, Wyatt. "The Black Loincloth and the Son of Nzambi Mpungu," *Research African Lit,* 5 (1974), 23–30.

ROALD DAHL

"An African Story"
Warren, Alan. *Roald Dahl,* 20–21.

"Ah! Sweet Mystery of Life, at Last I've Found Thee"
Warren, Alan. *Roald Dahl,* 60–61.

"Beware of the Dog"
Warren, Alan. *Roald Dahl,* 24–25.

"Bitch"
Warren, Alan. *Roald Dahl,* 54.

"The Bookseller"
Warren, Alan. *Roald Dahl,* 61–62.

"The Boy Who Talked to Animals"
Warren, Alan. *Roald Dahl,* 55.

"The Butler"
Warren, Alan. *Roald Dahl,* 58–59.

"The Champion of the World"
Warren, Alan. *Roald Dahl,* 48–49.

"Claud's Dog"
Warren, Alan. *Roald Dahl,* 40–42.

"Death of an Old, Old Man"
Warren, Alan. *Roald Dahl,* 20.

"Dip in the Pool"
Warren, Alan. *Roald Dahl,* 32–33.

"Edward the Conqueror"
Warren, Alan. *Roald Dahl,* 47.

"Galloping Foxley"
Warren, Alan. *Roald Dahl,* 33.

"Genesis and Catastrophe" [same as "A Fine Son"]
Warren, Alan. *Roald Dahl,* 47.

"Georgy Porgy"
Warren, Alan. *Roald Dahl,* 46.

"The Great Automatic Grammatisator"
Warren, Alan. *Roald Dahl,* 39–40.

"The Great Switcheroo"
Warren, Alan. *Roald Dahl,* 52.

"The Hitchhiker"
Warren, Alan. *Roald Dahl,* 55.

"Kalina"
Warren, Alan. *Roald Dahl,* 23.

"Lamb to Slaughter"
Warren, Alan. *Roald Dahl,* 28–29.

"The Landlady"
Warren, Alan. *Roald Dahl,* 42–43.

"The Last Act"
Warren, Alan. *Roald Dahl,* 52–53.

"Madame Rosette"
Warren, Alan. *Roald Dahl,* 22–23.

"Man from the South"
Warren, Alan. *Roald Dahl,* 29–30.

"The Mildenhall Treasure"
Warren, Alan. *Roald Dahl*, 55–56.

"Mr. Botibol"
Warren, Alan. *Roald Dahl*, 59.

"Mrs. Bixby and the Colonel's Coat"
Warren, Alan. *Roald Dahl*, 45.

"My Lady Love, My Dove"
Warren, Alan. *Roald Dahl*, 31–32.

"Neck"
Warren, Alan. *Roald Dahl*, 36–37.

"Nunc Dimittis" [originally titled "The Devious Bachelor"]
Warren, Alan. *Roald Dahl*, 38–39.

"Only This"
Warren, Alan. *Roald Dahl*, 25.

"Parson's Pleasure"
Warren, Alan. *Roald Dahl*, 44.

"Pig"
Warren, Alan. *Roald Dahl*, 47–48.

"Poison"
Warren, Alan. *Roald Dahl*, 34–36.

"Royal Jelly"
Warren, Alan. *Roald Dahl*, 45–46.

"The Ruins"
Warren, Alan. *Roald Dahl*, 60.

"Shot Down in Libya" [originally titled "A Piece of Cake"]
Warren, Alan. *Roald Dahl*, 21–22.

"Skin"
Warren, Alan. *Roald Dahl*, 33–34.

"The Soldier"
Warren, Alan. *Roald Dahl*, 30–31.

"Someone Like You"
Warren, Alan. *Roald Dahl*, 25–26.

"The Sound Machine"
Warren, Alan. *Roald Dahl*, 38.

"The Swan"
Warren, Alan. *Roald Dahl,* 56–57.

"Taste"
Warren, Alan. *Roald Dahl,* 27–28.

"They Shall Not Grow Old"
Warren, Alan. *Roald Dahl,* 24.

"Vengeance Is Mine, Inc."
Warren, Alan. *Roald Dahl,* 59–60.

"The Visitor"
Warren, Alan. *Roald Dahl,* 49–51.

"The Way up to Heaven"
Warren, Alan. *Roald Dahl,* 43–44.

"William and Mary"
Warren, Alan. *Roald Dahl,* 43.

"The Wish"
Warren, Alan. *Roald Dahl,* 36.

"The Wonderful Story of Henry Sugar"
Warren, Alan. *Roald Dahl,* 57.

"Yesterday Was Beautiful"
Warren, Alan. *Roald Dahl,* 23.

SEPTIMUS DALE

"The Little Girl Eater"
Büssing, Sabine. *Aliens in the Home . . . ,* 129.

AHMAT DANGOR

"Waiting for Leila"
Trump, Martin. "Black South African Short Fiction in English," *Research African Lit,* 19, i (1988), 47–48.

RUBÉNS DARÍO

"The Ruby"
Menton, Seymour. *El Cuento Hispanoamericano,* I, 185–187; 2nd ed., 185–187; 3rd ed., 185–187.

ALPHONSE DAUDET

"La Chèvre de M. Seguin"
Apostolides, Jean-Marie. "La Chèvre-Femme: Madame Bovary chez Monsieur
Seguin," in Guggenheim, Michel, Ed. *Women in French Literature*, 199–212.

GUY DAVENPORT

"Apples and Pears"
Bawer, Bruce. *Diminishing Fiction . . .* , 239–242.

"The Chain"
Bawer, Bruce. *Diminishing Fiction . . .* , 239.

ROBERTSON DAVIES

"Eisengrin"
Atwood, Margaret. "Canadian Monsters: Some Aspects of the Supernatural in
Canadian Fiction," in Staines, David, Ed. *The Canadian Imagination . . .* ,
116–119.

CHANDLER DAVIS

"To Still the Drums"
Franklin, H. Bruce. *War Stars . . .* , 172–173.

RICHARD DAVIS

"Guy Fawkes Night"
Büssing, Sabine. *Aliens in the Home . . .* , 87–88.

DAZAI OSAMU

"A Sound of Hammering"
Motofuji, Frank T. "Dazai Osamu," in Swan, Thomas E., and Kinya Truruta,
Eds. . . . *Modern Japanese Short Story*, 55–59.

"Villon's Wife"
Motofuji, Frank T. "Dazai Osamu," 47–54.

DESIDERIO T. DEFERIA

"Man Is Indeed a Slave"
Lucero, Rosario Cruz. "Notes on the Contemporary Hiligaynon Short Story,"
Solitary, 108–109 (1986), 169.

JOHN W. DeFOREST

"Della"
Hijiva, James A. *J. W. DeForest* . . . , 114–115.

"The Lauson Tragedy"
Hijiva, James A. *J. W. DeForest* . . . , 22–23.

SALVADOR M. DE JESÚS

"Lágrimas de mangle"
Melendez, Concha. *El arte del cuento* . . . , 335.

"La otra hija de Jairo"
Melendez, Concha. *El arte del cuento* . . . , 335–336.

SAMUEL R. DELANY

"Driftglass"
Dowling, Terry. "Catharsis among the Byzantines: Delany's 'Driftglass,'" *Sci Fiction*, 6, ii (1984), 42.

CHARLOTTE DELBO

"Spectres mes compagnons"
Lamont, Eosette C. "Charlotte Delbo, a Woman/Book," in Harris, Alice, and William McBrien, Eds. *Faith of a (Woman) Writer*, 247–252.

LESTER DEL REY

"The Faithful"
Bartter, Martha A. *The Way to Ground Zero* . . . , 84–85.

MANUEL DEL TORO

"My Father"
Melendez, Concha. *El arte del cuento* . . . , 160–161.

ANITA DESAI

"Games at Twilight"
Kumar, Shiv K. "Desai's *Games at Twilight*: A View," in Srivastava, Ramesh K., Ed. *Perspectives on Anita Desai*, 203–204.
Varady, Evelyn D. "The West Views Anita Desai: American and British Criticism of '*Games at Twilight*' and Other Stories," in Srivastava, Ramesh K., Ed. *Perspectives on Anita Desai*, 199–200.

"Sale"
Kumar, Shiv K. "Desai's *Games at Twilight* . . . ," 204–205.
Varady, Evelyn D. "The West Views Anita Desai . . . ," 201.

"Scholar and Gypsy"
Kumar, Shiv K. "Desai's *Games at Twilight* . . . ," 205–206.
Varady, Evelyn D. "The West Views Anita Desai . . . ," 197–198.

"Studies in the Park"
Kumar, Shiv K. "Desai's *Games at Twilight* . . . ," 204.
Varady, Evelyn D. "The West Views Anita Desai . . . ," 200–201.

"Surface Texture"
Varady, Evelyn D. "The West Views Anita Desai . . . ," 199.

MAHASVETA DEVI

"Breast-Giver"
Spivak, Gayatri Chakravorty. *In Other Words* . . . , 241–268.

"Draupadi"
Spivak, Gayatri Chakravorty. *In Other Words* . . . , 182–185.

AUGUSTO D'HALMAR

"En provincia"
Menton, Seymour. *El Cuento Hispanoamericano*, I, 163–164; 2nd ed., 163–164;
    3rd ed., 163–164.

ABELARDO DÍAZ ALFARO

"Bagazo"
Melendez, Concha. *El arte del cuento* . . . , 192.

"Los perros"
Melendez, Concha. *El arte del cuento* . . . , 192–193.

EMILIO DÍAZ VALCÁRCEL

"La mente en blanco"
Melendez, Concha. *El arte del cuento* . . . , 371–372.

"The Soldier Damián Sánchez"
Melendez, Concha. *El arte del cuento* . . . , 369–370.

"Two Men"
Melendez, Concha. *El arte del cuento* . . . , 368–369.

PHILIP K. DICK

"Adjustment Team"
Mackey, Douglas A. *Philip K. Dick,* 12–13.

"Autofac"
Mackey, Douglas A. *Philip K. Dick,* 9.

"Beyond Lies the Wub"
Warrick, Patricia S. *Mind in Motion . . . ,* 99–100.

"Cantata 140"
Gillespie, Bruce, Ed. . . . *Electric Shepherd,* 24–27.

"Colony"
Mackey, Douglas A. *Philip K. Dick,* 8.

"The Cosmic Poachers"
Mackey, Douglas A. *Philip K. Dick,* 7–8.

"The Electric Ant"
Warrick, Patricia S. *Mind in Motion . . . ,* 131–132.

"Exhibit Piece"
Wolf, Anthony. "The Sunstruck Forest: A Guide to the Short Fiction of
    Philip K. Dick," *Foundation,* 18 (January, 1980), 28–29.

"Faith of Our Fathers"
Mackey, Douglas A. *Philip K. Dick,* 107.
Warrick, Patricia S. *Mind in Motion . . . ,* 113–114.
Wolf, Anthony. "The Sunstruck Forest . . . ," 31–32.

"The Father-Thing"
Büssing, Sabine. *Aliens in the Home . . . ,* 130.

"The Hanging Stranger"
Mackey, Douglas A. *Philip K. Dick,* 8.

"Human Is"
Wolf, Anthony. "The Sunstruck Forest . . . ," 29–30.

"Misadjustment"
Mackey, Douglas A. *Philip K. Dick,* 13.

"The Mold of Yancy"
Mackey, Douglas A. *Philip K. Dick,* 9.

"Nanny"
Wolf, Anthony. "The Sunstruck Forest . . . ," 30.

"Oh To Be a Blobel"
Suvin, Darko. *Positions and Presuppositions . . . ,* 121–122.

"Precious Artifact"
Warrick, Patricia S. *Mind in Motion* . . . , 97–98.

"Rautavaara's Case"
Warrick, Patricia S. *Mind in Motion* . . . , 115–116.

"Roog"
Warrick, Patricia S. *Mind in Motion* . . . , 196–197.

"Small Town"
Warrick, Patricia S. *Mind in Motion* . . . , 100–101.

"Time Pawn"
Mackey, Douglas A. *Philip K. Dick,* 29.

"The Variable Man"
Suvin, Darko. *Positions and Presuppositions* . . . , 119–120.

"A World of Talent"
Mackey, Douglas A. *Philip K. Dick,* 10.

CHARLES DICKENS

"The Signalman"
Justin, Henri. "The Signalman's Signal-Man," *J Short Story Engl,* 7 (Autumn, 1986), 9–16.

"To Be Read at Dusk"
Glancy, Ruth. "'To Be Read at Dusk,'" *Dickensian,* 83, i (1987), 40–47.

GORDON DICKSON

"Jean Dupres"
Gillespie, Bruce R. "Vector Zero: The Science Fiction Short Story in the Seventies," in Chauvin, Cy, Ed. *A Multitude* . . . , 16–17.

ISAK DINESEN [BARONESS KAREN BLIXEN]

"Alkmene"
Stambaugh, Sara. *The Witch* . . . , 84–85.

"Babette's Feast"
Stambaugh, Sara. *The Witch* . . . , 79–81.

"The Bear and the Kiss"
Stambaugh, Sara. *The Witch* . . . , 50–55.

"The Blue Jar"
Charters, Ann, William E. Sheidley, and Martha Ramsey. *Instructor's Manual* . . . , 2nd ed., 87.

"The Blue Stones"
Charters, Ann, William E. Sheidley, and Martha Ramsey. *Instructor's Manual* . . . , 2nd ed., 86–87.

"The Cardinal's First Tale"
Stambaugh, Sara. *The Witch* . . . , 23–26.

"The Cardinal's Third Tale"
Stambaugh, Sara. *The Witch* . . . , 92–93.

"Carnival"
Stambaugh, Sara. *The Witch* . . . , 26.

"The Caryatids"
Stambaugh, Sara. *The Witch* . . . , 30–34.

"Copenhagen Season"
Stambaugh, Sara. *The Witch* . . . , 19–21.

"The Deluge at Norderney"
Stambaugh, Sara. *The Witch* . . . , 86–90.

"The Diver"
Stambaugh, Sara. *The Witch* . . . , 11–12.

"The Dreamers"
Stambaugh, Sara. *The Witch* . . . , 100–107.

"Echoes"
Stambaugh, Sara. *The Witch* . . . , 70–71.

"The Fish"
Stambaugh, Sara. *The Witch* . . . , 75–76.

"The Heroine"
Stambaugh, Sara. *The Witch* . . . , 13–14.

"The Immortal Story"
Stambaugh, Sara. *The Witch* . . . , 39–45.

"The Invincible Slave-Owners"
Stambaugh, Sara. *The Witch* . . . , 12–13.

"The Last Day"
Stambaugh, Sara. *The Witch* . . . , 37–38.

"The Old Chevalier"
Stambaugh, Sara. *The Witch* . . . , 5–7.

"Peter and Rosa"
Knapp, Bettina L. *Women in Twentieth-Century Literature* . . . , 49–67.
Stambaugh, Sara. *The Witch* . . . , 70–73.

"The Poet"
Stambaugh, Sara. *The Witch* . . . , 95–100.

"The Roads Round Pisa"
Stambaugh, Sara. *The Witch* . . . , 15–17.

"The Sailor-Boy's Tale"
Stambaugh, Sara. *The Witch* . . . , 55–57.

"Second Meeting"
Stambaugh, Sara. *The Witch* . . . , 51.

"Sorrow-Acre"
Richter, David H. "Covert Plot in Isak Dinesen's 'Sorrow-Acre,'" *J Narrative Technique*, 15 (1985), 82–90.

"The Supper at Elsinore"
Stambaugh, Sara. *The Witch* . . . , 8–11.

"Tales of Two Old Gentlemen"
Stambaugh, Sara. *The Witch* . . . , 60–61.

"Uncle Seneca"
Stambaugh, Sara. *The Witch* . . . , 90–91.

THOMAS DISCH

"The Asian Shore"
Gillespie, Bruce R. "Vector Zero: The Science Fiction Short Story in the Seventies," in Chauvin, Cy, Ed. *Multitude* . . . , 20–22.

"Planet of the Rapes"
Broege, Valerie. "Technology and Sexuality in Science Fiction: Creating New Erotic Interfaces," in Palumbo, Donald, Ed. *Erotic Universe* . . . , 117–118.

E. L. DOCTOROW

"The Foreign Legation"
Saltzman, Arthur M. "Doctorow's *Lives of the Poets* and the Problem of Witness," in Logsdon, Loren, and Charles W. Mayes, Eds. *Since Flannery O'Connor* . . . , 87–88.

"The Hunter"
Saltzman, Arthur M. "Doctorow's *Lives of the Poets* . . . ," 87.

"The Leather Man"
Levine, Paul. *E. L. Doctorow*, 82.

Saltzman, Arthur M. "Doctorow's *Lives of the Poets* . . . ," 88–89.

"Lives of the Poets"
Saltzman, Arthur M. "Doctorow's *Lives of the Poets* . . . ," 89–91.

"Willi"
Saltzman, Arthur M. "Doctorow's *Lives of the Poets* . . . ," 86–87.

"The Writer in the Family"
Levine, Paul. *E. L. Doctorow*, 81–82.
Saltzman, Arthur M. "Doctorow's *Lives of the Poets* . . . ," 85–86.

EMMA DOLUJANOFF

"La correría del venado"
Dorward, Frances R. "The Short Story as a Vehicle for Mexican Literary *Indigenismo*," *Letras Femeninas,* 13, i–ii (1987), 61.

"El huellero"
Dorward, Frances R. "The Short Story . . . ," 62.

"María Galdina"
Dorward, Frances R. "The Short Story . . . ," 62.

"Siéntate Teófilo"
Dorward, Frances R. "The Short Story . . . ," 64–65.

JOSÉ DONOSO

"Ana Maria"
Achugar, Hugo. *Ideología y estructuras* . . . , 52–54.
Bendezü, Edmundo. "Donoso: Fabulación y realidad," in Promis Ojeda, José, et al. [6]. *José Donoso* . . . , 166–168.
Gutiérrez Mouat, Ricardo. *José Donoso* . . . , 54–67.

"Gaspard de la nuit"
Bendezü, Edmundo. "Donoso: Fabulación . . . ," 168–169.

"Green Atom Number Five"
Bendezü, Edmundo. "Donoso: Fabulación . . . ," 168.
Gutiérrez Mouat, Ricardo. *José Donoso* . . . , 67–69.

"El guerro"
Munoz, Willy O. "The Past as Source for the Renewal of the Present: Modernity in José Donoso," *Revista/Review Interamericana,* 15 (1985), 47–60.

"El hombrecito"
Achugar, Hugo. *Ideología y estructuras* . . . , 54–58.

"Paseo"
Achugar, Hugo. *Ideología y estructuras . . .* , 118–121.
Gutiérrez Mouat, Ricardo. *José Donoso . . .* , 92–97.

"Pasos en la noche"
Achugar, Hugo. *Ideología y estructuras . . .* , 110–114.

"Santelices"
Achugar, Hugo. *Ideología y estructuras . . .* , 134–136.

"Veraneo"
Gutiérrez Mouat, Ricardo. *José Donoso . . .* , 90–92.

JOHN DOS PASSOS

"Revolution"
Clark, Michael. *Dos Passos's Early Fiction . . .* , 29–31.

"Romantic Education"
Clark, Michael. *Dos Passos's Early Fiction . . .* , 31–32.

FYODOR DOSTOEVSKY

"The Double"
Somerwil-Ayrton, S. K. *Poverty and Power . . .* , 104–113.

"The Duel"
Patterson, David. *The Affirming Flame . . .* , 58–73.

"The Eternal Husband"
Shechner, Mark. *After the Revolution . . .* , 126–127.

"Mr. Prokharchin"
Somerwil-Ayrton, S. K. *Poverty and Power . . .* , 121–134.

"Notes from Underground"
Axthelm, Peter M. . . . *Confessional Novel,* 13–15, 24–27.
Coates, Paul. *The Double and the Other . . .* , 107–111.
Conradi, Peter. *Fyodor Dostoevsky,* 38–41.
Gutierrez, Donald. *The Dark and the Light Gods . . .* , 2–26.
Levy, Michele F. "D. H. Lawrence and Dostoevsky: The Thirst for Risk and the Thirst for Life," *Mod Fiction Stud,* 33 (1987), 282–285.
Ponomareff, Constantin V. *On the Dark Side . . .* , 148–150.
Widmer, Kingsley. *Countering . . .* , 34–35.

"The Peasant Marey"
Slattery, Dennis P. "Memory, Metaphor and the Image of Christ in Dostoevsky's 'The Peasant Marei,'" *Renascence,* 39 (1987), 383–392; rpt., with changes, in Braendlin, Hans P., Ed. *Ambiguities in Literature . . .* , 23–32.

"Polzunkov"
Somerwil-Ayrton, S. K. *Poverty and Power* . . . , 134–146.

ARTHUR CONAN DOYLE

"The Adventure of Silver Blaze"
Manning, Rita C. "Why Sherlock Holmes Can't Be Replaced by an Expert System," *Philosophical Stud*, 51, i (1987), 19–28.
Shannon, James. " 'Silver Blaze': Did Sherlock Holmes *Fix* the Wessex Cup Race?" in Doyle, Pj, and E. W. McDiarmid, Eds. *The Baker Street Dozen*, 314–318.

"The Adventure of the Devil's Foot"
Keefauver, Brad. "Devilish Adventures," in Doyle, Pj, and E. W. McDiarmid, Eds. *The Baker Street Dozen*, 215–218.

"The Adventure of the Empty House"
Bengtsson, Hans-Uno. "A Norwegian Named Sigerson," *Baker Street J*, 37, iii (1987), 148–152.
Connors, Joseph B. " 'The Adventure of the Empty House,' " in Doyle, Pj, and E. W. McDiarmid, Eds. *The Baker Street Dozen*, 143–148.
Jaffe, Jacqueline A. *Arthur Conan Doyle*, 79–81.

"The Adventure of the Engineer's Thumb"
McClain, Donovan H. "The Curious Affair of the Counterfeit Consultant; Or, Holmes Was No Engineer," *Baker Street J*, 37, ii (1987), 101–106.

"The Adventure of the Missing Three-Quarter"
Berdan, M. S. "A Suggested Two-Thirds of 'The Missing Three-Quarter,' " *Baker Street J*, 38 (1988), 151–155.
Jaffe, Jacqueline A. *Arthur Conan Doyle*, 83–84.

"The Adventure of the Priory School"
Fletcher, George. " 'The Adventure of the Priory School,' " in Doyle, Pj, and E. W. McDiarmid, Eds. *The Baker Street Dozen*, 246–251.

"The Adventure of the Red Circle"
Griffin, Daniel. "Emilia Lucca's Story," *Baker Street J*, 15, ii (1965), 97–102.

"The Blanched Soldier"
Holly, Raymond L. "A Pythagorean Theory," *Baker Street J*, 37, ii (1987), 81–86.

"The Captain of the Polestar"
Batory, Dana M. "The Rime of the Polestar," *Riverside Q*, 7 (1985), 222–237.

"The Final Problem"
Liebouw, Ely. " 'The Final Problem,' " in Doyle, Pj, and E. W. McDiarmid, Eds. *The Baker Street Dozen*, 92–98.

"The Five Orange Pips"
Asimov, Isaac. "'The Five Orange Pips,'" in Doyle, Pj, and E. W. McDiarmid, Eds. *The Baker Street Dozen*, 165–168.

"His Last Bow"
Jaffe, Jacqueline A. *Arthur Conan Doyle*, 89–90.
Lellenberg, Jon L. "The *Magnum Opus* of His Latter Years," *Baker Street J*, 37, ii (1987), 71–74.

"The Lost Special"
Vatza, Edward. "The Apocryphal Letters Revisited," *Baker Street J*, 38 (1988), 84–87.

"The Man with the Watches"
Vatza, Edward. "The Apocryphal Letters . . . ," 84–87.

"The Musgrave Ritual"
Groves, Derham. "The Three Houses in 'The Musgrave Ritual,'" in Doyle, Pj, and E. W. McDiarmid, Eds. *The Baker Street Dozen*, 267–272.

"The Red-Headed League"
Byerly, Ann. "It Was an Adventure—'The Red-Headed League,'" in Doyle, Pj, and E. W. McDiarmid, Eds. *The Baker Street Dozen*, 47–51.

"The Reigate Squires"
Green, Richard L. "'The Reigate Squires,'" in Doyle, Pj, and E. W. McDiarmid, Eds. *The Baker Street Dozen*, 289–293.

"The Resident Patient"
Meyer, Charles A. "The Curious Incident of the Doctor in the Nighttime," *Baker Street J*, 38 (1988), 88–90.

"The Second Stain"
Crawford, Bryce. "'The Second Stain': The Second-Best Case of the Missing Classified Documents," in Doyle, Pj, and E. W. McDiarmid, Eds. *The Baker Street Dozen*, 190–195.

"The Speckled Band"
Rodin, Alvin E., and Jack D. Key. "'The Speckled Band': Poisonous Snakes and Evil Doctors," in Doyle, Pj, and E. W. McDiarmid, Eds. *The Baker Street Dozen*, 23–27.

"When the World Screamed"
Batory, Dana M. "The Climax of 'When the World Screamed,'" *Riverside Q*, 8, ii (1988), 124–128.

DAVID DRAKE

"Something Had To Be Done"
Senf, Carol A. *The Vampire . . .* , 3.

THEODORE DREISER

"McEwen of the Shining Slave Makers"
Lingeman, Richard. *Theodore Dreiser* . . . , 216–217.

"Nigger Jeff"
Good, Howard. *Acquainted with the Night* . . . , 31–32.
Lingeman, Richard. *Theodore Dreiser* . . . , 217–219.

"A Story of Stories"
Good, Howard. *Acquainted with the Night* . . . , 31.

ANNETTE VON DROSTE-HÜLSHOFF

"Die Judenbuche"
Kraft, Herbert. "Annette von Droste-Hülshoffs 'Judenbuche,'" *J Australian
   Univs Lang & Lit Assoc*, 69 (May, 1988), 78–87.
Lietina-Ray, Maruta. "Annette von Droste-Hülshoff and Critics of 'Die Juden-
   buch,'" in Goldberger, Avriel H., Ed. *Woman as Mediatrix* . . . , 123–125.

ANDRE DUBUS

"Adultery"
Kennedy, Thomas E. "The Progress from Hunger to Love: Three Novellas by
   Andre Dubus," *Hollins Critic*, 24, i (1987), 6–7.
Thomas, Kenneth E. *Andre Dubus* . . . , 63–69.

"Andromache"
Thomas, Kenneth E. *Andre Dubus* . . . , 135–136.

"Anna"
Thomas, Kenneth E. *Andre Dubus* . . . , 15–16.

"The Blackberry Patch"
Thomas, Kenneth E. *Andre Dubus* . . . , 52–53.

"Blessings"
Thomas, Kenneth E. *Andre Dubus* . . . , 50–52.

"Cadence"
Thomas, Kenneth E. *Andre Dubus* . . . , 110–111.

"Corporal of Artillery"
Thomas, Kenneth E. *Andre Dubus* . . . , 26–27.

"The Dark Men"
Thomas, Kenneth E. *Andre Dubus* . . . , 27–32.
Yarbrough, Steve. "Andre Dubus: From Detached Incident to Compressed
   Novel," *Critique*, 28, i (1986), 21–22.

"Deaths at Sea"
Thomas, Kenneth E. *Andre Dubus* . . . , 57–59.

"The Doctor"
Thomas, Kenneth E. *Andre Dubus* . . . , 57–59.
Yarbrough, Steve. "Andre Dubus . . . ," 20–21.

"Dressed Like Summer Leaves"
Thomas, Kenneth E. *Andre Dubus* . . . , 53–55.

"The Fat Girl"
Thomas, Kenneth E. *Andre Dubus* . . . , 16–18.
Yarbrough, Steve. "Andre Dubus . . . ," 26.

"A Father's Story"
Cassill, R. V. . . . *Instructor's Handbook,* 21–22.
Thomas, Kenneth E. *Andre Dubus* . . . , 74–78.

"Finding a Girl in America"
Kennedy, Thomas E. "The Progress . . . ," 7–9.

"Going Under"
Thomas, Kenneth E. *Andre Dubus* . . . , 72–73.

"Graduation"
Thomas, Kenneth E. *Andre Dubus* . . . , 18–19.

"His Lover"
Thomas, Kenneth E. *Andre Dubus* . . . , 47–49.

"Killings"
Thomas, Kenneth E. *Andre Dubus* . . . , 38–40.

"Land Where My Fathers Died"
Thomas, Kenneth E. *Andre Dubus* . . . , 42–44.

"Molly"
Thomas, Kenneth E. *Andre Dubus* . . . , 19–20.

"My Life"
Yarbrough, Steve. "Andre Dubus . . . ," 22–23.

"Rose"
Thomas, Kenneth E. *Andre Dubus* . . . , 44–47.

"Separate Flights"
Yarbrough, Steve. "Andre Dubus . . . ," 24–25.

"The Shooting"
Thomas, Kenneth E. *Andre Dubus* . . . , 34–36.

"The Sorrowful Mysteries"
Thomas, Kenneth E. *Andre Dubus* . . . , 55–56.

"Townies"
Thomas, Kenneth E. *Andre Dubus* . . . , 40–42.
Yarbrough, Steve. "Andre Dubus . . . ," 23–24.

"We Don't Live Here Anymore"
Kennedy, Thomas E. "The Progress . . . ," 5–6.
Thomas, Kenneth E. *Andre Dubus* . . . , 63–66.

"The Winter Father"
Thomas, Kenneth E. *Andre Dubus* . . . , 72–74.

MAURICE DUGGAN

"Along Rideout Road That Summer"
Besner, Neil. "Coming of Age in New Zealand: Busher O'Leary Among STC,
    Rhett Butler, Hell's Angels and Others," *Ariel,* 18, i (1987), 63–73.

HENRY DUMAS

"Ark of Bones"
Collier, Eugene. "Elemental Wisdom in *Goodbye Sweetwater*: Suggestions for Fur-
    ther Study," *Black Am Lit Forum,* 22 (1988), 195.
Pearse, Adetokunbo. "The Mystique Factor in Dumas's 'Ark of Bones,'" *Black
    Am Lit Forum,* 22 (1988), 325–327.

"Fon"
Halsey, William. "Signify(cant) Correspondence," *Black Am Lit Forum,* 22 (1988),
    260–261.

"Harlem"
de Jongh, James L. "Notes on Henry Dumas's Harlem," *Black Am Lit Forum,* 22
    (1988), 220.

"Rope of Wind"
Collier, Eugene. "Elemental Wisdom . . . ," 196.

"The Voice"
de Jongh, James L. "Notes . . . ," 218–220.
Mitchell, Carolyn A. "Henry Dumas and Jean Toomer," *Black Am Lit Forum,* 22
    (1988), 304–305.

ROGER DUNKLEY

"A Problem Called Albert"
Büssing, Sabine. *Aliens in the Home* . . . , 68.

LORD DUNSANY [EDWARD JOHN MORETON DRAX PLUNKETT]

"The Sword of Welleran"
Kroeber, Karl. *Romantic Fantasy,* 115–116.

MARGUERITE DURAS [MARGUERITE DONADIEU]

"Mr. Andesman's Afternoon"
Morgan, Jane. "The *caméra-stylo* of Marguerite Duras: The Translation of Literary Aesthetics into Film," *Perspectives on Contemp Lit,* 13 (1987), 34–37.

"Moderato cantabile"
Callander, Margaret M. "Reading Marguerite Duras's 'Moderato cantabile,'"
   Mod Langs, 69, iii (1988), 160–164.
Inal, Tanju. "Marguerite Duras: 'Moderato cantabile,'" *Fransiz Dili Edebiyati,* 3,
   ix (1982), 67–74.
Pierrot, Jean. "Histoire d'un fantôme," *Revue des Sciences Humaines,* 73 (April-
   June, 1986), 126–128.
Selous, Trista. *The Other Woman . . . ,* 97–111, 127–132.
Wight, Doris T. "A Game Played *Moderato Cantabile* by Marguerite Duras," *Lang
   Q,* 26, iii–iv (1988), 32–34.
Willis, Sharon. *Marguerite Duras . . . ,* 155–160.

SARIF EASMON

"The Black Madonna"
Palmer, Eustace. "New Fiction from Sierra Leone: A Study of Sarif Easmon's
   The Feud and Other Stories, Lucilda Hunter's *Road to Freedom,* and Prince
   Palmer's *The Mockingstone,*" *Fourah Bay Stud,* 3 (1986), 43.

"The Feud"
Palmer, Eustace. "New Fiction . . . ," 40, 42.

"For Love of Theresa"
Palmer, Eustace. "New Fiction . . . ," 39–40, 43.

"Koya"
Palmer, Eustace. "New Fiction . . . ," 38–39, 42–43.

"No. 2 to Maia's Tailor"
Palmer, Eustace. "New Fiction . . . ," 44.

"Under the Flamboyante Tree"
Palmer, Eustace. "New Fiction . . . ," 44.

AQUILEO J. ECHEVERRÍA

"Acuarlas"
Menton, Seymour. *El Cuento Costarricense,* 11.

ESTEBAN ECHEVERRÍA

"El matadero"
Menton, Seymour. *El Cuento Hispanoamericano*, I, 35–36; 2nd ed., 35–37; 3rd
    ed., 35–37.

GEORGE EGERTON

"The Regeneration of Two"
Gilbert, Sandra M., and Susan Gubar. *No Man's Land* . . . , 87–88.

"Wedlock"
Gilbert, Sandra M., and Susan Gubar. *No Man's Land* . . . , 84–85.

SUZETTE HADEN ELGIN

"For the Sake of Grace"
Allen, Virginia, and Terri Paul. "Science and Fiction: Ways of Theorizing about
    Women," in Palumbo, Donald, Ed. *Erotic Universe* . . . , 180–181.

GEORGE ELIOT [MARY ANN EVANS]

"Amos Barton"
Edwards, P. D. *Idyllic Realism* . . . , 88–94.

"Janet's Repentance"
Coney, Mary B. "The Meaning of Milby in 'Janet's Repentance,'" *George Eliot
    Fellowship R*, 13 (1982), 19–24.
Fenves, Peter. "Exiling the Encyclopedia: The Individual in 'Janet's Revenge,'"
    Nineteenth-Century Fiction, 41 (1987), 419–444.

"The Lifted Veil"
Baldick, Chris. *In Frankenstein's Shadow* . . . , 142–144.
Escuret, Annie. "G. Eliot: 'The Lifted Veil' ou le scandale de la mémoire
    trouée," *Cahiers Victoriens et Edouardiens*, 26 (October, 1987), 21–35.
Freadman, Richard. *Eliot, James* . . . , 129–134.

"Mr. Gilfil's Love Story"
Edwards, P. D. *Idyllic Realism* . . . , 95–97.

STANLEY ELKIN

"The Making of Ashenden"
Wilde, Alan. *Middle Grounds* . . . , 30–36.

"Plot"
McHale, Brian. *Postmodern Fiction*, 210–211.

HARLAN ELLISON

"A Boy and His Dog"
Francavilla, Joseph. "Mythic Hells in Harlan Ellison's Science Fiction," in Yoke,
    Carl B., Ed. *Phoenix from the Ashes . . .* , 162–163.

"The Deathbird"
Francavilla, Joseph. "Mythic Hells . . . ," 160–162.

"I Have No Mouth and I Must Scream"
Francavilla, Joseph. "Mythic Hells . . . ," 159–160.
Franklin, H. Bruce. *War Stars . . .* , 209–210.

"The Region Between"
Gillespie, Bruce R. "Vector Zero: The Science Fiction Short Story in the Sev-
    enties," in Chauvin, Cy, Ed. *A Multitude . . .* , 18–19.

RALPH ELLISON

"Battle Royal"
German, Norman. "Imagery in the 'Battle Royal' Chapter of Ralph Ellison's
    Invisible Man," Coll Lang Assoc J, 31 (1988), 394–399.
Perrine, Laurence, and Thomas R. Arp. *Instructor's Manual . . .* , 6th ed., 59–
    61; 7th ed., 56–58.
Sheidley, William E., and Ann Charters. *Instructor's Manual . . .* , 142–144;
    Charters, Ann, William E. Sheidley, and Martha Ramsey. *Instructor's Man-
    ual . . .* , 2nd ed., 143–144.

"Flying Home"
Dixon, Melvin. *Ride Out the Wilderness . . .* , 70–72.

ENCHI FUMIKO

"Boxcar of Chrysanthemums"
Tanaka, Yukiko. "Introduction," in Tanaka, Yukiko, and Elizabeth Hanson,
    Eds. *This Kind of Woman . . .* , xvi–xvii.

NAZLI ERAY

"Monte Kristo"
Gün, Güneli. "The Woman in the Darkroom: Contemporary Women Writers
    in Turkey," *World Lit Today,* 60 (1986), 276.

LOUISE ERDRICH

"The Red Convertible"
Charters, Ann, William E. Sheidley, and Martha Ramsey. *Instructor's Man-
    ual . . .* , 2nd ed., 231.

"Saint Marie"
Cassill, R. V. . . . *Instructor's Handbook,* 23–25.
Jaskoski, Helen. "From the Time Immemorial: Native American Traditions in
    Contemporary Short Fiction," in Logsdon, Loren, and Charles W. Mayes,
    Eds. *Since Flannery O'Connor . . . ,* 54–59.

AHMED ESSOP

"The Commandment"
Trump, Martin. "Black South African Short Fiction in English," *Research African
    Lit,* 19, i (1988), 57–59.

ZOË FAIRBANKS

"Relics"
Lefanu, Sarah. *Feminism and Science Fiction,* 74–75.

PAUL W. FAIRMAN

"Invasion from the Deep"
Roberts, Robin. "The Female Alien: Pulp Science Fiction's Legacy to Feminists,"
    J Pop Culture, 21, ii (1987), 38–46.

PHILIP JOSÉ FARMER

"The Lovers"
Roberts, Robin. "The Female Alien: Pulp Science Fiction's Legacy to Feminists,"
    J Pop Culture, 21, ii (1987), 37–38.

WILLIAM FAULKNER

"Barn Burning"
Ruzicka, William T. *Faulkner's Fictive Architecture . . . ,* 115–116.

"The Bear"
Barker, Stephen. "From Old Gold to I.O.U.'s: Ike McCaslin's Debased Geneal-
    ogical Coin," *Faulkner J,* 3, i (1987), 2–25.
Foster, Thomas C. *Form and Society . . . ,* 87–89, 92–93.
Howell, John M. "McCaslin and Macomber: From *Green Hills* to *Big Woods,*"
    Faulkner J, 2, i (1986), 29–36.
Ruzicka, William T. *Faulkner's Fictive Architecture . . . ,* 106–110.
Savolainen, Matti. *The Element of Stasis . . . ,* 344–349.
Schmidt, Rita T. "Two Theories of American Literature: Insights into Faulk-
    ner's Southern Garden," *Ilha do Desterro,* 15–16, i–ii (1986), 147–165.
Whitley, Dorothy C. "The Rites of Initiation in Faulkner's 'The Bear,'" *Mount
    Olive R,* 1, i (1987), 11–27.

"Delta Autumn"
Foster, Thomas C. *Form and Society* . . . , 86–87.

"Dry September"
Sheidley, William E., and Ann Charters. *Instructor's Manual* . . . , 107–108; Charters, Ann, William E. Sheidley, and Martha Ramsey. *Instructor's Manual* . . . , 2nd ed., 107–108.

"The Fire and the Hearth"
Ruzicka, William T. *Faulkner's Fictive Architecture* . . . , 90–96.

"Go Down, Moses"
Grover, Dorsy C. "Isaac McCaslin and Roth's Mistress," in Ford, Dan, Ed. *Heir and Prototype* . . . , 22–32.
Sowder, William J. "Young Ike McCaslin: Travels in Terra Incognita," in Ford, Dan, Ed. *Heir and Prototype* . . . , 34–47.
Tangum, Marion. "Rhetorical Clues to 'Go Down, Moses': Who Is Talking to Whom?" in Ford, Dan, Ed. *Heir and Prototype* . . . , 8–21.

"Knight's Gambit"
Kalfatovic, Martin R. "Faulkner's 'Knight's Gambit,'" *Explicator*, 45, iii (1987), 47–48.

"Miss Zilphia Gant"
Watson, James G. *William Faulkner* . . . , 96–97.

"Mistral"
Orlofsky, Michael. "Faulkner's Alpine Apprenticeship: 'Mistral' and 'Snow,'" *Iowa J Lit Stud*, 5 (1984), 97–101.

"Mountain Victory"
Bradford, M. E. "A Late Encounter: Faulkner's 'Mountain Victory,'" *Mississippi Q*, 40 (1987), 372–382.
Inscoe, John C. "Faulkner, Race and Appalachia," *So Atlantic Q*, 86 (1987), 244–246.

"Mule in the Yard"
Perrine, Laurence, and Thomas R. Arp. *Instructor's Manual* . . . , 6th ed., 45–48; 7th ed., 46–48.

"The Old People"
Foster, Thomas C. *Form and Society* . . . , 83–85.
Ruzicka, William T. *Faulkner's Fictive Architecture* . . . , 101–106.

"Pantaloon in Black"
Foster, Thomas C. *Form and Society* . . . , 81–83.
Polk, Noel. "Man in the Middle: Faulkner and the Southern White Moderate," in Fowler, Doreen, and Ann J. Abadie, Eds. *Faulkner and Race* . . . , 149–150.

"Race at Morning"
Dasher, Thomas. "William Faulkner," in Flora, Joseph M., and Robert Bain,
    Eds. *Fifty Southern Writers After 1900*, 166–167.

"A Rose for Emily"
Sheidley, William E., and Ann Charters. *Instructor's Manual . . .* , 104–105;
    Charters, Ann, William E. Sheidley, and Martha Ramsey. *Instructor's Manual . . .* , 2nd ed., 105–106.
Shiroma, Mikiu. "A Rose for Tobe: A New View of Faulkner's First Short
    Story," *Kyushu Am Lit,* 27 (1986), 21–27.

"Snow"
Orlofsky, Michael. "Faulkner's Alpine Apprenticeship . . . ," 102–104.

"Spotted Horses"
Perrine, Laurence, and Thomas R. Arp. *Instructor's Manual . . .* , 6th ed., 43–
    45; 7th ed., 43–45.

"The Tall Men"
Ruzicka, William T. *Faulkner's Fictive Architecture . . .* , 86–88.

"That Evening Sun"
*Perrine, Laurence, and Thomas R. Arp. *Instructor's Manual . . .* , 7th ed., 27–
    28.
Polk, Noel. "Man in the Middle . . . ," 146–147.

"Uncle Willy"
Ficken, Carl. *God's Story . . .* , 109–119.

"Vendee"
Ruzicka, William T. *Faulkner's Fictive Architecture . . .* , 25–27.

"Victory"
Halsall, Albert. " 'La Transition,' description et ambiguités narrativo-discursives
    dans 'Victoire' de William Faulkner," in Bessière, Jean, Ed. *L'Ordre du descriptif*, 159–172.
Watson, James G. *William Faulkner . . .* , 98.

"Was"
Foster, Thomas C. *Form and Society . . .* , 79–80.
Merrill, Robert. "Faulknerian Sleight of Hand: The Poker Game in 'Was,' " *Stud
    Short Fiction,* 25 (1988), 31–40.
Salmon, Webb. "Faulkner's *Go Down, Moses*," *Explicator,* 46, iv (1988), 29–32.

IRVIN FAUST

"Roar Lion Roar"
Cassill, R. V. *. . . Instructor's Handbook,* 25–27.

BRIAN FAWCETT

"Lowers"
Bowering, George. *Imaginary Hand* . . . , I, 50–52.

CRISTINA FERNÁNDEZ CUBAS

"Los altillos de Brumal"
Bretz, Mary L. "Cristina Fernández Cubas and the Recuperation of the Semiotic
   in *Los altillos de Brumal*," *Anales de la Literatura Española*, 13, iii (1988), 184–
   186.
Zatlin, Phyllis. "Tales from Fernández Cubas: Adventure in the Fantastic,"
   Monographic R, 3 (1987), 110–112.

"En el hemisferio sur"
Bretz, Mary L. "Cristina Fernández Cubas . . . ," 180–183.

"Lúnula and Violeta"
Rueda, Ana. "Cristina Fernández Cubas: Una narrativa de voces extinguidas,"
   Monographic R, 4 (1988), 261–262.
Zatlin, Phyllis. "Tales from Fernández Cubas . . . ," 112.

"Mi hermana Elba"
Zatlin, Phyllis. "Tales from Fernández Cubas . . . ," 108.

"La noche de Jezebel"
Bretz, Mary L. "Cristina Fernández Cubas . . . ," 178–180.
Zatlin, Phyllis. "Tales from Fernández Cubas . . . ," 116–117.

"El provocador de imágenes"
Zatlin, Phyllis. "Tales from Fernández Cubas . . . ," 113–114.

"El reloj de Bagdad"
Bretz, Mary L. "Cristina Fernández Cubas . . . ," 183–184.
Zatlin, Phyllis. "Tales from Fernández Cubas . . . ," 108.

"The Southern Hemisphere"
Rueda, Ana. "Cristina Fernández Cubas . . . ," 263–264.
Zatlin, Phyllis. "Tales from Fernández Cubas . . . ," 115–116.

"La ventana del jardín"
Zatlin, Phyllis. "Tales from Fernández Cubas . . . ," 112–113.

RAMÓN FERREIRA

"Cita a las nueve"
Menton, Seymour. *El Cuento Hispanoamericano*, II, 159–160; 2nd ed., 159–160;
   3rd ed., 53–54.

JORGE FERRETIS

"Hombres en tempestad"
Menton, Seymour. *El Cuento Hispanoamericano,* II, 45–47; 2nd ed., 45–47; 3rd
    ed., 359–361.

EDWIN FIGUEROA

"Lolo Manco"
Melendez, Concha. *El arte del cuento* . . . , 257–259.

"Raíz amarga"
Melendez, Concha. *El arte del cuento* . . . , 259–262.

"El sol de los muertos"
Melendez, Concha. *El arte del cuento* . . . , 256–257.

TIMOTHY FINDLEY

"Daybreak at Pisa"
Murray, Don. "Seeing and Surviving in Timothy Findley's Short Stories," *Stud
    Canadian Lit,* 13, ii (1988), 200–222.

"Dinner Among the Amazons"
Murray, Don. "Seeing and Surviving . . . ," 221–222.

"Hello Cheeverland, Goodbye"
Murray, Don. "Seeing and Surviving . . . ," 202–206.

"Lemonade"
Murray, Don. "Seeing and Surviving . . . ," 206–209.

"Losers, Finders, Strangers at the Door"
Murray, Don. "Seeing and Surviving . . . ," 212–214.

"Out of the Silence"
Murray, Don. "Seeing and Surviving . . . ," 220–221.

"War"
Murray, Don. "Seeing and Surviving . . . ," 209–211.

"What Mrs. Felton Knew"
Murray, Don. "Seeing and Surviving . . . ," 214–217.

LESLIE FISH

"The Deadly Innocence, or 'The End of the Hurt/Comfort Syndrome'"
Lamb, Patricia F. "Romantic Myth, Transcendence, and *Star Trek* Zones," in
    Palumbo, Donald, Ed. *Erotic Universe* . . . , 246–247.

RUDOLPH FISHER

"The City of Refuge"
McCluskey, John, Ed. *The City of Refuge* . . . , xxi–xxii.
Perry, Margaret. "A Fisher of Black Life: Short Stories of Rudolph Fisher," in
    Kramer, Victor, Ed. *The Harlem Renaissance* . . . , 260–261.
————. "Introduction," *The Short Fiction of Rudolph Fisher*, 16.

"Common Meter"
McCluskey, John, Ed. *The City of Refuge* . . . , xxvi–xxvii.

"Miss Cynthie"
McCluskey, John, Ed. *The City of Refuge* . . . , xxiv–xxv.
Perry, Margaret. "Introduction," 13–14.

"Ringtail"
Perry, Margaret. "A Fisher of Black Life . . . ," 256–257.

F. SCOTT FITZGERALD

"An Alcoholic Case"
Gilmore, Thomas B. *Equivocal Spirits* . . . , 105–106.

"The Baby Party"
Pinsker, Sanford. "Fitzgerald's 'The Baby Party,'" *Explicator*, 45, ii (1987), 52–
    55.

"Babylon Revisited"
Gilmore, Thomas B. *Equivocal Spirits* . . . , 108–109.
Sheidley, William E., and Ann Charters. *Instructor's Manual* . . . , 102; Charters,
    Ann, William E. Sheidley, and Martha Ramsey. *Instructor's Manual* . . . , 2nd
    ed., 103.

"Bernice Bobs Her Hair"
Roulston, Robert. "Rummaging Through F. Scott Fitzgerald's 'Trash': Early
    Stories in *The Saturday Evening Post*," *J Pop Culture*, 21, iv (1988), 157–160.

"The Camel's Back"
Roulston, Robert. "Rummaging . . . ," 156–157.

"Crazy Sunday"
Gilmore, Thomas B. *Equivocal Spirits* . . . , 112–115.

"Head and Shoulders"
Roulston, Robert. "Rummaging . . . ," 151–154.

"Her Last Case"
Gilmore, Thomas B. *Equivocal Spirits* . . . , 111–112.

"Myra Meets His Family"
Roulston, Robert. "Rummaging . . . ," 154–156.

"A New Leaf"
Gilmore, Thomas B. *Equivocal Spirits* . . . , 106–108.

"Pat Hobby's College Days"
Gilmore, Thomas B. *Equivocal Spirits* . . . , 117–118.

"The Rich Boy"
Nilsen, Helge N. "A Failure to Love: A Note on F. Scott Fitzgerald's 'The Rich Boy,'" *Int'l Fiction R*, 14, i (1987), 40–43.

GUSTAVE FLAUBERT

"Bouvard and Pécuchet"
Haig, Stirling. *Flaubert and the Gift* . . . , 160–169.
Wing, Nathaniel. "Detail and Narrative Dalliance in Flaubert's 'Bouvard et Pécuchet,'" *French Forum*, 13, i (1988), 47–56.

"St. Julien"
Bonaccorso, Giovanni. "Tra sogno e realtà: Il fantastico nella 'Légende de Saint Julien,'" *Studi di Letteratura Francese*, 13 (1987), 123–142.
Killick, Rachel. "Family Likeness in Flaubert and Maupassant: 'La Légende de Saint Julien l'Hospitalier' and 'Le Donneur d'eau bénite,'" *Forum Mod Lang Stud*, 24 (1988), 346–358.

"A Simple Heart"
Boilait, Marianne. "Pronominale Anapher und Ambiguitat im Entstehungsprozess von Flauberts 'Un Coeur simple,'" trans. Christine LeGal, *LiLi*, 17 (1987), 63–69.
Duncan, Phillip A. "Paul and Virginia/Flaubert and Bernardin," *Stud Short Fiction*, 24 (1987), 436–438.
Gelley, Alexander. *Narrative Crossings* . . . , 146–149.
Haig, Stirling. *The Madame Bovary Blues* . . . , 116–143.
Sheidley, William E., and Ann Charters. *Instructor's Manual* . . . , 14–15; Charters, Ann, William E. Sheidley, and Martha Ramsey. *Instructor's Manual* . . . , 2nd ed., 14–16.
Woodhull, Winifred. "Configurations of the Family in 'Un Coeur simple,'" *Comp Lit*, 39 (1987), 139–161.

PAUL FLEHR [FREDERIK POHL]

"A Life and A/Half"
Clareson, Thomas. *Frederick Pohl*, 39–40.

RUBEM FONSECA

"Happy New Year"
Ballantyne, Christopher J. "The Rhetoric of Violence in Rubem Fonseca," *Luso-Brazilian R*, 23, ii (1986), 6–12, 15–16.

"Large Intestine"
Ballantyne, Christopher J. "The Rhetoric of Violence . . . ," 2–4, 13–14, 16–
    17.

E. M. FORSTER

"Ansell"
Herz, Judith S. *The Short Narratives . . .* , 41.

"Arthur Snatchfold"
Herz, Judith S. *The Short Narratives . . .* , 62–63.

"The Celestial Omnibus"
Herz, Judith S. *The Short Narratives . . .* , 34–35.

"The Curate's Friend"
Herz, Judith S. *The Short Narratives . . .* , 50–52.

"The Eternal Moment"
Herz, Judith S. *The Short Narratives . . .* , 58–59.

"The Life To Come"
Herz, Judith S. *The Short Narratives . . .* , 43–47.

"The Machine Stops"
Dunn, Thomas. "The Deep Caves of Thought: Plato, Heinlein, and Le Guin,"
    in Palumbo, Donald, Ed. *Spectrum of the Fantastic,* 111.
Herz, Judith S. *The Short Narratives . . .* , 59–62.
Lesser, Wendy. *The Life Below the Ground . . .* , 175–182.
Pierce, John J. *Foundations . . .* , 171–172.

"Mr. Andrews"
Charters, Ann, William E. Sheidley, and Martha Ramsey. *Instructor's Man-
    ual . . .* , 2nd ed., 68–70.

"The Other Boat"
Goonetilleke, D. C. R. *Images of the Raj . . .* , 159–160.
Herz, Judith S. *The Short Narratives . . .* , 52–56.

"Other Kingdom"
Herz, Judith S. *The Short Narratives . . .* , 32–34.

"The Road from Colonus"
Herz, Judith S. *The Short Narratives . . .* , 49–50.

"The Story of a Panic"
Herz, Judith S. *The Short Narratives . . .* , 30–32.

"The Tomb of Pletone"
Herz, Judith S. *The Short Narratives . . .* , 19–21.

JOHN FOWLES

"The Cloud"
Holmes, Frederick. "The Novelist as Magus: John Fowles and the Function of
    Narrative," *Dalhousie R*, 68 (1988), 293–297.
McDaniel, Ellen. "Fowles as Collector: The Failed Artists of *The Ebony Tower*,"
    Papers Lang & Lit, 23 (1987), 79–82.

"The Ebony Tower"
McDaniel, Ellen. "Fowles as Collector . . . ," 74–76.

"The Enigma"
McDaniel, Ellen. "Fowles as Collector . . . ," 78–79.

"Poor Koko"
Holmes, Frederick. "The Novelist as Magus . . . ," 229, 297.
McDaniel, Ellen. "Fowles as Collector . . . ," 76–78.

MEDARDO FRAILE

"El álbum"
Brandenberger, Erna. *Estudios . . . ,* 279–280.

"La cabezota"
Brandenberger, Erna. *Estudios . . . ,* 233–236.

ULRICH FRANK [ULLA WOLFF]

"Simon Eichelkatz"
Kahn, Lothar. "Neglected Nineteenth-Century German-Jewish Historical Fic-
    tion," in Gelber, Mark H., Ed. *Identity and Ethos . . . ,* 166–167.

RAYMOND FRASER

"The Actor"
MacKendrick, Louis K. "A Voice Within the Tavern Cried: Crossing the Bar
    with Raymond Fraser and Ray Smith," in Struthers, J. A. (Tim), Ed. *The
    Montreal Story Tellers . . . ,* 111.

"Bertha and Bill"
MacKendrick, Louis K. "A Voice Within the Tavern . . . ," 109–110.

"A Cold Frosty Morning"
MacKendrick, Louis K. "A Voice Within the Tavern . . . ," 111–112.

"The Janitor's Wife"
MacKendrick, Louis K. "A Voice Within the Tavern . . . ," 113–114.

"The Newbridge Sighting"
MacKendrick, Louis K. "A Voice Within the Tavern . . . ," 107–108.

"On the Bus"
MacKendrick, Louis K. "A Voice Within the Tavern . . . ," 110–111.

"The Quebec Prison"
MacKendrick, Louis K. "A Voice Within the Tavern . . . ," 108–109.

"Spanish Jack"
MacKendrick, Louis K. "A Voice Within the Tavern . . . ," 107.

"They Came Here to Die"
MacKendrick, Louis K. "A Voice Within the Tavern . . . ," 112–113.

MARY E. WILKINS FREEMAN

"Christmas Jenny"
Johns, Barbara A. " 'Love-Cracked': Spinsters as Subversives in 'Anna Malann,' 'Christmas Jenny,' and 'An Object of Love,' " *Colby Lib Q,* 23, i (1987), 10–12.

"An Object of Love"
Johns, Barbara A. " 'Love-Cracked' . . . ," 12–15.

"Old Woman Magoun"
Gilbert, Sandra M., and Susan Gubar. *No Man's Land . . . ,* 84–86.

"The Revolt of Mother"
Aaron, Victoria. "A Community of Women Surviving Marriage in the Wilderness," *Rendezvous,* 22, ii (1986), 3–11.
Charters, Ann, William E. Sheidley, and Martha Ramsey. *Instructor's Manual . . . ,* 2nd ed., 38–39.
Gilbert, Sandra M., and Susan Gubar. *No Man's Land . . . ,* 86–87.

"Two Friends"
Koppelman, Susan. "About 'Two Friends' and Mary Eleanor Wilkins Freeman," *Am Lit Realism,* 21, i (1988), 43–57.

CELIA FREMLIN

"The Quiet Game"
Büssing, Sabine. *Aliens in the Home . . . ,* 33–34.

BARBARA FRISCHMUTH

"Let It Be"
Vansant, Jacqueline. *Against the Horizon . . . ,* 46.

"Tree of the Forgotten Dog"
Vansant, Jacqueline. *Against the Horizon* . . . , 59–60.

CARLOS FUENTES

"Chac Mool"
Duncan, Cynthia. "Carlos Fuentes' 'Chac Mool' and Todorov's Theory of the Fantastic: A Case for the Twentieth Century," *Hispanic J*, 8, i (1986), 125–133.
———. "The Living Past: The Mexican's History Returns to Haunt Him in Two Short Stories by Carlos Fuentes," in Morse, Donald E., Ed. *The Fantastic* . . . , 145–147.

"The Cost of Life"
Wing, George G. "A Gallery of Women in Carlos Fuentes' *Cantar de ciegos*," *R Contemp Fiction*, 8 (1988), 222.

"The Doll Queen"
Pérez, Janet. "Aspects of the Triple Lunar Goddess in Fuentes' Short Fiction," *Stud Short Fiction*, 24 (1987), 144–146.

"Mother's Day"
Valdes, M. E. de. "Fuentes on Mexican Feminophobia," *R Contemp Fiction*, 8 (1988), 225–233.

"The Old Morality"
Pérez, Janet. "Aspects of the Triple Lunar Goddess . . . ," 146–147.

"There Were Palaces"
McMurray, George R. *Spanish American Writing* . . . , 73–75.

"Tlactocatzine, the One from the Flemish Garden"
Duncan, Cynthia. "The Living Past . . . ," 143–145.
———. "Ghosts of the Past: The Return of Maximilian and Carlotta in Two Contemporary Mexican Short Stories," *Perspectives Contemp Lit*, 14 (1988), 98–100.
Pérez, Janet. "Aspects of the Triple Lunar Goddess . . . ," 141–143.

"To the Snake of the Sea"
Wing, George G. "A Gallery . . . ," 218.

"The Two Elenas"
Pérez, Janet. "Aspects of the Triple Lunar Goddess . . . ," 143.
Wing, George G. "A Gallery . . . ," 218–219.

HENRY BLAKE FULLER

"Dr. Gowdy and the Squash"
Scambray, Kenneth. *A Varied Harvest* . . . , 131–132.

"The Downfall of Abner Joyce"
Scambray, Kenneth. *A Varied Harvest* . . . , 128–131.

"Pasquale's Picture"
Griffin, Constance M. *Henry Blake Fuller* . . . , 50–51.

"The Pilgrim Sons"
Scambray, Kenneth. *A Varied Harvest* . . . , 109–110.

FÜRUZAN

"My Cinemas"
Gün, Güneli. "The Woman in the Darkroom: Contemporary Women Writers in Turkey," *World Lit Today,* 60 (1986), 277.

CARLOS GAGINI

"La bruja de Miramar"
Menton, Seymour. *El Cuento Costarricense,* 16.

ERNEST J. GAINES

"Just Like a Tree"
Cassill, R. V. . . . *Instructor's Handbook,* 28–29.
Perrine, Laurence, and Thomas R. Arp. *Instructor's Manual* . . . , 7th ed., 59–60.

"A Long Day in November"
Ficken, Carl. *God's Story* . . . , 131–140.

SERGIO GALINDO

"Cena en Dorrius"
Aponte, Barbara B. "Lo fantástico en los cuentos de Sergio Galindo," *Monographic R,* 4 (1988), 145–146.

"Querido Jim"
Aponte, Barbara B. "Lo fantástico . . . ," 144–145.

"El tío Quintín"
Aponte, Barbara B. "Lo fantástico . . . ," 140–141.

MAVIS GALLANT

"About Geneva"
Besner, Neil K. *The Light of Imagination* . . . , 22–25.

"Acceptance of Their Ways"
Bonheim, Helmut. "The Aporias of Lily Littel: Mavis Gallant's 'Acceptance of Their Ways,'" *Ariel*, 18, iv (1987), 69–78.
Dahlie, Hallvard. *Varieties of Exile* . . . , 127–128.

"August"
Besner, Neil K. *The Light of Imagination* . . . , 53–54.

"An Autobiography"
Besner, Neil K. *The Light of Imagination* . . . , 81–82.

"An Autumn Day"
Dahlie, Hallvard. *Varieties of Exile* . . . , 122–123.

"Bernadette"
Schrank, Bernice. "Celluloid Images and Social Control in Selected Short Stories by Mavis Gallant," in Jurak, Mirko, Ed. *Cross-Cultural Studies* . . . , 230–231.

"Bonaventure"
Besner, Neil K. *The Light of Imagination* . . . , 127–128.

"The Colonel's Child"
Besner, Neil K. *The Light of Imagination* . . . , 149–150.

"The Cost of Living"
Besner, Neil K. *The Light of Imagination* . . . , 37–42.

"The Deceptions of Marie-Blanche"
Besner, Neil K. *The Light of Imagination* . . . , 18–19.

"Ernst in Civilian Clothes"
Besner, Neil K. *The Light of Imagination* . . . , 75–80.

"A Flying Start"
Besner, Neil K. *The Light of Imagination* . . . , 145–146.

"The Four Seasons"
Besner, Neil K. *The Light of Imagination* . . . , 99–104.
Dahlie, Hallvard. *Varieties of Exile* . . . , 129.

"The Ice Wagon Going Down the Street"
Besner, Neil K. *The Light of Imagination* . . . , 124–127.
Dahlie, Hallvard. *Varieties of Exile* . . . , 121–122.

"In the Tunnel"
Besner, Neil K. *The Light of Imagination* . . . , 122–124.
Dahlie, Hallvard. *Varieties of Exile* . . . , 132–133.

"In Youth Is Pleasure"
Besner, Neil K. *The Light of Imagination* . . . , 132–135.
Dahlie, Hallvard. *Varieties of Exile* . . . , 140–141, 143.

"Its Image in the Mirror"
Besner, Neil K. *The Light of Imagination* . . . , 28–37.
Keith, W. J. "Dates and Details in Mavis Gallant's 'Its Image in the Mirror,'"
    Stud Canadian Lit, 12, i (1987), 156–159.
Schrank, Bernice. "Celluloid Images . . . ," 230.

"The Latehomecomers"
Besner, Neil K. *The Light of Imagination* . . . , 79–80.

"Lena"
Besner, Neil K. *The Light of Imagination* . . . , 150–151.

"Malcolm and Bea"
Dahlie, Hallvard. *Varieties of Exile* . . . , 125–127.

"The Moabitess"
Dahlie, Hallvard. *Varieties of Exile* . . . , 128.

"The Moslem Wife"
Besner, Neil K. *The Light of Imagination* . . . , 105–116.
Dahlie, Hallvard. *Varieties of Exile* . . . , 131–132.

"My Heart Is Broken"
Besner, Neil K. *The Light of Imagination* . . . , 42–45.
Schrank, Bernice. "Celluloid Images . . . ," 231–233.

"The Old Friends"
Besner, Neil K. *The Light of Imagination* . . . , 70–75.

"The Other Paris"
Besner, Neil K. *The Light of Imagination* . . . , 10–17.

"Overhead in a Balloon"
Besner, Neil K. *The Light of Imagination* . . . , 143–145.

"The Pegnitz Junction"
Besner, Neil K. *The Light of Imagination* . . . , 82–93.

"Potter"
Besner, Neil K. *The Light of Imagination* . . . , 94–99.

"The Remission"
Besner, Neil K. *The Light of Imagination* . . . , 104–105.
Dahlie, Hallvard. *Varieties of Exile* . . . , 130–131.

"Saturday"
Besner, Neil K. *The Light of Imagination* . . . , 119–122.

"Señor Pinedo"
Besner, Neil K. *The Light of Imagination* . . . , 19–20.

"Speck's Idea"
Besner, Neil K. *The Light of Imagination* . . . , 141–143.

"Varieties of Exile"
Besner, Neil K. *The Light of Imagination* . . . , 135–138.
Dahlie, Hallvard. *Varieties of Exile* . . . , 141.

"Virus X"
Besner, Neil K. *The Light of Imagination* . . . , 128–131.
Dahlie, Hallvard. *Varieties of Exile* . . . , 135–136.

"Wing's Chips"
Besner, Neil K. *The Light of Imagination* . . . , 17–18.

RÓMULO GALLEGOS

"The Beggar's Sweetheart"
Spell, Jefferson R. . . . *Spanish-American Fiction,* 208–209.

"The Miracle of the Year"
Spell, Jefferson R. . . . *Spanish-American Fiction,* 209.

"The Prop"
Spell, Jefferson R. . . . *Spanish-American Fiction,* 207–208.

JOAQUÍN GALLEGOS LARA

"Era la mamá"
Menton, Seymour. *El Cuento Hispanoamericano,* II, 65–66; 2nd ed., 65–66; 3rd
    ed., 279–280.

JOHN GALSWORTHY

"The Apple Tree"
Gindin, James. *John Galsworthy's Life and Art* . . . , 407–408.

"The Japanese Quince"
*Perrine, Laurence, and Thomas R. Arp. *Instructor's Manual* . . . , 7th ed., 5–6.

"A Knight"
Gindin, James. *John Galsworthy's Life and Art* . . . , 128–129.

"A Man of Devon"
Gindin, James. *John Galsworthy's Life and Art* . . . , 127–128.

"Salvation of a Forsythe"
Gindin, James. *John Galsworthy's Life and Art* . . . , 130–131.

"The Silence"
Gindin, James. *John Galsworthy's Life and Art* . . . , 129–130.

"A Stoic"
Gindin, James. *John Galsworthy's Life and Art* . . . , 406–407.

JOHN GALT

"A Rich Man"
Letley, Emma. *From Galt to Douglas Brown* . . . , 73–75.

EULALIA GALVARRIATO

"Descanso en primavera"
Alborg, Concha. "Eulalia Galvarriato cuentista," *Monographic R*, 4 (1988), 280–281.

"La espera"
Alborg, Concha. "Eulalia Galvarriato . . . ," 280.

"Final de jornada"
Alborg, Concha. "Eulalia Galvarriato . . . ," 281.

"La gota de agua"
Alborg, Concha. "Eulalia Galvarriato . . . ," 284.

"Los hijos"
Alborg, Concha. "Eulalia Galvarriato . . . ," 281–282.

"Un niño sueña"
Alborg, Concha. "Eulalia Galvarriato . . . ," 284.

"Raíces bajo el agua"
Alborg, Concha. "Eulalia Galvarriato . . . ," 282.

"Tantos días cualquiera"
Alborg, Concha. "Eulalia Galvarriato . . . ," 282–283.

"Los zapatos blancos"
Alborg, Concha. "Eulalia Galvarriato . . . ," 283–284.

EUGENE GARBER

"The Poets"
Cassill, R. V. . . . *Instructor's Handbook*, 30–32.

GABRIEL GARCÍA MÁRQUEZ

"Artificial Roses"
Carlos, Alberto J. "Aproximaciones a los cuentos de Gabriel García Márquez," in Giacoman, Helmy F., Ed. *Homenaje a G. García Márquez* . . . , 224–227.

Mendizábal, J. C. "Ceguerta clarividente en 'Rosas artificiales' de Gabriel García Márquez," *Káñina,* 4, i (1980), 77–80.

"Baltazar's Wonderful Afternoon"
Carlos, Alberto J. "Aproximaciones a los cuentos . . . ," 216–220.
Linker, Susan M. "Myth and Legend in Two Prodigious Tales of García Márquez," *Hispanic J,* 6, i (1987), 89–100.
McMurray, George R. *Gabriel García Márquez,* 13.

"Big Mama's Funeral"
Castillo, Debra A. "The Storyteller and the Carnival Queen: 'Funerales de la Mamá Grande,'" *Romance Q,* 35 (1988), 457–467.
Chase, Cida. "'La Violencia' and Political Oppression in the Stories of García Márquez," *J Pop Culture,* 22 (1988), 77–78.
Collazos, Oscar. *García Márquez . . . ,* 74–89.
McMurray, George R. *Gabriel García Márquez,* 13.
Paiewonsky-Conde, Edgar. "La escritura como acto revolucionario: 'Los funerales de la Mamá Grande,'" in Hernández de López, Ana M., Ed. *En el punto de mira . . . ,* 33–53.
Palencia-Roth, Michael. *Gabriel García Márquez . . . ,* 47–51.
Shaw, Donald L. *Nueva narrativa . . . ,* 2nd ed., 111–112.
Sims, Robert L. "The Creation of Myth in García Márquez's 'Los funerales de la Mamá Grande,'" *Hispania,* 61, i (1978), 14–23; rpt. in his *The Evolution of Myth . . . ,* 27–38.
———. "Matriarchal and Patriarchal Patterns in Gabriel García Márquez's *Leaf Storm,* 'Big Mama's Funeral,' and *One Hundred Years of Solitude:* The Synergetic, Mythic and *Bricolage* Synthesis," in Shaw, Bradley A., and Nora Vera-Godwin, Eds. *Critical Perspectives . . . ,* 37–38.

"Blacamán the Good, Vendor of Miracles"
Arrone-Amestoy, Lida. "Blacabunderías del método: El recurso al discurso en García Márquez," in Hernández de López, Ana M., Ed. *En el punto de mira . . . ,* 55–62.
Palencia-Roth, Michael. *Gabriel García Márquez . . . ,* 140–144.
Shivers, George R. "The Other Within and the Other Without: The Writer's Role and Personality in Works by Julio Cortázar and Gabriel García Márquez," in Rogers, Elizabeth S. and Timothy S., Eds. *In Retrospect . . . ,* 146.

"Chronicle of a Decade Foretold"
Sims, Robert L. "Narrating Violence and the Permutable Violence of Narration: The Evolution of Focalization in the Works of Gabriel García Márquez from 1947 to 1981," *Hispanic J,* 10, i (1988), 60–63.

"The Day after Saturday"
Palencia-Roth, Michael. *Gabriel García Márquez . . . ,* 57–59.

"Death Constant Beyond Love"
Palencia-Roth, Michael. *Gabriel García Márquez . . . ,* 149–151.

"Eva Is Inside Her Cat"
Chase, Cida. "'La Violencia' . . . ," 78–79.

"The Handsomest Drowned Man in the World"
Cassill, R. V. . . . *Instructor's Handbook,* 32–33.
McMurray, George R. *Gabriel García Márquez,* 14–15.
Palencia-Roth, Michael. *Gabriel García Márquez . . . ,* 136–140.
Rodríguez, Terensita. "'El ahogado más hermoso del mundo': La odisea más allá del Atlántico," *Iberoromania,* 27–28 (1988), 154–166.
Speratti-Piñero, Emma S. "De las fuentes y su utilización en 'El ahogado más hermoso del mundo,'" in Schwartz Lerner, Lía, and Isaías Lerner, Eds. *Homenaje a Ana María Barrenechea,* 549–555.

"The Incredible and Sad Tale of Innocent Eréndira and Her Heartless Grandmother"
Barwell, J. Timothy. "Science Fiction and the Semiotics of Realism," in Slusser, George E., and Eric S. Rabkin, Eds. *Intersections . . . ,* 41.
Benítez-Rojo, Antonio. "'Eréndira' o La Bella Durmiente de García Márquez," *Cuadernos Hispanoamericanos,* 448 (1987), 31–48.
Berg, Mary G. "The Presence and Subversion of the Past in Gabriel García Márquez' 'Eréndira,'" in Paolini, Gilbert, Ed. *LA CHISPA '87,* 23–31.
Boo, Matilde L. "'La incredíble y triste historia de la cándida Eréndira y de su abuela desalmada,' de García Márquez y *Tormento,* de Galdós: significación ironica de la irrealidad," in Hernández de López, Ana M., Ed. *En el punto de mira . . . ,* 71–82.
Cjamdadu, Amaryll B. "Las soledades y los solitarios en 'La incredíble y triste historia de la cándida Eréndira y de su abuela desalmada' de Gabriel García Márquez," *Symposium,* 40, iv (1986–1987), 297–307.
Collazos, Oscar. *García Márquez . . . ,* 171–184.
Jain, Jasbir. "Innocent Eréndira: The Reversal of a Fairy Tale," in Bhalla, Alok, Ed. *García Márquez . . . ,* 101–108.
McMurray, George R. *Gabriel García Márquez,* 14.
Méndez, José Luis. "La dialéctica del amo y el esclavo en 'La cándida Eréndira' de Gabriel García Márquez," *Torre,* 1, i (1987), 59–68.
Millington, Mark. "Aspects of Narrative Structure in 'The Incredible and Sad Story of the Innocent Eréndira and Her Heartless Grandmother,'" in McGuirk, Bernard, and Richard Cardwell, Eds. *Gabriel García Márquez . . . ,* 120–122.
Mottram, Eric. "Existential and Political Controls in the Fiction of García Márquez," in Bhalla, Alok, Ed. *García Márquez . . . ,* 6–7.
Palencia-Roth, Michael. *Gabriel García Márquez . . . ,* 152–162.
Penuel, Arnold M. "The Theme of Colonialization in García Márquez' 'La incredíble y triste historia de la cándida Eréndira y de su abuela desalmada,'" *Hispanic J,* 10, i (1988), 67–83.

"The Last Voyage of the Ghost Ship"
Kroeber, Karl. *Romantic Fantasy,* 129–139.
Palencia-Roth, Michael. *Gabriel García Márquez . . . ,* 144–149.
Shivers, George R. "The Other Within . . . ," 145–146.

"Leaf Storm"
Álverez Gardeazábal, Gustavo. "De 'Antígona' a 'La hojarasca,' verificación tragica," in Giacoman, Helmy F., Ed. *Homenaje a G. García Márquez . . . ,* 295–311.
Collazos, Oscar. *García Márquez . . . ,* 35–40.

Lastra, Pedro. "La tragedia como fundamentos estructural en 'La hojarasca,'" *Anales de la Universidad de Chile*, 124 (1966), 168–186; rpt. *Nueve asedios . . .*, 38–51; Giacoman, Helmy F., Ed. *Homenaje a G. García Márquez . . .*, 43–56.

Loveluck, Juan. "Gabriel García Márquez, narrador colombiano," *Duquesne Hispanic R*, 3 (1966), 135–154; rpt. *Nueve asedios . . .*, 52–73.

Maturo, Graciela. "El sentido religioso de 'La Hojarasca' de Gabriel García Márquez," *Eco*, 24 (1972), 217–235; rpt. in her *Claves simbólicas . . .*, 77–90.

Sims, Robert L. "García Márquez' 'La hojarasca': Paradigm of Time and Search for Myth," *Hispania*, 59 (1976), 810–819; rpt., revised, in his *The Evolution of Myth . . .*, 15–25.

Vargas Llosa, Mario. *García Márquez . . .*, 243–291.

"Monologue of Isabel Watching It Rain in Macondo"
Palencia-Roth, Michael. *Gabriel García Márquez . . .*, 42–43.
Shaw, Donald L. *Nueva narrativa . . .*, 2nd ed., 109–110.

"Montiel's Widow"
Arrington, Melvin S. "'La viuda de Montiel': Un relato en miniatura de Macondo," in Hernández de López, Ana M., Ed. *En el punto de mira . . .*, 63–69.
Chase, Cida. "'La Violencia' . . .," 75–76.
Linker, Susan M. "Myth and Legend . . .," 89–100.

"Nabo, the Black Who Made the Angels Wait"
Sims, Robert L. "Narrating Violence . . .," 55–56.

"The Night of the Curlews"
Chase, Cida. "'La Violencia' . . .," 79–80.

"One Day After Saturday"
Chase, Cida. "'La Violencia' . . .," 76.

"One of These Days"
Carlos, Alberto J. "Aproximaciones a los cuentos . . .," 220–224.
Chase, Cida. "'La Violencia' . . .," 75.
Kason, Nancy M. "El arte del ambiente psicológico en 'Un día de éstos,'" in Hernández de López, Ana M., Ed. *En el punto de mito . . .*, 83–90.
McMurray, George R. *Gabriel García Márquez*, 12–13.

"The Sea of Lost Time"
Chase, Cida. "'La Violencia' . . .," 76.
Mottram, Eric. "Existential and Political Controls . . .," 8.
Palencia-Roth, Michael. *Gabriel García Márquez . . .*, 51–54.
———. *Myth and the Modern Novel . . .*, 45–48.

"Tale of a Castaway"
Díez Huélamo, Beguña, Ed. *"Relato de un Naufrago" . . .*, 42–49.

"Tuesday Siesta"
Carlos, Alberto J. "Aproximaciones a los cuentos . . .," 227–232.

McMurray, George R. *Gabriel García Márquez*, 12.
Palencia-Roth, Michael. *Gabriel García Márquez* . . . , 54–57.
Pineda Botero, Alvaro. "Agresión y poesía: A propósito de dos cuentos de García Márquez," *Univ Dayton R*, 18, i (1986), 59–65.

"A Very Old Man with Enormous Wings"
Carrillo, Germán D. "Desenfado y comicidad: dos técnicas magicorrealistas de García Márquez en 'Un hombre muy viejo con unas alas enormes," in Giacoman, Helmy F., Ed. *Homenaje a G. García Márquez* . . . , 235–248.
Clark, John R. "Angel in Excrement: García Márquez's Innocent Tale ('A Very Old Man with Enormous Wings')," *Notes Contemp Lit*, 18, iii (1988), 2–3.
McMurray, George R. *Gabriel García Márquez*, 14.
Palencia-Roth, Michael. *Gabriel García Márquez* . . . , 132–136.
Sheidley, William E., and Ann Charters. *Instructor's Manual* . . . , 165–166; Charters, Ann, William E. Sheidley, and Martha Ramsey. *Instructor's Manual* . . . , 2nd ed., 177–178.
Yviricu, Jorge. "Trasposición y Subversión en 'Un señor muy viejo con unas alas enormes' de Gabriel García Márquez," in Bell-Villada, Gene H., Antonio Giménez, and George Pistorius, Eds. *From Dante to García Márquez* . . . , 384–390.

JOAQUÍN GARCÍA MONGE

"Tres viejos"
Menton, Seymour. *El cuento Costarricense*, 19.

FRANCISCO GARCÍA PAVÓN

"La novena"
Brandenberger, Erna. *Estudios* . . . , 204–206.

HAMLIN GARLAND

"Under the Lion's Paw"
Charters, Ann, William E. Sheidley, and Martha Ramsey. *Instructor's Manual* . . . , 2nd ed., 50–51.

ISABEL GARMA

"Consagración y secuestro"
Schlau, Stacey. "The Social Power of the Literary Word: Isabel Garma's *Cuentos de muerte y resurrección*," *Monographic R*, 4 (1988), 113–114.

"El hombre que pintaba la verdad"
Schlau, Stacey. "The Social Power . . . ," 108–109.

"El pueblo de los seres taciturnos"
Schlau, Stacey. "The Social Power . . . ," 109–111.

"Y cuando las pascuas fueron de sangre"
Schlau, Stacey. "The Social Power . . . ," 111–113.

GEORGE GARRETT

"An Evening Performance"
Cassill, R. V. . . . *Instructor's Handbook,* 34–35.

ELENA GARRO

"La culpa es de los tlaxcaltecas"
Meyer, Doris. "Alienation and Escape in Elena Garro's *La semana de colores,*"
    Hispanic R, 55, ii (1987), 153–164.

"El día que fuimos perros"
San Pedro, Teresa A. "La caída de los 'dioses' en el cuento de Elena Garro 'El
    día que fuimos perros,'" *Monographic R,* 4 (1988), 116–126.

ELIZABETH CLEGHORN GASKELL

"Sylvia's Lovers"
Keith, W. J. *Regions of the Imagination* . . . , 58–60.

WILLIAM GASS

"In the Heart of the Heart of the Country"
Cassill, R. V. . . . *Instructor's Handbook,* 36–37.
Hadella, Charlotte B. "The Winter Wasteland of William Gass's 'In the Heart
    of the Heart of the Country,'" *Critique S,* 30 (1988), 49–58.

"Order of Insects"
McHale, Brian. *Postmodern Fiction,* 81–82.

THÉOPHILE GAUTIER

"Le Chevalier double"
Gordon, Rae B. *"Le Merveilleux scientifique* and the Fantastic," *L'Esprit Créateur,*
    28, iii (1988), 12–14.

"Une larme du diable"
Smith, Albert B. "Romantic Irony in Théophile Gautier's 'Une larme du di-
    able,'" *French Lit Series,* 14 (1987), 75–81.

"La Morte amoureuse"
Gordon, Rae B. *"Le Merveilleux scientifique* . . . ," 14–16.

ANDRÉ GIDE

"El Hadj"
Meitinger, Serge. "Un Modèle de récit 'déceptif': 'El Hadj ou le traité du faux prophète,'" *Revue des Sciences Humaines*, 70, iii (1985), 59–77.

"The Immoralist"
Axthelm, Peter M. . . . *Confessional Novel*, 55–57.
Dollimore, Jonathan. "Different Desires: Subjectivity and Transgression in Wilde and Gide," *Genders*, 2 (July, 1988), 24–41.
Greene, Robert W. "Fading (Sacred) Texts and Dying (Guiding) Voices in Gide's Early *Récits*," *French Forum*, 12, i (1987), 77–82.
Pasco, Allan H. *Novel Configurations* . . . , 99–122.

"Isabelle"
Cancalon, Elaine. "'Isabelle': oeuvre de transition," *Australian J French Stud*, 24 (1987), 193–203.

"The Pastoral Symphony"
Crookes, David Z. "Gide's 'La Symphonie Pastorale,'" *Explicator*, 47, i (1988), 20.
Goulet, Alain. "L'Ironie pastorale en jeu," *Bull des Amis*, 16, ii (1988), 41–57.
Heuvel, Pierre van den. "Révélations d'un discours mensonger: Les Déictiques temporels dans 'La Symphonie pastorale' d'André Gide," *Neophilologus*, 73, iii (1988), 366–375.
Mahieu, M. Raymond. "'La Symphonie pastorale' et la lutte des tropes," *Bull des Amis*, 16 (April-July, 1988), 58–70.

"Strait Is the Gate"
Greene, Robert W. "Fading (Sacred) Texts . . . ," 82–89.
Kapetanovich, Myo. "Un récit d'André Gide entre l'ironie et la satire," *French Lit Series*, 14 (1987), 133–142.
Lachasse, Pierre. "Le Récit de Jérome dans 'La Porte étroite': Un Thématique de la séparation," *Revue d'Histoire Littéraire*, 88, i (1988), 67–81.
Marty, Eric. "À propos de 'La Porte étroite': Répétition et remémoration: *Le Nouvel Abailard*," *Revue des Sciences Humaines*, 70, iii (1985), 79–105.
Wegimont, Marie A. "Gide's 'La Porte étroite,'" *Explicator*, 46, ii (1988), 21–23.

ENRIQUE GIL GILBERT

"El malo"
Menton, Seymour. *El Cuento Hispanoamericano*, II, 78–80; 2nd ed., 78–80; 3rd ed., 292–294.

ELLEN GILCHRIST

"Victory Over Japan"
Perrine, Laurence, and Thomas R. Arp. *Instructor's Manual* . . . , 7th ed., 91–93.

ALFRED GILLESPIE

"The Evil Eye"
Büssing, Sabine. *Aliens in the Home . . .* , 129–130.

CHARLOTTE PERKINS GILMAN

"The Giant Wisteria"
Biamonte, Gloria A. " 'There is a story, if we could only find it': Charlotte
Perkins Gilman's 'The Giant Wisteria,' " *Legacy,* 5, ii (1988), 33–43.

"When I Was a Witch"
Gilbert, Sandra M., and Susan Gubar. *No Man's Land . . .* , 88–89.

"The Yellow Wallpaper"
Charters, Ann, William E. Sheidley, and Martha Ramsey. *Instructor's Man-
ual . . .* , 2nd ed., 47–48.
DeLamotte, Eugenia C. "Male and Female Mysteries in 'The Yellow Wall Pa-
per,' " *Legacy,* 5, i (1988), 3–14.
Michaels, Walter B. *The Gold Standard . . .* , 9–13.
Treichler, Paula A. "Escaping the Sentence: Diagnosis and Discourse in 'The
Yellow Wallpaper,' " in Benstock, Shari, Ed. *Feminist Issues . . .* , 62–71.
Veeder, William. "Who Is Jane? The Intricate Feminism of Charlotte Perkins
Gilman," *Arizona Q,* 44, iii (1988), 40–79.

GEORGE GISSING

"The Invincible Curate"
Brook, Clifford. " 'The Invincible Curate' and Penny Readings at Wakefield
Mechanics' Institution," *Gissing Newsletter,* 23, i (1987), 15–27.

"Joseph"
Coustillas, Pierre. " 'Joseph': A Forgotten Gissing Story of the Mid-Nineties,"
Gissing Newsletter, 24, i (1988), 6–7.

ELLEN GLASGOW

"The Greatest Good"
Pannill, Linda. "Ellen Glasgow's Allegory of Love and Death: 'The Greatest
Good,' " *Resources Am Lit Stud,* 14, i–ii (1984), 161–166.

GERALD M. GLASKIN

"The Return"
Büssing, Sabine. *Aliens in the Home . . .* , 133–134.

SUSAN GLASPELL

"A Jury of Her Peers"
*Perrine, Laurence, and Thomas R. Arp. *Instructor's Manual . . .*, 7th ed., 41–43.

ARTHUR DE GOBINEAU

"Adélaïde"
Smith, Annette, and David Smith. "Afterword," *"Mademoiselle Irnois" and Other Stories* [by Arthur de Gobineau], 283–286.

"Akrivie Phrangopoulo"
Smith, Annette, and David Smith. "Afterword," 280–283.

"Mademoiselle Irnois"
Smith, Annette, and David Smith. "Afterword," 277–279.

"A Traveling Life"
Smith, Annette, and David Smith. "Afterword," 288–290.

"The War with the Turcomans"
Smith, Annette, and David Smith. "Afterword," 286–288.

GAIL GODWIN

"Dream Children"
Charters, Ann, William E. Sheidley, and Martha Ramsey. *Instructor's Manual . . .*, 2nd ed., 203–204.

JOHANN WOLFGANG VON GOETHE

"Fairy Tale"
Niggl, Günter. "Verantwortliches Handeln als Utopie? Überlegungen zu Goethes 'Märchen,'" in Wittkowski, Wolfgang, Ed. *Verantwortung und Utopie . . .*, 91–104.

NIKOLAI GOGOL

"The Diary of a Madman"
Waszink, P. M. "*Such Things Happen . . .*," 254–300.

"Ivan Fyodorovich Shponka and His Aunt"
Andrews, Joe. *Women in Russian Literature . . .*, 81–85.

"The Nevsky Prospect"
Andrews, Joe. *Women in Russian Literature . . .*, 103–104.
Waszink, P. M. "*Such Things Happen . . .*," 77–133.

"The Nose"
Waszink, P. M. *"Such Things Happen . . . ,"* 147–188.

"Old World Landowners"
Feuer, Kathryn B. "Three Easy Pieces: Izmailov to Pushkin; Pushkin to Gogol; Gogol to Balzac," in Flier, Michael S., and Simon Karlinsky, Eds. *Language, Literature, Linguistics . . .* , 34–37.

"The Overcoat"
Connolly, Julian W. "Boris Vakhtin's 'The Sheepskin Coat' and Gogol's 'The Overcoat,'" in Connolly, Julian W., and Sonia I. Ketchian, Eds. *Studies in Russian Literature . . .* , 74–85.
Ponomareff, Constantin V. *On the Dark Side . . .* , 98–100.
Sheidley, William E., and Ann Charters. *Instructor's Manual . . .* , 7–8; Charters, Ann, William E. Sheidley, and Martha Ramsey. *Instructor's Manual . . .* , 2nd ed., 11.

"The Quarrel Between Ivan Ivanovich and Ivan Nikiforovich"
Gregg, Richard. "The Curse of Sameness and the Gogolian Esthetic: 'The Tale of the Two Ivans' as Parable," *Slavic & East European J,* 31, i (1987), 1–9.

"Taras Bulba"
Andrews, Joe. *Women in Russian Literature . . .* , 88–90.

"Viy"
Andrews, Joe. *Women in Russian Literature . . .* , 98–99.

WILLIAM GOLDING

"Clonk Clonk"
Gindin, James. *William Golding,* 64–65.

"Envoy Extraordinary"
Gindin, James. *William Golding,* 61–63.

"The Scorpion God"
Gindin, James. *William Golding,* 63–64.

PEDRO A. GÓMEZ VALDERRAMA

"La aventura de la nieve"
Pavón, Alfredo. "'La aventura de la nieve' o las deformaciones de la realidad," *Texto Crítico,* 13 (1987), 106–122.

JOSÉ LUIS GONZÁLEZ

"Una cajo de plumo que no se podía abrir"
Melendez, Concha. *El arte del cuento . . .* , 294–296.

"La carta"
Melendez, Concha. *El arte del cuento* . . . , 293–294.

"En el fondo del caño hay un negrito"
Melendez, Concha. *El arte del cuento* . . . , 296–297.

MANUEL GONZÁLEZ ZELEDÓN

"El clis de sol"
Menton, Seymour. *El Cuento Hispanoamericano,* I, 114–115; 2nd ed., 114–115; 3rd ed., 114–115.

NADINE GORDIMER

"Ah, Woe Is Me"
Smith, Rowland. "Leisure, Law and Loathing: Matrons, Mistresses, Mothers in the Fiction of Nadine Gordimer and Jillian Becker," *World Lit Written Engl,* 28 (1988), 42–43.

"Is There Nowhere Else We Can Meet?"
Clingman, Stephen. *The Novels of Nadine Gordimer* . . . , 210–212.

"Six Feet of the Country"
Clingman, Stephen. *The Novels of Nadine Gordimer* . . . , 140–141.

"Something Out There"
Jacobs, J. U. "Living Space and Narrative Space in Nadine Gordimer's 'Something Out There,'" *Engl Africa,* 14, ii (1987), 31–43.

"Town and Country Lovers"
Charters, Ann, William E. Sheidley, and Martha Ramsey. *Instructor's Manual* . . . , 2nd ed., 161–163.

MAXIM GORKY

"Chelkash"
Clowes, Edith W. *The Revolution* . . . , 182.

"Kain and Artem"
Clowes, Edith W. *The Revolution* . . . , 182–184.

"Man"
Clowes, Edith W. *The Revolution* . . . , 195–198.

"The Mistake"
Clowes, Edith W. *The Revolution* . . . , 188–189, 190–192.

"Song of the Falcon"
Clowes, Edith W. *The Revolution* . . . , 184–186.

ANGÉLICA GORODISCHER

"And the Vacant Street"
Mosier, M. Patricia. "Women in Power in Gorodischer's *Kalpa Imperial*," in Palumbo, Donald, Ed. *Spectrum of the Fantastic,* 156–157.

"The End of a Dynasty or The Natural History of Ferrets"
Mosier, M. Patricia. "Women in Power . . . ," 154–156.

"Portrait of the Empress"
Mosier, M. Patricia. "Women in Power . . . ," 157–158.

"El señor Caos"
Mosier, M. Patricia. "Comunicando la trascendencia en *Trafalgar* por Angélica Gorodischer," *Foro Literario,* 15–16 (1986), 50–56.

"Sensatez del circulo"
Mosier, M. Patricia. "Comunicando . . . ," 50–56.

"That's How the South Is"
Mosier, M. Patricia. "Women in Power . . . ," 158–160.

JEREMIAS GOTTHELF [ALBERT BITZIUS]

"The Black Spider"
Büssing, Sabine. *Aliens in the Home . . . ,* 97–98.
Reinhardt, George. "Swiss Animal Satire as Psychological Safety Valve," in Collings, Michael R., Ed. *Reflections on the Fantastic . . . ,* 12–13.

PATRICIA GRACE

"A Way of Talking"
New, W. H. *Dreams of Speech . . . ,* 224–228.

LAURENCE GRAFFTEY-SMITH

"The Locket"
Büssing, Sabine. *Aliens in the Home . . . ,* 104.

DANIIL A. GRANIN

"A Personal Opinion"
Lowe, David. *Russian Writing Since 1953 . . . ,* 79–80.

DAVID GRANT

"The Bats"
Büssing, Sabine. *Aliens in the Home . . . ,* 63–64.

THOMAS COLLEY GRATTAN

"The Priest and the Garde-du-Corps"
Krans, Horatio S. *Irish Life* . . . , 55–56.

MORAG GREEN

"Under the Flagstone"
Büssing, Sabine. *Aliens in the Home* . . . , 114.

GRAHAM GREENE

"The Basement Room"
O'Prey, Paul. *A Reader's Guide* . . . , 57–58.

"The Destructors"
O'Prey, Paul. *A Reader's Guide* . . . , 58–60.
*Perrine, Laurence, and Thomas R. Arp. *Instructor's Manual* . . . , 7th ed., 5.

"The Hint of an Explanation"
O'Prey, Paul. *A Reader's Guide* . . . , 60–62.

"The Innocent"
O'Prey, Paul. *A Reader's Guide* . . . , 60.

"Under the Garden"
Lesser, Wendy. *The Life Below the Ground* . . . , 182–192.
O'Prey, Paul. *A Reader's Guide* . . . , 63–66.
Thomas, Brian. *An Underground Fate* . . . , 107–125.

"A Visit to Morin"
O'Prey, Paul. *A Reader's Guide* . . . , 96.

JOSEPH GREENE

"Encounter with a Carnivore"
McGregor, Gaile. *The Noble Savage* . . . , 276–277.

GERALD GRIFFIN

"The Aylmers of Bally-Aylmer"
Krans, Horatio S. *Irish Life* . . . , 155–156.

"The Barber of Bantry"
Krans, Horatio S. *Irish Life* . . . , 161–164.

"Card-Drawing"
Krans, Horatio S. *Irish Life* . . . , 153–155.

"The Half Sir"
Krans, Horatio S. *Irish Life* . . . , 159–161.

"The Hand and the Word"
Krans, Horatio S. *Irish Life* . . . , 153–155.

"Suil Dhuv, or The Coiner"
Krans, Horatio S. *Irish Life* . . . , 157–158.

FRANZ GRILLPARZER

"The Poor Player"
Bahr, Ehrhard. "Geld und Liebe im 'Arme Spielmann': Versuch einer sozio-
    literarischen Interpretation," in Bernd, Clifford A., Ed. *Grillparzer's "Der
    arme Spielmann"* . . . , 300–310.
Cook, Roger F. "Relocating the Author: A New Perspective on the Narrator in
    'Der arme Spielmann,'" in Bernd, Clifford A., Ed. *Grillparzer's "Der arme
    Spielmann"* . . . , 322–326.
Fetzer, John F. "Jakob: Guardian of the Musical Threshold," in Bernd, Clifford
    A., Ed. *Grillparzer's "Der arme Spielmann"* . . . , 254–272.
Lindsey, Barbara. "Music in 'Der arme Spielmann,' with Special Consideration
    to the Elements of the Sacred and Profane," in Bernd, Clifford A., Ed.
    Grillparzer's "Der arme Spielmann" . . . , 272–286.
Thanner, Josef. "Causality and the Ideological Structure of 'Der arme Spiel-
    mann,'" in Bernd, Clifford A., Ed. *Grillparzer's "Der arme Spielmann"* . . . ,
    311–321.

FREDERICK PHILIP GROVE

"Snow"
MacCulloch, Clare. *The Neglected Genre* . . . , 46–50.

BEATRICE GUIDO

"Takeover"
Brunton, Rosanne. "A Note on Contemporary Argentine Women's Writing: A
    Discussion of *The Web*," *Int'l Fiction R*, 15 (1988), 10–11.

RALPH GUSTAFSON

"The Pigeon"
MacCulloch, Clare. *The Neglected Genre* . . . , 60–63.

MANUEL GUTIÉRREZ NÁJERA

"After the Races"
Fulk, Randal C. "Form and Style in the Short Stories of Manuel Gutiérrez
    Nájera," *Hispanic J*, 10, i (1988), 128–131.

Menton, Seymour. *El Cuento Hispanoamericano,* I, 174–177; 2nd ed., 174–177; 3rd ed., 174–177.

MARTÍN LUIS GUZMÁN

"La fiesta de las balas"
Menton, Seymour. *El Cuento Hispanoamericano,* II, 32–35; 2nd ed., 32–35; 3rd ed., 246–249.

OAKLEY HALL

"Horseman"
Cassill, R. V. . . . *Instructor's Handbook,* 38–39.

EDMOND HAMILTON

"The Comet Doom"
Kwasniewski, Elizabeth. "Thrilling Structures? Science Fiction from Early *Amazing* and Detective Fiction," *Foundation,* 38 (1987), 25–27.

DASHIELL HAMMETT

"The Girl with the Silver Eyes"
Day, Gary. "Investigating the Investigator: Hammett's Continental Op," in Docherty, Brian, Ed. *American Crime Fiction* . . . , 44–45.

"The Whosis Kid"
Day, Gary. "Investigating the Investigator . . . ," 40–41.

YAHYA HAQQI

"The Lamp of Umm Hashim"
Badawi, Mustafa. "*The Lamp of Umm Hashim*: The Egyptian Intellectual Between East and West," *J Arabic Lit,* 1 (1970), 145–146; rpt. Allen, Roger, Ed. *Modern Arabic Literature,* 128–129.

THOMAS HARDY

"The Fiddler of the Reels"
Alexander, Anne. *Thomas Hardy* . . . , 169.

"How I Built Myself a House"
Orel, Harold. *The Unknown Hardy* . . . , 16–18.

"An Imaginative Woman"
Bayley, John. *The Short Story* . . . , 139–141.

"Interlopers at the Knap"
Alexander, Anne. *Thomas Hardy . . .* , 183–184.

"On the Western Circuit"
Bayley, John. *The Short Story . . .* , 140–151.

"The Son's Veto"
Bayley, John. *The Short Story . . .* , 136–138.

"The Three Strangers"
Alexander, Anne. *Thomas Hardy . . .* , 170–171.

"The Withered Arm"
Alexander, Anne. *Thomas Hardy . . .* , 169–170.
Bayley, John. *The Short Story . . .* , 143–146.

GEORGE WASHINGTON HARRIS

"Eaves-Dropping a Lodge of Free-Masons"
Wenke, John. "*Sut Lovingood's Yarns* and the Politics of Performance," *Stud Am Fiction,* 15 (1988), 200–201.

"Frustrating a Funeral"
Wenke, John. "*Sut Lovingood's Yarns . . .* ," 205–206.

"Sut at a Negro Night Meeting"
Wenke, John. "*Sut Lovingood's Yarns . . .* ," 204–205.

"Sut Lovingood's Daddy, Acting Horse"
Wenke, John. "*Sut Lovingood's Yarns . . .* ," 201–202.

BRET HARTE

"The Luck of Roaring Camp"
Morrow, Patrick D. "Bret Harte," in Erisman, Fred, and Richard W. Etulain, Eds. *Fifty Western Writers,* 176–177.

"M'liss"
Chapman, Arnold. "The Barefoot Galateas of Bret Harte and Rómulo Gallegos," *Symposium,* 18 (1964), 333–341.

GERALD HASLAM

"Ace Low"
Locklin, Gerald. *Gerald Haslam,* 14.

"Before Dishonor"
Locklin, Gerald. *Gerald Haslam,* 12–13.

"California Christmas"
Locklin, Gerald. *Gerald Haslam,* 9–10.

"Companeros"
Locklin, Gerald. *Gerald Haslam,* 11–12.

"Cowboys"
Locklin, Gerald. *Gerald Haslam,* 12.

"Crossing the Valley"
Locklin, Gerald. *Gerald Haslam,* 44.

"The Doll"
Locklin, Gerald. *Gerald Haslam,* 8–9.

"Dust"
Locklin, Gerald. *Gerald Haslam,* 33–34.

"Earthquake Summer"
Locklin, Gerald. *Gerald Haslam,* 33.

"The Great Kern County Gator Hunt"
Locklin, Gerald. *Gerald Haslam,* 21.

"Growing Up at Babe's"
Locklin, Gerald. *Gerald Haslam,* 38.

"Happily Ever After"
Locklin, Gerald. *Gerald Haslam,* 26.

"Hawk Flights: An American Fable"
Locklin, Gerald. *Gerald Haslam,* 29–30.

"Heat"
Locklin, Gerald. *Gerald Haslam,* 26–27.

"Hey, Okie!"
Locklin, Gerald. *Gerald Haslam,* 35.

"Home to America"
Locklin, Gerald. *Gerald Haslam,* 34–35.

"The Horned Toad"
Locklin, Gerald. *Gerald Haslam,* 30–31.

"Jimmy Eight"
Locklin, Gerald. *Gerald Haslam,* 24–25.

"Joaquin"
Locklin, Gerald. *Gerald Haslam,* 35–36.

"The Souvenir"
Locklin, Gerald. *Gerald Haslam,* 42–43.

"Sweet Reason"
Locklin, Gerald. *Gerald Haslam,* 23–24.

"Trophies"
Locklin, Gerald. *Gerald Haslam,* 42.

"Vengeance"
Locklin, Gerald. *Gerald Haslam,* 44.

"Voice of a Place: The Great Central Valley"
Locklin, Gerald. *Gerald Haslam,* 36–37.

"The Wages of Sin"
Locklin, Gerald. *Gerald Haslam,* 22–23.

"Walls"
Locklin, Gerald. *Gerald Haslam,* 25–26.

"Who Can Write What"
Locklin, Gerald. *Gerald Haslam,* 37.

"Widder Maker"
Locklin, Gerald. *Gerald Haslam,* 31–32.

"Wild Goose: Memories of a Valley Summer"
Locklin, Gerald. *Gerald Haslam,* 13–14.

GERHART HAUPTMANN

"The Bassgeige"
Dussère, Carolyn T. *The Image of the Primitive Giant . . . ,* 56–57.

"Galahad"
Dussère, Carolyn T. *The Image of the Primitive Giant . . . ,* 84–85.

"Der Ketzer von Soana"
Dussère, Carolyn T. *The Image of the Primitive Giant . . . ,* 76–79.
McClain, William H. "The Case of Hauptmann's Fallen Priest," *Germ Q,* 30
    (1957), 167–183.

"Signalman Thiel"
Dussère, Carolyn T. *The Image of the Primitive Giant . . . ,* 22–32.
Heerdegen, Irene. "Gerhart Hauptmanns Novelle 'Bahnwärter Thiel,'" *Wei-
    marer Beiträge,* 4 (1958), 348–360.
Martini, Fritz. *Das Wagnis der Sprache . . . ,* 59–98.
———. "Der kleine Thiel und der grosse Thienwiebel: Das Erzählen auf der
    Schwelle zur Moderne," *Der Deutschunterricht,* 40, ii (1988), 65–76.

NATHANIEL HAWTHORNE

"Alice Doane's Appeal"
Budick, Emily. *Fiction* . . . , 99–102.
Swartzlander, Susan. "'Appealing to the Heart': The Use of History and the
    Role of Fiction in 'Alice Doane's Appeal,'" *Stud Short Fiction*, 25 (1988),
    121–128.
Twitchell, James B. *Forbidden Partners* . . . , 207–212.

"The Ancestral Footstep"
Newberry, Frederick. *Hawthorne's Divided Loyalties* . . . , 217–220.

"The Artist of the Beautiful"
Bowering, George. *The Mask* . . . , 10–13.
Newberry, Frederick. *Hawthorne's Divided Loyalties* . . . , 136–138.

"The Birthmark"
Bowering, George. *The Mask* . . . , 7–9.
Coleman, Arthur. "Hawthorne's Pragmatic Fantasies," *Coll Lang Assoc J*, 31
    (1988), 365–366.
Morse, David. *American Romanticism, I* . . . , 190–191.
Person, Leland S. *Aesthetic Headaches* . . . , 109–112.
Rucker, Mary E. "Science and Art in Hawthorne's 'The Birth-mark,'" *Nine-
    teenth-Century Fiction*, 41 (1987), 445–461.

"The Christmas Banquet"
Harris, Kenneth M. *Hypocrisy* . . . , 38–40.

"Drowne's Wooden Image"
Bowering, George. *The Mask* . . . , 5–7.
Newberry, Frederick. *Hawthorne's Divided Loyalties* . . . , 134–136.
Stout, Janis P. *Sodom in Eden* . . . , 93–94.

"Edward Randolph's Portrait"
Budick, Emily. *Fiction* . . . , 102–105.
Newberry, Frederick. *Hawthorne's Divided Loyalties* . . . , 76–85.

"Endicott and the Red Cross"
Franzosa, John. "Young Man Hawthorne: Scrutinizing the Discourse of His-
    tory," *Bucknell R*, 30, ii (1987), 72–94.
Newberry, Frederick. *Hawthorne's Divided Loyalties* . . . , 34–44.

"Ethan Brand"
Baldick, Chris. *In Frankenstein's Shadow* . . . , 70–72.
Harris, Kenneth M. *Hypocrisy* . . . , 40–42.
Marx, Leo. *The Pilot* . . . , 119–124.
Wegner, Gregory R. "Hawthorne's 'Ethan Brand' and the Structure of the
    Literary Sketch," *J Narrative Technique*, 17 (1987), 57–66.

"Fancy's Show Box"
Harris, Kenneth M. *Hypocrisy* . . . , 29–31.

"Feathertop"
Harris, Kenneth M. *Hypocrisy* . . . , 22–24.
Rucker, Mary E. "The Art of Witchcraft in Hawthorne's 'Feathertop: A Moralized Legend,'" *Stud Short Fiction*, 24 (1987), 31–39.

"Footprints on the Seashore"
See, Fred G. *Desire and the Sign* . . . , 18–21.

"The Gentle Boy"
Büssing, Sabine. *Aliens in the Home* . . . , 16–17.
Dekker, George. . . . *Historical Romance*, 152–154.
Harris, Kenneth M. *Hypocrisy* . . . , 31–34.
Newberry, Frederick. *Hawthorne's Divided Loyalties* . . . , 41–50.

"The Gray Champion"
Dekker, George. . . . *Historical Romance*, 134–151.
Newberry, Frederick. *Hawthorne's Divided Loyalties* . . . , 50–59.

"Lady Eleanore's Mantle"
Budick, Emily. *Fiction* . . . , 111–113.
Newberry, Frederick. *Hawthorne's Divided Loyalties* . . . , 85–99.
Pribek, Thomas. "Witchcraft in 'Lady Eleanore's Mantle,'" *Stud Am Fiction*, 15 (1987), 95–100.

"Little Annie's Ramble"
Van Tassel, Mary M. "Hawthorne, His Narrator, and His Readers in 'Little Annie's Ramble,'" *ESQ: J Am Renaissance*, 33 (1987), 168–179.

"The Man of Adamant"
Person, Leland S. *Aesthetic Headaches* . . . , 167–168.

"The Maypole of Merry Mount"
Dekker, George. . . . *Historical Romance*, 154–158.
Newberry, Frederick. *Hawthorne's Divided Loyalties* . . . , 25–34.

"The Minister's Black Veil"
Budick, Emily. *Fiction* . . . , 105–110.
German, Norman. "The Veil of Words in 'The Minister's Black Veil,'" *Stud Short Fiction*, 25 (1988), 41–47.
Harris, Kenneth M. *Hypocrisy* . . . , 34–38.
McCarthy, Judy. "'The Minister's Black Veil': Concealing Moses and the Holy of Holies," *Stud Short Fiction*, 24 (1987), 131–138.
Morse, David. *American Romanticism, I* . . . , 187–188.
Pribek, Thomas. "The 'Three Parts of the Visible Circle' and Hooper's Sin," *Nathaniel Hawthorne R*, 13, ii (1987), 16–18.

"Mrs. Bullfrog"
Harris, Kenneth M. *Hypocrisy* . . . , 21–22.

"My Kinsman, Major Molineux"
Budick, Emily. *Fiction* . . . , 113–118.
Dekker, George. . . . *Historical Romance*, 173–176.

Machor, James L. *Pastoral Cities* . . . , 193–198.
Marzec, Marcia S. "'My Kinsman, Major Molineux' as Theo-Political Allegory,"
     Am Transcendental Q, 1 N.S. (1987), 273–289.
Morse, David. *American Romanticism, I* . . . , 184–185.
Newberry, Frederick. *Hawthorne's Divided Loyalties* . . . , 62–65, 67–68.
Pearce, Roy H. *Gesta Humanorum* . . . , 62–65.
Portch, Stephen R. *Literature's Silent Language* . . . , 48–74.
Rowe, Joyce A. *Equivocal Endings* . . . , 14–28.
Stout, Janis P. *Sodom in Eden* . . . , 94–96.

"The New Adam and Eve"
Abel, Darrell. *The Moral Picturesque* . . . , 142–143.
Morse, David. *American Romanticism, I* . . . , 185–186.
Schriber, Mary S. *Gender* . . . , 45–46.
See, Fred G. *Desire and the Sign* . . . , 35–36.

"Old Esther Dudley"
Newberry, Frederick. *Hawthorne's Divided Loyalties* . . . , 99–110.

"Old Ticonderoga"
Smith, Judy R. "'Old Ticonderoga': An Early Example of Hawthorne's Nar-
     rative Strategy," *Hawthorne Soc Newsletter,* 10, ii (1984), 10–11.

"The Procession of Life"
Harris, Kenneth M. *Hypocrisy* . . . , 19–20.

"The Prophetic Pictures"
Coleman, Arthur. ". . . Pragmatic Fantasies," 368–370.

"Rappaccini's Daughter"
Bowering, George. *The Mask* . . . , 14–16.
Coleman, Arthur. ". . . Pragmatic Fantasies," 365.
Cuddy, Lois A. "The Purgatorial Gardens of Hawthorne and Dante: Irony and
     Redefinition in 'Rappaccini's Daughter,'" *Mod Lang Stud,* 17, i (1987), 39–
     53.
Hallissy, Margaret. *Venomous Woman* . . . , 133–141.
Haviland, Beverly. "The Sin of Synecdoche: Hawthorne's Allegory Against
     Symbolism in 'Rappaccini's Daughter,'" *Texas Stud Lit & Lang,* 29 (1987),
     278–301.
Jones, Deborah J. "Hawthorne's Post-Platonic Paradise: The Inversion of Al-
     legory in 'Rappaccini's Daughter,'" *J Narrative Technique,* 18 (1988), 153–
     169.
Morse, David. *American Romanticism, I* . . . , 186–187.
Person, Leland S. *Aesthetic Headaches* . . . , 115–121.

"Roger Malvin's Burial"
Budick, Emily. *Fiction* . . . , 39–54.
McIntosh, James. "Nature and Frontier in 'Roger Malvin's Burial,'" *Am Lit,* 60
     (1988), 188–204.
Masuda, Hideo. "'Roger Malvin's Burial': Sin and Its Expiation in Hawthorne,"
     Hiroshima Stud Engl Lang & Lit, 31 (1986), 39–48.

"The Shaker Bridal"
Harris, Kenneth M. *Hypocrisy* . . . , 26–28.

"The Threefold Destiny"
Harris, Kenneth M. *Hypocrisy* . . . , 24–25.

"Wakefield"
Enniss, Stephen C. "Told as Truth: 'Wakefield' as Archetypal Experience," *Nathaniel Hawthorne R*, 14, ii (1988), 7–9.
Gelley, Alexander. *Narrative Crossings* . . . , 155–171.
Morse, David. *American Romanticism, I* . . . , 189–190.

"The Wedding Knell"
St. Pierre, Ronald. "'The married of eternity': Hawthorne's 'The Wedding Knell,'" *Shoin Lit R*, 20 (1986), 87–100.

"Young Goodman Brown"
Abel, Darrell. *The Moral Picturesque* . . . , 130–140.
Budick, Emily. *Fiction* . . . , 85–97.
Hardt, John S. "Doubts in the American Garden: Three Cases of Paradisal Skepticism," *Stud Short Fiction*, 25 (1988), 252–255.
Harris, Kenneth M. *Hypocrisy* . . . , 42–45.
Martin, Terry. "Anti-Allegory and the Reader in 'Young Goodman Brown,'" *Mid-Hudson Lang Stud*, 11 (1988), 31–40.
Morris, Christopher D. "Deconstructing 'Young Goodman Brown,'" *Am Transcendental Q*, 2, i N.S. (1988), 23–33.
Perrine, Laurence, and Thomas R. Arp. *Instructor's Manual* . . . , 6th ed., 50–52; 7th ed., 37–39.
Portch, Stephen R. *Literature's Silent Language* . . . , 75–84.
Sheidley, William E., and Ann Charters. *Instructor's Manual* . . . , 1–2; Charters, Ann, William E. Sheidley, and Martha Ramsey. *Instructor's Manual* . . . , 2nd ed., 1–2.
Wilczynsky, Marek. "Nathaniel Hawthorne's 'Young Goodman Brown': An Attempt at Deconstruction," *Studia Anglica Posnaniensia*, 20 (1987), 227–239.

HAYASHI FUMIKO

"Late Chrysanthemums"
Brown, Janice. "Hayashi Fumiko," in Swann, Thomas E., and Kinya Tsuruta, Eds. . . . *Modern Japanese Short Story*, 63–70.

ERNEST HAYCOCK

"On Bakeoven Grade"
Etulian, Richard W. *Ernest Haycock*, 36–37.

"Stage to Lordsburg"
Etulian, Richard W. *Ernest Haycock*, 12–14.

HAYIM HAZAZ

"Rahamim the Porter"
Bargad, Warren. "Realism and Myth in the Works of Hazaz: 1933–1943," *Jewish Book Annual*, 41 (1983–1984), 142–145.

"The Sermon"
Bargad, Warren. "Realism and Myth . . . ," 145–147.

BESSIE HEAD

"The Deep River: A Story of Ancient Tribal Migration"
Trump, Martin. "Black South African Short Fiction in English," *Research African Lit*, 19, i (1988), 41.

"Heaven Is Not Closed"
Trump, Martin. "Black South African Short Fiction . . . ," 42.

"Life"
Trump, Martin. "Black South African Short Fiction . . . ," 42–43.

ANN HÉBERT

"The Coral Dress"
Blodgett, E. D. *Configuration* . . . , 55–56.

"The Death of Stella"
Blodgett, E. D. *Configuration* . . . , 56–57.

"The House on the Esplanade"
Blodgett, E. D. *Configuration* . . . , 57.

ROBERT HEINLEIN

"All You Zombies"
Schuyler, William M. "Sexes, Genders, and Discrimination," in Palumbo, Donald, Ed. *Erotic Universe* . . . , 49–50.

"Blowups Happen"
Bartter, Martha A. *The Way to Ground Zero* . . . , 76–77.
Berger, Albert I. "Theories of History and Social Order in *Astounding Science Fiction*, 1934–1955," *Sci-Fiction Stud*, 15 (1988), 24.

"By His Bootstraps"
Leiby, David A. "The Tooth That Gnaws: Reflections on Time Travel," in Slusser, George E., and Eric S. Rabkin, Eds. *Intersections* . . . , 112–114.

"If This Goes On"
Pierce, John J. *Foundations* . . . , 204–205.

"Project Nightmare"
Bartter, Martha A. *The Way to Ground Zero* . . . , 183–184.

"Requiem"
Berger, Albert I. "Theories of History . . . ," 23.

"The Roads Must Roll"
Berger, Albert I. "Theories of History . . . ," 24.

"Solution Unsatisfactory"
Bartter, Martha A. *The Way to Ground Zero* . . . , 177–178.
Franklin, H. Bruce. *War Stars* . . . , 141–145.

MARK HELPRIN

"A Dove of the East"
Field, Leslie. "Mark Helprin and Postmodern Jewish-American Fiction of Fantasy," *Yiddish*, 7, i (1987), 59–60.

"Ellis Island"
Boelhower, William. *Through a Glass Darkly* . . . , 84–85.
Field, Leslie. "Mark Helprin . . . ," 62–64.

"A Jew of Persia"
Field, Leslie. "Mark Helprin . . . ," 58–59.

"North Light"
Charters, Ann, William E. Sheidley, and Martha Ramsey. *Instructor's Manual* . . . , 2nd ed., 224–225.

"The Schreuderspitze"
Field, Leslie. "Mark Helprin . . . ," 61–62.

ERNEST HEMINGWAY

"An Alpine Idyll"
Putnam, Ann. "Dissemblings and Disclosure in Hemingway's 'An Alpine Idyll,'" *Hemingway R*, 6, ii (1987), 27–33.

"The Battler"
Lynn, Kenneth S. *Hemingway*, 271–272.

"Big Two-Hearted River"
Gaggin, John. *Hemingway* . . . *Aestheticism*, 25–26.
Lynn, Kenneth S. *Hemingway*, 102–106.

"Cat in the Rain"
Barbour, James. "Fugue State as a Literary Device in 'Cat in the Rain' and 'Hills Like White Elephants,'" *Arizona Q*, 44, ii (1988), 99–103.
Bayley, John. *The Short Story* . . . , 77–78.

Bennett, Warren. "The Poor Kitty and the Padrone and Tortoise-Shell Cat in 'Cat in the Rain,'" *Hemingway R,* 8, i (1988), 26–36.

"A Clean, Well-Lighted Place"
Johnston, Kenneth G. *The Tip . . . ,* 162–165.

"Cross-Country Snow"
Johnston, Kenneth G. *The Tip . . . ,* 64–68.

"The Denunciation"
Johnston, Kenneth G. *The Tip . . . ,* 218–227.

"The Doctor and the Doctor's Wife"
Hannum, Howard L. "The Case of Dr. Henry Adams," *Arizona Q,* 44, ii (1988), 43–45.

"The Faithful Bull"
Johnston, Kenneth G. *The Tip . . . ,* 235–237.

"Fathers and Sons"
Hannum, Howard L. "The Case . . . ," 52–54.
Johnston, Kenneth G. *The Tip . . . ,* 184–187.

"Fifty Grand"
Lynn, Kenneth S. *Hemingway,* 307–310.

"Get a Seeing-Eye Dog"
Johnston, Kenneth G. *The Tip . . . ,* 251–253.

"God Rest You Merry, Gentlemen"
Lynn, Kenneth S. *Hemingway,* 71–72.

"The Good Lion"
Johnston, Kenneth G. *The Tip . . . ,* 238–241.

"Hills Like White Elephants"
Barbour, James. "Fugue State . . . ," 103–106.
Brown, Nancy H. "Aspects of the Short Story: A Comparison of Jean Rhys's 'The Sound of the River' with Ernest Hemingway's 'Hills Like White Elephants,'" *Jean Rhys R,* 1, i (1986), 2–13.
Johnston, Kenneth G. *The Tip . . . ,* 126–131.
Passey, Laurie. "Hemingway's 'Hills Like White Elephants,'" *Explicator,* 46, iv (1988), 32–33.
*Perrine, Laurence, and Thomas R. Arp. *Instructor's Manual . . . ,* 7th ed., 19–20.
Portch, Stephen R. *Literature's Silent Language . . . ,* 100–110.
Smiley, Pamela. "Gender-Linked Miscommunication in 'Hills Like White Elephants,'" *Hemingway R,* 8, i (1988), 2–12.
Urgo, Joseph R. "Hemingway's 'Hills Like White Elephants,'" *Explicator,* 46, iii (1988), 35–37.

"In Another Country"
Johnston, Kenneth G. *The Tip* . . . , 115–120.
Robinson, Forrest. "Hemingway's Invisible Hero of 'In Another Country,'" *Essays Lit,* 15 (1988), 237–244.
Waldmeir, Joseph J. "And the Wench in Faith and Value," *Stud Short Fiction,* 24 (1987), 393–398.

"Indian Camp"
Bayley, John. *The Short Story* . . . , 78–80.
Cowan, James C. "The *Pharmakos* Figure in Modern American Stories of Physicians and Patients," *Lit & Med,* 6 (1987), 104–105.
Hannum, Howard L. "The Case . . . ," 40–43.
Johnston, Kenneth G. *The Tip* . . . , 50–58.
Meyers, Jeffrey. "Hemingway's Primitivism and 'Indian Camp,'" *Twentieth Century Lit,* 34 (1988), 211–222.

"The Killers"
Portch, Stephen R. *Literature's Silent Language* . . . , 91–100.

"The Last Good Country"
Spilka, Mark. "Original Sin in 'The Last Good Country'; or, The Return of Catherine Barkley," in Gamache, Lawrence B., and Ian S. MacNiven, Eds. *The Modernists* . . . , 210–233.

"Nobody Ever Dies"
Cooper, Stephen. "Politics Over Art: Hemingway's 'Nobody Ever Dies,'" *Stud Short Fiction,* 25 (1988), 117–120.

"Now I Lay Me"
Johnston, Kenneth G. *The Tip* . . . , 137–141.
Lynn, Kenneth S. *Hemingway,* 46–48.

"The Old Man and the Sea"
Kort, Wesley A. *Modern Fiction* . . . , 34–35.
Love, Glen A. "Hemingway's Indian Virtues: An Ecological Reconsideration," *Western Am Lit,* 22 (1987), 206–208.
Peck, Marie J. "José Pedro Díaz y Hemingway: Una mitología compartida," *Texto Crítico,* 12 (1986), 189–203.
Waldmeir, Joseph J. "And the Wench . . . ," 393–398.
West, Paul. *The Modern Novel,* II, 225–227.

"On the Quai at Smyrna"
Smith, Peter A. "Hemingway's 'On the Quai at Smyrna' and the Universe of *In Our Time,*" *Stud Short Fiction,* 24 (1987), 159–162.

"Out of Season"
Bayley, John. *The Short Story* . . . , 76–77.
Johnston, Kenneth G. *The Tip* . . . , 29–35.
Lynn, Kenneth S. *Hemingway,* 201–204.

"The Revolutionist"
Johnston, Kenneth G. *The Tip* . . . , 42–45.

"The Short Happy Life of Francis Macomber"
Howell, John M. "McCaslin and Macomber: From *Green Hills* to *Big Woods*," *Faulkner J*, 2, i (1986), 29–36.
Johnston, Kenneth G. *The Tip* . . . , 207–211.

"The Snows of Kilimanjaro"
Gaggin, John. *Hemingway . . . Aestheticism*, 35–36.
Johnston, Kenneth G. *The Tip* . . . , 196–201.
Sheidley, William E., and Ann Charters. *Instructor's Manual* . . . , 109–110; Charters, Ann, William E. Sheidley, and Martha Ramsey. *Instructor's Manual* . . . , 2nd ed., 109–110.

"Soldier's Home"
Johnston, Kenneth G. *The Tip* . . . , 75–79.
Myers, Thomas. *Walking Point* . . . , 186–188.

"The Strange Country"
Flora, Joseph M. "Hemingway's 'The Strange Country' in the Context of *The Complete Short Stories*," *Stud Short Fiction*, 25 (1988), 413–420.

"Ten Indians"
Hannum, Howard L. "The Case . . . ," 46–49.

"Three-Day Blow"
Johnston, Kenneth G. *The Tip* . . . , 95–101.

"The Undefeated"
Gaggin, John. *Hemingway . . . Aestheticism*, 47–48.
Johnston, Kenneth G. *The Tip* . . . , 85–89.

"A Way You'll Never Be"
Johnston, Kenneth G. *The Tip* . . . , 172–177.

"Wine of Wyoming"
Johnston, Kenneth G. *The Tip* . . . , 148–155.
Martin, Lawrence H. "Crazy in Sheridan: Hemingway's 'Wine of Wyoming' Reconsidered," *Hemingway R*, 8, i (1988), 13–25.

AMY HEMPEL

"In the Cemetery Where Al Jolson Is Buried"
Cassill, R. V. . . . *Instructor's Handbook*, 40–42.

ZENNA HENDERSON

"Things"
McGregor, Gaile. *The Noble Savage* . . . , 258–259.

FELISBERTO HERNÁNDEZ

"El acomodador"
Ferré, Rosario. *"El acomodador"* . . . , 47–49, 64–66, 81–88.
Lasarte, Francisco. *Felisberto Hernández* . . . , 177–181.

"El balcón"
Barrenechea, Ann M. "Excentricidad, di-vergencias y con-vergencias en Felisberto Hernández," *Mod Lang Notes*, 91 (1976), 319–320.
Ferré, Rosario. *"El acomodador"* . . . , 66–68, 75–81.

"La casa inundador"
Echavarren, Roberto. *El espacio de la verdad* . . . , 149–200.
Lasarte, Francisco. *Felisberto Hernández* . . . , 65–72.
Paternain, Alejandro. "La religion del agua," *Cuadernos Hispanoamericanos*, 256 (1971), 83–110.

"El cocodrilo"
Ferré, Rosario. *"El acomodador"* . . . , 49–50, 72–75.

"Las dos historias"
Barrenechea, Ann M. "Excentricidad . . . ," 327–329.

"La envenedada"
Ferré, Rosario. *"El acomodador"* . . . , 37–40.

"Historia de un cigarrillo"
Ferré, Rosario. *"El acomodador"* . . . , 35.

"Las hortensias"
Barrenechea, Ann M. "Excentricidad . . . ," 321–322.
Borinsky, Alicia. "Expectador y expectáculo en 'Las hortensias' y otros cuentos de Felisberto Hernández," *Cuadernos Americanos*, 189, iv (1973), 240–245.
Lasarte, Francisco. *Felisberto Hernández* . . . , 184–191.

"Menos Julia"
Antúnez, Rocío. *Felisberto Hernández* . . . , 80–81.
Lasarte, Francisco. *Felisberto Hernández* . . . , 182–184.

"Muebles el canario"
Antúnez, Rocío. *Felisberto Hernández* . . . , 60–61.

"Nadie encendía las lámparas"
Antúnez, Rocío. *Felisberto Hernández* . . . , 62–63.

"Tal vez un movimiento"
Echavarren, Roberto. *El espacio de la verdad* . . . , 36–37.

"Úrsula"
Echavarren, Roberto. "El suceso textual en 'Úrsula' de Felisberto Hernández,' in McDuffie, Keith, and Alfredo Roggiano, Eds. *Texto/Contexto* . . . , 71–78.
———. *El espacio de la verdad* . . . , 201–245.

"El vestido blanco"
Ferré, Rosario. *"El acomodador"* . . . , 33–34.

LUIS HERNÁNDEZ AQUINO

"Aire de guazábara"
Melendez, Concha. *El arte del cuento* . . . , 144–145.

"Un enigma y una clave"
Melendez, Concha. *El arte del cuento* . . . , 145.

HERMANN HESSE

"Siddhartha"
Kort, Wesley A. *Modern Fiction* . . . , 143–144.

PATRICIA HIGHSMITH

"Hamsters vs. Websters"
Büssing, Sabine. *Aliens in the Home* . . . , 62–63.

"Harry: A Ferret"
Büssing, Sabine. *Aliens in the Home* . . . , 61–62.

HIGUCHI ICHIYŌ

"Comparing Heights"
Rimer, J. Thomas. *A Reader's Guide* . . . , 110–111.

"Growing Up"
Makoto, Ueda. "Higuchi Ichiyō," in Swann, Thomas E., and Kinya Tsuruta,
    Eds. . . . *Modern Japanese Short Story*, 73–80.

E[RNEST] T[HEODOR] A[MADEUS] HOFFMANN

"The Entail"
Diebitz, Stefan. " 'Überhaupt eine gehässige Sache': E. T. A. Hoffmanns Erzäh-
    lung 'Das Majorat' als Dichtung der Hybris und der Niedertracht," *Mittei-
    lungen der E. T. A. Hoffmann*, 32 (1986), 35–49.
Woeller, Waltraud, and Bruce Cassiday. *The Literature of Crime* . . . , 53.

"The Golden Pot"
Birrell, Gordon. *The Boundless Present* . . . , 126–127.
Coates, Paul. *The Double and the Other* . . . , 106–107.
Ekfelt, Nils. "Style and Level of Reality in E. T. A. Hoffmann's 'Der goldne
    Topf,' " *Style*, 22, i (1988), 61–92.
Marhold, Hartmut. "Die Problematik dichterischen Schaffens in E. T. A. Hoff-

manns Erzählung 'Der goldne Topf,'" *Mitteilungen der E. T. A. Hoffmann,* 32 (1986), 50–73.

"Ignatz Denner"
Woeller, Waltraud, and Bruce Cassiday. *The Literature of Crime* . . . , 52–53.

"Mademoiselle de Scudery"
Woeller, Waltraud, and Bruce Cassiday. *The Literature of Crime* . . . , 53–54.

"The Mines of Falun"
Baldick, Chris. *In Frankenstein's Shadow* . . . , 66–68.

"The Sandman"
Cave, Terence. *Recognitions* . . . , 170–172.
Coates, Paul. *The Double and the Other* . . . , 104–106.
Heller, Terry. *The Delights of Terror* . . . , 88–95.
Kamla, Thomas A. "E. T. A. Hoffmann's 'Der Sandmann': The Narrative Poet as Romantic Solipsist," *Germ R,* 63 (1988), 94–102.
Koelb, Clayton. *Invention of Reading* . . . , 115–134.
Kroeber, Karl. *Romantic Fantasy,* 88–89.
Merkl, Helmut. "Der paralysierte Engel: Zur Erkundung der Automatenliebe in E. T. A. Hoffmanns Erzählung 'Der Sandmann,'" *Wirkendes Wort,* 38, ii (1988), 187–199.
Schmidt, Ricarda. "E. T. A. Hoffmann's 'Der Sandmann': An Early Example of *Écriture feminine—Critique of Trends in Feminist Literary Criticism,*" *Women Germ Yearbook,* 4 (1988), 21–45.
Siebers, Tobin. "'Whose Hideous Voice Is This?' The Reading Unconscious in Freud and Hoffmann," *New Orleans R,* 15, iii (1988), 80–87.

"Der Zusammenhang der Dinge"
Diebitz, Stefan. "Übersehen und verkannt Hoffmanns Vampirismuslung 'Der Zusammenhang der Dinge,'" *Mitteilungen der E. T. A. Hoffmann,* 33 (1987), 50–65.

MARY HOOD

"Finding the Chain"
Pope, Dan. "The Post-Minimalist American Story; or, What Comes after Carver?" *Gettysburg R,* 1 (1988), 341–342.

LUCILA HOSILLOS

"Baptism-Escape"
Lucero, Rosario Cruz. "Notes on the Contemporary Hiligaynon Short Story," *Solitary,* 108–109 (1986), 169.

ROBERT ERVIN HOWARD

"Beyond the Black River"
Cerasini, Marc A., and Charles Hoffman. *Robert E. Howard,* 93–95.

"Black Canaan"
Cerasini, Marc A., and Charles Hoffman. *Robert E. Howard*, 118–120.

"By This Axe I Rule"
Cerasini, Marc A., and Charles Hoffman. *Robert E. Howard*, 53–58.

"The Dark Man"
Cerasini, Marc A., and Charles Hoffman. *Robert E. Howard*, 102–104.

"The Footfall Within"
Cerasini, Marc A., and Charles Hoffman. *Robert E. Howard*, 40–42.

"For the Love of Barbara Allen"
Cerasini, Marc A., and Charles Hoffman. *Robert E. Howard*, 108–109.

"The Grey God Passes"
Cerasini, Marc A., and Charles Hoffman. *Robert E. Howard*, 101–102.

"King of the Night"
Cerasini, Marc A., and Charles Hoffman. *Robert E. Howard*, 20–22.

"Men of the Shadows"
Cerasini, Marc A., and Charles Hoffman. *Robert E. Howard*, 18–19.

"The Mirrors of Tuzun Thune"
Cerasini, Marc A., and Charles Hoffman. *Robert E. Howard*, 50–52.

"The Moon of Skulls"
Cerasini, Marc A., and Charles Hoffman. *Robert E. Howard*, 32–35.

"Nekht Semerkeht"
Cerasini, Marc A., and Charles Hoffman. *Robert E. Howard*, 134–135.

"Pigeons from Hell"
Cerasini, Marc A., and Charles Hoffman. *Robert E. Howard*, 116–117.

"Queen of the Black Coast"
Cerasini, Marc A., and Charles Hoffman. *Robert E. Howard*, 72–77.

"Red Nails"
Cerasini, Marc A., and Charles Hoffman. *Robert E. Howard*, 85–91.

"Red Shadows"
Cerasini, Marc A., and Charles Hoffman. *Robert E. Howard*, 27–31.

"Rogues in the House"
Cerasini, Marc A., and Charles Hoffman. *Robert E. Howard*, 69–72.

"The Shadow Kingdom"
Cerasini, Marc A., and Charles Hoffman. *Robert E. Howard*, 43–48.

"The Shadow of the Vulture"
Cerasini, Marc A., and Charles Hoffman. *Robert E. Howard,* 124–125.

"The Skull of Silence"
Cerasini, Marc A., and Charles Hoffman. *Robert E. Howard,* 48–50.

"The Thunder-Ride"
Cerasini, Marc A., and Charles Hoffman. *Robert E. Howard,* 107–108.

"The Vale of Lost Women"
Cerasini, Marc A., and Charles Hoffman. *Robert E. Howard,* 77–79.

"The Valley of the Lost"
Cerasini, Marc A., and Charles Hoffman. *Robert E. Howard,* 114–115.

"The Valley of the Worm"
Cerasini, Marc A., and Charles Hoffman. *Robert E. Howard,* 104–107.

"Wings in the Night"
Cerasini, Marc A., and Charles Hoffman. *Robert E. Howard,* 35–40.

"A Witch Shall Be Born"
Cerasini, Marc A., and Charles Hoffman. *Robert E. Howard,* 79–81.

"Worms of the Earth"
Cerasini, Marc A., and Charles Hoffman. *Robert E. Howard,* 22–25.

WILLIAM DEAN HOWELLS

"Editha"
Piacentino, Edward J. "Arms in Love and War in Howells' 'Editha,'" *Stud Short Fiction,* 24 (1987), 425–432.

LANGSTON HUGHES

"Feet Live Their Own Life"
Frank, Thomas L. "The Art of Verbal Performance: A Stylistic Analysis of Langston Hughes's 'Feet Live Their Own Life,'" *Lang & Style,* 19 (1986), 377–387.

"Slave on the Block"
Roberts, Edgar V., and Henry E. Jacobs. *Instructor's Manual . . . ,* 74.

TED HUGHES

"The Thought Fox"
Gilbert, Sandra M., and Susan Gubar. *No Man's Land . . . ,* 222.

ZORA NEALE HURSTON

"Drenched in Light"
Lowe, John. "Hurston, Humor, and the Harlem Renaissance," in Kramer, Victor, Ed. *The Harlem Renaissance . . .* , 292–293.

"The Gilded Six-Bits"
Lowe, John. "Hurston, Humor . . . ," 296–298.

"Muttsy"
Lowe, John. "Hurston, Humor . . . ," 294.

"Spunk"
Charters, Ann, William E. Sheidley, and Martha Ramsey. *Instructor's Manual . . .* , 2nd ed., 116–117.
Lowe, John. "Hurston, Humor . . . ," 293.

"Sweat"
Gilbert, Sandra M., and Susan Gubar. *No Man's Land . . .* , 95–96.
Lowe, John. "Hurston, Humor . . . ," 294–296.

IBUSE MASUJI

"The Carp"
Liman, Anthony V. "Ibuse Masuji," in Swann, Thomas E., and Kinya Tsuruta, Eds. . . . *Modern Japanese Short Story,* 83–93.
Treat, John W. *Pools of Water . . .* , 40–45.

"Chōhei on an Uninhabited Island"
Treat, John W. *Pools of Water . . .* , 166–167.

"Chōhei's Grave"
Treat, John W. *Pools of Water . . .* , 167–170.

"Confinement"
Treat, John W. *Pools of Water . . .* , 32–36.

"The Day of a Memorial Service for a Bell"
Treat, John W. *Pools of Water . . .* , 130–131.

"The Fire God"
Treat, John W. *Pools of Water . . .* , 214–215.

"A General Account of Aogashima"
Treat, John W. *Pools of Water . . .* , 97–101.

"A Guide to the Ravine"
Treat, John W. *Pools of Water . . .* , 145–147.

"Kuchisuke's Valley"
Treat, John W. *Pools of Water . . .* , 49–54.

"Lieutenant Lookeast"
Treat, John W. *Pools of Water* . . . , 150–153.

"Morikichi from Beppu Village on Oki Island"
Treat, John W. *Pools of Water* . . . , 107–108.

"Papaya"
Treat, John W. *Pools of Water* . . . , 129–130.

"Pilgrim's Inn"
Liman, Anthony V. "Ibuse Masuji," 94–101.

"Plum Blossom by Night"
Treat, John W. *Pools of Water* . . . , 39–40.

"The River"
Liman, Anthony V. "'The River': Ibuse's Poetic Cosmology," in Takeda, Kat-
    suhiko, Ed. . . . *Japanese Literature*, 129–145.
Treat, John W. *Pools of Water* . . . , 61–73.

"Sawan on the Roof"
Treat, John W. *Pools of Water* . . . , 61–73.

"The Sutra Case"
Treat, John W. *Pools of Water* . . . , 133–134.

"A Talk with Abu Bakr"
Treat, John W. *Pools of Water* . . . , 127–128.

"Wabisuke"
Treat, John W. *Pools of Water* . . . , 135–140.

"A Young Girl's Wartime Diary"
Treat, John W. *Pools of Water* . . . , 118–125.

JORGE ICAZA

"Disorientation"
Spell, Jefferson R. . . . *Spanish-American Fiction*, 244–245.

"Interpretation"
Spell, Jefferson R. . . . *Spanish-American Fiction*, 243–244.

"Thirst"
Spell, Jefferson R. . . . *Spanish-American Fiction*, 242–243.

"Whelps"
Spell, Jefferson R. . . . *Spanish-American Fiction*, 241–242.

YUSUF IDRIS

"City Dregs"
Allen, Roger. "The Artistry of Yusuf Idris," *World Lit Today,* 55 (1981), 44.

"Farahat's Republic"
Allen, Roger. "The Artistry . . . ," 44–45.

"House of Flesh"
Allen, Roger. "The Artistry . . . ," 46–47.

"The Omitted Letter"
Allen, Roger, Ed. *In the Eye of the Beholder* . . . , xxiii–xxiv; rpt. Allen, Roger,
     Ed. *Modern Arabic Literature,* 160.

IKEDA MASUO

"To the Aegean Sea"
Sakurai, Emiko. "Japan's New Generation of Writers," *World Lit Today,* 61
     (1988), 406.

WASHINGTON IRVING

"The Adventure of My Aunt"
Doubleday, Neal F. *Variety of Attempt* . . . , 42–43.

"The Adventure of My Uncle"
Doubleday, Neal F. *Variety of Attempt* . . . , 41–42.

"The Adventure of the German Student"
Daigrepont, Lloyd M. "Passion and Gnosticism in Irving's 'Adventure of the
     German Student,'" *Lamar J Humanities,* 13 (Spring, 1987), 19–29.
Rubin-Dorsky, Jeffrey. *Adrift in the Old World* . . . , 184–185.

"The Adventure of the Mysterious Picture"
Doubleday, Neal F. *Variety of Attempt* . . . , 43–44.

"The Devil and Tom Walker"
Rubin-Dorsky, Jeffrey. *Adrift in the Old World* . . . , 197–198.

"Dolph Heyliger"
Dekker, George. . . . *Historical Romance,* 119–121.

"The Legend of Sleepy Hollow"
Dekker, George. . . . *Historical Romance,* 116–119.
Rubin-Dorsky, Jeffrey. *Adrift in the Old World* . . . , 104–110.
von Frank, Albert J. "The Man That Corrupted Sleepy Hollow," *Stud Am Fiction,*
     15 (1988), 129–143.

"Rip Van Winkle"
Fraustino, Daniel. "'Rip Van Winkle' and Eighteenth-Century Social Psychology," *J Evolutionary Psych*, 9, i–ii (1988), 70–74.
Hardt, John S. "Doubts in the American Garden: Three Cases of Paradisal Skepticism," *Stud Short Fiction*, 25 (1988), 250–252.
Rubin-Dorsky, Jeffrey. *Adrift in the Old World . . .* , 110–115.

"The Storm Ship"
Doubleday, Neal F. *Variety of Attempt . . .* , 114–117.

"The Story of the Young Italian"
Rubin-Dorsky, Jeffrey. *Adrift in the Old World . . .* , 190–191.

"The Story of the Young Robber"
Rubin-Dorsky, Jeffrey. *Adrift in the Old World . . .* , 191–194.

"Wolfert Webber"
Rubin-Dorsky, Jeffrey. *Adrift in the Old World . . .* , 198–200.

FAZIL ABDULOVICH ISKANDER

"The Story of Old Xabug's Mule"
Ryan-Hayes, Karen. "Iskander and Tolstoj: The Parodical Implications of the Beast Narrator," *Slavic & East European J*, 32 (1988), 225–236.

MANJERI S. ISVARAN

"Immersion"
Venugopal, C. V. *The Indian Short Story . . .* , 34–35.

SHIRLEY JACKSON

"The Lottery"
Church, Joseph. "Getting Taken in 'The Lottery,'" *Notes Contemp Lit*, 18, iv (1988), 10–11.
Oehlschlaeger, Fritz. "The Stoning of Mistress Hutchinson: Meaning and Context in 'The Lottery,'" *Essays Lit*, 15 (1988), 259–265.
*Perrine, Laurence, and Thomas R. Arp. *Instructor's Manual . . .* , 7th ed., 21–22.
Sheidley, William E., and Ann Charters. *Instructor's Manual . . .* , 151–152; Charters, Ann, William E. Sheidley, and Martha Ramsey. *Instructor's Manual . . .* , 2nd ed., 156.
Terry, James S., and Peter C. Williams. "Literature and Bioethics: The Tension in Goals and Styles," *Lit & Med*, 7 (1988), 15–17.

RICARDO JAIMES FREYRE

"Justicia india"
Menton, Seymour. *El Cuento Hispanoamericano*, I, 219–220; 2nd ed., 219–220; 3rd ed., 219–220.

C[YRIL] L[IONEL] R[OBERT] JAMES

"Triumph"
Carby, Hazel V. "Proletarian or Revolutionary Literature: C. L. R. James and
  the Politics of the Trinidadian Renaissance," *So Atlantic Q*, 87 (1988), 47–
  48.

HENRY JAMES

"The Abasement of the Northmores"
Gage, Richard P. *Order and Design . . .* , 43–45.

"The Altar of the Dead"
Newman, Benjamin. *Searching for the Figure . . .* , 115–138.

"The Aspern Papers"
Bellringer, Alan W. *Henry James*, 72–76.
Krook, Dorothea. "'The Aspern Papers': A Counter-Introduction," in Bakker,
  J., J. A. Verleun, and J. van der Vriesenaerde, Eds. *Essays . . . and a Sheaf
  of Poems*, 223–234.
Marroni, Francesco. "Henry James e le possibilita dell'inganno: Una lettura di
  'The Aspern Papers,'" *Analysis*, 3 (1985), 101–119.
Newman, Benjamin. *Searching for the Figure . . .* , 27–40.

"The Author of 'Beltraffio'"
Freier, Mary P. "The Story of 'The Author of "Beltraffio,"'" *Stud Short Fiction*,
  24 (1987), 308–309.

"The Beast in the Jungle"
Bellringer, Alan W. *Henry James*, 109–111.
Ellis, James. "The Archaeology of Ancient Rome: Sexual Metaphor in 'The
  Beast in the Jungle,'" *Henry James R*, 6 (1984), 27–31.
Gage, Richard P. *Order and Design . . .* , 88–90.
Gutierrez, Donald. *The Dark and the Light Gods . . .* , 64–74.
Lindholdt, Paul J. "Pragmatism and 'The Beast in the Jungle,'" *Stud Short Fic-
  tion*, 25 (1988), 275–284.
Newman, Benjamin. *Searching for the Figure . . .* , 139–156.

"The Beldonald Holbein"
Gage, Richard P. *Order and Design . . .* , 65–67.

"The Bench of Desolation"
Bellringer, Alan W. *Henry James*, 121–122.
Gage, Richard P. *Order and Design . . .* , 257–274.
Satomi, Shigemi. "The Bench in 'The Bench of Desolation,'" *Kyushu Am Lit*, 29
  (1988), 23–30.

"The Birthplace"
Gage, Richard P. *Order and Design . . .* , 91–95.

"Broken Wings"
Gage, Richard P. *Order and Design* . . . , 62–63.

"Brooksmith"
Gage, Richard P. *Order and Design* . . . , 179–185.

"A Bundle of Letters"
Bishop, George. *When the Master Relents* . . . , 13–25.

"Collaboration"
Bishop, George. *When the Master Relents* . . . , 77–85.

"Covering End"
Gage, Richard P. *Order and Design* . . . , 32–33.

"The Coxon Fund"
Gage, Richard P. *Order and Design* . . . , 16–18.

"Crapy Cornelia"
Gage, Richard P. *Order and Design* . . . , 245–250.

"Daisy Miller"
Bellringer, Alan W. *Henry James*, 45–49.
Gage, Richard P. *Order and Design* . . . , 121–127.
Gooder, Jean, Ed. "Introduction," *"Daisy Miller" and Other Stories* [by Henry James], xv–xxi.
Lukacs, Paul. "Unambiguous Ambiguity: The International Theme of 'Daisy Miller,'" *Stud Am Fiction*, 16 (1988), 209–216.
Newman, Benjamin. *Searching for the Figure* . . . , 7–18.

"The Death of the Lion"
Bellringer, Alan W. *Henry James*, 82–85.
Gage, Richard P. *Order and Design* . . . , 15–16.

"The Figure in the Carpet"
Bishop, George. *When the Master Relents* . . . , 4–7.
Cave, Terence. *Recognitions* . . . , 201–202.
Gage, Richard P. *Order and Design* . . . , 21–22.
Johnson, Warren. "Parable, Secrecy and the Form of Fiction: The Example of 'The Figure in the Carpet' and *The Portrait of a Lady*," *J Engl & Germ Philol*, 87 (1988), 230–237.
Krook, Dorothea. "'As a man is, so he sees': The Reader in Henry James," *Neophilologus*, 73 (1988), 300–315.
Newman, Benjamin. *Searching for the Figure* . . . , 63–84.
Zgorzelski, Andrzej. "The Quest for the Indecipherable: Todorov's Non-Existent Mystery of 'The Figure in the Carpet,'" in Nowakowski, Jan, Ed. *Litterae et Lingua* . . . , 171–177.

"Four Meetings"
Gooder, Jean. "Introduction," xi–xiii.

"The Friends of the Friends" [originally titled "The Way It Came"]
Cesarani, Remo. "La maschera della medusa," *Belfagor,* 41 (November 30, 1986), 605–620.
Gage, Richard P. *Order and Design . . . ,* 27–30.

"The Ghostly Rental"
Varnado, S. L. *Haunted Presence . . . ,* 79–83.

"The Given Case"
Gage, Richard P. *Order and Design . . . ,* 45–46.

"Glasses"
Bishop, George. *When the Master Relents . . . ,* 27–41.
Gage, Richard P. *Order and Design . . . ,* 23–26.

"The Great Condition"
Gage, Richard P. *Order and Design . . . ,* 39–41.

"The Great Good Place"
Gage, Richard P. *Order and Design . . . ,* 34–35.

"Greville Fane"
Gilbert, Sandra M., and Susan Gubar. *No Man's Land . . . ,* 134–135.

"Hugh Merrow"
Bishop, George. *When the Master Relents . . . ,* 92–99.

"In the Cage"
Bauer, Dale M., and Andrew Lakritz. "Language, Class, and Sexuality in Henry James's 'In the Cage,'" *New Orleans R,* 14, iii (1987), 61–69.

"John Delavoy"
Gage, Richard P. *Order and Design . . . ,* 47–48.

"The Jolly Corner"
Bellringer, Alan W. *Henry James,* 121–122.
Benert, Annette L. "Dialogical Discourse in 'The Jolly Corner': The Entrepreneur as Language and Image," *Henry James R,* 8 (1987), 116–125.
Coates, Paul. *The Double and the Other . . . ,* 54–56.
Fogel, Daniel M. "A New Reading of Henry James's 'The Jolly Corner,'" in Gargano, James W., Ed. *Critical Essays . . . ,* 190–203.
Newman, Benjamin. *Searching for the Figure . . . ,* 157–184.

"A Landscape Painter"
Bayley, John. *The Short Story . . . ,* 40–48, 54–59.

"The Lesson of the Master"
Newman, Benjamin. *Searching for the Figure . . . ,* 41–54.

"The Liar"
Bishop, George. *When the Master Relents . . . ,* 41–55.
Newman, Benjamin. *Searching for the Figure . . . ,* 55–62.

"Louisa Pallant"
Levine, Peg. "Henry James's 'Louisa Pallant' and the Participant-Observer Nar-
    rator and Responsibility," *Mid-Hudson Lang Stud*, 10 (1987), 33–41.

"Madame de Mauves"
Bellringer, Alan W. *Henry James*, 27–32.

"The Marriages"
Gage, Richard P. *Order and Design . . .* , 153–166.

"Maud-Evelyn"
Bishop, George. *When the Master Relents . . .* , 82–88.
Bronfen, Elisabeth. "Dialogue with the Dead: The Deceased Beloved as Muse,"
    New Comparison, 6 (August, 1988), 114–116.
Gage, Richard P. *Order and Design . . .* , 50–51.

"The Middle Years"
Gage, Richard P. *Order and Design . . .* , 18–19.
Wegelin, Christof. "Art and Life in James's 'The Middle Years,'" *Mod Fiction
    Stud*, 33 (1987), 639–646.

"Miss Gunton of Poughkeepsie"
Gage, Richard P. *Order and Design . . .* , 52–53.

"Mrs. Medwin"
Gage, Richard P. *Order and Design . . .* , 78–81.

"A Most Extraordinary Case"
Aaron, Daniel. *The Unwritten War . . .* , 114.

"The Next Time"
Gage, Richard P. *Order and Design . . .* , 26–27.

"Pandora"
Gooder, Jean. "Introduction," xxi–xxvi.

"The Papers"
Gage, Richard P. *Order and Design . . .* , 95–100.
Howard, David. "Henry James and 'The Papers,'" in Bell, Ian F. A., Ed. *Henry
    James . . .* , 46–64.

"A Passionate Pilgrim"
Bellringer, Alan W. *Henry James*, 9–10.
Sweeney, Gerald M. "The Illness of the Passionate Pilgrim," *Am Lit Realism*, 21,
    i (1988), 3–18.

"Paste"
Gage, Richard P. *Order and Design . . .* , 36–38.

"The Patagonia"
Gage, Richard P. *Order and Design . . .* , 137–152.

"The Pension Beaurepas"
Bellringer, Alan W. *Henry James*, 49–51.

"Poor Richard"
Aaron, Daniel. *The Unwritten War...*, 114.

"The Pupil"
Newman, Benjamin. *Searching for the Figure...*, 19–26.

"The Real Right Thing"
Gage, Richard P. *Order and Design...*, 38–39.

"The Real Thing"
Gage, Richard P. *Order and Design...*, 166–179.
Sheidley, William E., and Ann Charters. *Instructor's Manual...*, 22–23; Charters, Ann, William E. Sheidley, and Martha Ramsey. *Instructor's Manual...*, 2nd ed., 25–26.

"A Round of Visits"
Gage, Richard P. *Order and Design...*, 231–245.

"The Special Type"
Gage, Richard P. *Order and Design...*, 75–77.

"The Story in It"
Gage, Richard P. *Order and Design...*, 85–87.

"The Story of a Masterpiece"
Bayley, John. *The Short Story...*, 61–62.

"The Story of a Year"
Aaron, Daniel. *The Unwritten War...*, 113–114.

"The Third Person"
Bishop, George. *When the Master Relents...*, 59–75.
Gage, Richard P. *Order and Design...*, 49–50.

"The Tone of Time"
Gage, Richard P. *Order and Design...*, 69–75.

"A Tragedy of Error"
Bellringer, Alan W. *Henry James*, 7–8.
Martin, W. R., and Warren U. Ober. "The Provenience of Henry James's First Tale," *Stud Short Fiction*, 24 (1987), 57–58.

"The Tree of Knowledge"
Bishop, George. *When the Master Relents...*, 55–57.
Gage, Richard P. *Order and Design...*, 41–43.

"The Turn of the Screw"
Bayley, John. *The Short Story...*, 50–54.
Bell, Millicent. "'The Turn of the Screw' and the 'Recherche de l'absolu,'" in Bell, Ian F. A., Ed. *Henry James...*, 65–81.

Bellringer, Alan W. *Henry James,* 99–104.

Bonnet, Michele. "Le Dessin dans le tapis: Les Jeux optiques de l'anamorphose dans 'The Turn of the Screw,'" in Mathé, Sylvie, Ed. *Morales . . . ,* 9–32.

Glasser, William. "'The Turn of the Screw,'" in Hogg, James, Ed. *Essays in Honour of Erwin Stürzl . . . ,* I, 212–231.

Hallab, Mary Y. "The Governess and the Demon Lover: The Return of a Fairy Tale," *Henry James R,* 8, ii (1987), 104–115.

Heller, Terry. *The Delights of Terror . . . ,* 147–161.

Krieg, Joann P. "A Question of Values: Culture and Cognition in 'The Turn of the Screw,'" *Langs & Communications,* 8 (1988), 147–154.

Loretelli, Rosamaria. "Un altro giro di vite: Attesa e strategie della suspense in *The Turn of the Screw* di Henry James," in Marucci, Franco, and Adriano Bruttini, Eds. *La Performance del testo,* 163–173.

Newman, Benjamin. *Searching for the Figure . . . ,* 85–114.

Renner, Stanley. "Sexual Hysteria, Physiognomical Bogeymen, and the 'Ghost' in 'The Turn of the Screw,'" *Nineteenth-Century Lit,* 43 (1988), 175–194.

Rosebury, Brian. *Art and Desire . . . ,* 119–132.

Rust, Richard D. "Liminality in 'The Turn of the Screw,'" *Stud Short Fiction,* 25 (1988), 441–446.

Singh, V. P. "The Facade of Innocence in 'The Turn of the Screw,'" *Panjab Univ Research Bull,* 18, ii (1987), 53–60.

Tintner, Adeline R. "The Sea of Asof in 'The Turn of the Screw' and Maurice Barrès's *Les Déracinés,*" *Essays Lit,* 14 (1987), 139–143.

Varnado, S. L. *Haunted Presence . . . ,* 86–94.

Whelan, Robert E. "Ordinary Human Virtue: The Key to 'The Turn of the Screw,'" *Renascence,* 40 (1988), 247–267.

"The Two Faces"
Gage, Richard P. *Order and Design . . . ,* 67–69.

"The Velvet Glove"
Gage, Richard P. *Order and Design . . . ,* 203–217.

"Washington Square"
Bellringer, Alan W. *Henry James,* 51–58.

M[ONTAGUE] R[HODES] JAMES

"The Mezzotint"
Rabkin, Eric. "Fantastic Verbal Portraits of Fantastic Visual Portraits," *Mosaic,* 21, iv (1988), 89–90.

"Oh, Whistle and I'll Come to You, My Lad"
Varnado, S. L. *Haunted Presence . . . ,* 42–43.

SARAH ORNE JEWETT

"A White Heron"
Sheidley, William E., and Ann Charters. *Instructor's Manual . . . ,* 25–26; Charters, Ann, William E. Sheidley, and Martha Ramsey. *Instructor's Manual . . . ,* 2nd ed., 27–28.

RUTH PRAWER JHABVALA

"A Bad Woman"
Albertazzi, Silvia. "'Shut In, Shut Off': Ruth Prawer Jhabvala's 'Mythology of Captivity,'" *Commonwealth Essays & Stud*, 8, i (1985), 46–47.

"A Course of English Studies"
Albertazzi, Silvia. "'Shut In, Shut Off' . . . ," 47–48.

"An Experience of India"
Albertazzi, Silvia. "'Shut In, Shut Off' . . . ," 48–49.

"The Housewife"
Albertazzi, Silvia. "'Shut In, Shut Off' . . . ," 51–52.

"Rose Petal"
Albertazzi, Silvia. "'Shut In, Shut Off' . . . ," 50–51.

COLIN JOHNSON

"A Missionary Would I Have Been"
Shoemaker, Adam. "'Fiction or Assumed Fiction': The Short Stories of Colin Johnson, Jack Davis and Archie Weller," in Neilson, Emmanuel, Ed. *Connections . . .* , 56.

DOROTHY JOHNSON

"The Hanging Tree"
Alter, Judy. "Dorothy Johnson," in Erisman, Fred, and Richard W. Etulain, Eds. *Fifty Western Writers*, 231–232.

"A Man Called Horse"
Alter, Judy. "Dorothy Johnson," 231.

C. I. JOHNSTONE

"Mrs. Mark Luke; or, West Country Exclusive"
Letley, Emma. *From Galt to Douglas Brown . . .* , 54–56.

H. R. JONES

"Suicide Durkee's Last Ride"
Kwasniewski, Elizabeth. "Thrilling Structures? Science Fiction from Early *Amazing* and Detective Fiction," *Foundation*, 38 (1987), 27.

JAMES JOYCE

"After the Race"

Herring, Phillip F. *Joyce's Uncertainty* . . . , 39–41.

Mosher, Harold F. "Ambiguity in the Reading Process: Narrative Mode in 'After the Race,'" *J Short Story Engl*, 7 (Autumn, 1986), 43–61.

Werner, Craig H. *Dubliners* . . . , 36–37.

"Araby"

Charters, Ann, William E. Sheidley, and Martha Ramsey. *Instructor's Manual* . . . , 2nd ed., 75–76.

Herring, Phillip F. *Joyce's Uncertainty* . . . , 26–34.

Lang, Frederick K. "Rite East of Joyce's 'Araby,'" *J Ritual Stud*, 1 (1987), 111–120.

Robinson, David W. "The Narration of Reading in Joyce's 'The Sisters,' 'An Encounter,' and 'Araby,'" *Texas Stud Lit & Lang*, 29 (1987), 387–392.

Werner, Craig H. *Dubliners* . . . , 53–54.

"The Boarding House"

Brooks, Cleanth. "'The Boarding House,'" *Stud Short Fiction*, 25 (1988), 405–408.

Perrine, Laurence, and Thomas R. Arp. *Instructor's Manual* . . . , 7th ed., 60–61.

"Clay"

Herring, Phillip F. *Joyce's Uncertainty* . . . , 63–65.

Norris, Margot. "Narration under Blindfold: Reading Joyce's 'Clay,'" *PMLA*, 102 (1987), 206–215.

Werner, Craig H. *Dubliners* . . . , 87–88.

"The Dead"

Bayley, John. *The Short Story* . . . , 150–168.

Billigheimer, Rachel V. "The Living in Joyce's 'The Dead,'" *Coll Lang Assoc J*, 31 (1988), 472–483.

Carpenter, William. *Death and Marriage* . . . , 56–60.

Foster, John W. *Fictions* . . . , 142–174.

Gottwald, Maria. "New Approaches and Techniques in the Short Story of James Joyce and Katherine Mansfield," in Zach, Wolfgang, and Heinz Kosak, Eds. *Literary Interrelations* . . . , II, 45–46.

Herring, Phillip F. *Joyce's Uncertainty* . . . , 71–75.

Maddox, Lucy B. "Gabriel and Otello: Opera in 'The Dead,'" *Stud Short Fiction*, 24 (1987), 271–277.

Meisel, Perry. *The Myth of the Modern* . . . , 123–128.

Morrissey, L. J. "Inner and Outer Perceptions in Joyce's 'The Dead,'" *Stud Short Fiction*, 25 (1988), 21–29.

Sheidley, William E., and Ann Charters. *Instructor's Manual* . . . , 72–74; Charters, Ann, William E. Sheidley, and Martha Ramsey. *Instructor's Manual* . . . , 2nd ed., 78–79.

Werner, Craig H. *Dubliners* . . . , 56–72.

Zimmermann, Georges-Denis. "Conflicting Contexts: Traditional Storytelling Performance in Irish Short Stories," in Forsyth, Neil, Ed. *Reading Contexts*, 110–111.

"An Encounter"
Herring, Phillip F. *Joyce's Uncertainty* . . . , 18–26.
Robinson, David W. "The Narration of Reading . . . ," 383–387.
Scott, Bonnie K. *James Joyce*, 22–24.
Werner, Craig H. *Dubliners* . . . , 93–94.

"Eveline"
Herring, Phillip F. *Joyce's Uncertainty* . . . , 34–38.
Knapp, Bettina L. *Music, Archetype* . . . , 95–108.
Tolentino, Magda V. F. "Family Bonds and Bondage within the Family: A Study of Family Ties in Clarice Lispector and James Joyce," *Mod Lang Stud*, 18, ii (1988), 73–78.
Werner, Craig H. *Dubliners* . . . , 37.

"Grace"
Herring, Phillip F. *Joyce's Uncertainty* . . . , 93–94.
Werner, Craig H. *Dubliners* . . . , 82–85.

"Ivy Day in the Committee Room"
Herring, Phillip F. *Joyce's Uncertainty* . . . , 69–70.
Larsen, Max D. "Joyce's Narrative Theater: 'Ivy Day in the Committee Room,'" in Rauchbauer, Otto, Ed. *A Yearbook . . . 1985/86*, 93–108.
Werner, Craig H. *Dubliners* . . . , 103–111.

"A Little Cloud"
Sugisaki, Shingo. "Narrative Counterpoint: James Joyce's 'A Little Cloud,'" *Univ Saga Stud Engl*, 15 (March, 1987), 1–19.
Werner, Craig H. *Dubliners* . . . , 112–200.

"A Mother"
Grace, Sherrill E. "Rediscovering Mrs. Kearney: An Other Reading of 'A Mother,'" in Benstock, Bernard, Ed. . . . *The Augmented Ninth*, 273–281.

"A Painful Case"
Herring, Phillip F. *Joyce's Uncertainty* . . . , 65–69.
Knapp, Bettina L. "Joyce's 'A Painful Case': The Train and an Epiphanic Experience," *Études Irlandaises*, 13, ii (1988), 45–60.
Loss, Archie K. "Another 'Gay Science,'" *James Joyce Q*, 25 (1988), 511–512.
Senn, Fritz. "Distancing in 'A Painful Case,'" *R Lettres Modernes (James Joyce 1)*, [n.v.] (1988), 25–38.
Werner, Craig H. *Dubliners* . . . , 51–54.

"The Sisters"
Carpenter, William. *Death and Marriage* . . . , 50–55.
Charters, Ann, William E. Sheidley, and Martha Ramsey. *Instructor's Manual* . . . , 2nd ed., 73–74.
Fischer, Andreas. "Context-Free and Context-Sensitive Literature: Sherwood Anderson's *Winesburg, Ohio* and James Joyce's *Dubliners*," in Forsyth, Neil, Ed. *Reading Contexts*, 21–22.
French, Marilyn. "Women in Joyce's Dublin," in Benstock, Bernard, Ed. . . . *The Augmented Ninth*, 267–272.
Herring, Phillip F. *Joyce's Uncertainty* . . . , 9–18.

Mahaffey, Vicki. *Reauthorizing Joyce*, 29–31.
Robinson, David W. "The Narration of Reading . . . ," 378–383.
Werner, Craig H. *Dubliners* . . . , 34–35.

FRANZ KAFKA

"Before the Law"
Binder, Hartmut. "Parabel als Problem: Eine Formbetrachtung zu Kafkas 'Vor
   dem Gesetz,'" *Wirkendes Wort*, 38, i (1988), 39–61.
Derrida, Jacques. "Devant la Loi," trans. Avital Ronell, in Udoff, Alan, Ed.
   . . . *Contemporary Critical Performance*, 128–134.
Lawson, Richard H. *Franz Kafka*, 141–143.
Nägele, Rainer. "Kafka and the Interpretive Desire," in Udoff, Alan, Ed.
   . . . *Contemporary Critical Performance*, 23–28.
Oates, Joyce C. *(Woman) Writer* . . . , 208–209.

"Ein Besuch im Bergwerk"
Fickert, Kurt. "First Person Narrators in Kafka's *Ein Landarzt* Stories," *Germ
   Notes*, 19, i–ii (1988), 16.

"Blumfeld, an Elderly Bachelor"
Mueller, Thomas. "Aspekte des Spiels bei Kafka," *Seminar*, 24, i (1988), 23–24.

"The Bridge"
Koelb, Clayton. *Invention of Reading* . . . , 134–140.

"The Burrow"
Lawson, Richard H. *Franz Kafka*, 130–132.
Lesser, Wendy. *The Life Below the Ground* . . . , 192–201.

"The Cares of a Family Man"
Fickert, Kurt. "First Person Narrators . . . ," 15.

"A Country Doctor"
Fickert, Kurt. "First Person Narrators . . . ," 19–20.
Heidsieck, Arnold. "Kafka's Narrative Ontology," *Philosophy & Lit*, 11 (1987),
   252.
Jofen, Jean. *The Jewish Mystic* . . . , 32–38.
Lawson, Richard H. *Franz Kafka*, 93–98.
Strelka, Peter J. "Elements of the Literary Self in Kafka's 'A Country Doctor,'"
   in Lazar, Moshe, and Ronald Gottesman, Eds. *The Dove and the Mole* . . . ,
   61–69.

"Description of a Struggle"
Heidsieck, Arnold. "Logic and Ontology in Kafka's Fiction," in Gottesman,
   Ronald, and Moshe Lazar, Eds. *The Dove and the Mole* . . . , 204–205.
———. "Kafka's Narrative Ontology," 247–248.
Lawson, Richard H. *Franz Kafka*, 15–16.
Sokel, Walter H. "Narcissism, Magic and the Function of Narration in 'Descrip-
   tion of a Struggle,'" in Udoff, Alan, Ed. . . . *Contemporary Critical Perfor-
   mance*, 98–110.

"Eleven Sons"
Fickert, Kurt. "First Person Narrators . . . ," 15–16.

"First Sorrow"
Ingram, Forrest L. *Representative Short Story Cycles . . .* , 85–89.

"Give It Up!"
Koelb, Clayton. *Invention of Reading . . .* , 5–8.
Lawson, Richard H. *Franz Kafka,* 147–148.

"The Great Wall of China"
Lawson, Richard H. *Franz Kafka,* 99–100.

"A Hunger Artist"
Heidsieck, Arnold. "Kafka's Narrative Ontology," 249–250.
Ingram, Forrest L. *Representative Short Story Cycles . . .* , 73–77, 88–91, 97–99.
Lawson, Richard H. *Franz Kafka,* 132–135.
Roberts, Edgar V., and Henry E. Jacobs. *Instructor's Manual . . .* , 75–76.

"The Hunter Gracchus"
Jofen, Jean. *The Jewish Mystic . . .* , 109–115.

"A Hybrid" [same as "A Crossbreed"]
Lawson, Richard E. *Franz Kafka,* 144–145.

"An Imperial Message"
Oates, Joyce C. *(Woman) Writer . . .* , 210–211.

"In the Gallery"
Thum, Reinhard H. "Generosity or Moral Posturing in Kafka's 'Auf der Ga-
      lerie,'" *Michigan Academician,* 19, ii (1987), 179–185.

"In the Penal Colony"
Dalton, Elizabeth. "Kafka as Saint," *Partisan R,* 54, iii (1987), 394–414.
Gunn, Daniel. *Psychoanalysis and Fiction . . .* , 27–30.
Lawson, Richard H. *Franz Kafka,* 87–93.
Schmidt, Ulrich. "'Tat-Beobachtung': Kafkas Erzählung 'In der Strafkolonie,'
      im literarisch-historischen Kontext," in Binder, Hartmut, Ed. *Franz
      Kafka . . .* , 55–69.
Weinstein, Arnold. *The Fiction of Relationship,* 157–174.

"Investigations of a Dog"
Jofen, Jean. *The Jewish Mystic . . .* , 101–105.
Lawson, Richard H. *Franz Kafka,* 125–130.
Leadbeater, Lewis W. "Platonic Elements in Kafka's 'Investigations of a Dog,'"
      Philosophy & Lit, 11 (1987), 104–116.
Ossar, Michael. "Kafka and the Reader: The World as Text in 'Forschungen
      eines Hundes,'" *Colloquia Germanica,* 20 (1987), 325–337.

"Jackals and Arabs"
Fickert, Kurt. "First Person Narrators . . . ," 17.

"Josephine the Singer"
Ingram, Forrest L. *Representative Short Story Cycles* . . . , 77–83, 91–92, 99–102.
Jofen, Jean. *The Jewish Mystic* . . . , 38–40.
Lawson, Richard H. *Franz Kafka,* 135–138.
Sattler, Emil E. "Kafka's Artist in a Society of Mice," *Germ Notes,* 9, iv (1978),
    49–53.

"The Judgment"
Corngold, Stanley. "Kafka's Other Metamorphosis," in Udoff, Alan, Ed.
    . . . *Contemporary Critical Performance,* 46–49.
————. *Franz Kafka* . . . , 24–46.
Gunn, Daniel. *Psychoanalysis and Fiction* . . . , 12–22.
Heidsieck, Arnold. "Logic and Ontology . . . ," 208–209.
————. "Kafka's Narrative Ontology," 251–252.
Jofen, Jean. *The Jewish Mystic* . . . , 50–53.
Lawson, Richard H. *Franz Kafka,* 18–25.
Leadbeater, Lewis W. "Euripidean Elements in Kafka's 'The Judgment,'" *Classical & Mod Lit,* 9, i (1988), 27–37.

"A Little Fable"
Lawson, Richard H. *Franz Kafka,* 146–147.

"A Little Woman"
Ingram, Forrest L. *Representative Short Story Cycles* . . . , 68–73, 86–88, 95–97.

"Metamorphosis"
Caldwell, Richard. "Kafka and Orpheus: 'The Metamorphosis,'" in Gottesman,
    Ronald, and Moshe Lazar, Eds. *The Dove and the Mole* . . . , 47–59.
Corngold, Stanley. *Franz Kafka* . . . , 47–89.
Green, Geoffrey. "Metamorphosing Kafka: The Example of Philip Roth," in
    Gottesman, Ronald, and Moshe Lazar, Eds. *The Dove and the Mole* . . . , 35–
    46.
Heidsieck, Arnold. "Kafka's Narrative Ontology," 248.
Olsen, Lance. *Ellipse of Uncertainty* . . . , 51–54.
Sheidley, William E., and Ann Charters. *Instructor's Manual* . . . , 78–79; Charters, Ann, William E. Sheidley, and Martha Ramsey. *Instructor's Manual* . . . , 2nd ed., 81–82.
Sokel, Walter H. "From Marx to Myth: The Structure and Function of Self-
    Alienation in Kafka's 'Metamorphosis,'" in Gottesman, Ronald, and Moshe
    Lazar, Eds. *The Dove and the Mole* . . . , 1–12.

"My Neighbor"
Lawson, Richard H. *Franz Kafka,* 143–144.

"The New Advocate"
Fickert, Kurt. "First Person Narrators . . . ," 17.

"The Next Village"
Fickert, Kurt. "First Person Narrators . . . ," 14–15.

"An Old Page" [same as "An Old Manuscript"]
Fickert, Kurt. "First Person Narrators . . . ," 17–18.

Lawson, Richard H. *Franz Kafka*, 98–99.
Olsen, Lance. *Ellipse of Uncertainty* . . . , 105–106.

"On the Tram"
Lawson, Richard H. *Franz Kafka*, 140–141.

"Prometheus"
Lawson, Richard H. *Franz Kafka*, 148–149.

"A Report to an Academy"
Fickert, Kurt. "First Person Narrators . . . ," 18.
Lawson, Richard H. *Franz Kafka*, 101–102.
Schönherr, Ulrich. "Vom Affen zur Maschine: Kafkas Erzählung 'Bericht für
    eine Akademie' im Spiegel der Machttheorien von Hegel und Foucault,"
    Neue Germanistik, 5, i–ii (1987–1988), 1–15.

"The Silence of the Sirens"
Koelb, Clayton. "Kafka and the Sirens: Writing as Lethetic Reading," in Koelb,
    Clayton, and Susan Noakes, Eds. *The Comparative Perspective* . . . , 300–314.
Weissberg, Liliane. "Singing of Tales: Kafka's Sirens," in Udoff, Alan, Ed.
    . . . *Contemporary Critical Performance*, 165–177.

"The Spinning Top"
Lawson, Richard H. *Franz Kafka*, 149–150.

"The Stoker"
Lawson, Richard H. *Franz Kafka*, 35–38.

"Unhappiness"
Heidsieck, Arnold. "Logic and Ontology . . . ," 205–206.

"Wedding Preparations in the Country"
Lawson, Richard H. *Franz Kafka*, 16–18.

AMALIA KAHANA-CARMON

"The Bright Light"
Fuchs, Esther. *Israeli Mythologies* . . . , 100.

"If I Found Favor in Your Eyes"
Fuchs, Esther. *Israeli Mythologies* . . . , 98–100.

"Neima Sasson Writes Poems"
Fuchs, Esther. *Israeli Mythologies* . . . , 97–98.

"To Build Herself a Home in the Land of Shinar"
Fuchs, Esther. *Israeli Mythologies* . . . , 100–101.

KANAI MIEKO

"Platonic Love"
Heinrich, Amy V. "Double Weave: The Fabric of Japanese Women's Writing,"
    World Lit Today, 62 (1988), 412.

NIKOLAY KARAMZIN

"Poor Liza"
Hammarberg, Gitta. "Poor Liza, Poor Erast, Lucky Narrator," *Slavic & East
    European J*, 31 (1987), 305–321.

KASAI ZENZŌ

"In the Same Boat"
Fowler, Edward. *The Rhetoric of Confession* . . . , 261–263.

"A Mad Drunk's Monologue"
Fowler, Edward. *The Rhetoric of Confession* . . . , 284–288.

"Morning Pilgrimage"
Fowler, Edward. *The Rhetoric of Confession* . . . , 263–265.

"The Oppressed One"
Fowler, Edward. *The Rhetoric of Confession* . . . , 282–284.

"A Stillbirth"
Fowler, Edward. *The Rhetoric of Confession* . . . , 267–269.

"An Unhappy Father"
Fowler, Edward. *The Rhetoric of Confession* . . . , 253–257.

"With the Children in Tow"
Fowler, Edward. *The Rhetoric of Confession* . . . , 259–260.

"Wriggling Creatures"
Fowler, Edward. *The Rhetoric of Confession* . . . , 266–267.

"Young Pasania Leaves"
Fowler, Edward. *The Rhetoric of Confession* . . . , 271–273.

KAWABATA YASUNARI

"The House of the Sleeping Beauties"
Swann, Thomas E. "Kawabata Yasunari," in Swann, Thomas E., and Kinya
    Tsuruta, Eds. . . . *Modern Japanese Short Story*, 113–128.

"The Izu Dancer"
Swann, Thomas E. "Kawabata Yasunari," 105–112.

"One Arm"
Swann, Thomas E. "Kawabata Yasunari," 129–137.
Takeda, Katsuhiko. "Kawabata Literature: Harmony and Conflict," in Takeda,
    Katsuhiko, Ed. . . . *Japanese Literature,* 124–127.

GOTTFRIED KELLER

"Clothes Make the Man"
Lehrer, Mark. "Keller's Anthropological Realism: The Scientific Underpinning
    of the Early Prose," *Germ Q,* 60 (1987), 570–574.

"The Misused Love Letter"
Radcliffe, Stanley. "Gottfried Keller's 'Keltische Knochen' and William Raabe's
    Mammoth," *Germ Life & Letters,* 41 (1988), 99–105.

MICHAEL KERNAN

"The Doll Named Silvio"
Büssing, Sabine. *Aliens in the Home* . . . , 78–80.

DANIIL KHARMS

"Elizabeth Bam"
Gibian, George, Ed. *The Man in the Black Coat* . . . , 40.

"The Old Woman"
Gibian, George, Ed. *The Man in the Black Coat* . . . , 34–36.

"Vindication"
Gibian, George, Ed. *The Man in the Black Coat* . . . , 32–33.

BENEDICT KIELY

"A Ball of Malt and Madame Butterfly"
Kersnowski, Frank. "Ben Kiely and His Ball of Malt," *J Short Story Engl,* 7
    (August, 1986), 23–25.

"God's Own People"
Kersnowski, Frank. "Ben Kiely . . . ," 22–23.

"Maiden's Leap"
Kersnowski, Frank. "Ben Kiely . . . ," 26.

"A Room in Linden"
Kersnowski, Frank. "Ben Kiely . . . ," 17–22.

JAMAICA KINCAID

"Girl"
Charters, Ann, William E. Sheidley, and Martha Ramsey. *Instructor's Manual . . .* , 2nd ed., 228.
Niesen de Abruña, Laura. "Twentieth-Century Women Writers from the English-Speaking Caribbean," *Mod Fiction Stud,* 34 (1988), 91–92.

"Windless"
Niesen de Abruña, Laura. "Twentieth-Century Women Writers . . . ," 91.

GRACE KING

"Madriène; or, The Festival of the Dead"
Juncker, Clara. "Grace King: Woman-as-Artist," *Southern Lit J,* 20, i (1987), 40–43.

"Monsieur Motte"
Kirby, David. "Grace King," in Bain, Robert, and Joseph M. Flora, Eds. *Fifty Southern Writers Before 1900,* 297–298.

STEPHEN KING

"Apt Pupil"
Reino, Joseph. *Stephen King . . .* , 120–126.

"Body"
Reino, Joseph. *Stephen King . . .* , 126–134.

"Breathing Method"
Reino, Joseph. *Stephen King . . .* , 119–120.

"Children of the Corn"
Büssing, Sabine. *Aliens in the Home . . .* , 37–41.
Reino, Joseph. *Stephen King . . .* , 109–112.

"I Am the Doorway"
Reino, Joseph. *Stephen King . . .* , 112–116.

"Jerusalem's Lot"
Reino, Joseph. *Stephen King . . .* , 18–21.

"Last Rung on the Ladder"
Reino, Joseph. *Stephen King . . .* , 103.

"The Mangler"
Heller, Terry. *The Delights of Terror . . .* , 45–46.

"Night Surf"
Reino, Joseph. *Stephen King . . .* , 103–109.

"Rita Hayworth and Shawshank Redemption"
Reino, Joseph. *Stephen King . . . ,* 117–119.

MAXINE HONG KINGSTON

"The Ghost-Mate"
Lim, Shirley G. "Twelve Asian American Writers: In Search of Self-Definition,"
    MELUS, 13, i–ii (1986), 70–71.

W[ILLIAM] P[ATRICK] KINSELLA

"The Ballad of the Public Trustee"
Murray, Don. *The Fiction of W. P. Kinsella . . . ,* 23–24.

"Barefoot and Pregnant in Des Moines"
Murray, Don. *The Fiction of W. P. Kinsella . . . ,* 41–42.

"Baseball Spurs"
Murray, Don. *The Fiction of W. P. Kinsella . . . ,* 41.

"The Battery"
Murray, Don. *The Fiction of W. P. Kinsella . . . ,* 43.

"The Bear Went Over the Mountain"
Murray, Don. *The Fiction of W. P. Kinsella . . . ,* 26.

"Black Wampum"
Murray, Don. *The Fiction of W. P. Kinsella . . . ,* 16–17.

"Caraway"
Murray, Don. *The Fiction of W. P. Kinsella . . . ,* 13–14.

"Dr. Don"
Murray, Don. *The Fiction of W. P. Kinsella . . . ,* 23.

"Fiona the First"
Murray, Don. *The Fiction of W. P. Kinsella . . . ,* 36–37.

"First Names and Empty Pockets"
Murray, Don. *The Fiction of W. P. Kinsella . . . ,* 37–38.

"The Four-Sky-Thunder Bundle"
Murray, Don. *The Fiction of W. P. Kinsella . . . ,* 17.

"Fugitives"
Murray, Don. *The Fiction of W. P. Kinsella . . . ,* 24–25.

"Horse Collars"
Murray, Don. *The Fiction of W. P. Kinsella . . . ,* 12–13.

"Indian Joe"
Murray, Don. *The Fiction of W. P. Kinsella* . . . , 28.

"Jokemaker"
Murray, Don. *The Fiction of W. P. Kinsella* . . . , 19.

"Lark Song"
Murray, Don. *The Fiction of W. P. Kinsella* . . . , 14.

"The Last Pennant Before Armageddon"
Murray, Don. *The Fiction of W. P. Kinsella* . . . , 42.

"The Managers"
Murray, Don. *The Fiction of W. P. Kinsella* . . . , 26–27.

"The Mother's Dance"
Murray, Don. *The Fiction of W. P. Kinsella* . . . , 24.

"The Night Mammy Mota Tied the Record"
Murray, Don. *The Fiction of W. P. Kinsella* . . . , 42–43.

"Panache"
Murray, Don. *The Fiction of W. P. Kinsella* . . . , 14–15.

"Parts of the Eagle"
Murray, Don. *The Fiction of W. P. Kinsella* . . . , 22–23.

"Pretend Dinners"
Murray, Don. *The Fiction of W. P. Kinsella* . . . , 20–21.

"The Rattlesnake Express"
Murray, Don. *The Fiction of W. P. Kinsella* . . . , 16.

"Scars"
Murray, Don. *The Fiction of W. P. Kinsella* . . . , 17.

"Shoeless Joe Jackson Comes to Iowa"
Murray, Don. *The Fiction of W. P. Kinsella* . . . , 38–40.

"Sister Ann of the Cornfields"
Murray, Don. *The Fiction of W. P. Kinsella* . . . , 40.

"The Thrill of the Grass"
Murray, Don. *The Fiction of W. P. Kinsella* . . . , 43–44.

"Weasels and Ermines"
Murray, Don. *The Fiction of W. P. Kinsella* . . . , 19–20.

"Yellow Scarf"
Murray, Don. *The Fiction of W. P. Kinsella* . . . , 20.

RUDYARD KIPLING

"As Easy as A.B.C."
Laski, Marghanita. *From Palm to Pine* . . . , 152–153.

"At the End of the Passage"
Bayley, John. *The Short Story* . . . , 66–67.
Falls, Cyril B. *Rudyard Kipling* . . . , 124–125.

"Baa, Baa, Black Sheep"
Bayley, John. *The Short Story* . . . , 186–187.
Cornell, Louis L., Ed. *"The Man Who Would Be King"* . . . , xxi–xxii.
Kemp, Sandra. *Kipling's Hidden Narratives*, 2–5.
Lerner, Laurence. *The Frontiers* . . . , 20–22.

"Below the Mill Dam"
Parry, Ann. "'Take away that bauble!': Political Allegory in 'Below the Mill
    Dam,'" *Kipling J*, 62, ii (1988), 10–24.

"Bertran and Bimi"
Falls, Cyril B. *Rudyard Kipling* . . . , 130–132.

"Beyond the Pale"
Kemp, Sandra. *Kipling's Hidden Narratives*, 12–13.
Raine, Craig, Ed. *A Choice* . . . , 9.

"The Bridge Builders"
Ramachandra, R. "Kipling's 'The Bridge Builders'—An Excursion into Value
    Structure," *Lit Criterion*, 22, iv (1987), 87–91.
Sharma, S. T. "Kipling's India: A Study of Some Short Stories," *Lit Criterion*,
    22, iv (1987), 57–59.

"The Brushwood Boy"
Kemp, Sandra. *Kipling's Hidden Narratives*, 51–53.
Laski, Marghanita. *From Palm to Pine* . . . , 92–93.
Parfitt, George. . . . *First World War*, 32–33.
Sullivan, Zohreh T. "Kipling the Nightwalker," in Bloom, Harold, Ed. *Rudyard
    Kipling*, 58–68.

"The Bull That Thought"
Kemp, Sandra. *Kipling's Hidden Narratives*, 68–69.
Stewart, David H. "Kipling's Portraits of the Artist," *Engl Lit Transition*, 31
    (1988), 273.

"Children of the Zodiac"
Stewart, David H. "Kipling's Portraits . . . ," 270.

"The Church That Was at Antioch"
Kemp, Sandra. *Kipling's Hidden Narratives*, 94–95.

"The Conversion of St. Wilfred"
Bayley, John. *The Short Story* . . . , 72–73.

Kemp, Sandra. *Kipling's Hidden Narratives*, 85–89.

"Dayspring Mishandled"
Raine, Craig, Ed. *A Choice* . . . , 18–22.

"The Devil and the Deep Sea"
Moorhouse, C. E. "Mr. Wardrop's Problem: Excerpts from a Talk on Kipling
    and Technology," *Kipling J*, 61 (March, 1987), 10–22.

"The Dog Hervey"
Kemp, Sandra. *Kipling's Hidden Narratives*, 59–60.

"The Dreams of Duncan Parrenness"
Kemp, Sandra. *Kipling's Hidden Narratives*, 16–17.

"Dymchurch"
Raine, Craig, Ed. *A Choice* . . . , 5–6.

"The Eye of Allah"
Laski, Marghanita. *From Palm to Pine* . . . , 83–85.
Raine, Craig, Ed. *A Choice* . . . , 28–30.

"Fairy Kist"
Kemp, Sandra. *Kipling's Hidden Narratives*, 75–78.

"The Finest Story in the World"
Kemp, Sandra. *Kipling's Hidden Narratives*, 33–35.
Laski, Marghanita. *From Palm to Pine* . . . , 144–145.
Lee, Hermione, Ed. "Introduction," *Traffics and Discoveries*, 25–27.
Raine, Craig, Ed. *A Choice* . . . , 3–4.

"The Gardener"
Bayley, John. *The Short Story* . . . , 94–95.
Kemp, Sandra. *Kipling's Hidden Narratives*, 120–123.
Laski, Marghanita. *From Palm to Pine* . . . , 167–169.

"The Gate of the Hundred Sorrows"
Goonetilleke, D. C. R. *Images of the Raj* . . . , 22–24.
Kemp, Sandra. *Kipling's Hidden Narratives*, 14–15.

"An Habitation Enforced"
Kemp, Sandra. *Kipling's Hidden Narratives*, 63–65.

"His Chance in Life"
Laski, Marghanita. *From Palm to Pine* . . . , 41–42.

"The House Surgeon"
Kemp, Sandra. *Kipling's Hidden Narratives*, 56–59.

"In the Interests of the Brethren"
Kemp, Sandra. *Kipling's Hidden Narratives*, 75.

"In the Same Boat"
Kemp, Sandra. *Kipling's Hidden Narratives*, 60–63.
Raine, Craig, Ed. *A Choice . . .* , 11–12.

"The Judgment of Dungara"
Cornell, Louis L., Ed. *"The Man Who Would Be King" . . .* , xxii–xxiv.

"The Knife and the Naked Chalk"
Kemp, Sandra. *Kipling's Hidden Narratives*, 103–106.

"The Limitations of Pambe Serang"
Kemp, Sandra. *Kipling's Hidden Narratives*, 22–24.

"Lispeth"
Goonetilleke, D. C. R. *Images of the Raj . . .* , 33–34.

"Love-o'-Women"
Laski, Marghanita. *From Palm to Pine . . .* , 91–92.
Raine, Craig, Ed. *A Choice . . .* , 4–5.

"A Madonna of the Trenches"
Bayley, John. *The Short Story . . .* , 95–96.
Kemp, Sandra. *Kipling's Hidden Narratives*, 118–120.

"The Maltese Cat"
Sharma, S. T. "Kipling's India . . . ," 55–56.

"The Man Who Would Be King"
Bascom, Tim. "Secret Imperialism: The Reader's Response to the Narrator in
    'The Man Who Would Be King,'" *Engl Lit Transition*, 31 (1988), 162–173.
Boone, Joseph A. *Tradition Counter Tradition . . .* , 237–238.
Cornell, Louis L., Ed. *"The Man Who Would Be King" . . .* , xxxiv–xxxvii.
Young, Michael. "Rewriting the Classic Romance: Kipling's 'The Man Who
    Would Be King,'" *Genre*, 20, i (1987), 45–66.

"The Manner of Men"
Kemp, Sandra. *Kipling's Hidden Narratives*, 95–97.

"The Mark of the Beast"
Falls, Cyril B. *Rudyard Kipling . . .* , 120–124.

"Mary Postgate"
Bayley, John. *The Short Story . . .* , 84–95.
Hewitt, Douglas. *English Fiction . . .* , 62–64.
Laski, Marghanita. *From Palm to Pine . . .* , 163–164.
Parfitt, George. *. . . First World War*, 93–94.
Raine, Craig, Ed. *A Choice . . .* , 23–25.

"A Matter of Fact"
Stewart, David H. "Kipling's Portraits . . . ," 270–271.

"The Miracle of Purun Shagat"
Goonetilleke, D. C. R. *Images of the Raj* . . . , 41–42.

"The Miracle of St. Jubanus"
Kemp, Sandra. *Kipling's Hidden Narratives,* 80–81.

"Miss Youghal's Sais"
Karlin, Danny. "Plain Tales?" in Mallett, Phillip, Ed. *Kipling Considered,* 9–12.

"Mrs. Bathurst"
Bayley, John. "'Mrs. Bathurst' Again," *Essays Crit,* 38 (1988), 233–236.
———. *The Short Story* . . . , 97–108.
Lee, Hermione, Ed. "Introduction," 23–24.
Raine, Craig, Ed. *A Choice* . . . , 15–18.
Stinton, T. C. W. "What Really Happened in 'Mrs. Bathurst'?" *Essays Crit,* 38, i (1988), 57–74.
Waterhouse, Ruth. "'The Blindish Look': Signification of Meaning in 'Mrs. Bathurst,'" *Studia Neophilologica,* 60 (1988), 193–206.

"On Greenhow Hill"
Hewitt, Douglas. *English Fiction* . . . , 59–61.

"On the City Wall"
Cornell, Louis L., Ed. *"The Man Who Would Be King"* . . . , xxxii–xxxiv.

"On the Gate"
Kemp, Sandra. *Kipling's Hidden Narratives,* 91–94.

"The Phantom Rickshaw"
Bayley, John. *The Short Story* . . . , 81–83.
Kemp, Sandra. *Kipling's Hidden Narratives,* 54–56.

"The Return of Imray"
Kemp, Sandra. *Kipling's Hidden Narratives,* 19–20.
Leithauser, Brad. "Dead Forms: The Ghost Story Today," *New Criterion,* 6, iv (1987), 34–35.

"The Ship That Found Herself"
Falls, Cyril B. *Rudyard Kipling* . . . , 144–146.

"Simple Simon"
Trotter, David. "Kipling's England . . . ," 63–64.

"The Story of Muhammad Din"
Karlin, Danny. "Plain Tales?" 13–17.

"The Strange Ride of Morrowbie Jukes"
Bayley, John. *The Short Story* . . . , 66–67.
Falls, Cyril B. *Rudyard Kipling* . . . , 129–130.
Goonetilleke, D. C. R. *Images of the Raj* . . . , 24–26.
Kemp, Sandra. *Kipling's Hidden Narratives,* 15–16.

A. M. KLEIN

"The Bells of Sobor Spasitula"
New, W. H. *Dreams of Speech* . . . , 90–91.

HEINRICH VON KLEIST

"The Duel"
Cave, Terence. *Recognitions* . . . , 388–390.
Ellis, John M. "Kleist's 'Der Zweikampf,'" *Monatshefte*, 65 (1973), 48–60; rpt.,
   revised, in his *Heinrich von Kleist* . . . , 54–66.

"The Earthquake in Chile"
Ellis, John M. *Heinrich von Kleist* . . . , 36–53.
Kroeber, Karl. *Romantic Fantasy*, 132–133.

"The Engagement in Santo Domingo"
Glenny, Robert E. *The Manipulation of Reality* . . . , 104–109, 145–150, 186–190.

"The Foundling"
Cave, Terence. *Recognitions* . . . , 390–392.
Ellis, John M. *Heinrich von Kleist* . . . , 1–20.
Glenny, Robert E. *The Manipulation of Reality* . . . , 152–158.

"The Marquise of O——"
Cave, Terence. *Recognitions* . . . , 392–393, 394–395.
Ellis, John M. *Heinrich von Kleist* . . . , 21–35.
Furst, Lilian. "Double-Dealing: Irony in Kleist's 'Die Marquise von O——,'" in
   Batts, Michael S., Anthony W. Riley, and Heinz Wetzel, Eds. *Echoes and
   Influences* . . . , 85–95.
Glenny, Robert E. *The Manipulation of Reality* . . . , 62–64, 118–127, 150–152,
   178–184.

"Michael Kohlhaas"
Ellis, John M. *Heinrich von Kleist* . . . , 67–88.
Kroeber, Karl. *Romantic Fantasy*, 118–129.
McGhee, Patricia O. "*Ragtime*'s Coalhouse Walker, Jr.: *Déjà vu*," *Lit/Film Q*, 16
   (1988), 272–275.

"Über das Marionettentheater"
Rushing, James A. "The Limitations of the Fencing Bear: Kleist's 'Über das
   Marionettentheater' as Ironic Fiction," *Germ Q*, 61 (1988), 528–539.

ALEXANDER KLUGE

"Eingemachte Elefantenwünsche"
Stadler, Ulrich. "Die Kohärenz eines Papierigers: Zu einem Text Alexander
   Kluges und zu dessen Realismuskonzeption," *Text & Kontext*, 15, i (1987),
   124–144.

"Ein Liebesversuch"
Müller, Michael. "Gefangen vom Text: Überlegungen zur Lesersteuerung am
    Beispiel eines Textes von Alexander Kluge," *Der Deutschunterricht,* 40, iv
    (1988), 59–67.

EDWARD KNATCHBULL-HUGESSON

"The Pig-Faced Queen"
Honig, Edith L. *Breaking the Angelic Image* . . . , 44.

NIGEL KNEALE

"Oh, Mirror, Mirror"
Büssing, Sabine. *Aliens in the Home* . . . , 90.

DAMON FRANCIS KNIGHT

"The Country of the Kind"
Blish, James. "The Arts in Science Fiction," in Chauvin, Cy, Ed. *A Multitude* . . . ,
    61–62.

"Stranger Station"
McGregor, Gaile. *The Noble Savage* . . . , 237–238.

RAYMOND KNISTER

"The Dance at Corncob Corners"
Stevens, Peter, Ed. "Introduction," *The First Day of Spring: Stories and Other Prose*
    [by Raymond Knister], xx.

"The First Day of Spring"
Stevens, Peter, Ed. "Introduction," xxiii–xxiv.

"Grapes"
Stevens, Peter, Ed. "Introduction," xxiii.

"Hackman's Night"
Stevens, Peter, Ed. "Introduction," xx–xxi.

"Indian Summer"
Stevens, Peter, Ed. "Introduction," xxv.

"Innocent Man"
Stevens, Peter, Ed. "Introduction," xxi–xxii.

"The Strawstack"
Stevens, Peter, Ed. "Introduction," xxii.

KOBAYASHI TAKIJI

"The Factory Ship"
Rimer, J. Thomas. *A Reader's Guide* . . . , 162–163.

KŌDA ROHAN

"The Bearded Samurai"
Rimer, J. Thomas. *A Reader's Guide* . . . , 107.

"Encounter with a Skull"
Rimer, J. Thomas. *A Reader's Guide* . . . , 106.

"The Five-Storied Pagoda"
Rimer, J. Thomas. *A Reader's Guide* . . . , 106–107.

KŌNO TAEKO

"The Last Time"
Tanaka, Yukiko. "Introduction," in Tanaka, Yukiko, and Elizabeth Hanson,
    Eds. *This Kind of Woman* . . . , xx.

JINCY KORNHAUSER

"Melinda Falling"
Cassill, R. V. . . . *Instructor's Handbook,* 42–43.

WILLIAM KOTZWINKLE

"Follow the Eagle"
Cassill, R. V. . . . *Instructor's Handbook,* 43–44.

HENRY KREISEL

"The Almost Meeting"
Dahlie, Hallvard. *Varieties of Exile* . . . , 188.

"The Broken Globe"
Blodgett, E. D. *Configuration* . . . , 88–89.

MILAN KUNDERA

"The Hitchhiking Game"
Sheidley, William E., and Ann Charters. *Instructor's Manual* . . . , 167–168;
    Charters, Ann, William E. Sheidley, and Martha Ramsey. *Instructor's Manual* . . . , 2nd ed., 181–182.

KUNIKIDA DOPPO

"Meat and Potatoes"
Buckstead, Richard C. "Kunikida Doppo," in Swann, Thomas E., and Kinya
 Tsuruta, Eds. . . . *Modern Japanese Short Story,* 155–166.

"Old Gen"
Buckstead, Richard C. "Kunikida Doppo," 141–154.

KURAHASHI YUKIMO

"Partei"
Tanaka, Yukiko. "Introduction," in Tanaka, Yukiko, and Elizabeth Hanson,
 Eds. *This Kind of Woman . . . ,* xx.

R[APHAEL] A[LOYSIUS] LAFFERTY

"All But the Words"
Smith, Sheryl. "Lafferty's Short Stories: Some Mystagogic Goshwow," *Riverside
 Q,* 7, ii (1982), 80.

"Bubbles When They Burst"
Smith, Sheryl. "Lafferty's Short Stories . . . ," 78.

"The Cliff Climbers"
Smith, Sheryl. "Lafferty's Short Stories . . . ," 77.

"Configuration of the North Shore"
Smith, Sheryl. "Lafferty's Short Stories . . . ," 77.

"Continued on the Next Rock"
Smith, Sheryl. "Lafferty's Short Stories . . . ," 76.

"Days of Grass, Days of Straw"
Smith, Sheryl. "Lafferty's Short Stories . . . ," 76.

"Hog-Belly Honey"
Smith, Sheryl. "Lafferty's Short Stories . . . ," 80.

"Interurban Queen"
Smith, Sheryl. "Lafferty's Short Stories . . . ," 80.

"Rivers of Damascus"
Smith, Sheryl. "Lafferty's Short Stories . . . ," 78.

"Thus We Frustrate Charlemagne"
Smith, Sheryl. "Lafferty's Short Stories . . . ," 81.

"The Weird World"
Smith, Sheryl. "Lafferty's Short Stories . . . ," 79.

ENRIQUE A. LAGUERRE

"The Enemy"
Melendez, Concha. *El arte del cuento . . .* , 119.

"Shipwreck"
Melendez, Concha. *El arte del cuento . . .* , 117–118.

RING LARDNER

"Haircut"
*Perrine, Laurence, and Thomas R. Arp. *Instructor's Manual . . .* , 7th ed., 17–
    18.

JOSÉ VICTORINO LASTARRÍA

"Rosa"
Menton, Seymour. *El Cuento Hispanoamericano,* I, 55–56; 2nd ed., 55–56; 3rd
    ed., 55–56.

IRVING LATTON

"Vacation in La Voiselle"
MacCulloch, Clare. *The Neglected Genre . . .* , 63–67.

KEITH LAUMER

"The War Against the Yukks"
Bogert, Judith. "From Barsoom to Giffard: Sexual Comedy in Science Fiction
    and Fantasy," in Palumbo, Donald, Ed. *Erotic Universe . . .* , 91–92.

MARGARET LAURENCE

"A Bird in the House"
Buss, Helen M. *Mother and Daughter . . .* , 62–63.

"Horses of the Night"
Buss, Helen M. *Mother and Daughter . . .* , 61.
New, W. H. *Dreams of Speech . . .* , 196–198.

"The Loons"
Buss, Helen M. *Mother and Daughter . . .* , 60–61.

"Uncertain Flowering"
Keith, W. J. " 'Uncertain Flowering': An Overlooked Short Story by Margaret
    Laurence," *Canadian Lit,* 112 (Spring, 1987), 202–205.

MARY LAVIN

"The Becker Wives"
Asbee, Susan. "In Mary Lavin's 'The Becker Wives': Narrative Strategy and
    Reader Response," *J Short Story Engl*, 8 (Spring, 1987), 93–101.

"The Shrine"
Donovan, Katie. *Irish Women Writers . . .* , 18.

D. H. LAWRENCE

"The Blind Man"
Bayley, John. *The Short Story . . .* , 125–127.

"The Border Line"
Bayley, John. *The Short Story . . .* , 128–129.

"The Captain's Doll"
Kumar, Akhilesh. "D. H. Lawrence's *Sons and Lovers* and 'The Captain's Doll':
    A Study in Thematic Link," in Sharma, T. R., Ed. *Essays on D. H. Lawrence*,
    95–103.

"The Christening"
Modiano, Marko. *Domestic Disharmony . . .* , 63–64.

"Daughters of the Vicar"
Modiano, Marko. *Domestic Disharmony . . .* , 64–68.

"Delilah and Mr. Bircumshaw"
Sharma, Susheel K. "Antifeminism in D. H. Lawrence's Short Stories," in
    Sharma, T. R., Ed. *Essays on D. H. Lawrence*, 141.

"The Fly in the Ointment"
Sharma, Susheel K. "Antifeminism . . . ," 142–143.

"The Fox"
Bayley, John. "Lawrence and the Modern English Novel," in Meyers, Jeffrey,
    Ed. *The Legacy . . .* , 27–28.
Coates, Paul. *The Double and the Other . . .* , 120–122.
Devlin, Albert J. "The 'Strange and Fiery' Course of 'The Fox': D. H. Law-
    rence's Aesthetics of Composition and Revision," in Salgado, Gamini, and
    G. K. Das, Eds. *The Spirit . . .* , 75–91.
Lakshmi, Vijaya. "Dialectics of Consciousness in the Short Fiction of Lawrence,"
    in Sharma, T. R., Ed. *Essays on D. H. Lawrence*, 128–130.
Singh, A. K. "War and Lawrence: A Study of His Short Story 'The Fox,'" in
    Sharma, T. R., Ed. *Essays on D. H. Lawrence*, 134–138.

"Goose Fair"
Modiano, Marko. *Domestic Disharmony . . .* , 44–45.

"Her Turn"
Modiano, Marko. *Domestic Disharmony* . . . , 61.
Sharma, Susheel K. "Antifeminism . . . ," 142.

"The Ladybird" [originally titled "The Thimble"]
Coates, Paul. *The Double and the Other* . . . , 118–120.

"The Lovely Lady"
Sharma, Susheel K. "Antifeminism . . . ," 144.

"The Man Who Died"
Rakhi [full name]. "'The Man Who Died': A Jungian Interpretation," in
    Sharma, T. R., Ed. *Essays on D. H. Lawrence*, 116–124.

"The Man Who Loved Islands"
Kearney, Martin F. "Spirit, Place and Psyche: Integral Integration in D. H.
    Lawrence's 'The Man Who Loved Islands,'" *Engl Stud*, 69, ii (1988), 158–
    162.
Widmer, Kingsley. *Countering* . . . , 11–14.

"The Miner at Home"
Modiano, Marko. *Domestic Disharmony* . . . , 60–61.
Sharma, Susheel K. "Antifeminism . . . ," 140–141.

"None of That"
Whiteley, Patrick J. *Knowledge* . . . , 139–142.

"Odour of Chrysanthemums"
Kenner, Hugh. *A Sinking Island* . . . , 116–118.
Lakshmi, Vijaya. "Dialectics of Consciousness . . . ," 130–131.
McCabe, T. H. "The Otherness of D. H. Lawrence's 'Odour of Chrysanthe-
    mums,'" *D. H. Lawrence R*, 19 (1987), 149–156.
Modiano, Marko. *Domestic Disharmony* . . . , 45–47.
Naugrette, Jean-Pierre. "Le Mythe et le réel: Lecture de 'Odour of Chrysan-
    themums,'" in Roy, Ginette, Ed. *Études lawrenciennes*, 7–27.

"A Prelude"
Modiano, Marko. *Domestic Disharmony* . . . , 43.

"The Rocking-Horse Winner"
Büssing, Sabine. *Aliens in the Home* . . . , 96.
McDermott, John V. "Faith and Love: Twin Forces in 'The Rocking-Horse
    Winner,'" *Notes Contemp Lit*, 18, i (1988), 6–8.
*Perrine, Laurence, and Thomas R. Arp. *Instructor's Manual* . . . , 7th ed., 36.
Sheidley, William E., and Ann Charters. *Instructor's Manual* . . . , 78–79; Char-
    ters, Ann, William E. Sheidley, and Martha Ramsey. *Instructor's Man-
    ual* . . . , 2nd ed., 81–82.
Watkins, Daniel P. "Labor and Religion in D. H. Lawrence's 'The Rocking-
    Horse Winner,'" *Stud Short Fiction*, 24 (1987), 295–301.
Wilson, Keith. "D. H. Lawrence's 'The Rocking-Horse Winner': Parable and
    Structure," *Engl Stud Canada*, 13 (1987), 438–450.

"St. Mawr"

Galván Reula, J. F. "'St. Mawr' a través de sus imágenes," *Revista Canaria*, 11 (November, 1985), 25–34.

Levy, Michele F. "D. H. Lawrence and Dostoevsky: The Thirst for Risk and the Thirst for Life," *Mod Fiction Stud*, 33 (1987), 285–287.

McDowell, Frederick P. "'Pioneering into the Wilderness of Unopened Life': Lou Witt in America," in Salgado, Gamini, and G. K. Das, Eds. *The Spirit* . . . , 92–105.

Sabin, Margery. *The Dialect of the Tribe* . . . , 162–178.

"A Sick Collier"

Modiano, Marko. *Domestic Disharmony* . . . , 62.

"Smile"

Bayley, John. *The Short Story* . . . , 131–132.

"Strike Pay"

Modiano, Marko. *Domestic Disharmony* . . . , 59–60.

"The Thimble" [later titled "The Ladybird"]

Sharma, Susheel K. "Antifeminism . . . ," 142.

"The Thorn in the Flesh" [same as "Vin Ordinaire"]

Cowan, James C. "Phobia and Psychological Development in D. H. Lawrence's 'The Thorn in the Flesh,'" in Gamache, Lawrence B., and Ian S. Mac-Niven, Eds. *The Modernists* . . . , 163–170.

"A White Stocking"

Bassein, Beth A. *Women and Death* . . . , 156–157.

"The Wilful Woman"

Sharma, Susheel K. "Antifeminism . . . ," 143.

"The Woman Who Rode Away"

Galea, Ilena. "D. H. Lawrence: The Value of Myth," *Cahiers Roumains*, 3 (1987), 72–78.

González Groba, Constante. "D. H. Lawrence y 'The Woman Who Rode Away': La imposible conexión entre dos mundos opuestos," *Revista Canaria*, 11 (November, 1985), 35–46.

Lakshmi, Vijaya. "Dialectics of Consciousness . . . ," 127–128.

Renaux, Sigrid. "D. H. Lawrence's 'The Woman Who Rode Away': An Exploration," *Estudos Anglo-Americanos*, 9–11 (1985–1987), 68–88.

HENRY LAWSON

"The Drover's Wife"

Barnes, John. "'Through Clear Australian Eyes': Landscape and Identity in Australian Writing," in Eaden, P. R., and F. H. Mares, Eds. *Mapped But Unknown* . . . , 98–99.

"The Loaded Dog"
Jones, Dorothy. "Serious Laughter: On Defining Australian Humour," *J Commonwealth Lit,* 23 (1988), 78–79.

"The Union Buries Its Dead"
Kiernan, Brian, Ed. "Introduction," *The Portable Henry Lawson,* xv–xvi.

STEPHEN LEACOCK

"The Arrested Philanthropy of Mr. Tomlinson"
Lynch, Gerald. *Stephen Leacock . . . ,* 130–136.

"The Beacon on the Hill"
Lynch, Gerald. *Stephen Leacock . . . ,* 95–100.

"The Candidacy of Mr. Smith"
Lynch, Gerald. *Stephen Leacock . . . ,* 79–81.

"L'Envoi: The Train to Mariposa"
Lynch, Gerald. *Stephen Leacock . . . ,* 111–120.

"The Extraordinary Entanglement of Mr. Pupkin"
Lynch, Gerald. *Stephen Leacock . . . ,* 100–104.

"The Great Election in Missinaba County"
Lynch, Gerald. *Stephen Leacock . . . ,* 76–79.

"The Hostelry of Mr. Smith"
Lynch, Gerald. *Stephen Leacock . . . ,* 65–72.

"A Little Dinner with Mr. Lucullus Fyshe"
Lynch, Gerald. *Stephen Leacock . . . ,* 126–130.

"The Love Story of Mr. Peter Spillikins"
Lynch, Gerald. *Stephen Leacock . . . ,* 134–151.

"The Marine Excursion of the Knights of Pythias"
Lynch, Gerald. *Stephen Leacock . . . ,* 81–84.
MacCulloch, Clare. *The Neglected Genre . . . ,* 43–45.

"The Mariposa Bank Mystery"
Lynch, Gerald. *Stephen Leacock . . . ,* 106–111.

"The Ministrations of the Rev. Mr. Drone"
Lynch, Gerald. *Stephen Leacock . . . ,* 86–91.

"The Ministrations of the Reverend Uttermust Dumfarthing"
Lynch, Gerald. *Stephen Leacock . . . ,* 152–155.

"The Rival Churches of St. Asaph and St. Osoph"
Bush, Douglas. "Stephen Leacock," in Staines, David, Ed. *The Canadian Imagination . . . ,* 146–147.

Lynch, Gerald. *Stephen Leacock . . .* , 152–157.

"The Speculations of Jefferson Thorpe"
Lynch, Gerald. *Stephen Leacock . . .* , 72–76.

"The Whirlwind Campaign in Mariposa"
Lynch, Gerald. *Stephen Leacock . . .* , 92–95.

"The Wizard of Finance"
Lynch, Gerald. *Stephen Leacock . . .* , 130–136.

"The Yahi-Bahi Oriental Society of Mrs. Rasselyer-Brown"
Lynch, Gerald. *Stephen Leacock . . .* , 140–145.

DAVID LEAVITT

"Family Dancing"
Haviland, Beverly. "Minimal Manners; or, The Novel of Manners in an Age
    with Few," *Southwest R*, 73 (1988), 457–459.

"Territory"
Charters, Ann, William E. Sheidley, and Martha Ramsey. *Instructor's Man-
    ual . . .* , 2nd ed., 232–233.
Haviland, Beverly. "Minimal Manners . . . ," 459–460.

VERNON LEE [VIOLET PAGET]

"Prince Alberic and the Snake Lady"
Gardner, Burdett. *The Lesbian Imagination . . .* , 1–28.

JOSEPH SHERIDAN LE FANU

"Carmilla"
Carter, Margaret L. *Specter or Delusion? . . .* , 91–93.
Rickels, Laurence A. *Aberrations of Mourning . . .* , 68–70.
Senf, Carol A. *The Vampire . . .* , 48–57.

"The Familiar"
Carter, Margaret L. *Specter or Delusion? . . .* , 88–90.

"The Fortunes of Sir Robert Ardagh"
Gates, Barbara T. "Blue Devils and Green Tea: Sheridan Le Fanu's Haunted
    Suicides," *Stud Short Fiction*, 24 (1987), 16–17.
———. *Victorian Suicide . . .* , 109–111.

"Green Tea"
Carter, Margaret L. *Specter or Delusion? . . .* , 84–88.
Gates, Barbara T. "Blue Devils . . . ," 20–23.
———. *Victorian Suicide . . .* , 114–117.

"The Watcher"
Gates, Barbara T. "Blue Devils . . . ," 18.
――――. *Victorian Suicide . . .* , 111–112.

URSULA K. LE GUIN

"The Masters"
Dunn, Thomas. "The Deep Caves of Thought: Plato, Heinlein, and Le Guin,"
    in Palumbo, Donald, Ed. *Spectrum of the Fantastic,* 110–111.

"Mazes"
McGregor, Gaile. *The Noble Savage . . .* , 275–276.

"The New Atlantis"
Cassill, R. V. . . . *Instructor's Handbook,* 44–46.

"The Ones Who Walk Away from Omelas"
Charters, Ann, William E. Sheidley, and Martha Ramsey. *Instructor's Man-
    ual . . .* , 2nd ed., 183–184.

"The Word for World Is Forest"
McGregor, Gaile. *The Noble Savage . . .* , 271–275.

MARCUS LEHMANN

"Der Fürst von Coucy"
Kahn, Lothar. "Neglected Nineteenth-Century German-Jewish Historical Fic-
    tion," in Gelber, Mark H., Ed. *Identity and Ethos . . .* , 162–163.

FRITZ LEIBER

"The Girl with the Hungry Eyes"
Senf, Carol A. *The Vampire . . .* , 7.

"The Ship Sails at Midnight"
Heldreth, Leonard G. "Close Encounters of the Carnal Kind: Sex with Aliens
    in Science Fiction," in Palumbo, Donald, Ed. *Erotic Universe . . .* , 138–139.

MURRAY LEINSTER

"Exploration Team"
McGregor, Gaile. *The Noble Savage . . .* , 249–250.

"The Power Planet"
Bartter, Martha A. *The Way to Ground Zero . . .* , 79.

194 JOSÉ ANTONIO LÉON REY

JOSÉ ANTONIO LÉON REY

"La casita del Alto"
Léon Rey, José Antonio. "Comentario al cuento 'La casita del Alto,'" *Boletín de la Academia Colombiana,* 36 (1986), 277–285.

ALEXANDER LERNET-HOLENIA

"Baron Bagge"
Schmidt, Hugo. "Alexander Lernet-Holenia," in Daviau, Donald G., Ed. ... *Modern Austrian Literature,* 300–301.

"Der Herr von Paris"
Bolla, Elisabetta. "Der Erzähler als Historiograph menschlicher Zeitgeschichtlichkeit: Alexander Lernet-Holenia," in Adam, Wolfgang, Ed. *Das achtzehnte Jahrhundert...*, 167–175.

NIKOLAI LESKOV

"Beauteous Aza"
Ziolkowski, Margaret. *Hagiography...*, 103–104.

"Deathless Golovan"
Ziolkowski, Margaret. *Hagiography...*, 180–181.

"The Enchanted Wanderer"
Ziolkowski, Margaret. *Hagiography...*, 177–178.

"Episcopal Justice"
Ziolkowski, Margaret. *Hagiography...*, 171–173.

"The Felon of Ashkelon"
Ziolkowski, Margaret. *Hagiography...*, 107–108.

"The Legend of Conscience-Stricken Daniil"
Ziolkowski, Margaret. *Hagiography...*, 99–101.

"The Little Things in a Bishop's Life"
Ziolkowski, Margaret. *Hagiography...*, 171–172.

"The Monognome"
Ziolkowski, Margaret. *Hagiography...*, 178–179.

"The Mountain"
Ziolkowski, Margaret. *Hagiography...*, 101–102.

"Pamphalon the Mountebank"
Jakobsh, F. K. "The Saints of Leskov and Böll," *Germano-Slavica,* 6, ii (1988), 91–102.

"The Sealed Angel"
McDuff, David, Ed. "Introduction," *"Lady Macbeth of Mtsensk"* . . . [by Nikolai Leskov], 19–21.
Ziolkowski, Margaret. *Hagiography* . . . , 174–176.

"The Tale of Fedor the Christian and His Friend Abraham the Jew"
Ziolkowski, Margaret. *Hagiography* . . . , 105–107.

"The Tale of the God-Pleasing Woodcutter"
Ziolkowski, Margaret. *Hagiography* . . . , 95–99.

"The White Eagle"
Ingham, Norman W. "The Case of the Unreliable Narrator: Leskov's 'White Eagle,'" in Connolly, Julian W., and Sonia I. Ketchian, Eds. *Studies in Russian Literature* . . . , 153–165.

DORIS LESSING

"The De Wets Come to Kloof Grange"
Budhos, Shirley. *The Theme of Enclosure* . . . , 48.

"Each Other"
Abel, Elizabeth. "Resisting the Exchange: Brother-Sister Incest in Fiction by Doris Lessing," in Kaplan, Carey, and Ellen C. Rose, Eds. *Doris Lessing* . . . , 120–124.
Hanson, Clare. "Each Other: Images of Otherness in the Short Fiction of Doris Lessing, Jean Rhys, and Angela Carter," *J Short Story Engl,* 10 (Spring, 1988), 71–72.

"Not a Very Nice Story"
Hanson, Clare. "Each Other . . . ," 70–71.

"The Old Chief Mshlanga"
Roberts, Edgar V., and Henry E. Jacobs. *Instructor's Manual* . . . , 76–77.

"Old John's Place"
Budhos, Shirley. *The Theme of Enclosure* . . . , 35–36.

"One Off the Short List"
Bassein, Beth A. *Women and Death* . . . , 157–159.

"The Other Woman"
Hanson, Clare. "Each Other . . . ," 69–70.

"Our Friend Judith"
Budhos, Shirley. *The Theme of Enclosure* . . . , 96.
Gardiner, Judith K. "Gender, Values, and Lessing's Cats," in Benstock, Shari, Ed. *Feminist Issues* . . . , 117–120.

"Report on a Threatened City"
Parrinder, Patricia. *The Failure of Theory* . . . , 157–158.

"To Room Nineteen"
Hunter, Eva. "Madness in Doris Lessing's 'To Room Nineteen,'" *Engl Stud Africa*, 30 (1987), 91–104.
Sheidley, William E., and Ann Charters. *Instructor's Manual* . . . , 148; Charters, Ann, William E. Sheidley, and Martha Ramsey. *Instructor's Manual* . . . , 2nd ed., 154.

"An Unposted Love Letter"
Budhos, Shirley. *The Theme of Enclosure* . . . , 97–98.

"Winter in July"
Budhos, Shirley. *The Theme of Enclosure* . . . , 93.

NORMAN LEVINE

"A Canadian Upbringing"
Dahlie, Hallvard. *Varieties of Exile* . . . , 111.

"Class of 1949"
Dahlie, Hallvard. *Varieties of Exile* . . . , 112.

"The Dilettante"
Dahlie, Hallvard. *Varieties of Exile* . . . , 110–111.

"The Playground"
Dahlie, Hallvard. *Varieties of Exile* . . . , 109–110.

"Ringa Ringa Rosie"
Dahlie, Hallvard. *Varieties of Exile* . . . , 108–109.

LUISA LEVINSON

"The Clearing"
Brunton, Rosanne. "A Note on Contemporary Argentine Women's Writing: A Discussion of *The Web*," *Int'l Fiction R*, 15 (1988), 9–10.

BALDOMERO LILLO

"La compuerta numéro 12"
Menton, Seymour. *El Cuento Hispanoamericano*, I, 150–151; 2nd ed., 150–151; 3rd ed., 150–151.

CLARICE LISPECTOR

"The Body"
Vieira, Nelson H. "The Stations of the Body, Clarice Lispector's *Abertura* and Renewal," *Stud Short Fiction*, 25 (1988), 62–64.

"The Buffalo"
Wheeler, A. M. "Animal Imagery as Reflection of Gender in Clarice Lispector's Family Ties," *Critique S*, 28 (1987), 128–129.

"The Chicken"
Wheeler, A. M. "Animal Imagery . . . ," 125–126.

"The Crime of the Mathematics Professor"
Wheeler, A. M. "Animal Imagery . . . ," 126–127.

"The Imitation of a Rose"
Douglass, Ellen H. "Myth and Gender in Clarice Lispector: Quest as a Feminist Statement in 'A Imitação da Rosa,'" *Luso-Brazilian R*, 25, ii (1988), 15–31.
Tolentino, Magda Velloso Fernandes de. "Family Bonds and Bondage within the Family: A Study of Family Ties in Clarice Lispector and James Joyce," *Mod Lang Stud*, 18, ii (1988), 73–78.

"The Man Who Appeared"
Vieira, Nelson H. "The Stations . . . ," 68.

"Miss Ruth Algrave"
Vieira, Nelson H. "The Stations . . . ," 61–62.

"Por Enquanto"
Vieira, Nelson H. "The Stations . . . ," 66–67.

"Praça Mauá"
Vieira, Nelson H. "The Stations . . . ," 64–65.

"A Quest for Dignity"
Aquino Gariglio, María Cristina de. "An Epiphany Inside an Epiphany? Clarice Lispector's 'A procura de uma Dignidade,'" *Romance Notes*, 28, ii (1987), 163–168.

"The Smallest Woman in the World"
Wheeler, A. M. "Animal Imagery . . . ," 129–131.

LIU BINYAN

"At the Building Site of the Bridge"
Wagner, Rudolf G. "The Cog and the Scout—Functional Concepts of Literature in Socialist Political Culture: The Chinese Debate in the Mid-Fifties," in Kubin, Wolfgang, and Rudolf G. Wagner, Eds. *Essays in Modern Chinese Literature . . .* , 357–360.

LIU XINWU

"Class Teacher"
Jenner, W. J. F. "Is a Modern Chinese Literature Possible?" in Kubin, Wolfgang, and Rudolf G. Wagner, Eds. *Essays in Modern Chinese Literature . . .* , 222.

CHARLES LLOYD

"Special Diet"
Büssing, Sabine. *Aliens in the Home . . .* , 93–94.

MARÍA LOMBARDO DE CASO

"La culebra tapó el rio"
Dorward, Frances R. "The Short Story as a Vehicle for Mexican Literary *In-digenismo*," *Letras Femeninas*, 13, i–ii (1987), 59–61.

JACK LONDON

"Bâtard"
Lundquist, James. *Jack London . . .* , 101–102.

"The Call of the Wild"
Fusco, Richard. "On Primitivism in 'The Call of the Wild,'" *Am Lit Realism*, 20 (1987), 76–80.

"Koolau the Leper"
Lundquist, James. *Jack London . . .* , 163–164.

"The League of Old Men"
Lundquist, James. *Jack London . . .* , 91–92.

"Mauki"
Lundquist, James. *Jack London . . .* , 164–165.

"On the Makaloa Mat"
Stasz, Clarice. *American Dreamers . . .* , 303–306.

"The Red One"
Stasz, Clarice. *American Dreamers . . .* , 311–312.

"To Build a Fire"
Sheidley, William E., and Ann Charters. *Instructor's Manual . . .* , 60–61; Charters, Ann, William E. Sheidley, and Martha Ramsey. *Instructor's Manual . . .* , 2nd ed., 62–63.

"The Unparalleled Invasion"
Franklin, H. Bruce. *War Stars . . .* , 37–39.

"The Water Baby"
Reesman, Jeanne C. "The Problem of Knowledge in Jack London's 'The Water Baby,'" *Western Am Lit*, 23 (1988), 201–215.
Stasz, Clarice. *American Dreamers . . .* , 312–314.

"The White Silence"
Lundquist, James. *Jack London . . .* , 83–86.

"The Wit of Porportuk"
Lundquist, James. *Jack London . . .* , 92–95.

AUGUSTUS BALDWIN LONGSTREET

"The Chase"
Newlin, Keith. *"Georgia Scenes*: The Satiric Artistry of Augustus Baldwin Long-
street," *Mississippi Q,* 41 (1987–1988), 32–33.

"The Dance"
Newlin, Keith. *"Georgia Scenes . . . ,"* 27–28.

"The Fight"
Brown, Carolyn S. *The Tall Tale . . .* , 48–50.

"The Fox Hunt"
Newlin, Keith. *"Georgia Scenes . . . ,"* 31–32.

"The Gander Pulling"
Newlin, Keith. *"Georgia Scenes . . . ,"* 29–30.

"Georgia Theatrics"
Newlin, Keith. *"Georgia Scenes . . . ,"* 27.

"The Shooting Match"
Brown, Carolyn S. *The Tall Tale . . .* , 50–53.
Newlin, Keith. *"Georgia Scenes . . . ,"* 33.

"The Song"
Newlin, Keith. *"Georgia Scenes . . . ,"* 34–36.

"The Turf"
Newlin, Keith. *"Georgia Scenes . . . ,"* 30–31.

BARRY LONGYEAR

"Enemy Mine"
Cooke, Leighton B. "The Human Alien: In-Groups and Outbreaking in 'Enemy Mine,'" in Slusser, George E., and Eric S. Rabkin, Eds. *Aliens . . . ,*
179–198.

JOSÉ LÓPEZ PORTILLO Y ROJAS

"Reloj sin dueño"
Menton, Seymour. *El Cuento Hispanoamericano,* I, 90–91; 2nd ed., 90–91; 3rd
ed., 90–91.

H. P. LOVECRAFT

"The Call of Cthulhu"
Lévy, Maurice. *Lovecraft . . .* , 93–94.
Tierney, Richard L. "When the Stars Are Right," in Schweitzer, Darrell, Ed.
    Discovering . . . , 85–90.

"The Dunwich Horror"
Lévy, Maurice. *Lovecraft . . .* , 95–96.

"The Festival"
Lévy, Maurice. *Lovecraft . . .* , 66–67.

"The Horror at Red Hook"
Lévy, Maurice. *Lovecraft . . .* , 93–94.

"The Music of Erich Zann"
Lévy, Maurice. *Lovecraft . . .* , 47–48.

"The Outsider"
Mosig, Dirk W. "The Four Faces of the Outsider," in Schweitzer, Darrell, Ed.
    Discovering . . . , 18–41.

"Rats in the Wall"
Lévy, Maurice. *Lovecraft . . .* , 67–68.

"The Shadow over Innsmouth"
Lévy, Maurice. *Lovecraft . . .* , 99–100.

"The Silver Key"
Lévy, Maurice. *Lovecraft . . .* , 112–113.

"The Terrible Old Man"
Burleson, Donald R. "'The Terrible Old Man': A Deconstruction," *Lovecraft
    Stud*, 6, ii (1987), 65–68.

"Through the Gates of the Silver Key"
Lévy, Maurice. *Lovecraft . . .* , 105–106.

"The White Ship"
Schweitzer, Darrell. "Lovecraft and Lord Dunsany," in Schweitzer, Darrell, Ed.
    Discovering . . . , 97–99.

MALCOLM LOWRY

"The Bravest Boat"
Dahlie, Hallvard. *Varieties of Exile . . .* , 162.

"Elephant and Colosseum"
Dahlie, Hallvard. *Varieties of Exile . . .* , 165–166.

"The Forest Path to the Spring"
Dahlie, Hallvard. *Varieties of Exile . . .* , 167–168.

"Present Estate of Pompeii"
Dahlie, Hallvard. *Varieties of Exile . . .* , 166–167.

"Through the Panama"
Dahlie, Hallvard. *Varieties of Exile . . .* , 164–165.

LU XÜN [LU HSÜN or CHOU SHU-JEN]

"Diary of a Madman"
Lee, Leo Ou-fan. *Voices from the Iron House . . .* , 53–57.

"In the Tavern"
Lee, Leo Ou-fan. *Voices from the Iron House . . .* , 81–83.

"Kong Yiji"
Lee, Leo Ou-fan. *Voices from the Iron House . . .* , 61–62, 73.

"Medicine"
Lee, Leo Ou-fan. *Voices from the Iron House . . .* , 65–68.

"The Misanthrope"
Lee, Leo Ou-fan. *Voices from the Iron House . . .* , 83–86.

"My Old Home"
Lee, Leo Ou-fan. *Voices from the Iron House . . .* , 80–81.

"The New Year Sacrifice"
Lee, Leo Ou-fan. *Voices from the Iron House . . .* , 75–76.

"The Story of Hair"
Lee, Leo Ou-fan. *Voices from the Iron House . . .* , 79–80.

"Tomorrow"
Lee, Leo Ou-fan. *Voices from the Iron House . . .* , 73–75.

"The True Story of Ah Q"
Lee, Leo Ou-fan. *Voices from the Iron House . . .* , 76–78.

BRIAN LUMLEY

"David's Worm"
Büssing, Sabine. *Aliens in the Home . . .* , 67–68.

MARTA LYNCH

"Latin Lover"
Brunton, Rosanne. "A Note on Contemporary Argentine Women's Writing: A
  Discussion of *The Web*," *Int'l Fiction R*, 15 (1988), 11.

JOHN McCLUSKY

"Chicago Jubilee Rag"
Johnson, Charles. *Being & Race . . .* , 71–72.

CARSON McCULLERS

"The Ballad of the Sad Café"
Gervin, Mary A. "McCullers' Frames of Reference in 'The Ballad of the Sad
  Café,'" *Pembroke Mag*, 20 (1988), 37–42.
Gilbert, Sandra M., and Susan Gubar. *No Man's Land . . .* , 105–112.
Stebbins, Todd. "McCullers' 'The Ballad of the Sad Café,'" *Explicator*, 46, ii
  (1988), 36–38.
Walsh, Margaret. "Carson McCullers' Anti-Fairy Tale: 'The Ballad of the Sad
  Café,'" *Pembroke Mag*, 20 (1988), 43–48.

"A Domestic Dilemma"
Perrine, Laurence. "Restoring 'A Domestic Dilemma,'" *Stud Short Fiction*, 11
  (1974), 101–104; rpt., abbreviated, in Perrine, Laurence, and Thomas R.
  Arp. *Instructor's Manual . . .* , 7th ed., 12–13.

"Wunderkind"
Petry, Alice H. "Carson McCullers's Precocious 'Wunderkind,'" *Southern Q*, 26,
  iii (1988), 31–39.

HUGH MacDIARMID [CHRISTOPHER MURRAY GRIEVE]

"Cerebral"
Bold, Alan. *MacDiarmid . . .* , 90–91.

ANSON MacDONALD [ROBERT HEINLEIN]

"Solution Unsatisfactory"
Berger, Albert I. "Theories of History and Social Order in *Astounding Science
  Fiction*, 1934–1955," *Sci-Fiction Stud*, 15 (1988), 24–25.

GEORGE MacDONALD

"The Day Boy and the Night Girl"
Honig, Edith L. *Breaking the Angelic Image . . .* , 22–23.

"The Light Princess"
Sammons, Martha C. *"A Better Country"* . . . , 66–67.

GWENDOLYN MacEWEN

"Kingsmere"
Atwood, Margaret. "Canadian Monsters: Some Aspects of the Supernatural in
    Canadian Fiction," in Staines, David, Ed. *The Canadian Imagination* . . . ,
    110–111.

"Noman"
Atwood, Margaret. "Canadian Monsters . . . ," 111–114.

"The Second Coming of Julian the Magician"
Atwood, Margaret. "Canadian Monsters . . . ," 114–116.

R. J. McGREGOR

"The Perfect Gentleman"
Broege, Valerie. "Technology and Sexuality in Science Fiction: Creating New
    Erotic Interfaces," in Palumbo, Donald, Ed. *Erotic Universe* . . . , 124–125.

ARTHUR MACHEN

"The Bright Boy"
Soula, Jean-Pierre. "Du féérique au fantastique chez Arthur Machen," *Caliban,*
    16 (1979), 127.

"The Happy Children"
Büssing, Sabine. *Aliens in the Home* . . . , 48–50.

"The Novel of the White Powder"
Soula, Jean-Pierre. "Du féérique au fantastique . . . ," 128–129.

"Out of the Earth"
Soula, Jean-Pierre. "Du féérique au fantastique . . . ," 124.

"The Shining Pyramid"
Soula, Jean-Pierre. "Du féérique au fantastique . . . ," 129.

"The White People"
Büssing, Sabine. *Aliens in the Home* . . . , 85–86.
Soula, Jean-Pierre. "Du féérique au fantastique . . . ," 124–125.

CLAUDE McKAY

"The Agricultural Show"
Cooper, Wayne F. *Claude McKay* . . . , 271–272.

"Color Scheme"
Cooper, Wayne F. *Claude McKay* . . . , 222.

RICHARD McKENNA

"Hunter, Come Home"
McGregor, Gaile. *The Noble Savage* . . . , 243–244.

BERNARD MacLAVERTY

"Between Two Shores"
Saxton, Arnold. "An Introduction to the Stories of Bernard MacLaverty," *J Short Story Engl,* 8 (Spring, 1987), 118–119.

"My Dear Palestrina"
Saxton, Arnold. "An Introduction . . . ," 119–120.

"Phonefun Limited"
Saxton, Arnold. "An Introduction . . . ," 117.

"St. Paul Could Hit the Nail on the Head"
Saxton, Arnold. "An Introduction . . . ," 116–117.

"Secrets"
Saxton, Arnold. "An Introduction . . . ," 114–115.

"Umberto Verdi, Chimney-Sweep"
Saxton, Arnold. "An Introduction . . . ," 120–123.

MICHAEL McLAVERTY

"A Schoolmaster"
Dunleavy, Janet E. "Mary Lavin, Elizabeth Bowen, and a New Generation: The Irish Short Story at Midcentury," in Kilroy, James F., Ed. *The Irish Short Story* . . . , 163.

"Stone"
Dunleavy, Janet E. "Mary Lavin . . . ," 164–165.

KATHERINE McLEAN

"The Other"
Büssing, Sabine. *Aliens in the Home* . . . , 18–19.

ALISTAIR MacLEOD

"As Birds Bring Forth the Sun"
Davidson, Arnold E. "As Birds Bring Forth the Story: The Elusive Art of Alistair MacLeod," *Canadian Lit,* [n.v.], cxix (1988), 33–35.

Ditsky, John. "'Such Meticulous Brightness': The Fiction of Alistair MacLeod," *Hollins Critic*, 25, i (1988), 7–8.

"The Boat"
Ditsky, John. "'Such Meticulous Brightness' . . . ," 4–5.

"The Closing Down of Summer"
Ditsky, John. "'Such Meticulous Brightness' . . . ," 6.

"In the Fall"
Ditsky, John. "'Such Meticulous Brightness' . . . ," 3.

"Island"
Ditsky, John. "'Such Meticulous Brightness' . . . ," 8–9.

"The Last Salt Gift"
Davidson, Arnold E. "As Birds Bring Forth . . . ," 35–37.

"The Return"
Ditsky, John. "'Such Meticulous Brightness' . . . ," 4.

"The Road to Rankin's Point"
Ditsky, John. "'Such Meticulous Brightness' . . . ," 6.

"Second Spring"
Ditsky, John. "'Such Meticulous Brightness' . . . ," 7.

"To Every Thing There Is a Season"
Davidson, Arnold E. "As Birds Bring Forth . . . ," 37–38.
Ditsky, John. "'Such Meticulous Brightness' . . . ," 7.

"The Vastness of the Dark"
Davidson, Arnold E. "As Birds Bring Forth . . . ," 38–39.
Ditsky, John. "'Such Meticulous Brightness' . . . ," 3–4.

"Vision"
Davidson, Arnold E. "As Birds Bring Forth . . . ," 39–41.
Ditsky, John. "'Such Meticulous Brightness' . . . ," 8.

"Winter Dog"
Ditsky, John. "'Such Meticulous Brightness' . . . ," 6–7.

JAMES ALAN McPHERSON

"Elbow Room"
Blicksilver, Edith. "Interracial Relationships in Three Short Stories by James Alan McPherson," *Coll Engl Assoc Critic*, 50, ii–iv (1987), 84–87.
Wallace, Jon. "The Story Behind the Story in James Alan McPherson's 'Elbow Room,'" *Stud Short Fiction*, 25 (1988), 447–451.

"Gold Coast"
Blicksilver, Edith. "Interracial Relationships . . . ," 80–82.

"Hue and Cry"
Blicksilver, Edith. "Interracial Relationships . . . ," 83–84.

"Just Enough for the City"
Wallace, Jon. "The Politics of Style in Three Stories by James Alan McPherson," *Mod Fiction Stud,* 34 (1988), 24–26.

"The Story of a Dead Man"
Wallace, Jon. "The Politics of Style . . . ," 18–21.

"The Story of a Scar"
Wallace, Jon. "The Politics of Style . . . ," 21–24.

DAVID MADDEN

"No Trace"
Cassill, R. V. . . . *Instructor's Handbook,* 46–48.

WILLIAM MAGINN

"The Man in the Bell"
Heller, Terry. *The Delights of Terror . . . ,* 27–28.

NAJIB MAHFUZ

"Al-Karnak"
Allen, Roger. "Najib Mahfuz," *J Am Research Center,* 14 (1977), 106–107; rpt. Allen, Roger, Ed. *Modern Arabic Literature,* 202–203.

"The Mosque in the Alley"
Ayyad, Shukri. "Najib Mahfuz," trans. Roger Allen, in Allen, Roger, Ed. *Modern Arabic Literature,* 194–195.

"Story with No Beginning and No End"
Mikhail, Mona N. "Broken Ideals: The Death of Religion in Two Stories by Idris and Mahfuz," *J Arabic Lit,* 5 (1974), 152, 157; rpt. Allen, Roger, Ed. *Modern Arabic Literature,* 198–199.

MAMADALI MAHMUDOV

"The Immortal Cliffs"
Paksoy, H. B. "Central Asia's New *Dastans,*" *Central Asian Survey,* 6, i (1987), 77–79.

NORMAN MAILER

"A Calculus of Heaven"
Harap, Louis. *In the Mainstream* . . . , 151–152.

VLADIMIR MAKANIN

"Where the Sky Met the Hills"
Lowe, David. *Russian Writing Since 1953* . . . , 113–114.
Shneidman, N. N. *Soviet Literature* . . . , 54–56.

BERNARD MALAMUD

"Angel Levine"
Chard-Hutchinson, Martine. "Bernard Malamud: Les petits Miracles du Quotidien," *Caliban*, 23 (1988), 40–43.
Freese, Peter. *Die amerikanische Kurzgeschichte* . . . , 206–209.

"The Bill"
Freese, Peter. *Die amerikanische Kurzgeschichte* . . . , 196–197.

"Black Is My Favorite Color"
Freese, Peter. *Die amerikanische Kurzgeschichte* . . . , 202–205.

"The First Seven Years"
Freese, Peter. *Die amerikanische Kurzgeschichte* . . . , 193–196.

"Idiots First"
Freese, Peter. *Die amerikanische Kurzgeschichte* . . . , 211–213.
Lyons, Bonnie K. "American-Jewish Fiction Since 1945," in Fried, Lewis, Ed. *Handbook of American-Jewish Literature* . . . , 78–79.

"The Jewbird"
Charters, Ann, William E. Sheidley, and Martha Ramsey. *Instructor's Manual* . . . , 2nd ed., 146–147.
Freese, Peter. *Die amerikanische Kurzgeschichte* . . . , 213–216.

"The Lady of the Lake"
Freese, Peter. *Die amerikanische Kurzgeschichte* . . . , 226–229.

"The Last Mohican"
Freese, Peter. *Die amerikanische Kurzgeschichte* . . . , 232–235.

"The Loan"
Freese, Peter. *Die amerikanische Kurzgeschichte* . . . , 197–199.

"The Magic Barrel"
Dessner, Lawrence J. "The Playfulness of Bernard Malamud's 'The Magic Barrel,'" *Essays Lit*, 15 (1988), 87–101.
Freese, Peter. *Die amerikanische Kurzgeschichte* . . . , 216–234.

Lyons, Bonnie K. "American-Jewish Fiction . . . ," 69–70.

"Man in the Drawer"
Milbauer, Asher Z. "Eastern Europe in American-Jewish Writing," in Fried, Lewis, Ed. *Handbook of American-Jewish Literature* . . . , 384–385.

"The Mourners"
Freese, Peter. *Die amerikanische Kurzgeschichte* . . . , 191–193.
Halperin, Irving. "The Theme of Responsibility in Bernard Malamud's 'The Mourners,'" *Judaism*, 36 (1987), 460–465.
Lyons, Bonnie K. "American-Jewish Fiction . . . ," 69.

"Pictures of the Artist"
Freese, Peter. *Die amerikanische Kurzgeschichte* . . . , 239–240.

"A Pimp's Revenge"
Freese, Peter. *Die amerikanische Kurzgeschichte* . . . , 238–239.

"The Silver Crown"
Chard-Hutchinson, Martine. "Bernard Malamud . . . ," 42–43.

"Still Life"
Freese, Peter. *Die amerikanische Kurzgeschichte* . . . , 235–237.

"Take Pity"
Freese, Peter. *Die amerikanische Kurzgeschichte* . . . , 199–202.

"Talking Horse"
Chard-Hutchinson, Martine. "Bernard Malamud . . . ," 44–45.

EDUARDO MALLEA

"Conversation"
Menton, Seymour. *El Cuento Hispanoamericano*, II, 242–243; 2nd ed., 242–243; 3rd ed., 136–137.

ANDRÉ PIEYRE DE MANDIARGUES

"The Capital Vision"
Lowrie, Joyce O. "Dissolution and Discovery in the Fantastic Fiction of André Pieyre de Mandiargues," in Morse, Donald E., Ed. *The Fantastic* . . . , 158–159.

"The Little Stone Women"
Lowrie, Joyce O. "Dissolution and Discovery . . . ," 149–153.

HEINRICH MANN

"Pippo Spano"
Bennett, Timothy A. "Heinrich Mann's 'Pippo Spano': The Problem of the Aura and the Work of Art," *Mod Lang Notes*, 108 (1988), 60–63.

Fiorioli, Elena. "Il Decadentismo: Proiezione dell' 'io' nell'oggetto artistico," *Cristallo*, 29, ii (1987), 41–50.

THOMAS MANN

"Death in Venice"
Boschert, Bernhard, and Ulf Schramm. "Literatur und Literaturwissenschaft als Medium der Bearbeitung von Verdrängung: Beobachtungen an Thomas Manns 'Der Tod in Venedig'—ein Beitrag zur Germanistik als Friedens- und Konfliktforschung," in Oellers, Norbert, Ed. *Politische Aufgaben . . .* , 19–34.
Cohn, Dorrit. "The Second Author of 'Der Tod in Venedig,'" in Bennett, Benjamin, Anton Kaes, and William Lillyman, Eds. *Probleme der Moderne . . .* , 223–245; rpt. Ezergaillis, Inta, Ed. *Critical Essays . . .* , 124–143.
Eggenschwiler, David. "The Very Glance of Art: Ironic Narrative in Mann's *Novellen*," *Mod Lang Q*, 48, i (1987), 65–77.
Palencia-Roth, Michael. *Myth and the Modern Novel . . .* , 109–113.
Reilly, Patrick. *The Literature of Guilt . . .* , 69–91.
Rotkin, Charlotte. "Form and Function: The Art and Architecture of 'Death in Venice,'" *Midwest Q*, 29 (1988), 497–505.
Weiner, Marc A. "Silence, Sound, and Song in 'Der Tod in Venedig': A Study in Psycho-Social Progression," *Seminar*, 23 (1987), 137–155.
Woodward, Kathleen. "Youthfulness as a Masquerade," *Discourse*, 11, i (1988–1989), 119–142.

"Mario and the Magician"
Eggenschwiler, David. "The Very Glance of Art . . . ," 77–83.

"Tonio Kröger"
Eggenschwiler, David. "The Very Glance of Art . . . ," 60–65.
Malmgren, Carl D. "'From Work to Text': The Modernist and Postmodernist *Künstlerroman*," *Novel*, 21, i (1987), 5–28.
Reed, T. J. "Text and History: 'Tonio Kröger' and the Politics of Four Decades," *Pubs Engl Goethe Soc*, 57 (1988), 39–54.

"The Transposed Heads"
Renner, Rolf G. "Thomas Mann als phantastischer Realist: Eine Überlegung anlässlich der 'vertauschten Köpfe,'" in Helftrich, Eckhard, and Hans Wysling, Eds. *Internationales Thomas-Mann-Kolloquium . . .* , 73–91.

KATHERINE MANSFIELD [KATHERINE BEAUCHAMP]

"The Advanced Ladies"
Nathan, Rhoda B. *Katherine Mansfield*, 55–56.

"The Aloe"
Nathan, Rhoda B. *Katherine Mansfield*, 145–146.

"At Lehmann's"
Nathan, Rhoda B. *Katherine Mansfield*, 64.

"At the Bay"
New, W. H. *Dreams of Speech* . . . , 211–220.

"A Birthday"
Nathan, Rhoda B. *Katherine Mansfield*, 63–64.

"A Blaze"
Nathan, Rhoda B. *Katherine Mansfield*, 68–69.

"Bliss"
Nathan, Rhoda B. *Katherine Mansfield*, 72–75.
Sheidley, William E., and Ann Charters. *Instructor's Manual* . . . , 88–89; Charters, Ann, William E. Sheidley, and Martha Ramsey. *Instructor's Manual* . . . , 2nd ed., 94.
Williams, Merryn. *Six Women Novelists*, 67–68.

"The Child-Who-Was-Tired"
Harmat, Andrée-Marie. "Un très mansfieldien plagiat de Tchékov: 'L'Enfant-qui-était-fatiguée' de Katherine Mansfield," *Littérature*, 16 (Spring, 1987), 49–68.
Nathan, Rhoda B. *Katherine Mansfield*, 60–62.

"A Cup of Tea"
Nathan, Rhoda B. *Katherine Mansfield*, 82–83.

"The Daughters of the Late Colonel"
Nathan, Rhoda B. *Katherine Mansfield*, 95–99.

"A Dill Pickle"
Nathan, Rhoda B. *Katherine Mansfield*, 69–72.

"The Doll's House"
Nathan, Rhoda B. *Katherine Mansfield*, 38–40.
Sheidley, William E., and Ann Charters. *Instructor's Manual* . . . , 90–91; Charters, Ann, William E. Sheidley, and Martha Ramsey. *Instructor's Manual* . . . , 2nd ed., 96.

"Escape"
Nathan, Rhoda B. *Katherine Mansfield*, 104–106.

"The Fly"
Nathan, Rhoda B. *Katherine Mansfield*, 101–103.

"Frau Brechenmacher Attends a Wedding"
Nathan, Rhoda B. *Katherine Mansfield*, 64–65.

"Frau Fischer"
Nathan, Rhoda B. *Katherine Mansfield*, 58–60.

"The Garden Party"
Bell, Barbara C. "Non-Identical Twins: Nature in 'The Garden Party' and 'The Grave,'" *Comparatist*, 12 (May, 1988), 58–66.

Nathan, Rhoda B. *Katherine Mansfield*, 40–46.
New, W. H. *Dreams of Speech . . .* , 136–137.
Williams, Merryn. *Six Women Novelists*, 74–76.

"Germans at Meat"
Nathan, Rhoda B. *Katherine Mansfield*, 53–54.

"Her First Ball"
Nathan, Rhoda B. *Katherine Mansfield*, 46–50.

"How Pearl Buttons Was Kidnapped"
Nathan, Rhoda B. *Katherine Mansfield*, 121–122.

"An Ideal Family"
Nathan, Rhoda B. *Katherine Mansfield*, 101–103.

"Je ne parle pas français"
Nathan, Rhoda B. *Katherine Mansfield*, 106–112.

"The Life of Ma Parker"
Nathan, Rhoda B. *Katherine Mansfield*, 93–95.

"The Little Girl"
Nathan, Rhoda B. *Katherine Mansfield*, 33–35.

"A Little Governess"
Williams, Merryn. *Six Women Novelists*, 66–67.

"The Man Without a Temperament"
Nathan, Rhoda B. *Katherine Mansfield*, 78–81.

"Marriage à la Mode"
Nathan, Rhoda B. *Katherine Mansfield*, 75–78.

"A Married Man's Story"
Nathan, Rhoda B. *Katherine Mansfield*, 84–85.

"Millie" [expanded to become "The Woman at the Store"]
Nathan, Rhoda B. *Katherine Mansfield*, 120–121.

"Miss Brill"
Nathan, Rhoda B. *Katherine Mansfield*, 91–92.
New, W. H. *Dreams of Speech . . .* , 132–133.
*Perrine, Laurence, and Thomas R. Arp. *Instructor's Manual . . .* , 7th ed., 8–
    10.

"The Modern Soul"
Nathan, Rhoda B. *Katherine Mansfield*, 57–58.

"New Dresses"
Nathan, Rhoda B. *Katherine Mansfield*, 35–38.

"Pictures"
Nathan, Rhoda B. *Katherine Mansfield,* 90–91.

"Poison"
Nathan, Rhoda B. *Katherine Mansfield,* 80–81.

"Prelude"
Nathan, Rhoda B. *Katherine Mansfield,* 15–25.
New, W. H. *Dreams of Speech . . . ,* 135–136.

"Revelations"
Nathan, Rhoda B. *Katherine Mansfield,* 103–104.

"The Sister of the Baroness"
Nathan, Rhoda B. *Katherine Mansfield,* 56–57.

"Sixpence"
Nathan, Rhoda B. *Katherine Mansfield,* 149–151.

"The Stranger"
Breuer, Hannelore and Horst. "Psychoanalytische Bemerkungen zu Katherine
    Mansfields Erzählung 'The Stranger,'" *Literatur in Wissenschaft,* 20 (1987),
    505–517.
Nathan, Rhoda B. *Katherine Mansfield,* 81–82.

"The Woman at the Store" [originally, in shorter form, titled "Millie"]
Nathan, Rhoda B. *Katherine Mansfield,* 115–120.

"Youth"
Nathan, Rhoda B. *Katherine Mansfield,* 123.

JUANITO MARCELLA

"The Cry of One Pierced by a Lance"
Lucero, Rosario Cruz. "Notes on the Contemporary Hiligaynon Short Story,"
    Solitary, 108–109 (1986), 168.

JOSÉ MARÍN CAÑAS

"Rota la ternura"
Menton, Seymour. *El Cuento Costarricense,* 22–23.

RENÉ MARQUÉS

"Death"
Melendez, Concha. *El arte del cuento . . . ,* 220.

"La sala"
Melendez, Concha. *El arte del cuento . . . ,* 221–222.

"Three Men Near the River"
Melendez, Concha. *El arte del cuento* . . . , 222–223.

JULIO MARRERO NUÑEZ

"Requiem for a Soldier of the King of Spain"
Melendez, Concha. *El arte del cuento* . . . , 154–155.

GEORGE R. R. MARTIN

"A Song for Lya"
McGregor, Gaile. *The Noble Savage* . . . , 237.

GREGORIO MARTÍNEZ

"The Cross of Bolivar"
Higgins, James. . . . *Peruvian Literature*, 323.

BOBBIE ANN MASON

"The Climber"
Wilhelm, Albert E. "Private Rituals: Coping with Change in the Fiction of
  Bobbie Ann Mason," *Midwest Q*, 28, ii (1987), 274–275.

"Detroit Skyline, 1949"
Barnes, Linda A. "The Freak Endures: The Southern Grotesque from Flan-
  nery O'Connor to Bobbie Ann Mason," in Logsdon, Loren, and Charles W.
  Mayes, Eds. *Since Flannery O'Connor* . . . , 139–140.
Wilhelm, Albert E. "Private Rituals . . . ," 273–274.

"Drawing Names"
Wilhelm, Albert E. "Private Rituals . . . ," 280–281.

"Graveyard Day"
Wilhelm, Albert E. "Private Rituals . . . ," 279–280.

"The Ocean"
Wilhelm, Albert E. "Private Rituals . . . ," 275–278.

"Old Things"
Barnes, Linda A. "The Freak Endures . . . ," 139–140.

"Residents and Transients"
Perrine, Laurence, and Thomas R. Arp. *Instructor's Manual* . . . , 7th ed., 87–
  88.

"The Retreat"
Wilhelm, Albert E. "Private Rituals . . . ," 278–279.

"Shiloh"
Barnes, Linda A. "The Freak Endures . . . ," 138.
Charters, Ann, William E. Sheidley, and Martha Ramsey. *Instructor's Manual . . .* , 2nd ed., 220–221.

RICHARD MATHESON

"Drink My Blood"
Büssing, Sabine. *Aliens in the Home . . .* , 64–65.

"Pattern for Survival"
Bartter, Martha A. *The Way to Ground Zero . . .* , 227.

MTUTUZELI MATSHOBA

"Three Days in the Land of a Dying Illusion"
Trump, Martin. "Black South African Short Fiction in English," *Research African Lit,* 19, i (1988), 39–40.

BRANDER MATTHEWS

"An Interview with Miss Marlenspuyk"
Good, Howard. *Acquainted with the Night . . .* , 35–36.

JAMES MATTHEWS

"A Case of Guilt"
Trump, Martin. "Black South African Short Fiction in English," *Research African Lit,* 19, i (1988), 35–36.

ANA MARÍA MATUTE

"El incendio"
Nichols, Geraldine C. "Stranger Than Fiction: Fantasy in Short Stories by Matute, Rodoreda, Riera," *Monographic R,* 4 (1988), 36.
Valis, Noël M. "La 'Pipá' de Clarín y 'El incendio' de Ana María Matute: Una infancia traicionada," *Cuadernos del Norte,* 2 (May–June, 1981), 72–77.

"Sin of Omission"
Vásquez, Mary S. "Two Mourners for the Human Spirit: Ana María Matute and Flannery O'Connor," *Monographic R,* 4 (1988), 51–59.

W. SOMERSET MAUGHAM

"The Fall of Edward Barnard"
Loss, Archie K. *W. Somerset Maugham,* 65–67.

"Mr. Know-all"
Mortimer, Armine K. "Second Stories: The Example of 'Mr. Know-all,'" *Stud Short Fiction,* 25 (1988), 307–314.

"Rain"
Loss, Archie K. *W. Somerset Maugham,* 73–76.

"The Taipan"
Leithauser, Brad. "Dead Forms: The Ghost Story Today," *New Criterion,* 6, iv (1987), 34.

GUY DE MAUPASSANT

"Allouma"
Coste, Didier. "'Allouma,' ou ce que la main gauche n'a pas dit à la main droite," *French Forum,* 13, ii (1988), 229–242.

"Berthe"
Lintvelt, Jaap. "L'Animalisation humaine et l'amour dans 'Berthe' de Maupassant," in Briosi, Sandro, and Jaap Lintvelt, Eds. *L'Homme et l'animal,* 65–71.

"Un Coup d'état"
Donaldson-Evans, Mary. "Doctoring History: Maupassant's 'Un Coup d'état,'" *Nineteenth-Century French Stud,* 16 (1988), 351–360.

"Le Donneur d'eau bénite"
Killick, Rachel. "Family Likeness in Flaubert and Maupassant: 'La Légende de Saint Julien l'Hospitalier' and 'Le Donneur d'eau bénite,'" *Forum Mod Lang Stud,* 24 (1988), 346–358.

"The Hand"
Godfrey, Sima. "Lending a Hand: Nerval, Gautier, Maupassant and the Fantastic," *Romanic R,* 78 (1987), 82–83.

"The Horla"
Heller, Terry. *The Delights of Terror . . . ,* 95–100.
Schaffner, Alain. "Pourquoi 'Horla'? Ou le passage du miroir," *Temps Modernes,* 43 (1988), 150–164.

"Madame Hermet"
Büssing, Sabine. *Aliens in the Home . . . ,* 13–14.

"Mademoiselle Fifi"
Zappel, Kristiane. "Vainqueurs et vaincus: La Structure argumentative de 'Mademoiselle Fifi,'" *Orbis Litterarum,* 43, i (1988), 58–68.

"Miss Harriet"
Sheidley, William E., and Ann Charters. *Instructor's Manual . . . ,* 29–30; Charters, Ann, William E. Sheidley, and Martha Ramsey. *Instructor's Manual . . . ,* 2nd ed., 31–32.

"The Orphan"
Büssing, Sabine. *Aliens in the Home* . . . , 2–3.

"A Piece of String"
Sheidley, William E., and Ann Charters. *Instructor's Manual* . . . , 27–28; Charters, Ann, William E. Sheidley, and Martha Ramsey. *Instructor's Manual* . . . , 2nd ed., 29–30.

"Queen Hortense"
Büssing, Sabine. *Aliens in the Home* . . . , 132–133.

"The Skinned Hand"
Godfrey, Sima. "Lending a Hand . . . ," 81–82.

"A Widow"
Büssing, Sabine. *Aliens in the Home* . . . , 90.

S. P. MEEK

"The Red Peril"
Bartter, Martha A. *The Way to Ground Zero* . . . , 77–79.

HERMAN MELVILLE

"The Apple-Tree Table"
*Slater, Judith. "The Domestic Adventurer in Melville's Tales," in Budd, Louis J., and Edwin H. Cady, Eds. *On Melville* . . . , 92–94.

"Bartleby the Scrivener"
Adler, Irving. "Equity, Law and Bartleby," *Sci & Soc,* 51 (1987–1988), 468–474.
Brown, Gilliam. "The Empire of Agoraphobia," *Representations,* 20 (Fall, 1987), 134–157.
Forst, Graham N. "Up Wall Street Towards Broadway: The Narrator's Pilgrimage in Melville's 'Bartleby the Scrivener,'" *Stud Short Fiction,* 24 (1987), 263–270.
Hattenhauer, Darryl. "Bartleby as Horological Chronometer: Yet Another View of Bartleby the Doubloon," *Am Transcendental Q,* 2, i N.S. (1988), 35–40.
Hildebrand, William K. "'Bartleby' and the Black Conceit," *Stud Romanticism,* 27 (1988), 289–313.
Kopley, Richard. "The Circle and Its Center in 'Bartleby the Scrivener,'" *Am Transcendental Q,* 2 (September, 1988), 191–206.
McCarthy, Paul. "Rascally Characters in Melville's Stories," *No Dakota Q,* 53, iii (1985), 77–78.
Perry, Dennis R. "'Ah, humanity': Compulsion Neuroses in Melville's 'Bartleby,'" *Stud Short Fiction,* 24 (1987), 407–415.
Rogers, Douglas. "Unamuno's Don Sandalio and Melville's Bartleby: Two Literary Enigmas," in Brancafore, Benito, Edward R. Mulvihill, and Roberto G. Sánchez, Eds. *Homenaje a Antonio Sánchez Barbudo* . . . , 187–201.

Rovit, Earl. "Purloined, Scarlet, and Dead Letters in Classic American Literature," *Sewanee R*, 96 (1988), 426–430.

Schaffer, Carl. "Unadmitted Impediments, Unmarried Minds: Melville's 'Bartleby' and 'I and My Chimney,'" *Stud Short Fiction*, 24 (1987), 93–96.

Sheidley, William E., and Ann Charters. *Instructor's Manual* ... , 12–13; Charters, Ann, William E. Sheidley, and Martha Ramsey. *Instructor's Manual* ... , 2nd ed., 13.

Smith, Peter A. "Entropy in Melville's 'Bartleby the Scrivener,'" *Centennial R*, 32 (1988), 155–162.

Stout, Janis P. *Sodom in Eden* ... , 136–138.

"Benito Cereno"

Bryant, John. "Melville's Comic Debate: Geniality and Aesthetics of Repose," *Am Lit*, 55 (1983), 164–168; rpt. Budd, Louis J., and Edwin H. Cady, Eds. *On Melville* ... , 267–271.

Dekker, George. ... *Historical Romance*, 197–207.

Hauss, Jon. "Masquerade of Language in Melville's 'Benito Cereno,'" *Arizona Q*, 44, ii (1988), 5–21.

Richardson, William D. *Melville's "Benito Cereno"* ... , 69–93.

Simpson, Eleanor E. "Melville and the Negro: From *Typee* to 'Benito Cereno,'" *Am Lit*, 41 (1969), 19–38; rpt. Budd, Louis J., and Edwin H. Cady, Eds. *On Melville* ... , 148–154.

Stuckey, Sterling, and Joshua Leslie. "Aftermath: Captain Delano's Claim against Benito Cereno," *Mod Philol*, 85 (1988), 265–287.

Thomas, Brook. *Cross-Examinations* ... , 93–114.

Weinstein, Arnold. *The Fiction of Relationship*, 174–183.

"Billy Budd"

Boone, Joseph A. *Tradition Counter Tradition* ... , 259–260.

Budick, Emily. *Fiction* ... , 58–62.

Chai, Leon. *The Romantic Foundations* ... , 215–227.

Dekker, George. ... *Historical Romance*, 208–219.

Garrison, Joseph M. "'Billy Budd': A Reconsideration," *Ball State Univ Forum*, 27, i (1986), 30–41.

Milder, Robert. "Melville's Later Poetry and 'Billy Budd': From Nostalgia to Transcendence," *Philol Q*, 66, iv (1987), 498–507.

Mizruchi, Susan L. *The Power of Historical Knowledge* ... , 65–67.

Radloff, Bernhard. "The Truth of Indirection and the Possibility of the Holy in 'Billy Budd,'" *Religion & Lit*, 20, iii (1988), 49–70.

Reynolds, David S. *Beneath the American Renaissance* ... , 305–308.

*Sten, Christopher W. "Vere's Use of the 'Forms': Means and Ends in 'Billy Budd,'" in Budd, Louis J., and Edwin H. Cady, Eds. *On Melville* ... , 188–202.

Thomas, Brook. *Cross-Examinations* ... , 211–233.

*Watters, R. E. "Melville's 'Sociality,'" in Budd, Louis J., and Edwin H. Cady, Eds. *On Melville* ... , 38–39.

"Cock-A-Doodle-Doo!"

McCarthy, Paul. "Rascally Characters ... ," 79.

*Moss, Sidney P. "'Cock-a-Doodle-Doo!' and Some Legends in Melville Scholarship," in Budd, Louis J., and Edwin H. Cady, Eds. *On Melville* ... , 116–134.

*Slater, Judith. "The Domestic Adventurer . . . ," 85–87.

"Daniel Orme"
Young, Philip. "Melville's Good-Bye: 'Daniel Orme,'" *Stud Am Fiction,* 6, i (1988), 1–11.

"The Encantadas"
Bryant, John. "Melville's Comic Debate . . . ," 160–161; rpt. Budd, Louis J., and Edwin H. Cady, Eds. *On Melville . . . ,* 263–264.
Hattenhauer, Darryl. "Ambiguity of Space and Place in Melville's 'The Encantadas,'" *No Dakota Q,* 55, ii (1987), 114–126.
Kellner, Robert S. "Slaves and Shrews: Women in Melville's Short Stories," *Univ Mississippi Stud Engl,* 5 (1984–1987), 301–303.
Lutwack, Leonard. *The Role of Place . . . ,* 132–134.
McCarthy, Paul. "Rascally Characters . . . ," 83–85.
Watson, Charles N. "Melville and the Theme of Timonism: From *Pierre* to *The Confidence Man,*" *Am Lit,* 44 (1972), 401–402; rpt. Budd, Louis J., and Edwin H. Cady, Eds. *On Melville . . . ,* 175–176.

"I and My Chimney"
Bryant, John. "Melville's Comic Debate . . . ," 169–170; rpt. Budd, Louis J., and Edwin H. Cady, Eds. *On Melville . . . ,* 272–273.
Kellner, Robert S. "Slaves and Shrews . . . ," 306–308.
Schaffer, Carl. "Unadmitted Impediments . . . ," 96–101.
*Sealts, Merton M. "Herman Melville's 'I and My Chimney,'" in Budd, Louis J., and Edwin H. Cady, Eds. *On Melville . . . ,* 10–22.

"Jimmy Rose"
McCarthy, Paul. "Rascally Characters . . . ," 78–79.
*Slater, Judith. "The Domestic Adventurer . . . ," 90–92.
Watson, Charles N. "Melville and the Theme of Timonism . . . ," 404–406; rpt. Budd, Louis J., and Edwin H. Cady, Eds. *On Melville . . . ,* 10–22.

"The Lightning-Rod Man"
McCarthy, Paul. "Rascally Characters . . . ," 80–81.
*Slater, Judith. "The Domestic Adventurer . . . ," 87–90.

"The Paradise of Bachelors and the Tartarus of Maids"
Kellner, Robert S. "Slaves and Shrews . . . ," 298–300.
Lutwack, Leonard. *The Role of Place . . . ,* 129–131.
Person, Leland S. *Aesthetic Headaches . . . ,* 88–91.
*Rowland, Beryl. "Melville's Bachelors and Maids: Interpretation Through Symbol and Metaphor," in Budd, Louis J., and Edwin H. Cady, Eds. *On Melville . . . ,* 155–171.
Thomas, Brook. *Cross-Examinations . . . ,* 177–180.

"The Piazza"
Dryden, Edgar A. *The Form . . . ,* 67–75.
Kellner, Robert S. "Slaves and Shrews . . . ," 303–306.
Person, Leland S. *Aesthetic Headaches . . . ,* 91–93.
*Slater, Judith. "The Domestic Adventurer . . . ," 94–96.

"The Two Temples"
McCarthy, Paul. "Rascally Characters . . . ," 79–80.

ALFRED MENDES

"Boodhoo"
Carby, Hazel V. "Proletarian or Revolutionary Literature: C. L. R. James and
the Politics of the Trinidadian Renaissance," *So Atlantic Q,* 87 (1988), 48–
49.

MIGUEL MÉNDEZ [same as C. MIGUEL MÉNDEZ and M. MIGUEL MÉNDEZ]

"Tata Casehua"
Alarcón, Justo. "La aventura del héroe como estructura mitica en 'Tata Casehua' de Miguel Méndez," *Explicación de Textos Literarios,* 15, ii (1986–1987),
77–91.
Lerat, Christian. "Problématique de la survie et de la Renaissance dans 'Tata
Casehua' de Miguel Méndez," in Beranger, Jean, et al. [3], Eds. *Multilinguisme et multiculturalisme . . . ,* 21–32.

ALVARO MENÉNDEZ LEAL [same as ALVARO MENÉN DESLEAL]

"Fire and Ice"
Menton, Seymour. *El Cuento Hispanoamericano,* II, 3rd ed., 270–272.

JUDITH MERRIL

"Daughters of Earth"
Barr, Marleen S. *Alien to Femininity . . . ,* 6–7.

"That Only a Mother"
Bartter, Martha A. *The Way to Ground Zero . . . ,* 145.
Franklin, H. Bruce. *War Stars . . . ,* 177–178.

JOHN METCALF

"The Eastmill Reception Centre"
Giltrow, Janet. "Life Expectancies," *West Coast R,* 22, i (1987), 64–67.

"The Estuary"
Garebian, Keith. "In the End, a Beginning: The Montreal Story Tellers," in
Struthers, J. R. (Tim), Ed. *The Montreal Story Tellers . . . ,* 199.

"Gentle as Flowers Make the Stones"
Cameron, Barry. "An Approximation of Poetry: Three Stories by John Metcalf," in Struthers, J. R. (Tim), Ed. *The Montreal Story Tellers . . . ,* 160–163.

"The Lady Who Sold Furniture"
Garebian, Keith. "In the End . . . ," 199.

"Polly Ongle"
Garebian, Keith. "In the End . . . ," 201–203.
Giltrow, Janet. "Life Expectancies," 56–61.

"Single Gents Only"
Giltrow, Janet. "Life Expectancies," 62–64.

"The Teeth of My Father"
Cameron, Barry. "An Approximation of Poetry . . . ," 165–168.
Rooke, Constance. "Between the World and the Word: John Metcalf's 'The
     Teeth of My Father,'" *New Q,* 7, i–ii (1987), 240–246.

"Travelling Northward"
Giltrow, Janet. "Life Expectancies," 67–69.

"The Years in Exile"
Cameron, Barry. "An Approximation of Poetry . . . ," 163–165.

JOHN METCALFE [WILLIAM JOHN METCALFE]

"Funeral March of a Marionette"
Büssing, Sabine. *Aliens in the Home . . .* , 87.

CHARLOTTE MEWS

"A White Night"
Gilbert, Sandra M., and Susan Gubar. *No Man's Land . . .* , 82–84.

CONRAD FERDINAND MEYER

"The Amulet"
McCort, Dennis. *States of Unconsciousness . . .* , 17–32.

"Gustav Adolf's Page"
McCort, Dennis. *States of Unconsciousness . . .* , 33–76.

"The Sufferings of a Boy"
McCort, Dennis. *States of Unconsciousness . . .* , 77–109.

GUSTAV MEYRINK

"The Urn of St. Gingolph"
Büssing, Sabine. *Aliens in the Home . . .* , 92.

P. SCHUYLER MILLER

"The Cave"
McGregor, Gaile. *The Noble Savage* . . . , 254–255.

SUE MILLER

"Tyler and Brina"
Zinman, Toby S. "The Good Old Days in *The Good Mother*," *Mod Fiction Stud*,
    34 (1988), 410.

SUSAN MINOT

"Lust"
Cassill, R. V. . . . *Instructor's Handbook,* 49–50.

MISHIMA YUKIO

"Death in Midsummer"
Yoshio, Iwamoto. "Mishima Yukio," in Swann, Thomas E., and Kinya Tsuruta,
    Eds. . . . *Modern Japanese Short Story,* 168–177.

"Onnagata"
Yoshio, Iwamoto. "Mishima Yukio," 178–187.

"Patriotism"
Yoshio, Iwamoto. "Mishima Yukio," 188–197.

"Three Million Yen"
Charters, Ann, William E. Sheidley, and Martha Ramsey. *Instructor's Man-
    ual* . . . , 2nd ed., 164–166.

NICHOLASA MOHR

"Herman and Alice"
Mohr, Eugene V. *The Nuyorican Experience* . . . , 81–84.

"Love with Aleluya"
Mohr, Eugene V. *The Nuyorican Experience* . . . , 79.

"Mr. Mendelsohn"
Mohr, Eugene V. *The Nuyorican Experience* . . . , 80.

"The Perfect Little Flower Girl"
Mohr, Eugene V. *The Nuyorican Experience* . . . , 87–88.

"Uncle Claudio"
Mohr, Eugene V. *The Nuyorican Experience* . . . , 78–79.

"A Very Special Pet"
Mohr, Eugene V. *The Nuyorican Experience* . . . , 80–81.

BRIAN MOORE

"Grieve for the Dear Departed"
Dahlie, Hallvard. *Varieties of Exile* . . . , 170–171.

"Uncle T"
Dahlie, Hallvard. *Varieties of Exile* . . . , 171–172.

C[ATHERINE] L. MOORE

"Shambleau"
Lefanu, Sarah. *Feminism and Science Fiction*, 16–17.

GEORGE MOORE

"The Curse of Julia Cahill"
Zimmermann, Georges-Denis. "Conflicting Contexts: Traditional Storytelling
    Performance in Irish Short Stories," in Forsyth, Neil, Ed. *Reading Contexts*,
    111.

"The Wild Goose"
Foster, John W. *Fictions* . . . , 131–133.

WARD MOORE

"Flying Dutchman"
Bartter, Martha A. *The Way to Ground Zero* . . . , 219–220.

"Lot"
Bartter, Martha A. *The Way to Ground Zero* . . . , 224–225.
Franklin, H. Bruce. *War Stars* . . . , 175–176.

"Lot's Daughter"
Bartter, Martha A. *The Way to Ground Zero* . . . , 225.
Franklin, H. Bruce. *War Stars* . . . , 176–177.

MARVEL MORENO

"Algo tan feo en la vida de una señora bien"
Ortega, José. "La alienación femenina en los cuentos de Marvel Moreno," *Mono-
    graphic R*, 4 (1988), 44–47.

"La noche feliz de Madame Yvonne"
Ortega, José. "La alienación femenina . . . ," 48–49.

MORI ŌGAI

"The Dancing Girl"
Rimer, J. Thomas. "Mori Ōgai," in Swann, Thomas E., and Kinya Tsuruta, Eds.
. . . *Modern Japanese Short Story,* 201–209.

"Delusion"
Rimer, J. Thomas. "Mori Ōgai," 214–222.

"The Japanese Neptune"
Okazaki, Yoshie. *Japanese Literature . . . ,* 302–303.

"Under Reconstruction"
Rimer, J. Thomas. "Mori Ōgai," 210–213.

WILLIAM MORRIS

"A Dream"
Hodgson, Amanda. *The Romances . . . ,* 20–23.

"Frank's Sealed Letter"
Hodgson, Amanda. *The Romances . . . ,* 25–26.

"Gertha's Lovers"
Hodgson, Amanda. *The Romances . . . ,* 34–35.

"The Hill of Venus"
Hodgson, Amanda. *The Romances . . . ,* 79–80.

"The Hollow Land"
Hodgson, Amanda. *The Romances . . . ,* 39–44.

"The Story of the Unknown Church"
Hodgson, Amanda. *The Romances . . . ,* 23–25.

"Svend and His Brethren"
Hodgson, Amanda. *The Romances . . . ,* 32–34.

LAZLO MOUSSONG

"Orugananda"
Moussong, Lazlo. "El desenlace de un cuento," *Plural,* 16 (June, 1987), 40–42.

WILLIAM MUDFORD

"The Iron Shroud"
Heller, Terry. *The Delights of Terror . . . ,* 27–28.

MANUEL MÚJICA LÁINEZ

"La galera"
Vidal, Sorkunde F. *La narrativa* . . . , 88–89.

"La gran favorita"
Vidal, Sorkunde F. *La narrativa* . . . , 105.

"La hechizada"
Vidal, Sorkunde F. *La narrativa* . . . , 89–91.

"El hombrecito del azulejo"
Vidal, Sorkunde F. *La narrativa* . . . , 91–96.

"La navegantes"
Vidal, Sorkunde F. *La narrativa* . . . , 103–105.

"La princesa de los camafeos"
Vidal, Sorkunde F. *La narrativa* . . . , 106–107.

"El rey artificial"
Vidal, Sorkunde F. *La narrativa* . . . , 101–102.

"El rey picapedrero"
Vidal, Sorkunde F. *La narrativa* . . . , 99–100.

ALICE MUNRO

"Accident"
Blodgett, E. D. *Alice Munro*, 115–116.
Martin, W. R. *Alice Munro* . . . , 137–141.

"Age of Faith"
Martin, W. R. *Alice Munro* . . . , 200–202.
Stouck, David. *Major Canadian Authors*, 268.

"At the Other Place"
Martin, W. R. *Alice Munro* . . . , 22–25.

"Baptizing"
Stouck, David. *Major Canadian Authors*, 268–269.

"Bardon Bus"
Blodgett, E. D. *Alice Munro*, 116–119.
Irvine, Lorna. *Sub-version* . . . , 102–105.
Martin, W. R. *Alice Munro* . . . , 141–144.

"A Basket of Strawberries"
Martin, W. R. *Alice Munro* . . . , 20–22.

Irvine, Lorna. "Questioning Authority: Alice Munro's Fiction," *Coll Engl Assoc Critic*, 50, i (1987), 59–63.
Martin, W. R. *Alice Munro . . .* , 79–80.

"Memorial"
Blodgett, E. D. *Alice Munro*, 83–84.
Irvine, Lorna. "Questioning Authority . . . ," 63–64.
Martin, W. R. *Alice Munro . . .* , 88–89.

"Miles City, Montana"
Blodgett, E. D. *Alice Munro*, 135–136.

"Mischief"
Martin, W. R. *Alice Munro . . .* , 111–114.

"Mrs. Cross and Mrs. Kidd"
Blodgett, E. D. *Alice Munro*, 122–123.
Martin, W. R. *Alice Munro . . .* , 149–152.

"Monsieur les Deux Chapeaux"
Blodgett, E. D. *Alice Munro*, 137–139.

"The Moon in the Orange Street Skating Rink"
Blodgett, E. D. *Alice Munro*, 131–133.
Martin, W. R. *Alice Munro . . .* , 180–183.

"The Moons of Jupiter"
Blodgett, E. D. *Alice Munro*, 126–129.
Irvine, Lorna. *Sub-version . . .* , 108–109.
Martin, W. R. *Alice Munro . . .* , 157–163.

"The Office"
Blodgett, E. D. *Alice Munro*, 28–29.
Martin, W. R. *Alice Munro . . .* , 53–55.

"The Ottawa Valley"
Blodgett, E. D. *Alice Munro*, 71–72.
Martin, W. R. *Alice Munro . . .* , 89–91.
Stouck, David. *Major Canadian Authors*, 271–272.

"An Ounce of Cure"
Dahlie, Hallvard. *Alice Munro . . .* , 17–18.
Martin, W. R. *Alice Munro . . .* , 37–38.

"The Peace of Utrecht"
Blodgett, E. D. *Configuration . . .* , 68–70.
———. *Alice Munro*, 23–27.
Martin, W. R. *Alice Munro . . .* , 39–45.

"Postcard"
Dahlie, Hallvard. *Alice Munro . . .* , 19.
Martin, W. R. *Alice Munro . . .* , 55–56.

Martin, W. R. *Alice Munro* . . . , 32–34.

"The Time of Death"
Dahlie, Hallvard. *Alice Munro* . . . , 20.
Martin, W. R. *Alice Munro* . . . , 32.

"A Trip to the Coast"
Dahlie, Hallvard. *Alice Munro* . . . , 22–23.

"The Turkey Season"
Blodgett, E. D. *Alice Munro*, 113–114.
Martin, W. R. *Alice Munro* . . . , 136–137.

"Visitors"
Blodgett, E. D. *Alice Munro*, 121–122.
Martin, W. R. *Alice Munro* . . . , 154–157.

"Walker Brothers Cowboys"
Blodgett, E. D. *Alice Munro*, 16–20.
Dahlie, Hallvard. *Alice Munro* . . . , 14–15.
Martin, W. R. *Alice Munro* . . . , 51–52.

"Walking on Water"
Blodgett, E. D. *Configuration* . . . , 70–71.
———. *Alice Munro*, 62–65.
Dahlie, Hallvard. *Alice Munro* . . . , 25.
Martin, W. R. *Alice Munro* . . . , 94–96.
New, W. H. *Dreams of Speech* . . . , 205–207.

"White Dump"
Blodgett, E. D. *Alice Munro*, 142–143.
Martin, W. R. *Alice Munro* . . . , 183–186.

"Who Do You Think You Are?"
Martin, W. R. *Alice Munro* . . . , 122–126.

"The Widower"
Martin, W. R. *Alice Munro* . . . , 17–18.

"Winter Wind"
Martin, W. R. *Alice Munro* . . . , 198–199.

"Wood"
Martin, W. R. *Alice Munro* . . . , 168–170.

ROBERT MUSIL

"Grigia"
Bangerter, Lowell A. *Robert Musil*, 78–83.
Jennings, Michael W. "Robert Musil," in Daviau, Donald G., Ed. . . . *Modern Austrian Literature*, 327–328.

"The Perfection of Love"
Bangerter, Lowell A. *Robert Musil*, 45–51.
Minguez, José M. "La perfección del amor: Sobre un inedito de Musil," *Quimera*, 4 (February, 1981), 4–7.
Nuvoloni, Elena. "Metafora e Silenzio nelle 'Vereinigungen' di Robert Musil," *Quaderni di Lingue e Letteratura*, 11 (1986), 289–313.

"The Portuguese Lady"
Bangerter, Lowell A. *Robert Musil*, 83–90.

"The Temptation of Silent Veronica"
Allais, Kai. "'Geräusche'—Textlichkeit und Serialität: Musils novelle 'Die Versuchung der stillen Veronika,'" in Strutz, Josef, Ed. *Robert Musils "Kakanien"*..., 77–94.
Nuvoloni, Elena. "Metafora e Silenzio...," 289–313.

"Tonka"
Bangerter, Lowell A. *Robert Musil*, 91–96.
Jennings, Michael W. "Robert Musil," 328.
Kontje, Todd. "Motivating Silence: The Recreation of the 'Eternal Feminine' in Robert Musil's 'Tonka,'" *Monatshefte*, 79 (1987), 161–171.
Willemsen, Roger. "Devotionalien—über Musils 'Tonka' und Godards 'Je vous salue, Marie,'" in Strutz, Josef, Ed. *Kunst, Wissenschaft und Politik*..., 81–103.

MBULELO VIZIKHUNGO MZAMANE

"My Cousin and His Pick-up"
Trump, Martin. "Black South African Short Fiction in English," *Research African Lit*, 19, i (1988), 50–51.

VLADIMIR NABOKOV

"Cloud, Castle, Lake"
Parker, Stephen J. ... *Vladimir Nabokov*, 132.

"Lance"
Nicol, Charles. "Nabokov and Science Fiction: 'Lance,'" *Sci-Fiction Stud*, 14, i (1987), 9–20.

"Lik"
Grossmith, Robert. "The Twin Abysses of 'Lik,'" *Nabokovian*, 19 (Fall, 1987), 46–50.

"Lips to Lips"
Barnstead, John A. "Nabokov, Kuzmin, Chekhov, and Gogol: Systems of Reference in 'Lips to Lips,'" in Connolly, Julian W., and Sonia I. Ketchian, Eds. *Studies in Russian Literature*..., 50–60.

"The Return of Chorb"
Green, Geoffrey. *Freud and Nabokov,* 13–17.

"Signs and Symbols"
Dole, Carol M. "Innocent Trifles, or 'Signs and Symbols,'" *Stud Short Fiction,* 24
     (1987), 303–305.
Field, David. "Sacred Dangers: Nabokov's Distorted Reflection in 'Signs and
     Symbols,'" *Stud Short Fiction,* 25 (1988), 285–293.
Parker, Stephen J. . . . *Vladimir Nabokov,* 132–134.
Tookey, Mary. "Nabokov's 'Signs and Symbols,'" *Explicator,* 46, ii (1988), 34–
     36.

"Spring in Fialta"
Parker, Stephen J. . . . *Vladimir Nabokov,* 131–132.
Saputelli, Linda N. "The Long-Drawn Sunset of Fialta," in Connolly, Julian W.,
     and Sonia I. Ketchian, Eds. *Studies in Russian Literature . . . ,* 233–242.

"That in Aleppo Once"
Green, Geoffrey. *Freud and Nabokov,* 65–70.

"Torpid Smoke"
Toker, Leona. "Nabokov's 'Torpid Smoke,'" *Stud Twentieth Century Lit,* 12, ii
     (1988), 239–248.

"The Vane Sisters"
Parker, Stephen J. . . . *Vladimir Nabokov,* 134–135.

NAGAI KAFŪ

"The River Sumida"
Rabson, Steve. "Nagai Kafū," in Swann, Thomas E., and Kinya Tsuruta, Eds.
     . . . *Modern Japanese Short Story,* 225–232.

"A Strange Tale from East of the River"
Rabson, Steve. "Nagai Kafū," 233–240.
Rimer, J. Thomas. *A Reader's Guide . . . ,* 119–120.

YURY NAGIBIN

"The Fiery Archpriest"
Ziolkowski, Margaret. *Hagiography . . . ,* 215–216.

MIKHAIL NAIMY [or NUAYMA]

"Her New Year"
Naimy, Nadim. *Mikhail Naimy . . . ,* 155–156; rpt. Allen, Roger, Ed. *Modern Arabic Literature,* 240–241.

V[IDIADHAR] S[URAJPRASAD] NAIPAUL

"A Christmas Story"
Cudjoe, Selwyn R. *V. S. Naipaul . . .* , 95–96.
Thieme, John. *The Web of Tradition . . .* , 142–143.

"Circus at Luxor"
Nightingale, Peggy. *Journey Through Darkness . . .* , 169–171.

"A Family Reunion"
Cudjoe, Selwyn R. *V. S. Naipaul . . .* , 26–27.

"A Flag on the Island"
Nightingale, Peggy. *Journey Through Darkness . . .* , 95–98.
Thieme, John. *The Web of Tradition . . .* , 144–145.

"Greenie and Yellow"
Thieme, John. *The Web of Tradition . . .* , 143–144.

"Hat"
Thieme, John. *The Web of Tradition . . .* , 28–30.

"In a Free State"
Cudjoe, Selwyn R. *V. S. Naipaul . . .* , 151–156.
Nightingale, Peggy. *Journey Through Darkness . . .* , 161–169.

"Love, Love, Love Alone"
Thieme, John. *The Web of Tradition . . .* , 25–26.

"The Mourners"
Thieme, John. *The Web of Tradition . . .* , 140–141.

"My Aunt Gold Teeth"
Cudjoe, Selwyn R. *V. S. Naipaul . . .* , 27–28.
Thieme, John. *The Web of Tradition . . .* , 141–142.

"The Old Man"
Cudjoe, Selwyn R. *V. S. Naipaul . . .* , 24–26.

"One out of Many"
Cudjoe, Selwyn R. *V. S. Naipaul . . .* , 146–151.
Nightingale, Peggy. *Journey Through Darkness . . .* , 151–156.
Thieme, John. *The Web of Tradition . . .* , 152–154.

"Potatoes"
Cudjoe, Selwyn R. *V. S. Naipaul . . .* , 22–24.

"A Second Visit"
Cudjoe, Selwyn R. *V. S. Naipaul . . .* , 129–130.

"Tell Me Who to Kill"
Nightingale, Peggy. *Journey Through Darkness . . .* , 156–161.

Thieme, John. *The Web of Tradition* . . . , 154–155.

"The Tramp at Piraeus"
Nightingale, Peggy. *Journey Through Darkness* . . . , 150–151.

"Until the Soldiers Came"
Thiem, John. *The Web of Tradition* . . . , 26–27.

NAKAGAMI KENJI

"The Promontory"
Sakurai, Emiko. "Japan's New Generation of Writers," *World Lit Today*, 61
    (1988), 404.

"The Sea of Kareki"
Sakurai, Emiko. "Japan's New Generation . . . ," 404.

R. K. NARAYAN

"An Astrologer's Day"
Jeurkar, R. K. "Narrative Techniques in the Short Stories of R. K. Narayan,"
    in Amur, G. S., V. R. N. Prasad, B. V. Nemade, and N. K. Nihalani, Eds.
    Indian Reading . . . , 111–114.

"A Breach of Promise"
Jeurkar, R. K. "Narrative Techniques . . . ," 114.

"The Roman Image"
Jeurkar, R. K. "Narrative Techniques . . . ," 108–111.

"Under the Banyan Tree"
Charters, Ann, William E. Sheidley, and Martha Ramsey. *Instructor's Man-
    ual* . . . , 2nd ed., 127–128.

ISAAC R. NATHANSON

"The World Aflame"
Bartter, Martha A. *The Way to Ground Zero* . . . , 57–58.

NATSUME SŌSEKI

"Botchan"
Yu, Beongcheon. *Natsume Sōseki*, 46–48.

"The Grass Pillow"
Yu, Beongcheon. *Natsume Sōseki*, 49–51.

"Hearing Things"
Viglielmo, Valdo H. "Natsume Sōseki," in Swann, Thomas E., and Kinya Tsu-
    ruta, Eds. . . . *Modern Japanese Short Story,* 243–254.

"The 'Storm Day'"
Yu, Beongcheon. *Natsume Sōseki,* 51.

"Ten Nights of Dreams"
Viglielmo, Valdo H. "Natsume Sōseki," 255–265.
Yu, Beongcheon. *Natsume Sōseki,* 69–71.

"The Wintry Blast"
Yu, Beongcheon. *Natsume Sōseki,* 51–52.

NJABULOS NDEBELE

"Uncle"
Trump, Martin. "Black South African Short Fiction in English," *Research African
    Lit,* 19, i (1988), 37–38.

JOHN G. NEIHARDT

"The Fading Shadow Flower"
Sundquist, Asebrit. *Pocahontas & Co.* . . . , 110–111.

"The Look in the Face"
Sundquist, Asebrit. *Pocahontas & Co.* . . . , 110.

GÉRARD DE NERVAL [GÉRARD LABRUNIE]

"The Bewitched Hand"
Godfrey, Sima. "Lending a Hand: Nerval, Gautier, Maupassant and the Fan-
    tastic," *Romanic R,* 78 (1987), 75–77.

AMADO NERVO

"Las Casas"
Meléndez, Gloria S. "Reincarnation and Metempsychosis in Amado Nervo's
    Fiction of Fantasy," in Collings, Michael R., Ed. *Reflections on the Fantas-
    tic* . . . , 42–43.

"Diálogos pitagóricos: La proxima encarnación"
Meléndez, Gloria S. "Reincarnation . . . ," 41–42.

EDITH NESBIT

"The Bristol Bowl"
Stetz, Margaret D. "Turning Point: E. Nesbit," *Turn-of-the-Century Women,* 4, ii
    (1987), 2–3.

F. TERRY NEWMAN

"Marius the Doll"
Büssing, Sabine. *Aliens in the Home* . . . , 84–85.

ANAÏS NIN

"Hejda"
Broderick, Catherine. "The Song of the Womanly Soul: Mask and Revelation
   in Japanese Literature and in the Fiction of Anaïs Nin," in Spencer, Sharon,
   Ed. *Anaïs, Art and Artist* . . . , 179–180.

LARRY NIVEN

"The Soft Weapon"
Pierce, John J. *Foundations* . . . , 207.

LINO NOVÁS CALVO

"No le sé desil"
Lichtblau, Myron I. "Modalidades irónicas en 'No le sé desil' de Lino Novás
   Calvo," in Kossoff, A. David, et al. [3], Eds. *Actas del VIII Congreso* . . . , II,
   161–164.

"La noche de Ramón Yendía"
Menton, Seymour. *El Cuento Hispanoamericano*, II, 277–279; 2nd ed., 277–279;
   3rd ed., 171–173.

BETH NUGENT

"City of Boys"
Cassill, R. V. . . . *Instructor's Handbook*, 52–53.

JOYCE CAROL OATES

"At the Seminary"
Allen, Mary. *The Necessary Blankness* . . . , 139; rpt. Bloom, Harold, Ed. *Joyce
   Carol Oates*, 66.
Dean, Sharon. "Oates's 'At the Seminary,'" *Explicator*, 46, ii (1988), 51–52.

"Bodies"
*Sullivan, Walter. "The Artificial Demon: Joyce Carol Oates and the Dimen-
   sions of the Real," in Bloom, Harold, Ed. *Joyce Carol Oates*, 9–10.

"The Children"
Allen, Mary. *The Necessary Blankness* . . . , 149–150; rpt. Bloom, Harold, Ed. *Joyce
   Carol Oates*, 73–74.

"The Dead"
Allen, Mary. *The Necessary Blankness* . . . , 150–151; rpt. Bloom, Harold, Ed. *Joyce Carol Oates,* 74–75.
Bender, Eileen T. *Joyce Carol Oates* . . . , 103–104.
Showalter, Elaine. "Joyce Carol Oates's 'The Dead' and Feminist Criticism," in Kessler-Harris, Alice, and William McBrien, Eds. *Faith of a (Woman) Writer,* 13–19.

"Détente"
Johnson, Greg. *Understanding* . . . , 191–192.

"How I Contemplated the World from the Detroit House of Correction and Began My Life Over Again"
Cassill, R. V. . . . *Instructor's Handbook,* 53–56.
Johnson, Greg. *Understanding* . . . , 109–115.

"In the Region of Ice"
Bender, Eileen T. *Joyce Carol Oates* . . . , 169–173.
Johnson, Greg. *Understanding* . . . , 95–98.

"The Lady with the Pet Dog"
Sheidley, William E., and Ann Charters. *Instructor's Manual* . . . , 188–189; Charters, Ann, William E. Sheidley, and Martha Ramsey. *Instructor's Manual* . . . , 2nd ed., 213–214.

"Last Days"
Bender, Eileen T. *Joyce Carol Oates* . . . , 173–175.
Johnson, Greg. *Understanding* . . . , 183–187.

"The Man Whom Women Adored"
Johnson, Greg. *Understanding* . . . , 187–190.

"My Warszawa: 1980"
Johnson, Greg. *Understanding* . . . , 194–199.

"Normal Love"
Allen, Mary. *The Necessary Blankness* . . . , 144–146; rpt. Bloom, Harold, Ed. *Joyce Carol Oates,* 70–71.

"Old Budapest"
Johnson, Greg. *Understanding* . . . , 193–194.

"Our Wall"
Johnson, Greg. *Understanding* . . . , 190–191.

"Pastoral Blood"
Petite, Joseph. "The Destruction of the Female Eunuch," *J Evolutionary Psych,* 8, iii–iv (1987), 191–193.

"Puzzle"
Allen, Mary. *The Necessary Blankness* . . . , 146–147; rpt. Bloom, Harold, Ed. *Joyce Carol Oates,* 71–72.

"The Sacred Marriage"
Martin, Carol A. "Art and Myth in Joyce Carol Oates's 'The Sacred Marriage,'"
    Midwest Q, 28 (1987), 540–552.

"The Turn of the Screw"
Rüdell, Lioba. "Joyce Carol Oates: 'The Turn of the Screw'—The Writer as
    Mythographer," *Literatur in Wissenschaft,* 20 (1987), 523–539.

"The Wheel of Love"
Johnson, Greg. *Understanding . . . ,* 103–109.

"Where Are You Going, Where Have You Been?"
Allen, Mary. *The Necessary Blankness . . . ,* 141–143; rpt. Bloom, Harold, Ed. *Joyce
    Carol Oates,* 68–70.
Gratz, David K. "Oates's 'Where Are You Going, Where Have You Been?'"
    Explicator, 45, iii (1987), 55–56.
Hurley, C. Harold. "Cracking the Secret Code in Oates's 'Where Are You
    Going, Where Have You Been?'" *Stud Short Fiction,* 24 (1987), 62–66.
Johnson, Greg. *Understanding . . . ,* 98–103.
Petry, Alice H. "Who Is Ellie? Oates' 'Where Are You Going, Where Have You
    Been?'" *Stud Short Fiction,* 25 (1988), 155–157.
Sheidley, William E., and Ann Charters. *Instructor's Manual . . . ,* 182–185;
    Charters, Ann, William E. Sheidley, and Martha Ramsey. *Instructor's Man-
    ual . . . ,* 2nd ed., 209–211.
*Sullivan, Walter. "The Artificial Demon . . . ," 7–8.
Weinberger, G. J. "Who Is Arnold Friend? The Other Self in Joyce Carol
    Oates's 'Where Are You Going, Where Have You Been?'" *Am Imago,* 45
    (1988), 205–215.

"Wild Saturday"
*Sullivan, Walter. "The Artificial Demon . . . ," 8–9.

"You"
*Sullivan, Walter. "The Artificial Demon . . . ," 11.

ŌBA MINAKO

"The Three Crabs"
Tanaka, Yukiko. "Introduction," in Tanaka, Yukiko, and Elizabeth Hanson,
    Eds. *This Kind of Woman . . . ,* xxi.

FITZ-JAMES O'BRIEN

"The Diamond Lens"
Wentworth, Michael. "A Matter of Taste: Fitz-James O'Brien's 'The Diamond
    Lens' and Poe's Aesthetic of Beauty," *Am Transcendental Q,* 2 N.S. (1988),
    271–284.

"A Legend of Barlagh Cave"
Salmonson, Jessica A., Ed. *The Supernatural Tales . . . ,* 156.

"The Lost Room"
Salmonson, Jessica A., Ed. *The Supernatural Tales* . . . , 151–152.

"Seeing the World"
Salmonson, Jessica A., Ed. *The Supernatural Tales* . . . , 154.

TIM O'BRIEN

"Going after Cacciato"
Cassill, R. V. . . . *Instructor's Handbook,* 57–59.

SILVINA OCAMPO

"Autobiography of Irene"
Klingenberg, Patricia N. "The Twisted Mirror: The Fantastic Stories of Silvina
    Ocampo," *Letras Femeninas,* 13, i–ii (1987), 69–70.

"La casa de azúcar"
Klingenberg, Patricia N. "The Twisted Mirror . . . ," 73–74.

"Esparanza en Flores"
Klingenberg, Patricia N. "A Portrait of the Writer as Artist: Silvina Ocampo,"
    Perspectives Contemp Lit, 13 (1987), 60–61.

"Keif"
Perassi, Emilia. "Mito e folclore in Silvina Ocampo," *Quaderni Ibero-Americani,*
    59–60 (1985–1986), 106.

"La liebre dorada"
Perassi, Emilia. "Mito e folclore . . . ," 108–109.

"Malva"
Klingenberg, Patricia N. "The Twisted Mirror . . . ," 76–77.

"Mimoso"
Perassi, Emilia. "Mito e folclore . . . ," 107.

"Nueve Perros"
Perassi, Emilia. "Mito e folclore . . . ," 107–108.

"El vestido de terciopelo"
Klingenberg, Patricia N. "The Twisted Mirror . . . ," 74–78.

"El vestido verde aceituna"
Klingenberg, Patricia N. "A Portrait of the Writer . . . ," 59–60.

"Las vestiduras pelgrosas"
Klingenberg, Patricia N. "A Portrait of the Writer . . . ," 61–63.

FLANNERY O'CONNOR

"The Artificial Nigger"
Desmond, John. *Risen Sons . . .* , 49–50.
Fiondella, Maris G. "Augustine, the 'Letter,' and the Failure of Love in Flannery
    O'Connor's 'The Artificial Nigger,' " *Stud Short Fiction,* 24 (1987), 119–129.
Giannone, Richard. " 'The Artificial Nigger' and the Redemptive Quality of
    Suffering," *Flannery O'Connor Bull,* 12 (1983), 5–16.
————. "The City: Flannery O'Connor's No Kind of Place," *Thought,* 62 (1987),
    31–32.
Paulson, Suzanne M. *Flannery O'Connor . . .* , 75–82.
Strickland, Edward. "The Penitential Quest in 'The Artificial Nigger,' " *Stud
    Short Fiction,* 25 (1988), 453–459.

"The Capture"
Paulson, Suzanne M. *Flannery O'Connor . . .* , 19–21.

"A Circle in the Fire"
Paulson, Suzanne M. *Flannery O'Connor . . .* , 94–96.

"The Comforts of Home"
Paulson, Suzanne M. *Flannery O'Connor . . .* , 31–37.

"The Crop"
Desmond, John. *Risen Sons . . .* , 35.

"The Displaced Person"
Castex, Peggy H. "Demonic Grotesque in Flannery O'Connor's 'The Displaced
    Person': An Exercise in Subversive Ambiguity," in Santraud, Jeanne-Marie,
    Ed. *Le Sud . . .* , 7–20.
Gretlund, Jan N. "The Side of the Road: Flannery O'Connor's Social Sensitiv-
    ity," in Westarp, Karl-Heinz, and Jan N. Gretlund, Eds. *Realist of Dis-
    tances . . .* , 197–207.
Olschner, Leonard M. "Annotations on History and Society in Flannery O'Con-
    nor's 'The Displaced Person,' " *Flannery O'Connor Bull,* 16 (1987), 62–78.
Paulson, Suzanne M. *Flannery O'Connor . . .* , 63–68.
Young, Thomas D. "Flannery O'Connor's View of the South: God's Earth and
    His Universe," *Stud Lit Imagination,* 20, ii (1987), 5–14.

"The Enduring Chill"
Paulson, Suzanne M. *Flannery O'Connor . . .* , 36–39.

"Everything That Rises Must Converge"
Desmond, John. *Risen Sons . . .* , 69–70.
Jauss, David. "Flannery O'Connor's Inverted Saint's Legend," *Stud Short Fiction,*
    25 (1988), 76–78.
Paulson, Suzanne M. *Flannery O'Connor . . .* , 82–84.
Petry, Alice H. "Julian and O'Connor's 'Everything That Rises Must Con-
    verge,' " *Stud Am Fiction,* 15 (1987), 101–108.
————. "O'Connor's 'Everything That Rises Must Converge,' " *Explicator,* 45, iii
    (1987), 51–54.

"The Geranium"

Baumgaertner, Jill P. *Flannery O'Connor.* . . , 25–26.

Darretta, John L. "From 'The Geranium' to 'Judgement Day': Retribution in the Fiction of Flannery O'Connor," in Logsdon, Loren, and Charles W. Mayes, Eds. *Since Flannery O'Connor.* . . , 21–28.

Giannone, Richard. "Flannery O'Connor's Consecration of the End," in Logsdon, Loren, and Charles W. Mayes, Eds. *Since Flannery O'Connor.* . . , 10–13.

———. "The City . . . ," 31.

Paulson, Suzanne M. *Flannery O'Connor.* . . , 16–19.

"Good Country People"

Baumgaertner, Jill P. *Flannery O'Connor.* . . , 33–40.

Burke, William M. "Protagonists and Antagonists in the Fiction of Flannery O'Connor," *Southern Lit J,* 20, ii (1988), 103–107.

Currie, Sheldon. "Freaks and Folks: Comic Imagery in the Fiction of Flannery O'Connor," *Antigonish R,* 62–63 (Summer–Fall, 1985), 134–137.

Montgomery, Marion. "Flannery O'Connor and Onnie Jay Holy and the Trouble with You Innerleckchuls," *Stud Lit Imagination,* 20, ii (1987), 67–70.

Paulson, Suzanne M. *Flannery O'Connor.* . . , 49–53.

Portch, Stephen R. *Literature's Silent Language* . . . , 118–135.

"A Good Man Is Hard to Find"

Desmond, John. *Risen Sons* . . . , 30–31.

Paulson, Suzanne M. *Flannery O'Connor.* . . , 86–91.

Roberts, Edgar V., and Henry E. Jacobs. *Instructor's Manual* . . . , 77–79.

Schenck, Mary J. "Deconstructed Meaning in Two Short Stories by Flannery O'Connor," in Braendlin, Hans P., Ed. *Ambiguities in Literature* . . . , 126–130.

Sheidley, William E., and Ann Charters. *Instructor's Manual* . . . , 158–159; Charters, Ann, William E. Sheidley, and Martha Ramsey. *Instructor's Manual* . . . , 2nd ed., 167–168.

Thompson, Terry. "Doodlebug, Doodlebug: The Misfit in 'A Good Man Is Hard to Find,'" *Notes Contemp Lit,* 17, iv (1987), 8–9.

Walls, Doyle W. "O'Connor's 'A Good Man Is Hard to Find,'" *Explicator,* 46, ii (1988), 43–45.

"Greenleaf"

Desmond, John. *Risen Sons* . . . , 66–68.

Paulson, Suzanne M. *Flannery O'Connor.* . . , 40–45.

*Perrine, Laurence, and Thomas R. Arp. *Instructor's Manual* . . . , 7th ed., 24–26.

"Judgement Day"

Darretta, John L. "From 'The Geranium' . . . ," 21–28.

Giannone, Richard. "Flannery O'Connor's Consecration . . . ," 14–19.

Paulson, Suzanne M. *Flannery O'Connor.* . . , 72–75.

Westarp, Karl-Heinz. "Flannery O'Connor's Development: An Analysis of the Judgment-Day Material," in Westarp, Karl-Heinz, and Jan N. Gretlund, Eds. *Realist of Distances* . . . , 46–54.

"The Lame Shall Enter First"
Paulson, Suzanne M. *Flannery O'Connor...*, 21–24.

"A Late Encounter with the Enemy"
Paulson, Suzanne M. *Flannery O'Connor...*, 56–60.

"The Life You Save May Be Your Own"
Currie, Sheldon. "Freaks and Folks...," 133–134.
Paulson, Suzanne M. *Flannery O'Connor...*, 91–94.
Portch, Stephen R. *Literature's Silent Language...*, 135–143.

"The Misfit"
Vásquez, Mary S. "Two Mourners for the Human Spirit: Ana María Matute and Flannery O'Connor," *Monographic R*, 4 (1988), 51–59.

"Parker's Back"
Archer, Emily. "Naming in the Neighborhood of Being: O'Connor and Percy on Language," *Stud Lit Imagination*, 20, ii (1987), 107–108.
Burke, William M. "Protagonists and Antagonists...," 107–110.
Burns, Dan G. "Flannery O'Connor's 'Parker's Back': The Key to the End," *Notes Contemp Lit*, 17, ii (1987), 11–12.
Desmond, John. *Risen Sons...*, 76–78.
Ficken, Carl. *God's Story...*, 120–130.
Oliver, Bill. "Flannery O'Connor's Compassion," *Flannery O'Connor Bull*, 15 (1986), 9–12.
Paulson, Suzanne M. *Flannery O'Connor...*, 103–111.
Petry, Alice H. "O'Connor's 'Parker's Back,'" *Explicator*, 46, ii (1988), 38–43.

"The Partridge Festival"
Paulson, Suzanne M. *Flannery O'Connor...*, 53–56.

"The Peeler"
Desmond, John. *Risen Sons...*, 39–41.

"Revelation"
Archer, Emily. "Naming in the Neighborhood...," 104–105.
Burke, William M. "Protagonists and Antagonists...," 102–103.
Heher, Michael. "Grotesque Grace in the Factious Commonwealth," *Flannery O'Connor Bull*, 15 (1986), 69–81.
McMillan, Norman. "Dostoevskian Vision in Flannery O'Connor's 'Revelation,'" *Flannery O'Connor Bull*, 16 (1987), 16–22.
Martin, W. R. "A Note on Ruby and Revelation," *Flannery O'Connor Bull*, 16 (1987), 23–25.
Paulson, Suzanne M. *Flannery O'Connor...*, 59–63.
Sloan, LaRue L. "The Rhetoric of the Seer: Eye Imagery in Flannery O'Connor's 'Revelation,'" *Stud Short Fiction*, 25 (1988), 135–145.

"The River"
Baumgaertner, Jill P. *Flannery O'Connor...*, 86–88.
Giannone, Richard. "The City...," 37.
Koelb, Clayton. *Invention of Reading...*, 188–202.
Paulson, Suzanne M. *Flannery O'Connor...*, 96–100.
Schenck, Mary J. "Deconstructed Meaning...," 130–133.

"A Stroke of Good Fortune"
Paulson, Suzanne M. *Flannery O'Connor . . .* , 14–15.

"A Temple of the Holy Ghost"
Oliver, Bill. "Flannery O'Connor's Compassion," 5, 7–9.
Paulson, Suzanne M. *Flannery O'Connor . . .* , 100–103.

"The Train"
Desmond, John. *Risen Sons . . .* , 37–39.

"The Turkey"
Desmond, John. *Risen Sons . . .* , 35–36.

"A View of the Woods"
Budick, Emily. *Fiction . . .* , 65–68.
Coulthard, A. R. "Flannery O'Connor's 'A View of the Woods': A View of the Worst," *Notes Contemp Lit,* 17, i (1987), 7–9.
Desmond, John. *Risen Sons . . .* , 71–73.
Magistrale, Tom. "An Explication of Flannery O'Connor's 'A View of the Woods,'" *Notes Contemp Lit,* 17, i (1987), 6–7.
Paulson, Suzanne M. *Flannery O'Connor . . .* , 24–27.

"The Wildcat"
Desmond, John. *Risen Sons . . .* , 34–35.

FRANK O'CONNOR [MICHAEL O'DONOVAN]

"The Drunkard"
*Perrine, Laurence, and Thomas R. Arp. *Instructor's Manual . . .* , 7th ed., 30–31.

"Guests of the Nation"
Liberman, Michael. "Unforeseen Duty in Frank O'Connor's 'Guests of the Nation,'" *Stud Short Fiction,* 24 (1987), 438–441.
Rafroidi, Patrick. "'Guests of the Nation': 'The Seminal Story of Modern Irish Literature'?" *J Short Story Engl,* 8 (Spring, 1987), 51–57.
Sheidley, William E., and Ann Charters. *Instructor's Manual . . .* , 122–123; Charters, Ann, William E. Sheidley, and Martha Ramsey. *Instructor's Manual . . .* , 2nd ed., 122–123.

"The Mass Island"
Zeiss, Cecelia. "Aspects of the Short Story: A Consideration of Selected Works of Frank O'Connor and Herman Charles Bosman," in Zach, Wolfgang, and Heinz Kosak, Eds. *Literary Interrelations . . .* , II, 127.

"Unapproved Route"
Zeiss, Cecelia. "Aspects of the Short Story . . . ," 124–126.

EUNICE ODIO

"Once There Was a Man"
Vallbona, Rima. "Eunice Odio, a Homeless Writer," trans. Roberto Olivera, in
Urbano, Victoria, Ed. *Five Women Writers . . .*, 45–48.

ŌE KENZABURŌ

"Aghwee the Sky Monster"
Iwamoto, Yoshio. "The 'Mad' World of Ōe Kenzaburō," *J Assoc Teachers Japanese,*
14, i (1979), 71–74.
Wilson, Michiko N. "Ōe's Obsessive Metaphor, Mori, the Idiot Son: Toward the
Imagination of Satire, Regeneration, and Grotesque Realism," *J Japanese
Stud,* 7, i (1981), 29–31.
———. *The Marginal World . . .*, 84–85.

"Cheers"
Wilson, Michiko N. *The Marginal World . . .*, 28–29.

"A Dark River, Heavy Oars"
Wilson, Michiko N. *The Marginal World . . .*, 28.

"The Day He Himself Shall Wipe My Tears Away"
Iwamoto, Yoshio. "The 'Mad' World . . . ," 78–82.

"Father, Where Are You Going?"
Wilson, Michiko N. *The Marginal World . . .*, 61–67.

"Lavish Are the Dead"
Rolf, Robert. "Ōe Kenzaburō," in Swann, Thomas E., and Kinya Tsuruta, Eds.
. . . Modern Japanese Short Story, 269–276.

"Leap Before You Look"
Wilson, Michiko N. *The Marginal World . . .*, 26–28.

"A Political Boy Is Now Dead"
Wilson, Michiko N. *The Marginal World . . .*, 78.

"Prize Stock"
Iwamoto, Yoshio. "The 'Mad' World . . . ," 67–71.
Rolf, Robert. "Ōe Kenzaburō," 277–285.
Wilson, Michiko N. *The Marginal World . . .*, 14–16.

"Sheep"
Wilson, Michiko N. *The Marginal World . . .*, 24–27.

"A Strange Job"
Wilson, Michiko N. *The Marginal World . . .*, 46.

"Teach Us to Outgrow Our Madness"
Iwamoto, Yoshio. "The 'Mad' World . . . ," 74–78.

Wilson, Michiko N. "Ōe's Obsessive Metaphor . . . ," 33–35.
—————. *The Marginal World* . . . , 86–87.

SEAN O'FAOLAIN

"The Bombshop"
Bonaccorso, Richard. . . . *Irish Vision*, 12–13.

"A Broken World"
Bonaccorso, Richard. . . . *Irish Vision*, 55–56.
Murphy, Daniel. *Imagination and Religion* . . . , 77–78.

"The End of the Record"
Bonaccorso, Richard. . . . *Irish Vision*, 95–96.

"Falling Rocks, Narrowing Road, Cul-de-sac, Stop"
Bonaccorso, Richard. . . . *Irish Vision*, 66–67.

"Fugue"
Bonaccorso, Richard. . . . *Irish Vision*, 108–110.

"Hymeneal"
Bonaccorso, Richard. . . . *Irish Vision*, 85–87.

"In the Bosom of the Country"
Bonaccorso, Richard. . . . *Irish Vision*, 98–100.

"A Letter"
Bonaccorso, Richard. . . . *Irish Vision*, 84–85.

"Lord and Master"
Bonaccorso, Richard. . . . *Irish Vision*, 128–129.

"Lovers of the Lake"
Murphy, Daniel. *Imagination and Religion* . . . , 71–73.
Tamplin, Ronald. "Sean O'Faolain's 'Lovers of the Lake,'" *J Short Story Engl*, 8
    (Spring, 1987), 59–69.

"The Man Who Invented Sin"
Murphy, Daniel. *Imagination and Religion* . . . , 75–77.

"Murder at Cobbler's Hulk"
Bonaccorso, Richard. . . . *Irish Vision*, 78–79.

"The Old Master"
Bonaccorso, Richard. . . . *Irish Vision*, 24–25.

"One Man, One Boat, One Girl"
Bonaccorso, Richard. . . . *Irish Vision*, 90–91.

"The Silence of the Valley"
Murphy, Daniel. *Imagination and Religion . . .* , 73–75.

"Teresa"
Bonaccorso, Richard. . . . *Irish Vision,* 80–81.

"A Touch of Autumn in the Air"
Bonaccorso, Richard. . . . *Irish Vision,* 75–76.

"The Trout"
Bonaccorso, Richard. . . . *Irish Vision,* 82–83.

"Up the Bare Stairs"
Bonaccorso, Richard. . . . *Irish Vision,* 3–4.

LIAM O'FLAHERTY

"The Fall of Joseph Timmins"
Gonzalez, Alexander. "Liam O'Flaherty's Urban Short Stories," *Études Irlandaises,* 12, i (1987), 86–91.

"Mackerel for Sale"
Gonzalez, Alexander. ". . . Urban Short Stories," 86–91.

"The Salted Goat"
Murphy, Maureen. "'The Salted Goat': Devil's Bargain or Fable of Faithfulness," *Canadian J Irish Stud,* 5, ii (1979), 60–61.

"The Tramp"
Gonzalez, Alexander. ". . . Urban Short Stories," 86–91.

JOHN O'HARA

"A Family Party"
Monteiro, George. "All in the Family: John O'Hara's Story of a Doctor's Life," *Stud Short Fiction,* 24 (1987), 305–308.

O. HENRY [WILLIAM SYDNEY PORTER]

"According to Their Lights"
Blansfield, Karen C. *Cheap Rooms . . .* , 120.

"Brickdust Row"
Blansfield, Karen C. *Cheap Rooms . . .* , 97–98.

"The Complete Life of John Hopkins"
Blansfield, Karen C. *Cheap Rooms . . .* , 73–75.

"The Cop and the Anthem"
Blansfield, Karen C. *Cheap Rooms . . .* , 118.

"The Ferry of Unfulfillment"
Blansfield, Karen C. *Cheap Rooms* . . . , 96.

"The Green Door"
Blansfield, Karen C. *Cheap Rooms* . . . , 80–82.

"The Guilty Party"
Blansfield, Karen C. *Cheap Rooms* . . . , 116–117.

"A Lickpenny Lover"
Blansfield, Karen C. *Cheap Rooms* . . . , 96–97.

"A Madison Square Arabian Night"
Blansfield, Karen C. *Cheap Rooms* . . . , 111–112.

"Mammon and the Archer"
Blansfield, Karen C. *Cheap Rooms* . . . , 111.

"Man About Town"
Blansfield, Karen C. *Cheap Rooms* . . . , 77–79.

"A Municipal Report"
*Perrine, Laurence, and Thomas R. Arp. *Instructor's Manual* . . . , 7th ed., 40–41.

"Past One at Rooney's"
Blansfield, Karen C. *Cheap Rooms* . . . , 115–116.

"The Pendulum"
Blansfield, Karen C. *Cheap Rooms* . . . , 70–72.

"Proof of the Pudding"
Blansfield, Karen C. *Cheap Rooms* . . . , 56–57.

"Romance of a Busy Broker"
Blansfield, Karen C. *Cheap Rooms* . . . , 106.

"Roses, Ruses and Romance"
Blansfield, Karen C. *Cheap Rooms* . . . , 64–67.

"The Skylight Room"
Blansfield, Karen C. *Cheap Rooms* . . . , 93.

"The Social Triangle"
Blansfield, Karen C. *Cheap Rooms* . . . , 61–64.

"The Third Ingredient"
Blansfield, Karen C. *Cheap Rooms* . . . , 94–95.

"Tobin's Palm"
Blansfield, Karen C. *Cheap Rooms* . . . , 46–47.

"The Voice of the City"
Blansfield, Karen C. *Cheap Rooms* . . . , 76–77.

"While the Auto Waits"
Blansfield, Karen C. *Cheap Rooms* . . . , 55–56.

"The Yellow Day"
Blansfield, Karen C. *Cheap Rooms* . . . , 103–104.

SEUMAS O'KELLY

"The Weaver's Grave"
Tracy, Robert. "Ghosts in the Churchyard: *Ó Cadhain* and Patterns," in Eyler, Audrey, and Robert F. Garratt, Eds. *The Uses of the Past,* 88–89.

PETER OLDALE

"The Problem Child"
Büssing, Sabine. *Aliens in the Home* . . . , 108–109.

MARGARET OLIPHANT

"The Library Window"
Gilbert, Sandra M., and Susan Gubar. *No Man's Land* . . . , 172–173.

ANTONIO OLIVER FRAU

"Chemán el Correcostas"
Melendez, Concha. *El arte del cuento* . . . , 33–34.

"Juan Perdío"
Melendez, Concha. *El arte del cuento* . . . , 36–38.

BOB OLSEN

"The Space Marines and the Slaves"
Kwasniewski, Elizabeth. "Thrilling Structures? Science Fiction from Early *Amazing* and Detective Fiction," *Foundation,* 38 (1987), 27.

TILLIE OLSEN

"Hey Sailor, What Ship?"
Orr, Elaine N. *Tillie Olsen* . . . , 85–92.

"I Stand Here Ironing"
Orr, Elaine N. *Tillie Olsen* . . . , 77–85.

Roberts, Edgar V., and Henry E. Jacobs. *Instructor's Manual . . .* , 79–80.
Sheidley, William E., and Ann Charters. *Instructor's Manual . . .* , 140–141;
    Charters, Ann, William E. Sheidley, and Martha Ramsey. *Instructor's Manual . . .* , 2nd ed., 141–142.

"O Yes"
Orr, Elaine N. *Tillie Olsen . . .* , 92–103.

"Requa"
Orr, Elaine N. *Tillie Olsen . . .* , 121–137.

"Tell Me a Riddle"
Niehus, Edward L., and Teresa Jackson. "Polar Stars, Pyramids, and 'Tell Me a Riddle,'" *Am Notes & Queries*, 24, v–vi (1986), 77–83.

JUAN CARLOS ONETTI

"Dreaded Hell"
Ocampo, Aurora M. "La mujer en 'El infierno tan temido,'" *Texto Crítico*, 6 (July–December, 1980), 223–234.
Rodríguez Alonso, Pilar. "Un aspect del tiempo en los cuentos de Juan Carlos Onetti: Análisis de 'El infierno tan temido,'" *Lexis*, 11, ii (1987), 183–208.

"A Dream Come True"
Turner, Harriet S. "Dinámica reflexiva en dos cuentos de Onetti," in Kossoff, A. David, et al. [3], Eds. *Actas del VIII Congreso . . .* , II, 650–652.

"Jacob and the Other"
Fernández, María L. "Los puntos de vista narrativos en 'Jacob y el otro' de Juan Carlos Onetti," *Letras*, 15–16 (April–August, 1986), 64–75.

"Welcome, Bob"
Turner, Harriet S. "Dinámica reflexiva . . . ," 646–650.

OLIVER ONIONS

"The Beckoning Fair One"
Heller, Terry. *The Delights of Terror . . .* , 57.

YOLANDA OREAMUNO

"High Valley"
Urbano, Victoria. "Reality in the Fiction of 'High Valley,'" trans. Vivian Gruber, in Urbano, Victoria, Ed. *Five Women Writers . . .* , 75–76.

"The Tide Returns at Night"
Bellver, Catherine G. "'The Tide Returns at Night,'" in Urbano, Victoria, Ed. *Five Women Writers . . .* , 77–78.

VLADIMIR ORLOVSKY

"The Revolt of the Atoms"
Pierce, John J. *Foundations . . .* , 180–181.

GEORGE ORWELL

"Animal Farm"
Smyer, Richard I. *Animal Farm . . .* , 39–66.
Wykes, David. *A Preface to Orwell*, 124–133.

SEMBÉNE OUSMANE

"Le Mandat"
Harrow, Kenneth. "The Money Order: False Treasure or True Benefice," in
Anyidoho, Kofi, Abioseh M. Porter, Daniel Racine, and Janice Spleth, Eds.
Interdisciplinary Dimensions . . . , 75–87.

MICHELE OWENS

"We Find Harris Again"
Simpson, Mona. "Michele Owens," in Miller, John H., Ed. *Hot Type . . .* , 128–
129.

AMOS OZ

"Nomads and Viper"
Fuchs, Esther. *Israeli Mythologies . . .* , 63–65.

"Strange Fire"
Fuchs, Esther. *Israeli Mythologies . . .* , 65–67.

"The Trappist Monastery"
Fuchs, Esther. *Israeli Mythologies . . .* , 65.

"Upon This Evil Earth"
Fuchs, Esther. "The Representation of Biblical Women in Israeli Narrative Fic-
tion: Some Transformations and Continuities," in Gelber, Mark H., Ed.
Identity and Ethos . . . , 365–367.

"The Way of the Wind"
Fuchs, Esther. *Israeli Mythologies . . .* , 62–63.

CYNTHIA OZICK

"At Fumicaro"
Lowin, Joseph. *Cynthia Ozick*, 163.

"Bloodshed"
Epstein, Joseph. "Cynthia Ozick, Jewish Writer," *Commentary,* 77, iii (1984), 67–68.
Gertel, Elliot B. "Cynthia Ozick and the 'Jewish' Short Story," *Midstream,* 29, x (1983), 45.
Lowin, Joseph. *Cynthia Ozick,* 59–66.
Pinsker, Sanford. *The Uncompromising Fictions . . . ,* 55–65.
Wisse, Ruth B. "American Jewish Writing, Act II," *Commentary,* 61, vi (1976), 42.

"The Doctor's Wife"
Kauvar, Elaine M. "The Dread of Moloch: Idolatry as Metaphor in Cynthia Ozick's Fiction," *Stud Am Jewish Lit,* 6 (Fall, 1987), 114–116.

"Dreams of Jewish Magic/The Magic of Jewish Dreams"
Pinsker, Sanford. *The Uncompromising Fictions . . . ,* 86–87.

"An Education"
Gertel, Elliot B. "Cynthia Ozick . . . ," 45–46.
Pinsker, Sanford. *The Uncompromising Fictions . . . ,* 72–77.

"Envy; or, Yiddish in America"
Lowin, Joseph. *Cynthia Ozick,* 20–31.
Pinsker, Sanford. *The Uncompromising Fictions . . . ,* 41–47.
Shaked, Gershon. "Shadows of Identity: German-Jewish and American-Jewish Literature—A Comparative Study," trans. Jeffrey Green, in Fried, Lewis, Ed. *Handbook of American-Jewish Literature . . . ,* 405–406.

"Levitation"
Epstein, Joseph. "Cynthia Ozick . . . ," 67.
Lowin, Joseph. "Cynthia Ozick and the Jewish Fantastic," in Gelbert, Mark H., Ed. *Identity and Ethos . . . ,* 317–321; rpt., with changes, in his *Cynthia Ozick,* 73–78.

"A Mercenary"
Gertel, Elliot B. "Cynthia Ozick . . . ," 44–45.
Pinsker, Sanford. *The Uncompromising Fictions . . . ,* 65–72.
Wisse, Ruth B. "American Jewish Writing . . . ," 42.

"The Pagan Rabbi"
Gertel, Elliot B. "Cynthia Ozick . . . ," 45.
Lowin, Joseph. ". . . Jewish Fantastic," 313–317; rpt., with changes, in his *Cynthia Ozick,* 69–73.
Lyons, Bonnie. "Cynthia Ozick as a Jewish Writer," *Stud Am Jewish Lit,* 6 (Fall, 1987), 18–19.
———. "American Jewish Fiction Since 1945," in Fried, Lewis, Ed. *Handbook of American-Jewish Literature . . . ,* 71–72.
Pinsker, Sanford. *The Uncompromising Fictions . . . ,* 33–41.
Rush, Jeffrey. "Talking to Trees: Address as Metaphor in 'The Pagan Rabbi,'" *Stud Am Jewish Lit,* 6 (Fall, 1987), 44–52.
Uffen, Ellen S. "The Levity of Cynthia Ozick," *Stud Am Jewish Lit,* 6 (Fall, 1987), 54–56.

Wisse, Ruth B. "American Jewish Writing . . . ," 41–42.

"Puttermesser and Xanthippe"
Lowin, Joseph. *Cynthia Ozick*, 132–143.
Lyons, Bonnie. "Cynthia Ozick . . . ," 20–22.
Pinsker, Sanford. *The Uncompromising Fictions . . .* , 92–94.
Uffen, Ellen S. "The Levity . . . ," 59.

"Puttermesser: Her Work History, Her Ancestry, Her Afterlife"
Lowin, Joseph. *Cynthia Ozick*, 124–132.

"Rosa"
Bilik, Dorothy S. "Fiction of the Holocaust," in Fried, Lewis, Ed. *Handbook of American-Jewish Literature . . .* , 425–426.
Kauvar, Elaine M. "The Dread of Moloch . . . ," 116–119.
Lowin, Joseph. "Cynthia Ozick, Rewriting Herself: The Road from 'The Shawl' to 'Rosa,'" in Logsdon, Loren, and Charles W. Mayes, Eds. *Since Flannery O'Connor . . .* , 105–111; rpt., with changes, in Lowin, Joseph. *Cynthia Ozick*, 109–121.

"The Sewing Harem"
Pinsker, Sanford. *The Uncompromising Fictions . . .* , 89–90.

"The Shawl"
Charters, Ann, William E. Sheidley, and Martha Ramsey. *Instructor's Manual . . .* , 2nd ed., 179–180.
Lowin, Joseph. "Cynthia Ozick, Rewriting Herself . . . ," 101–105; rpt., with changes, in Lowin, Joseph. *Cynthia Ozick*, 106–109.
Martin, Margot L. "The Theme of Survival in Cynthia Ozick's 'The Shawl,'" *RE: Artes Liberales*, 14, i (1988), 31–36.

"Shots"
Chertok, Haim. "Ozick's Hoofprints," *Yiddish*, 6, iv (1987), 8–11.

"Usurpation (Other People's Stories)"
Criswell, Jeanne S. "Cynthia Ozick and Grace Paley: Diverse Visions in Jewish and Women's Literature," in Logsdon, Loren, and Charles W. Mayes, Eds. *Since Flannery O'Connor . . .* , 93–95.
Gertel, Elliot B. "Cynthia Ozick . . . ," 44.
Lowin, Joseph. *Cynthia Ozick*, 90–105.
Pinsker, Sanford. *The Uncompromising Fictions . . .* , 77–85.
Wisse, Ruth B. "American Jewish Writing . . . ," 42–43.

"Virility"
Criswell, Jeanne S. "Cynthia Ozick and Grace Paley . . . ," 98.
Pinsker, Sanford. *The Uncompromising Fictions . . .* , 47–54.
Uffen, Ellen S. "The Levity . . . ," 57–58.

CRISTINA PACHECO

"La dicha conyugal"
De Valdés, María E. "Feminist Testimonial Literature: Cristina Pacheco, Witness to Women," *Monographic R*, 4 (1988), 157–159.

"La esclavitud"
De Valdés, María E. "Feminist Testimonial . . . ," 156.

"Esposa y mártir"
De Valdés, María E. "Feminist Testimonial . . . ," 155–156.

"Los trabajos perdidos"
De Valdés, María E. "Feminist Testimonial . . . ," 156–157.

JOSÉ EMILIO PACHECO

"August Afternoon"
Jiménez de Báez, Yvette, Diana Morán, and Edith Negrín. *Ficción e historia* . . . , 44–49.

"El castillo en la aguja"
Jiménez de Báez, Yvette, Diana Morán, and Edith Negrín. *Ficción e historia* . . . , 116–118.

"La cautiva"
Bockus Aponte, Barbara. "José Emilio Pacheco, Cuentista," *J Spanish Stud*, 7, i (1979), 15–16; rpt. Verani, Hugo, Ed. *José Emilio Pacheco* . . . , 146–147.

"Civilización y barbarie"
Jiménez de Báez, Yvette, Diana Morán, and Edith Negrín. *Ficción e historia* . . . , 29–33.

"Cuando sali de Habana"
Bockus Aponte, Barbara. "José Emilio Pacheco . . . ," 16–17; rpt. Verani, Hugo, Ed. *José Emilio Pacheco* . . . , 148–149.

"The Fierce Sport"
Bockus Aponte, Barbara. "José Emilio Pacheco . . . ," 18–19; rpt. Verani, Hugo, Ed. *José Emilio Pacheco* . . . , 150–151.
Jiménez de Báez, Yvette, Diana Morán, and Edith Negrín. *Ficción e historia* . . . , 147–153.

"Jericó"
Jiménez de Báez, Yvette, Diana Morán, and Edith Negrín. *Ficción e historia* . . . , 123–124.

"Langenhaus"
Bockus Aponte, Barbara. "José Emilio Pacheco . . . ," 17; rpt. Verani, Hugo, Ed. *José Emilio Pacheco* . . . , 149.

"La luna decapitada"
Jiménez de Báez, Yvette, Diana Morán, and Edith Negrín. *Ficción e historia* . . . , 75–81.

"Parque de diversiones"
Jiménez de Báez, Yvette, Diana Morán, and Edith Negrín. *Ficción e historia* . . . , 59–64.

"El principio del placer"
Bockus Aponte, Barbara. "José Emilio Pacheco . . . ," 10–11; rpt. Verani, Hugo,
    Ed. *José Emilio Pacheco . . .* , 140–141.
Jiménez de Báez, Yvette, Diana Morán, and Edith Negrín. *Ficción e historia . . .* ,
    133–135.

"Tenga para que se entretenda"
Duncan, Cynthia K. "Ghosts of the Past: The Return of Maximilian and Car-
    lotta in Two Contemporary Mexican Short Stories," *Perspectives Contemp Lit,*
    14 (1988), 100–105.

"El viento distante"
Jiménez de Báez, Yvette. "Del texto literario al texto social: 'El viento distante,'"
    in Verani, Hugo, Ed. *José Emilio Pacheco . . .* , 153–170.

NANCY HUDDLESTON PACKER

"Early Morning, Lonely Ride"
Perrine, Laurence, and Thomas R. Arp. *Instructor's Manual . . .* , 7th ed., 61–
    64.

P. K. PAGE

"The Green Bird"
MacCulloch, Clare. *The Neglected Genre . . .* , 57–60.

GRACE PALEY

"A Conversation with My Father"
Criswell, Jeanne S. "Cynthia Ozick and Grace Paley: Diverse Visions in Jewish
    and Women's Literature," in Logsdon, Loren, and Charles W. Mayes, Eds.
    Since Flannery O'Connor . . . , 95–96.
Sheidley, William E., and Ann Charters. *Instructor's Manual . . .* , 154–155;
    Charters, Ann, William E. Sheidley, and Martha Ramsey. *Instructor's Man-
    ual . . .* , 2nd ed., 159–160.

"Goodbye and Good Luck"
Criswell, Jeanne S. "Cynthia Ozick and Grace Paley . . . ," 98–99.
Roberts, Edgar V., and Henry E. Jacobs. *Instructor's Manual . . .* , 80–81.

"The Loudest Voice"
Criswell, Jeanne S. "Cynthia Ozick and Grace Paley . . . ," 96–97.

"Love"
Tracy, Laura. *"Catching the Drift" . . .* , 200–201.

"Ruth and Edie"
Lyons, Bonnie K. "American-Jewish Fiction Since 1945," in Fried, Lewis, Ed.
    Handbook of American-Jewish Literature . . . , 81–82.
Wilde, Alan. *Middle Grounds . . .* , 178–180.

"Love Note"
Kason, Nancy M. *Breaking Traditions* . . . , 57–59.

"Mythological Fantasies"
Kason, Nancy M. *Breaking Traditions* . . . , 43–46.

"The Necromancer"
Kason, Nancy M. *Breaking Traditions* . . . , 60–62.

"Parábola"
Kason, Nancy M. *Breaking Traditions* . . . , 39–41.

"Un paseo extraño"
Kason, Nancy M. *Breaking Traditions* . . . , 75–77.

"Prince Alacrán"
Kason, Nancy M. *Breaking Traditions* . . . , 85–87.

"Las queridas de humo"
Kason, Nancy M. *Breaking Traditions* . . . , 59–60.

"Tengo una gata blanca"
Kason, Nancy M. *Breaking Traditions* . . . , 64–65.

"The Tragic Day"
Kason, Nancy M. *Breaking Traditions* . . . , 48–53.

"La ultima rubia"
Kason, Nancy M. *Breaking Traditions* . . . , 65–67.

"Walpurgis"
Kason, Nancy M. *Breaking Traditions* . . . , 80–81.

"The White Farm"
Kason, Nancy M. *Breaking Traditions* . . . , 93–96.

VANCE PALMER

"The Catch"
Torre, Stephen. "Psyche as Text: The Short Stories of Vance Palmer," *Lit No Queensland,* 15, i (1987), 65–68.

"Father and Son"
Torre, Stephen. "Psyche as Text . . . ," 75–77.

"The Foal"
Torre, Stephen. "Psyche as Text . . . ," 71–72.

"Josie"
Torre, Stephen. "Psyche as Text . . . ," 72–73.

"Mathieson's Wife"
Torre, Stephen. "Psyche as Text . . . ," 68–71.

"The Red Truck"
Torre, Stephen. "Psyche as Text . . . ," 73–75.

ALEXANDROS PAPADIAMANDIS

"Christos Milionis"
Beaton, Roderick. "Realism and Folklore in Nineteenth-Century Greek Fiction," *Byzantine & Mod Greek Stud,* 8 (1983), 117–119.

EMILIA PARDO BAZÁN

"The Drop of Blood"
Hart, Patricia. *The Spanish Sleuth . . .* , 19–20.

DOROTHY PARKER

"The Waltz"
Walker, Nancy A. *A Very Serious Thing . . .* , 32–33.

BORIS PASTERNAK

"The Childhood of Luvers"
Greber, Erika. "Pasternak's 'Detstvo lyuyers' and Dostoevsky's 'Netochka Nezvanova': An Intertextual Approach," *Irish Slavonic Stud,* 9 (1988), 62–79.

WALTER PATER

"Apollo in Picardy"
Buckley, William E. *Walter Pater . . .* , 229–237.
Keefe, Robert and Janice A. *Walter Pater . . .* , 136–143.

"The Child in the House"
Buckley, William E. *Walter Pater . . .* , 186–191.

"Denys L'Auxerrois"
Buckley, William E. *Walter Pater . . .* , 213–220.

"Duke Carl of Rosemold"
Buckley, William E. *Walter Pater . . .* , 220–224.

"Emerald Uthwart"
Buckley, William E. *Walter Pater . . .* , 196–202.

"Sebastian van Storck"
Buckley, William E. *Walter Pater . . .* , 208–213.
Keefe, Robert and Janice A. *Walter Pater . . .* , 28–29.

MANUEL PAYNO

"Amor secreto"
Menton, Seymour. *El Cuento Hispanoamericano,* I, 46–47; 2nd ed., 46–47; 3rd ed., 46–47.

THOMAS LOVE PEACOCK

"Headlong Hall"
Baron, Michael. "Introduction," *"Headlong Hall" and "Gryll Grange,"* xv–xviii.

JONATHAN PENNER

"Emotion Recollected in Tranquillity"
Cassill, R. V. . . . *Instructor's Handbook,* 59–60.

JOSÉ MARÍA DE PEREDA

"Un sabio"
Feeny, Thomas. "Burlesque Krausist Type in Pereda and Clarín," *Hispanic J,* 9, ii (1988), 45–46.

S. J. PERELMAN

"The Idol Eye"
Gale, Steven H. *S. J. Perelman . . .* , 30–31.

ITZAK LEIB PERETZ

"The Pious Cat"
Knox, Israel. "Yitzhok [sic] Leib Peretz: On the Fiftieth Anniversary of His Death," *Jewish Book Annual,* 22 (1964), 81.

RAMÓN PÉREZ DE AYALA

"Miguelín y Margarita"
Casaprima Collera, Adolfo. "La elección de la 'historia' y el 'discurso' en el cuento 'Miguelín y Margarita' de Ramón Pérez de Ayala," *Boletín del Instituto de Estudios Asturianos,* 41 (1987), 283–298.

CRISTINA PERI ROSSI

"El museo de los esfuerzos inútiles"
Rodríguez, Mercedes M. de. "Variaciones del tema del exilio en el mundo alegórico de 'El museo de los esfuerzos inútiles,'" *Monographic R,* 4 (1988), 69–77.

"Unidentified Flying Objects"
Castillo, Debra A. "(De)ciphering Reality in 'Los extraños objetos voladores,'" *Letras Femeninas,* 13, i–ii (1987), 31–41.

LEVI S. PETERSON

"Road to Damascus"
Sondrup, Steven. "Levi Peterson's 'Road to Damascus' and the Language of
    Grace," *Lit & Belief*, 5 (1985), 79–93.

ANN LANE PETRY

"Has Anybody Here Seen Miss Dora Dean?"
Washington, Gladys J. "A World Made Cunningly: A Closer Look at Ann Pe-
    try's Short Fiction," *Coll Lang Assoc J*, 30 (1986), 21.

"In Darkness and Confusion"
Washington, Gladys J. "A World Made Cunningly . . . ," 22.

"Miss Muriel"
Washington, Gladys J. "A World Made Cunningly . . . ," 18–21.

"Mother Africa"
Washington, Gladys J. "A World Made Cunningly . . . ," 21.

"The New Mirror"
Washington, Gladys J. "A World Made Cunningly . . . ," 17–18.

ELIZABETH STUART PHELPS

"The Angel Over the Right Shoulder"
Holly, Carol. "Shaming the Self in 'The Angel Over the Right Shoulder,' " *Am
    Lit*, 60 (1988), 42–60.

LUDWIG PHILIPPSON

"Die Marannen"
Kahn, Lothar. "Neglected Nineteenth-Century German-Jewish Historical Fic-
    tion," in Gelber, Mark H., Ed. *Identity and Ethos* . . . , 164–165.

JAYNE ANNE PHILLIPS

"Cheers"
Charters, Ann, William E. Sheidley, and Martha Ramsey. *Instructor's Man-
    ual* . . . , 2nd ed., 229.

"Counting"
Friedman, Ellen G., and Miriam Fuchs. "Contexts and Continuities: An Intro-
    duction to Women's Experimental Fiction in English," in Friedman,
    Ellen G., and Miriam Fuchs, Eds. *Breaking the Sequence* . . . , 36–37.

"Souvenir"
Cassill, R. V. . . . *Instructor's Handbook*, 60–62.

LOIS PHILLIPS

"The Loop of Time"
Putnam, Ann. "Betrayal and Redemption in the Fiction of Lois Phillips," *So
    Dakota R*, 26, iii (1988), 20–21.

VIRGILIO PIÑERA

"The Album"
Balderston, Daniel. "Lo grotesco en Piñera: Lectura de 'El álbum,'" *Texto Crítico*,
    12 (1986), 174–178.

LUIGI PIRANDELLO

"The Difficulty of Living Like This"
Caputi, Anthony. *Pirandello* . . . , 51–52.

"The Epistle Singer"
Valesio, Paolo. "A Remark on Silence and Listening," *Oral Tradition*, 2, i (1987),
    286–300.

"The First Night"
Caputi, Anthony. *Pirandello* . . . , 40–41.

"A Little Wine"
Caputi, Anthony. *Pirandello* . . . , 121–122.

"Puberty"
Caputi, Anthony. *Pirandello* . . . , 72–73.

"Sunlight and Shadow"
Caputi, Anthony. *Pirandello* . . . , 38–40.

"Visiting the Sick"
Caputi, Anthony. *Pirandello* . . . , 74–75.

"A Voice"
Caputi, Anthony. *Pirandello* . . . , 86–87.

EDGAR ALLAN POE

"The Assignation"
Ketterer, David. "The Sexual Abyss: Consummation in 'The Assignation,'" *Poe
    Stud*, 19, i (1986), 7–10.
Person, Leland S. *Aesthetic Headaches* . . . , 25–28.
Stout, Janis P. *Sodom in Eden* . . . , 60–61.
Wuletich-Brinberg, Sybil. *Poe* . . . , 127–130.

"Berenice"
Bassein, Beth A. *Women and Death* . . . , 50–51.
Dayan, Joan. *Fables of Mind* . . . , 135–158.
Kennedy, J. Gerald. *Poe, Death* . . . , 77–80.
Person, Leland S. *Aesthetic Headaches* . . . , 28–29.
Williams, Michael J. S. *A World of Words* . . . , 83–90.
Wuletich-Brinberg, Sybil. *Poe* . . . , 130–133.

"The Black Cat"
Chai, Leon. *The Romantic Foundations* . . . , 29–38.
Heller, Terry. *The Delights of Terror* . . . , 100–107.
Kennedy, J. Gerald. *Poe, Death* . . . , 135–137.
Morse, David. *American Romanticism, I* . . . , 116–117.
Weaver, Aubrey M. "And Then My Heart with Pleasure Fills . . . ," *J Evolutionary Psych*, 9 (1988), 317–320.
Wuletich-Brinberg, Sybil. *Poe* . . . , 212–213.

"Bon-Bon"
Dayan, Joan. *Fables of Mind* . . . , 203–205.

"The Cask of Amontillado"
Kennedy, J. Gerald. *Poe, Death* . . . , 138–143.
Kirkham, E. Bruce. "Poe's Amontillado, One More Time," *Am Notes & Queries*, 24, ix–x (1986), 144–145.
Perrine, Laurence, and Thomas R. Arp. *Instructor's Manual* . . . , 7th ed., 65–68.
Pribek, Thomas. "The Serpent and the Heel," *Poe Stud*, 20, i (1987), 22–23.
Robertson, Patricia. "Poe's 'The Cask of Amontillado'—Again," *Pubs Arkansas Philol Assoc*, 14, i (1988), 39–49.
Sheidley, William E., and Ann Charters. *Instructor's Manual* . . . , 4–5; Charters, Ann, William E. Sheidley, and Martha Ramsey. *Instructor's Manual* . . . , 2nd ed., 7–8.
Stewart, Kate. "The Supreme Madness: Revenge and the Bells in 'The Cask of Amontillado,'" *Univ Mississippi Stud Engl*, 5 (1984–1987), 51–57.
Wuletich-Brinberg, Sybil. *Poe* . . . , 201–202.

"The Colloquy of Monos and Una"
Kennedy, J. Gerald. *Poe, Death* . . . , 51–53.

"The Conversation of Eiros and Charmion"
Williams, Michael J. S. *A World of Words* . . . , 11–13.

"A Descent into the Maelström"
Madden, Fred. "'A Descent into the Maelström': Suggestions of a Tall Tale," *Stud Hum*, 4, ii (1987), 127–138.
Varnado, S. L. *Haunted Presence* . . . , 71–76.
Wuletich-Brinberg, Sybil. *Poe* . . . , 187–188.

"The Domain of Arnheim"
Dayan, Joan. *Fables of Mind* . . . , 83–104.
Tatsumi, Takayuki. "Poe's Idea of Art: A Study of 'The Domain of Arnheim,'" *Sophia Engl Stud*, 5 (1980), 45–61.
Wuletich-Brinberg, Sybil. *Poe* . . . , 141–143.

"A Dream"
Dayan, Joan. *Fables of Mind* . . . , 194–200.

"The Facts in the Case of M. Valdemar"
Bloom, Clive. *The Occult Experience* . . . , 45–53.
Williams, Michael J. S. *A World of Words* . . . , 106–113.

Wuletich-Brinberg, Sybil. *Poe . . .* , 177–178.

"The Fall of the House of Usher"
Allison, John. "Coleridgean Self-Development: Entrapment and Incest in 'The Fall of the House of Usher,'" *So Central R,* 5, i (1988), 40–47.
Anspach, Sílvia S. "Poe's Pictorial Writing," *Estudios Anglo-Americanos,* 9–11 (1985–1987), 19–20, 21–22, 24.
Bassein, Beth A. *Women and Death . . .* , 52–53.
Beiganowski, Ronald. "The Self-Consuming Narrator in Poe's 'Ligeia' and 'Usher,'" *Am Lit,* 60 (1988), 182–185.
Brunel, Pierre. "Claude Debussy interprète d'Edgar Poe: 'La chute de la maison Usher,'" *Revue de Littérature Comparée,* 243 (1987), 359–368.
Goldman, Arnold. "Poe's Stories of Premature Burial: 'That Ere Kind of Style,'" in Lee, A. Robert, Ed. *Edgar Allan Poe . . .* , 56–60.
Haggerty, George E. *Gothic Fiction . . .* , 91–105.
Hardt, John S. "Doubts in the American Garden: Three Cases of Paradisal Skepticism," *Stud Short Fiction,* 25 (1988), 255–259.
Heller, Terry. *The Delights of Terror . . .* , 126–139.
Jordan, Cynthia S. "Poe's Re-Vision: The Recovery of the Second Story," *Am Lit,* 59 (1987), 5–12.
Kennedy, J. Gerald. *Poe, Death . . .* , 86–88.
Kinkead-Weekes, Mark. "Reflection on, and in, 'The Fall of the House of Usher,'" in Lee, A. Robert, Ed. *Edgar Allan Poe . . .* , 17–34.
Morse, David. *American Romanticism, I . . .* , 109–113.
Person, Leland S. *Aesthetic Headaches . . .* , 34–41.
Reynolds, David S. *Beneath the American Renaissance . . .* , 235–237.
Rosenblat, María. "La nostalgia de la unidad en el cuento fantástico: 'The Fall of the House of Usher' y 'Casa tomada,'" in Burgos, Fernando, Ed. *Los ochenta mundos . . .* , 199–209.
Twitchell, James B. *Forbidden Partners . . .* , 205–206.
Voloshin, Beverly R. "Poe's 'The Fall of the House of Usher,'" *Explicator,* 46, iii (1988), 13–15.
Wuletich-Brinberg, Sybil. *Poe . . .* , 143–148.

"The Gold Bug"
Morse, David. *American Romanticism, I . . .* , 103–105.
Williams, Michael J. S. *A World of Words . . .* , 127–140.

"Hop-Frog"
Shulman, Robert. *Social Criticism . . .* , 178–180.
Williams, Michael J. S. *A World of Words . . .* , 70–71.

"The Imp of the Perverse"
Kennedy, J. Gerald. *Poe, Death . . .* , 137–138.
Williams, Michael J. S. *A World of Words . . .* , 32–36.

"King Pest"
Stout, Janis P. *Sodom in Eden . . .* , 59–60.

"Landor's Cottage"
Dayan, Joan. *Fables of Mind . . .* , 104–129.

"Ligeia"
Andriano, Joseph. "Archetypal Projection in 'Ligeia': A Post-Jungian Reading,"
    Poe Stud, 19, ii (1986), 27–31.
Bassein, Beth A. *Women and Death . . . ,* 51–52.
Beiganowski, Ronald. "The Self-Consuming Narrator . . . ," 178–182.
Chai, Leon. *The Romantic Foundations . . . ,* 23–29.
Dayan, Joan. *Fables of Mind . . . ,* 172–191.
Heller, Terry. *The Delights of Terror . . . ,* 110–119.
Kennedy, J. Gerald. *Poe, Death . . . ,* 82–86.
Morse, David. *American Romanticism, I . . . ,* 107–109.
Person, Leland S. *Aesthetic Headaches . . . ,* 29–34.
Williams, Michael J. S. *A World of Words . . . ,* 90–104.
Wuletich-Brinberg, Sybil. *Poe . . . ,* 138–141.

"Loss of Breath"
Dayan, Joan. *Fables of Mind . . . ,* 205–210.
Williams, Michael J. S. *A World of Words . . . ,* 50–54.

"The Man of the Crowd"
Kennedy, J. Gerald. *Poe, Death . . . ,* 118–119.
Stout, Janis P. *Sodom in Eden . . . ,* 61–62.

"The Man That Was Used Up"
Bloom, Clive. *The Occult Experience . . . ,* 39–40.
Boelhower, William. *Through a Glass Darkly . . . ,* 76–78.
Williams, Michael J. S. *A World of Words . . . ,* 21–24.

"MS. Found in a Bottle"
Beaver, Harold. "Doodling America: Poe's 'MS. Found in a Bottle,'" in Druce,
    Robert, Ed. *A Centre of Excellence . . . ,* 15–27.
Kennedy, J. Gerald. *Poe, Death . . . ,* 23–29.
Varnado, S. L. *Haunted Presence . . . ,* 66–69.
Wuletich-Brinberg, Sybil. *Poe . . . ,* 183–187.

"The Masque of the Red Death"
Cassuto, Leonard. "The Coy Reaper: Unmasque-ing the Red Death," *Stud Short
    Fiction,* 25 (1988), 317–320.
Goodwin, Sarah W. "Poe's 'Masque of the Red Death' and the Dance of Death,"
    in Rosenthal, Bernard, and Paul E. Szarmach, Eds. *Medievalism in American
    Culture . . . ,* 17–28.
Kennedy, J. Gerald. *Poe, Death . . . ,* 201–203.

"Mellonta Tauta"
Williams, Michael J. S. *A World of Words . . . ,* 123–125.

"Metzengerstein"
Kennedy, J. Gerald. *Poe, Death . . . ,* 200–201.
Wuletich-Brinberg, Sybil. *Poe . . . ,* 124–127.

"Morella"
Büssing, Sabine. *Aliens in the Home . . . ,* 82–83.
Dayan, Joan. *Fables of Mind . . . ,* 158–172.

Fukuchi, Curtis. "Repression and Guilt in Poe's 'Morella,'" *Stud Short Fiction*, 24 (1987), 149–154.
Kennedy, J. Gerald. *Poe, Death . . .* , 104–105.
Morse, David. *American Romanticism, I . . .* , 106–107.
Williams, Michael J. S. *A World of Words . . .* , 25–32.
Wuletich-Brinberg, Sybil. *Poe . . .* , 134–138.

"The Murders in the Rue Morgue"
Conger, Syndy M. "Another Secret of the Rue Morgue: Poe's Transformation of the *Geistersehr* Motif," *Stud Short Fiction*, 24 (1987), 9–14.
Day, Leroy T. *Narrative Transgression . . .* , 24–65.
Grella, George. "Poe's Tangled Web," *Armchair Detective*, 21 (1988), 268–275.
Morse, David. *American Romanticism, I . . .* , 98–101.
Rollason, Christopher. "The Detective Myth in Edgar Allan Poe's Dupin Trilogy," in Docherty, Brian, Ed. *American Crime Fiction . . .* , 8–11.
Williams, Michael J. S. *A World of Words . . .* , 141–146.
Woeller, Waltraud, and Bruce Cassiday. *The Literature of Crime . . .* , 56.

"The Mystery of Marie Roget"
Chai, Leon. *The Romantic Foundations . . .* , 116–120.
Jordan, Cynthia S. "Poe's Re-Vision . . . ," 15–16.
Rollason, Christopher. "The Detective Myth . . . ," 12–13.
Woeller, Waltraud, and Bruce Cassiday. *The Literature of Crime . . .* , 56–57.

"The Narrative of Arthur Gordon Pym"
Black, Lynette C. "Pym's Vision Transcribed by 'Le Bateau ivre,'" *Mississippi Q*, 41, i (1987–1988), 3–19.
Goldman, Arnold. "Poe's Stories . . . ," 53–55.
Kennedy, J. Gerald. *Poe, Death . . .* , 145–176.
Lee, A. Robert. "'Impudent and Ingenious Action': Poe's 'The Narrative of Arthur Gordon Pym,'" in Lee, A. Robert, Ed. *Edgar Allan Poe . . .* , 112–134.
Pease, Donald E. *Visionary Compacts . . .* , 195–202.
Richard, Claude. "Le Démon de la perversité," *Dires*, 4 (January, 1986), 29–38.
Smith, Herbert F. "P/P . . . Tekelili: 'Pym' Decoded," *Engl Stud Canada*, 14, i (1988), 82–93.
Tanner, Tony. *Scenes of Nature . . .* , 15–16.
Williams, Michael J. S. *A World of Words . . .* , 125–126.
Wuletich-Brinberg, Sybil. *Poe . . .* , 188–198.

"Never Bet the Devil Your Head"
Williams, Michael J. S. *A World of Words . . .* , 18–19.

"The Oval Portrait"
Aldrich, Elizabeth K. "Musing on the Model, or An American Tradition of Female Life into Art: Henry James in Context," in Forsyth, Neil, Ed. *Reading Contexts*, 167–169.
Anspach, Sílvia S. "Poe's Pictorial Writing," 20–21, 22–23, 24–25.
Bassein, Beth A. *Women and Death . . .* , 53–54.
Kennedy, J. Gerald. *Poe, Death . . .* , 60–63.
Person, Leland S. *Aesthetic Headaches . . .* , 41–44.

Rabkin, Eric. "Fantastic Verbal Portraits of Fantastic Visual Portraits," *Mosaic*, 21, iv (1988), 95.
Sheidley, William E., and Ann Charters. *Instructor's Manual* . . . , 6; Charters, Ann, William E. Sheidley, and Martha Ramsey. *Instructor's Manual* . . . , 2nd ed., 9–10.

"The Pit and the Pendulum"
Haggerty, George E. *Gothic Fiction* . . . , 86–89.
Heller, Terry. *The Delights of Terror* . . . , 30–31.
Marx, Wolfgang. "Des Teufels Skinnerbox," *Horen*, 32, iv (1987), 116–119.

"The Power of Words"
Williams, Michael J. S. *A World of Words* . . . , 13–15.

"A Predicament"
Williams, Michael J. S. *A World of Words* . . . , 19–21.

"The Premature Burial"
Goldman, Arnold. "Poe's Stories . . . ," 60–61.
Kennedy, J. Gerald. *Poe, Death* . . . , 55–59.
Williams, Michael J. S. *A World of Words* . . . , 66–70.

"The Purloined Letter"
*Babener, Liahna K. "The Shadow's Shadow: The Motif of the Double in Edgar Allan Poe's 'The Purloined Letter,'" in Muller, John P., and William J. Richardson, Eds. *The Purloined Poe* . . . , 323–334.
Holland, Norman N. "Re-Covering 'The Purloined Letter': Reading as a Personal Transaction," in Suleiman, Susan R., and Inge Crossman, Eds. *The Reader in the Text* . . . , 350–370; rpt. Muller, John P., and William J. Richardson, Eds. *The Purloined Poe* . . . , 307–322.
Jordan, Cynthia S. "Poe's Re-Vision . . . ," 16–17.
Lacan, Jacques. "Le séminaire sur 'La lettre volée," *Le Psychanalyse*, 2 (1956), 1–44; rpt. in his *Écrits*, 11–61; "Seminar on 'The Purloined Letter,'" trans. Jeffrey Mehlman, *Yale French Stud*, 48 (1972), 39–72; Muller, John P., and William J. Richardson, Eds. *The Purloined Poe* . . . , 28–54.
Morse, David. *American Romanticism, I* . . . , 101–103.
Muller, John. "Negation in 'The Purloined Letter': Hegel, Poe, and Lacan," in Muller, John P., and William J. Richardson, Eds. *The Purloined Poe* . . . , 343–368.
Peraldi, François. "A Note on Time in 'The Purloined Letter,'" in Muller, John P., and William J. Richardson, Eds. *The Purloined Poe* . . . , 335–342.
Porter, Dennis. "Of Poets, Politicians, Policemen, and the Power of Analysis," *New Lit Hist*, 19 (1988), 501–519.
Rollason, Christopher. "The Detective Myth . . . ," 11–12.
Williams, Michael J. S. *A World of Words* . . . , 141–146.
Woeller, Waltraud, and Bruce Cassiday. *The Literature of Crime* . . . , 57.
Wuletich-Brinberg, Sybil. *Poe* . . . , 158–174.

"Shadow—A Parable"
Williams, Michael J. S. *A World of Words* . . . , 54–61.

"Some Words with a Mummy"
Williams, Michael J. S. *A World of Words* . . . , 113–121.

"The Spectacles"
Person, Leland S. *Aesthetic Headaches* . . . , 44–46.
Twitchell, James B. *Forbidden Partners* . . . , 194–199.

"The Tell-Tale Heart"
Heller, Terry. *The Delights of Terror* . . . , 31–32.
Kennedy, J. Gerald. *Poe, Death* . . . , 132–135.
Rajan, Gita. "A Feminist Rereading of Poe's 'The Tell-Tale Heart,'" *Papers Lang
    & Lit*, 24 (1988), 283–300.
Weaver, Aubrey M. "And Then My Heart . . . ," 317–320.
Williams, Michael J. S. *A World of Words* . . . , 36–38.

"Thou Art the Man"
Woeller, Waltraud, and Bruce Cassiday. *The Literature of Crime* . . . , 57.

"The Unparalleled Adventures of One Hans Pfaall"
Wuletich-Brinberg, Sybil. *Poe* . . . , 176–177.

"William Wilson"
Joswick, Thomas. "Who's Master in the House of Poe? A Reading of 'William
    Wilson,'" *Criticism*, 30 (1988), 225–251.
Kennedy, J. Gerald. *Poe, Death* . . . , 128–132.
Morse, David. *American Romanticism, I* . . . , 113–116.
Reynolds, David S. *Beneath the American Renaissance* . . . , 234–235.
Williams, Michael J. S. *A World of Words* . . . , 38–44.
Wuletich-Brinberg, Sybil. *Poe* . . . , 203–212.

FREDERIK POHL

"The Abominable Earthman"
Clareson, Thomas. *Frederik Pohl*, 57–58.

"The Candle Lighter"
Clareson, Thomas. *Frederik Pohl*, 44–45.

"The Census-Taker"
Clareson, Thomas. *Frederik Pohl*, 36–38.

"The Children of the Night"
Clareson, Thomas. *Frederik Pohl*, 77–78.

"The Day of the Boomer Dukes"
Clareson, Thomas. *Frederik Pohl*, 41.

"The Day the Icicle Works Closed"
Clareson, Thomas. *Frederik Pohl*, 52–53.

"The Deadly Mission of Phineas Snodgrass"
Clareson, Thomas. *Frederik Pohl*, 72–73.

"Earth, Farewell!"
Clareson, Thomas. *Frederik Pohl*, 4–5.

"Father of the Stars"
Clareson, Thomas. *Frederik Pohl*, 78–79.

"Fermi and Frost"
Clareson, Thomas. *Frederik Pohl*, 158–159.

"The Five Hells of Orion"
Clareson, Thomas. *Frederik Pohl*, 74–76.

"The Gold at the Starbow's End"
Clareson, Thomas. *Frederik Pohl*, 91–92.

"Happy Birthday, Dear Jesus"
Clareson, Thomas. *Frederik Pohl*, 32–34.

"I Plingot, Who You?"
Clareson, Thomas. *Frederik Pohl*, 47–48.

"Let the Ants Try"
Clareson, Thomas. *Frederik Pohl*, 6–7.

"The Man Who Ate the World"
Clareson, Thomas. *Frederik Pohl*, 50–51.

"The Mapmakers"
Clareson, Thomas. *Frederik Pohl*, 42–43.

"The Midas Plague"
Clareson, Thomas. *Frederik Pohl*, 27–30.

"The Middle of Nowhere"
Clareson, Thomas. *Frederik Pohl*, 46–47.

"My Lady Greensleeves"
Clareson, Thomas. *Frederik Pohl*, 51–52.

"Rafferty's Reasons"
Clareson, Thomas. *Frederik Pohl*, 34–35.

"The Richest Man in Levittown" [originally titled "The Bitterest Pill"]
Clareson, Thomas. *Frederik Pohl*, 55–56.

"The Schematic Man"
Clareson, Thomas. *Frederik Pohl*, 84.

"Shaffery Among the Immortals"
Clareson, Thomas. *Frederik Pohl*, 88–89.

"The Snowmen"
Clareson, Thomas. *Frederik Pohl*, 38–39.

"Some Joys under the Star"
Clareson, Thomas. *Frederik Pohl*, 89–90.

"To See Another Mountain"
Clareson, Thomas. *Frederik Pohl*, 43–44.

"The Tunnel under the World"
Clareson, Thomas. *Frederik Pohl*, 30–32.
Pierce, John J. *Foundations . . .*, 191–192.

"Under Two Moons"
Clareson, Thomas. *Frederik Pohl*, 80–81.

"The Waging of the Peace"
Clareson, Thomas. *Frederik Pohl*, 55.

"Way Up Yonder"
Clareson, Thomas. *Frederik Pohl*, 56–57.

"The Wizards of Pung's Corners"
Clareson, Thomas. *Frederik Pohl*, 53–54.

FREDERIK POHL and CYRIL KORNBLUTH

"Best Friend"
Clareson, Thomas. *Frederik Pohl*, 8–9.

"The Engineer"
Clareson, Thomas. *Frederik Pohl*, 22–23.

JOHN POLIDORI

"The Vampyre"
Senf, Carol A. *The Vampire . . .*, 24–25, 33–41.

MARIO POMILIO

"Cimitero cinesi"
Doni, Rodolfo. "Per una rilettura del 'Cimitero cinesi,'" *Italian Q*, 26 (Winter–
    Spring–Summer, 1985), 51–55.

KATHERINE ANNE PORTER

"The Circus"
Unrue, Darlene H. *Understanding Katherine Anne Porter*, 55–56.

"The Cracked Looking Glass"
Malik, Meera. "Love and Marriage in Katherine Anne Porter," *Panjab Univ Research Bull*, 17, i (1986), 53–54.
Unrue, Darlene H. *Understanding Katherine Anne Porter*, 96–101.

"A Day's Work"
Malik, Meera. "Love and Marriage . . . ," 54–55.
Unrue, Darlene H. *Understanding Katherine Anne Porter*, 101–103.

"The Downward Path to Wisdom"
Unrue, Darlene H. *Understanding Katherine Anne Porter*, 84–86.

"The Fig Tree"
Gibbons, Kaye. "Planes of Language and Time: The Surfaces of the Miranda Stories," *Kenyon R*, 10 N.S. (1988), 77–78.
Scott, Shirley. "Origins of Power in the Fiction of Katherine Anne Porter," *J Evolutionary Psych*, 7, i–ii (1986), 51–52.
Titus, Mary. " 'Mingled Sweetness and Corruption': Katherine Anne Porter's 'The Fig Tree' and 'The Grave,' " *So Atlantic R*, 53, ii (1988), 122–124.
Unrue, Darlene H. *Understanding Katherine Anne Porter*, 56–58.

"Flowering Judas"
Sheidley, William E., and Ann Charters. *Instructor's Manual* . . . , 94–95; Charters, Ann, William E. Sheidley, and Martha Ramsey. *Instructor's Manual* . . . , 2nd ed., 97–99.
Unrue, Darlene H. *Understanding Katherine Anne Porter*, 34–38.

"The Grave"
Bell, Barbara C. "Non-Identical Twins: Nature in 'The Garden Party' and 'The Grave,' " *Comparatist*, 12 (May, 1988), 58–66.
Cheatham, George. "Literary Criticism, Katherine Anne Porter's Consciousness, and the Silver Dove," *Stud Short Fiction*, 25 (1988), 112–114.
Gibbons, Kaye. "Planes of Language . . . ," 79.
Scott, Shirley. "Origins of Power . . . ," 52–55.
Titus, Mary. " 'Mingled Sweetness . . . ,' " 118–122.
Unrue, Darlene H. *Understanding Katherine Anne Porter*, 58–61.

"Hacienda"
Unrue, Darlene H. *Understanding Katherine Anne Porter*, 38–42.

"He"
Unrue, Darlene H. *Understanding Katherine Anne Porter*, 71–74.

"Holiday"
Unrue, Darlene H. *Understanding Katherine Anne Porter*, 86–88.

"The Jilting of Granny Weatherall"
Brinkmeyer, Robert H. " 'Endless Remembering': The Artistic Vision of Katherine Anne Porter," *Mississippi Q*, 40 (1987), 11–15.
Perrine, Laurence, and Thomas R. Arp. *Instructor's Manual* . . . , 7th ed., 69–70.
Unrue, Darlene H. *Understanding Katherine Anne Porter*, 75–78.

"The Journey"
Unrue, Darlene H. *Understanding Katherine Anne Porter,* 52–54.

"The Leaning Tower"
Unrue, Darlene H. *Understanding Katherine Anne Porter,* 112–119.

"Magic"
Unrue, Darlene H. *Understanding Katherine Anne Porter,* 48–50.

"María Concepción"
Unrue, Darlene H. *Understanding Katherine Anne Porter,* 24–28.

"The Martyr"
Unrue, Darlene H. *Understanding Katherine Anne Porter,* 28–31.

"Noon Wine"
Unrue, Darlene H. *Understanding Katherine Anne Porter,* 78–84.

"Old Mortality"
Gibbons, Kaye. "Planes of Language . . . ," 78.
Sullivan, Walter. *A Requiem . . . ,* 3–9.
Unrue, Darlene H. *Understanding Katherine Anne Porter,* 62–67.

"The Old Order"
Brinkmeyer, Robert H. "'Endless Remembering' . . . ," 17–18.
Stout, Janis P. "Miranda's Guarded Speech: Porter and the Problem of Truth-Telling," *Philol Q,* 66 (1987), 259–278.

"Pale Horse, Pale Rider"
Cheatham, George. "Fall and Redemption in 'Pale Horse, Pale Rider,'" *Renascence,* 39 (1987), 396–405.
———. "Literary Criticism . . . ," 114.
Gibbons, Kaye. "Planes of Language . . . ," 78–79.
Malik, Meera. "Love and Marriage . . . ," 55–56.
Unrue, Darlene H. *Understanding Katherine Anne Porter,* 105–112.

"Rope"
Malik, Meera. "Love and Marriage . . . ," 53.
Unrue, Darlene H. *Understanding Katherine Anne Porter,* 91–94.

"The Source"
Unrue, Darlene H. *Understanding Katherine Anne Porter,* 51–52.

"That Tree"
Malik, Meera. "Love and Marriage . . . ," 53.
Unrue, Darlene H. *Understanding Katherine Anne Porter,* 42–44.

"Theft"
Malik, Meera. "Love and Marriage . . . ," 52–53.
Unrue, Darlene H. *Understanding Katherine Anne Porter,* 94–96.

"Virgin Violeta"
Unrue, Darlene H. *Understanding Katherine Anne Porter,* 31–34.

"The Witness"
Gibbons, Kaye. "Planes of Language . . . ," 76–77.

ESTELA PORTILLO TRAMBLEY

"Duende"
Schiavones, James D. "Distinct Voices in the Chicano Short Story: Anaya's Out-
reach, Portillo Trambley's Outcry, Rosaura Sánchez's Outrage," *Americas,*
16, ii (1988), 75–76.

"The Paris Gown"
Parotti, Phillip. "Nature and Symbol in Estela Portillo [Trambley]'s 'The Paris
Gown,'" *Stud Short Fiction,* 24 (1987), 417–424.
Schiavones, James D. "Distinct Voices . . . ," 73–75.

RICHARD POSNER

"Vacation"
McGregor, Gaile. *The Noble Savage . . . ,* 283–284.

J. F. POWERS

"The Lord's Day"
Walters, Kerry S. "The Virago and the Bully: Soul-Paralyzed 'Spouses' in J. F.
Powers' *Prince of Darkness,*" *Cithara,* 28, i (1988), 18–21, 25.

"The Valiant Woman"
Walters, Kerry S. "The Virago and the Bully . . . ," 15–18, 24–25.

REYNOLDS PRICE

"A Chain of Love"
Ficken, Carl. *God's Story . . . ,* 152–161.

V[ICTOR] S[AWDON] PRITCHETT

"Blind Love"
Baldwin, Dean R. *V. S. Pritchett,* 85–87.
Oumhani, Cécile. "Water in V. S. Pritchett's Art of Revealing," *J Short Story
Engl,* 6 (Spring, 1986), 78–81.

"The Camberwell Beauty"
Baldwin, Dean R. *V. S. Pritchett,* 89–90.

"The Cuckoo Clock"
Baldwin, Dean R. *V. S. Pritchett,* 41–42.

"The Diver"
Aquien, Pascal. "'The Diver'; Or, The Plunge into Fantasy," *J Short Story Engl,* 6 (Spring, 1986), 47–57.
Baldwin, Dean R. *V. S. Pritchett,* 87–88.
Oumhani, Cécile. "Water . . . ," 75–77.

"A Family Man"
Baldwin, Dean R. *V. S. Pritchett,* 91–92.

"The Fly in the Ointment"
Baldwin, Dean R. *V. S. Pritchett,* 64–65.
Yvard, Pierre. "V. S. Pritchett and the Short Narrative in 'The Fly in the Ointment,'" *J Short Story Engl,* 6 (Spring, 1986), 111–121.

"Greek Theatre Tragedy"
Baldwin, Dean R. *V. S. Pritchett,* 39–40.

"Handsome Is as Handsome Does"
Baldwin, Dean R. *V. S. Pritchett,* 59–60.
Oumhani, Cécile. "Water . . . ," 84–87.

"The Liars"
Larrière, Claire. "Explosions and Catharses," *J Short Story Engl,* 6 (Spring, 1986), 68–69.

"Many Are Disappointed"
Doze, Genevieve. "Two Tentative Readings of 'Many Are Disappointed' by V. S. Pritchett," *J Short Story Engl,* 6 (Spring, 1986), 59–66.

"The Marvellous Gift"
Baldwin, Dean R. *V. S. Pritchett,* 88–89.

"The Night Worker"
Baldwin, Dean R. *V. S. Pritchett,* 63–64.

"Noise in the Doghouse"
Baldwin, Dean R. *V. S. Pritchett,* 81–82.

"On the Edge of the Cliff"
Baldwin, Dean R. *V. S. Pritchett,* 92–94.
Oumhani, Cécile. "Water . . . ," 81–84.

"Page and Monarch"
Baldwin, Dean R. *V. S. Pritchett,* 56–57.

"Pocock Passes"
Baldwin, Dean R. *V. S. Pritchett,* 65–66.

"The Sailor"
Baldwin, Dean R. *V. S. Pritchett,* 68–71.

"The Saint"
Baldwin, Dean R. *V. S. Pritchett,* 66–68.
Oumhani, Cécile. "Water . . . ," 87–89.

"The Scapegoat"
Baldwin, Dean R. *V. S. Pritchett,* 55–56.

"The Skeleton"
Baldwin, Dean R. *V. S. Pritchett,* 84–85.

"The Spanish Virgin"
Baldwin, Dean R. *V. S. Pritchett,* 38–39.

"The Speech"
Baldwin, Dean R. *V. S. Pritchett,* 83.

"The Two Brothers"
Baldwin, Dean R. *V. S. Pritchett,* 58–59.

"The Voice"
Larrière, Claire. "Explosions and Catharses," 69–70.

"The Wheelbarrow"
Baldwin, Dean R. *V. S. Pritchett,* 79–80.

"The White Rabbit"
Baldwin, Dean R. *V. S. Pritchett,* 40–41.

"You Make Your Own Life"
Baldwin, Dean R. *V. S. Pritchett,* 57–58.

MARCEL PROUST

"Mélancolique villégiature de Mme de Breyves"
Keller, Luzius. "Prousts Erzählung 'Mélancolique villégiature de Mme de
    Breyves,'" in Keller, Luzius, and André Oeschger, Eds. *Marcel Proust . . . ,*
    116–131.

"La Mort de Baldassare Silvande"
Oeschger, André. "Die Funktion der Epigraphe in 'La Mort de Baldassare
    Silvande,'" in Keller, Luzius, and André Oeschger, Eds. *Marcel Proust . . . ,*
    132–159.

"Le Petit Pan de mur jaune"
La Grenadière, Philippe de. "Pour en finir avec Oedipe," *La Quinzaine Littéraire,*
    481 (March 1–15, 1987), 12.

"A Young Girl's Confession"
Gunn, Daniel. *Psychoanalysis and Fiction . . . ,* 198–200.

JAMES PURDY

"Color of Darkness"
Freese, Peter. *Die amerikanische Kurzgeschichte* . . . , 337–339.

"Don't Call Me by My Right Name"
Freese, Peter. *Die amerikanische Kurzgeschichte* . . . , 344–345.

"Encore"
Freese, Peter. *Die amerikanische Kurzgeschichte* . . . , 342–343.

"Eventide"
Freese, Peter. *Die amerikanische Kurzgeschichte* . . . , 341–342.

"Man and Wife"
Freese, Peter. *Die amerikanische Kurzgeschichte* . . . , 345–346.

"Night and Day"
Freese, Peter. *Die amerikanische Kurzgeschichte* . . . , 339–340.

"Plan Now to Attend"
Fick, Thomas H. "Reading a Dummy: James Purdy's 'Plan Now to Attend,'"
    Stud Short Fiction, 25 (1988), 13–19.

"Why Can't They Tell You Why?"
Freese, Peter. *Die amerikanische Kurzgeschichte* . . . , 332–337.

ALEXANDER PUSHKIN

"The Queen of Spades"
Žekulin, Gleb. "And in Conclusion, Who Is Tomsky?: Rereading 'The Queen
    of Spades,'" *Transcriptions/Zapiski*, 20 (1988), 71–79.

"The Stationmaster" [same as "The Post-Stage Master"]
Dimri, J. P., and Charumati Ramdas. "Socio-Historical Context of Literature:
    The Response of Indian Readers to A. S. Pushkin's 'The Stationmaster,'"
    Lit Criterion, 22, i (1987), 10–17.
Feuer, Kathryn B. "Three Easy Pieces: Izmailov to Pushkin; Pushkin to Gogol;
    Gogol to Balzac," in Flier, Michael S., and Simon Karlinsky, Eds. *Language,
    Literature, Linguistics* . . . , 33–34.

BARBARA PYM

"Across a Crowded Room"
Ross, Janice. *The World* . . . , 39–40.

THOMAS PYNCHON

"Entropy"
Moore, Thomas. *The Style of Connectedness* . . . , 161–165.
Seed, David. *The Fictional Labyrinths* . . . , 35–52.

"Low-Lands"
Seed, David. *The Fictional Labyrinths* . . . , 23–35.

"Mortality and Mercy in Vienna"
Seed, David. *The Fictional Labyrinths* . . . , 18–23.
Tylee, Claire M. " 'Spot This Mumbo Jumbo': Thomas Pynchon's Emblems for
    American Culture in 'Mortality and Mercy in Vienna,' " *Pynchon Notes*, 17
    (Fall, 1985), 52–72.

"The Secret Integration"
Seed, David. *The Fictional Labyrinths* . . . , 63–70.

"Under the Rose"
Seed, David. *The Fictional Labyrinths* . . . , 52–63.

ABD AL-HAKIM QASIM

"The Journey"
Khashaba, Sami. "Abd al-Hakim Qasim," trans. Roger Allen, in Allen, Roger,
    Ed. *Modern Arabic Literature*, 249–250.

LUIS QUERO CHIESA

"Detrás de aquella lucesita"
Melendez, Concha. *El arte del cuento* . . . , 166–167.

"La protesta"
Melendez, Concha. *El arte del cuento* . . . , 165–166.

HORACIO QUIROGA

"Anaconda"
Spell, Jefferson R. . . . *Spanish-American Fiction*, 170–171.

"The Dead Man"
Menton, Seymour. *El Cuento Hispanoamericano*, II, 15–17; 2nd ed., 15–17; 3rd
    ed., 229–231.

"Hired Hands"
Spell, Jefferson R. . . . *Spanish-American Fiction*, 167–168.

"Juan Darién"
Echevarría, Evelio. "Jack London y Horacio Quiroga," *Revista Iberoamericana*,
    53 (1987), 637–638.

"Las rayas"
Puccini, Darío. "Otra nueva lectura de 'Las rayas' de Horacio Quiroga," *His-
    pamerica*, 17 (August, 1988), 109–114.

JUAN ANTONIO RAMOS

"Elpidia Figueroa"
Lugo Filippi, Carmen. "Juan Antonio Ramos: A Feminist Writer?" in Rodríguez
de Laguna, Asela, Ed. *Images and Identities . . .* , 147–149.

"Había una vez y dos son tres"
Rosa, William. "El narrador-niño en 'Había una vez y dos son tres,'" *Círculo,*
17 (1988), 123–128.

RAJA RAO

"Akkaya"
Venugopal, C. V. *The Indian Short Story . . .* , 64.

"The Cow of the Barricades"
Harrex, S. C. "Typology and Modes: Raja Rao's Experiments in Short Story,"
World Lit Today, 62 (1988), 592.
Venugopal, C. V. *The Indian Short Story . . .* , 66.

"Javni"
Venugopal, C. V. *The Indian Short Story . . .* , 63–64.

"The Policeman and the Rose"
Harrex, S. C. "Typology and Modes . . . ," 593–595.

VALENTIN GRIGOREVICH RASPUTIN

"Borrowed Time"
Lowe, David. *Russian Writing Since 1953 . . .* , 88.

"Live and Love"
Winchell, Margaret. "'Live and Love': The Spiritual Path of Valentin Rasputin,"
Slavic & East European J, 31 (1987), 533–547.

"Money for Maria"
Lowe, David. *Russian Writing Since 1953 . . .* , 88.

"The Old Woman"
Porter, Robert. "Animal Magic in Solzhenitsyn, Rasputin, and Voynovich," *Mod
Lang R,* 82 (1987), 680–681.

"Parting with Matera"
Lowe, David. *Russian Writing Since 1953 . . .* , 88–89.

ISHMAEL REED

"Cab Calloway Stands in for the Moon"
Fox, Robert E. *Conscientious Sorcerers . . .* , 51.

KIT REED

"Winter"
Cassill, R. V. . . . *Instructor's Handbook*, 63–64.

JOSÉ REVUELTAS

"God on This Earth"
Menton, Seymour. *El Cuento Hispanoamericano*, II, 56–58; 2nd ed., 56–58; 3rd
ed., 270–272.

JEAN RHYS [ELLA GWENDOLEN REES WILLIAMS]

"The Bishop's Feast"
Hagley, Carol R. "Ageing in the Fiction of Jean Rhys," *World Lit Written Engl*,
28 (1988), 122–123.

"From a French Prison"
Hagley, Carol R. "Ageing . . . ," 121–122.

"Let Them Call It Jazz"
Hanson, Clare. "Each Other: Images of Otherness in the Short Fiction of Doris
Lessing, Jean Rhys, and Angela Carter," *J Short Story Engl*, 10 (Spring,
1988), 75–77.

"Rapunzel, Rapunzel"
Hagley, Carol R. "Ageing . . . ," 123.

"The Sound of the River"
Brown, Nancy H. "Aspects of the Short Story: A Comparison of Jean Rhys's
'The Sound of the River' with Ernest Hemingway's 'Hills Like White Ele-
phants,'" *Jean Rhys R*, 1, i (1986), 2–13.

"Tigers Are Better Looking"
Hanson, Clare. "Each Other . . . ," 74–75.

"Till September Petronella"
Hagley, Carol R. "Ageing . . . ," 120–121.
Hanson, Clare. "Each Other . . . ," 73–74.

JACK RICHARDSON

"In the Final Year of Grace"
Callens, Jonah. "Initiation in Jack Richardson's 'In the Final Year of Grace,'"
in Debusscher, Gilbert, and Marc Maufort, Eds. *American Literature . . . ,*
163–174.

CARME RIERA

"Te deix, amor, la mar com a penyora"
Nichols, Geraldine C. "Stranger Than Fiction: Fantasy in Short Stories by Matute, Rodoreda, Riera," *Monographic R,* 4 (1988), 40–41.

RICHARD RIVE

"Advance, Retreat" [originally titled "Black Macbeth"]
Trump, Martin. "Black South African Short Fiction in English," *Research African
Lit,* 19, i (1988), 52–53.

"A Man from the Board"
Trump, Martin. "Black South African Short Fiction . . . ," 52–53.

TOMÁS RIVERA

"And the Earth Did Not Part"
Reed, Michael D. "Structural Motif in the Stories of Tomás Rivera," *J Am Stud
Assoc Texas,* 18 (1987), 43–45.
Urioste, Donaldo W. "The Child's Process of Alienation in Tomás Rivera's 'Y
no se lo trago la tierra'," in García, John A., Theresa Córdova, and Juan R.
García, Eds. *The Chicano Struggle . . . ,* 188–190.

"First Holy Communion"
Urioste, Donaldo W. "The Child's Process . . . ," 185–187.

"It Is Painful"
Urioste, Donaldo W. "The Child's Process . . . ," 183–185.

"It Was a Silvery Night"
Reed, Michael D. "Structural Motif . . . ," 42–43.

"The Lost Year"
Urioste, Donaldo W. "The Child's Process . . . ," 180–182.

"The Night of the Blackout"
Urioste, Donaldo W. "The Child's Process . . . ," 187–188.

AUGUSTO ROA BASTOS

"Ajuste de cuentas"
Herszenhorn, Jaime. "Reflexiones sobre la temática de los cuentos de Augusto
Roa Bastos," in Giacoman, Helmy F., Ed. *Homenaje a Augusto Roa Bastos . . . ,*
264.

"Borrador de un informe"
*Rodríguez-Alcalá, Hugo. "Verdad oficial y verdad verdadera: 'Borrador de un
informe,'" in Giacoman, Helmy F., Ed. *Homenaje a Augusto Roa Bastos . . . ,*

279–294; rpt., with changes, in Rodríguez-Alcalá, Hugo. *Narrativa Hispanoamericana*, 39–62.

"Cigarrillos Mauser"
Alegria, Fernando. "'Cigarrillos Mauser,'" in Giacoman, Helmy F., Ed. *Homenaje a Augusto Roa Bastos* . . . , 15–18.

"Contar un cuento"
Ruiz, Mario E. "La introspección auto-crítica en 'Contar un cuento,'" in Giacoman, Helmy F., Ed. *Homenaje a Augusto Roa Bastos* . . . , 269–276.

"Kurupí"
Herszenhorn, Jaime. "Reflexiones . . . ," 265–266.

"Niño-azoté"
Herszenhorn, Jaime. "Reflexiones . . . ," 264–265.

"Pajáro Mosca"
Castillo, Debra A. "Claustrofobia en la academia: 'Pajáro Mosca,'" in Burgos, Fernando, Ed. *Las voces del karaí* . . . , 187–195.
Rodríguez-Alcalá, Hugo. *Narrativa Hispanoamericana*, 63–81.

"The Prisoner"
Menton, Seymour. *El Cuento Hispanoamericano*, II, 291–292; 2nd ed., 291–292; 3rd ed., 185–187.

ALAIN ROBBE-GRILLET

"The Secret Room"
Hayman, David. *Re-Forming the Narrative* . . . , 61–62.

TOM ROBBINS

"The Chink and the Clock People"
Cassill, R. V. . . . *Instructor's Handbook*, 64–65.

CHARLES G. D. ROBERTS

"Strayed"
MacCulloch, Clare. *The Neglected Genre* . . . , 35–37.

KEITH ROBERTS

"The Beautiful One"
Kincaid, Paul. "The Touch of Phantom Hands," in Kincaid, Paul, and Geoff Rippington, Eds. *Keith Roberts*, 30–31.

"Brother John"
Kincaid, Paul. "The Touch . . . ," 17–18.

"The Death of Libby Maynard"
Kincaid, Paul. "The Touch . . . ," 23–24.

"The Everything Man"
Kincaid, Paul. "The Touch . . . ," 24.

"Fragments"
Kincaid, Paul. "The Touch . . . ," 27.

"The God House"
Kincaid, Paul. "The Touch . . . ," 29–30.

"The Grain Kings"
Kincaid, Paul. "The Touch . . . ," 22–23.

"The Inner Wheel"
Kincaid, Paul. "The Touch . . . ," 23.

"The Lady Margaret"
Kincaid, Paul. "The Touch . . . ," 16.

"Lords and Ladies"
Kincaid, Paul. "The Touch . . . ," 18–19.

"The Ministry of Children"
Kincaid, Paul. "The Touch . . . ," 34.

"Monkey and Pru and Sal"
Kincaid, Paul. "The Touch . . . ," 27–29.

"Rand"
Kincaid, Paul. "The Touch . . . ," 31–32.

"The Signaller"
Kincaid, Paul. "The Touch . . . ," 16–17.

"The Sun over a Low Hill"
Kincaid, Paul. "The Touch . . . ," 26–27.

"Usk and Jokeman"
Kincaid, Paul. "The Touch . . . ," 32.

"Weihnachtabend"
Kincaid, Paul. "The Touch . . . ," 20–21.

FRANK M. ROBINSON

"The Fire and the Sword"
McGregor, Gaile. *The Noble Savage* . . . , 256–257.

MARY ROBISON

"Coach"
Cassill, R. V. . . . *Instructor's Handbook,* 66–67.

MERCÈ RODOREDA

"Una carta"
Nichols, Geraldine C. "Stranger Than Fiction: Fantasy in Short Stories by Matute, Rodoreda, Riera," *Monographic R,* 4 (1988), 38–40.

JOSÉ RODRIGUES MIGUÉIS

"Léah"
Kerr, John A. "Some Considerations on Rodrigues Miguéis's 'Léah,'" *World Lit
Today,* 51 (1977), 220–223.

MANUEL ROJAS

"The Glass of Milk"
Menton, Seymour. *El Cuento Hispanoamericano,* II, 110–112; 2nd ed., 110–112;
3rd ed., 324–326.
Scott, Robert. "The Psychological Conflict in Manuel Rojas' 'El vaso de leche,'"
Stud Short Fiction, 24 (1987), 49–56.

JOÃO GUIMARÃES ROSA

"Field of the High Plain"
Perrone, Charles A. "João Guimarães Rosa: An Endless Passage," in King, John,
Ed. *On Modern Latin American Fiction,* 121–122.

"The Third Bank of the River"
Perrone, Charles A. "João Guimarães Rosa . . . ," 129–130.

ROLANDO P. ROSELL

"Reflection of the Times"
Baguio, Tiburcio. "Cebuano Short Stories in the Last Twenty Years," *Solidarity,*
108–109 (1986), 138–139.

ISAAC ROSENFELD

"The Hand That Fed Me"
Harap, Louis. *In the Mainstream . . . ,* 95–96.

"King Solomon"
Harap, Louis. *In the Mainstream* . . . , 96.

J. H. ROSNY [pseudonym JOSEPH HENRI BOEX]

"Another World"
Pierce, John J. *Foundations* . . . , 70–71.

"The Shapes"
Pierce, John J. *Foundations* . . . , 70.

"The Xipéhuz"
Ducommun, Pascal. "Alien Aliens," in Slusser, George E., and Eric S. Rabkin,
Eds. *Aliens* . . . , 37–39.

PHILIP ROTH

"The Conversion of the Jews"
Searles, George J. "The Mouths of Babes: Childhood Epiphany in Roth's 'Conversion of the Jews' and Updike's 'Pigeon Feathers,'" *Stud Short Fiction*, 24 (1987), 59–62.

"Defender of the Faith"
Harap, Louis. *In the Mainstream* . . . , 133–135.
Lyons, Bonnie K. "American-Jewish Fiction Since 1945," in Fried, Lewis, Ed. *Handbook of American-Jewish Literature* . . . , 66–67.
*Perrine, Laurence, and Thomas R. Arp. *Instructor's Manual* . . . , 7th ed., 14–16.
Wirth-Nesher, Hana. "From Newark to Prague: Roth's Place in the American-Jewish Literary Tradition," in Milbauer, Asher, and Donald G. Watson, Eds. *Reading Philip Roth*, 21–22.

"Eli the Fanatic"
Kartiganer, Donald. "Fictions of Metamorphosis: From *Goodbye, Columbus* to *Portnoy's Complaint*," in Millbauer, Asher, and Donald G. Watson, Eds. *Reading Philip Roth*, 86–88.
Novak, Estelle G. "Strangers in a Strange Land: The Homelessness of Roth's Protagonists," in Milbauer, Asher, and Donald G. Watson, Eds. *Reading Philip Roth*, 50–54.
Wirth-Nesher, Hana. "From Newark to Prague . . . ," 22–23.

"Goodbye, Columbus"
Nilsen, Helge N. "On Love and Identity: Neil Klugman's Quest in 'Goodbye, Columbus,'" *Engl Stud*, 68, i (1987), 79–88.

"I Always Wanted You to Admire My Fasting"
Shechner, Mark. *After the Revolution* . . . , 207–209.

"The Prague Orgy"
Milbauer, Asher Z. "Eastern Europe in American-Jewish Writing," in Fried,
    Lewis, Ed. *Handbook of American-Jewish Literature* . . . , 385–386.

GABRIELLE ROY

"L'alouette"
Boucher, Jean-Pierre. "Un receuil de récits briefs: *Ces enfants de ma vie* de Ga-
    brielle Roy," *Canadian Lit,* [n.v.], cxix (1988), 47–48.

"De la truite dans l'eau glacée"
Boucher, Jean-Pierre. "Un receuil . . . ," 50–51.

"Demetrioff"
Boucher, Jean-Pierre. "Un receuil . . . ," 47–49.

"La maison gardée"
Boucher, Jean-Pierre. "Un receuil . . . ," 49–50.

"Vincento"
Boucher, Jean-Pierre. "Un receuil . . . ," 47.

MURILO RUBIÃO

"The Ex-Magician from the Minhota Tavern"
DiAntonio, Robert E. "Biblical Correspondences and Eschatological Question-
    ing in the Metafiction of Murilo Rubião," *World Lit Today,* 62, i (1988), 62–
    64.

"Zacarias the Pyrotechnist"
DiAntonio, Robert E. "Biblical Correspondences . . . ," 65–66.

JUAN RULFO

"En la madrugada"
Rodríguez-Alcalá, Hugo. *Narrativa Hispanoamericana,* 106–124.

"The Heritage of Matilde Archangel"
Mathieu, Corina S. "Algunas observaciones sobre 'La herencia de Matilde Arc-
    ángel' de Juan Rulfo," *Explicación de Textos Literarios,* 16, i (1987–1988), 28–
    37.

"The Hill of the *Comadres*"
Rodríguez-Alcalá, Hugo. *Narrativa Hispanoamericana,* 91–92.

"El llano en llamas"
Rodríguez-Alcalá, Hugo. *Narrativa Hispanoamericana,* 139–172.

"Luvina"
Bruce-Novoa, Juan D. "Rulfo y Arreola: Dos vias hacia lo mismo," *Monographic R*, 4 (1988), 25–32.

"Macario"
Rodríguez-Alcalá, Hugo. *Narrativa Hispanoamericana*, 91.

"The Night They Left Him Alone"
Rodríguez-Alcalá, Hugo. *Narrativa Hispanoamericana*, 92–93.

"No Dogs Bark"
Rodríguez-Alcalá, Hugo. *Narrativa Hispanoamericana*, 125–138.

"Tell Them Not to Kill Me!"
Menton, Seymour. *El Cuento Hispanoamericano*, II, 199–201; 2nd ed., 199–201; 3rd ed., 94–95.

"They Gave Us the Land"
Lorente-Murphy, Silvia. "'Nos han dado la tierra' de Juan Rulfo: Síntesis de una frustración," *Confluencia*, 3, i (1987), 95–100.
Rodríguez-Alcalá, Hugo. *Narrativa Hispanoamericana*, 91.

"We Are Very Poor"
McMurray, George R. *Spanish American Writing . . .* , 49–50.

JOANNA RUSS

"Sword Blades and Poppy Seed"
Lefanu, Sarah. *Feminism and Science Fiction*, 195–198.

"When It Changed"
Lefanu, Sarah. *Feminism and Science Fiction*, 183–185.

MARK RUTHERFORD [WILLIAM HALE WHITE]

"Confessions of a Self-Tormentor"
Harland, Catherine R. *Mark Rutherford . . .* , 95–97.

"A Dream of Two Dimensions"
Harland, Catherine R. *Mark Rutherford . . .* , 148–153.

PINHAS SADEH

"The Death of Abimelech and His Ascent to Heaven in His Mother's Arms"
Fuchs, Esther. "The Representation of Biblical Women in Israeli Narrative Fiction: Some Transformations and Continuities," in Gelber, Mark H., Ed. *Identity and Ethos . . .* , 367–371.

GEORGE SAIKO

"The Bathtub"
Achberger, Friedrich. "George Saiko," in Daviau, Donald G., Ed. . . . *Modern Austrian Literature*, 388–389.

SAKI [HECTOR HUGH MUNRO]

"The Lumber Room"
Büssing, Sabine. *Aliens in the Home* . . . , 70–71.

"The Penance"
Büssing, Sabine. *Aliens in the Home* . . . , 65–66.

"Sredni Vashtar"
Büssing, Sabine. *Aliens in the Home* . . . , 59–61.

SALVADOR SALAZAR ARRUÉ

"La botija"
Menton, Seymour. *El Cuento Hispanoamericano*, II, 85–86; 2nd ed., 85–86; 3rd ed., 299–300.

CARLOS SALAZAR HERRERA

"La saca"
Menton, Seymour. *El Cuento Costarricense*, 24–25.

PEDRO SALINAS

"Cita de los tres"
Spires, Robert C. *Transparent Simulacra* . . . , 135–140.

"Mundo cerrado"
Spires, Robert C. *Transparent Simulacra* . . . , 130–135.

J. D. SALINGER

"Blue Melody"
French, Warren. *J. D. Salinger, Revisited*, 26–28.

"De Daumier-Smith's Blue Period"
Coy, Juan José. *J. D. Salinger*, 69–75.
Freese, Peter. *Die amerikanische Kurzgeschichte* . . . , 161–162.
French, Warren. *J. D. Salinger, Revisited*, 80–83.
*Galloway, David G. "The Love Ethic," in Bloom, Harold, Ed. *J. D. Salinger*, 34–36.

*Goldstein, Bernice and Sanford. "Zen and *Nine Stories*," in Bloom, Harold, Ed. *J. D. Salinger*, 89–92.

"Down at the Dinghy"
Coy, Juan José. *J. D. Salinger*, 41–46.
Freese, Peter. *Die amerikanische Kurzgeschichte . . .* , 147–148.
French, Warren. *J. D. Salinger, Revisited*, 74–76.

"Elaine"
French, Warren. *J. D. Salinger, Revisited*, 22–23.

"For Esmé—With Love and Squalor"
Bawer, Bruce. *Diminishing Fiction . . .* , 170.
Coy, Juan José. *J. D. Salinger*, 53–61.
Freese, Peter. *Die amerikanische Kurzgeschichte . . .* , 129–138.
*French, Warren. *J. D. Salinger, Revisited*, 76–78.
*Galloway, David G. "The Love Ethic," 38–39.
*Goldstein, Bernice and Sanford. "Zen . . . ," 88–89.
Wenke, John. "Sergeant X, Esmé, and the Meaning of Words," *Stud Short Fiction*, 18 (1981), 251–259; rpt. Bloom, Harold, Ed. *J. D. Salinger*, 111–118.
*Wiegand, William. "J. D. Salinger: Seventy-Eight Bananas," in Bloom, Harold, Ed. *J. D. Salinger*, 11.

"Franny"
Aikant, Satish C. "From Alienation to Accommodation: Salinger's *Franny and Zooey*," *Kyushu Am Lit*, [n.v.], (October, 1987), 39–44.
Alsen, Eberhard. *Salinger's Glass Stories . . . ,*" 21–32.
Bawer, Bruce. *Diminishing Fiction . . .* , 175–176.
Coy, Juan José. *J. D. Salinger*, 94–103.
*Galloway, David G. "The Love Ethic," 41–43.
*Wiegand, William. ". . . Seventy-Eight Bananas," 13.

"A Girl I Knew"
French, Warren. *J. D. Salinger, Revisited*, 28–29.

"Hapworth 16, 1924"
Alsen, Eberhard. *Salinger's Glass Stories . . .* , 78–96.
Bawer, Bruce. *Diminishing Fiction . . .* , 180–181.
French, Warren. *J. D. Salinger, Revisited*, 93–94.

"The Inverted Forest"
French, Warren. *J. D. Salinger, Revisited*, 29–32.

"Just Before the War with the Eskimos"
Coy, Juan José. *J. D. Salinger*, 47–52.
Freese, Peter. *Die amerikanische Kurzgeschichte . . .* , 123–127.
French, Warren. *J. D. Salinger, Revisited*, 70–72.

"The Laughing Man"
Coy, Juan José. *J. D. Salinger*, 33–40.
Freese, Peter. *Die amerikanische Kurzgeschichte . . .* , 118–123.
French, Warren. *J. D. Salinger, Revisited*, 72–74.

*Goldstein, Bernice and Sanford. "Zen . . . ," 84–85.

"The Long Debut of Lois Taggett"
French, Warren. *J. D. Salinger, Revisited,* 20–22.

"Once a Week Won't Kill You"
French, Warren. *J. D. Salinger, Revisited,* 22.

"A Perfect Day for Bananafish"
Alsen, Eberhard. *Salinger's Glass Stories . . . ,* 9–20, 202–208.
Bawer, Bruce. *Diminishing Fiction . . . ,* 170–172.
Coy, Juan José. *J. D. Salinger,* 21–26.
Freese, Peter. *Die amerikanische Kurzgeschichte . . . ,* 150–161.
French, Warren. *J. D. Salinger, Revisited,* 66–69.
*Galloway, David G. "The Love Ethic," 36–37.
*Goldstein, Bernice and Sanford. "Zen . . . ," 86–88.
*Wiegand, William. ". . . Seventy-Eight Bananas," 7–8.

"Pretty Mouth and Green My Eyes"
Coy, Juan José. *J. D. Salinger,* 62–68.
Freese, Peter. *Die amerikanische Kurzgeschichte . . . ,* 109–117.

"Raise High the Roof Beam, Carpenters"
Alsen, Eberhard. *Salinger's Glass Stories . . . ,* 33–47.
Bawer, Bruce. *Diminishing Fiction . . . ,* 178–179.
Coy, Juan José. *J. D. Salinger,* 117–128.
French, Warren. *J. D. Salinger, Revisited,* 101–106.
O'Connor, Dennis L. "J. D. Salinger's Religious Pluralism: The Example of 'Raise High the Roof Beam, Carpenters,'" *Southern R,* 20 (1984), 316–322; rpt. Bloom, Harold, Ed. *J. D. Salinger,* 119–134.
*Wiegand, William. ". . . Seventy-Eight Bananas," 13–14.

"Seymour: An Introduction"
Alsen, Eberhard. *Salinger's Glass Stories . . . ,* 63–77.
Bawer, Bruce. *Diminishing Fiction . . . ,* 179–180.
Coy, Juan José. *J. D. Salinger,* 129–141.
French, Warren. *J. D. Salinger, Revisited,* 107–109.
*Schulz, Max F. "Epilogue to 'Seymour: An Introduction': Salinger and the Crisis of Consciousness," in Bloom, Harold, Ed. *J. D. Salinger,* 53–61.

"Slight Rebellion Off Madison"
French, Warren. *J. D. Salinger, Revisited,* 38–39.

"Teddy"
Alsen, Eberhard. *Salinger's Glass Stories . . . ,* 124–125.
Coy, Juan José. *J. D. Salinger,* 76–81.
Freese, Peter. *Die amerikanische Kurzgeschichte . . . ,* 162–165.
French, Warren. *J. D. Salinger, Revisited,* 84–87.
*Goldstein, Bernice and Sanford. "Zen . . . ," 92–93.
*Wiegand, William. ". . . Seventy-Eight Bananas," 12–13.

"Uncle Wiggily in Connecticut"
Coy, Juan José. *J. D. Salinger*, 27–32.
Freese, Peter. *Die amerikanische Kurzgeschichte . . .* , 139–147.
French, Warren. *J. D. Salinger, Revisited*, 69–70.
*Goldstein, Bernice and Sanford. "Zen . . .," 83–84.
*Wiegand, William. ". . . Seventy-Eight Bananas," 10.

"The Varioni Brothers"
French, Warren. *J. D. Salinger, Revisited*, 23–24.

"The Young Folks"
French, Warren. *J. D. Salinger, Revisited*, 18–20.

"A Young Girl in 1941 with No Waist at All"
French, Warren. *J. D. Salinger, Revisited*, 25–26.

"Zooey"
Aikant, Satish C. "From Alienation to Accommodation . . . ," 39–44.
Alsen, Eberhard. *Salinger's Glass Stories . . .* , 48–56.
Bawer, Bruce. *Diminishing Fiction . . .* , 176–178.
Coy, Juan José. *J. D. Salinger*, 104–116.
*Galloway, David G. "The Love Ethic," 43–49.
*Wiegand, William. ". . . Seventy-Eight Bananas," 14–15.

ROSAURA SÁNCHEZ

"Crónica del barrio"
Schiavones, James D. "Distinct Voices in the Chicano Short Story: Anaya's Out-
    reach, Portillo Trambley's Outcry, Rosauro Sánchez's Outrage," *Americas*,
    16, ii (1988), 78–79.

"Una Noche . . ."
Schiavones, James D. "Distinct Voices . . . ," 78.

"Se Arremango Las Mangas"
Schiavones, James D. "Distinct Voices . . . ," 77–78.

GEORGE SAND [ARMANDINE AURORE LUCILE DUPIN]

"Coax"
Crecelius, Kathryn J. "Female Fantastic: The Case of George Sand," *L'Esprit
    Créateur*, 28, iii (1988), 54–55.

"Le Gnome des huîtres"
Crecelius, Kathryn J. "Female Fantastic . . . ," 55.

"L'Orgue"
Crecelius, Kathryn J. "Female Fantastic . . . ," 52.

"Pictordu"
Crecelius, Kathryn J. "Female Fantastic . . . ," 52–53.

"Rêveur"
Crecelius, Kathryn J. "Female Fantastic . . . ," 52.

MANUEL SAN MARTÍN

"Salut y otros misterios"
Brandenberger, Erna. *Estudios . . .* , 290–292.

WILLIAM SANSOM

"A Contest of Ladies"
Peden, William H. "The Short Stories of William Sansom: A Retrospective
    Commentary," *Stud Short Fiction,* 25 (1988), 427.

"Fireman Flower"
Peden, William H. "The Short Stories . . . ," 423.

"Through the Quinquina Glass"
Kirk, Gerald A. "'Through the Quinquina Glass': William Sansom's Coda,"
    Conference Coll Teachers Engl Stud, 51 (September, 1986), 66–72.

"The Wall"
Peden, William H. "The Short Stories . . . ," 422–423.

SAPPER [HERMAN CYRIL McNEILE]

"The Land of Topsy-Turvy"
Parfitt, George. . . . *First World War,* 34–35, 38–39.

FRANK SARGESON

"Beau"
Rhodes, H. Winston. *Frank Sargeson,* 74–75.

"Conversation with My Uncle"
New, W. H. *Dreams of Speech . . .* , 221–224.

"The Hole That Jack Dug"
Daalder, Joost. "'The Hole . . .' as Romance," in Daalder, Joost, Simon During,
    and Peter Simpson. "Three Readings of Sargeson's 'The Hole That Jack
    Dug,'" *SPAN,* 22 (April, 1986), 73–78.
During, Simon. "Reading New Zealand Literature," *Southern R* (Adelaide), 18,
    i (1985), 65–85; rpt., in part, Daalder, Joost, Simon During, and Peter
    Simpson, "Three Readings . . . ," 78–89.
Simpson, Peter. "'The Hole . . .' as Literary Parable," in Daalder, Joost, Simon
    During, and Peter Simpson, "Three Readings . . . ," 89–92.

"I've Lost My Pal"
Rhodes, H. Whitney. *Frank Sargeson*, 69.

"Just Trespassing, Thanks"
Rhodes, H. Whitney. *Frank Sargeson*, 72–73.

"A Man of Good Will"
Rhodes, H. Whitney. *Frank Sargeson*, 55–56.

"Old Man's Story"
Rhodes, H. Whitney. *Frank Sargeson*, 62–63.

"A Piece of Yellow Soap"
Rhodes, H. Whitney. *Frank Sargeson*, 52.

"Sale Day"
Rhodes, H. Whitney. *Frank Sargeson*, 69–70.

"That Summer"
Rhodes, H. Whitney. *Frank Sargeson*, 77–91.

"Three Men"
Rhodes, H. Whitney. *Frank Sargeson*, 64.

"Tod"
Rhodes, H. Whitney. *Frank Sargeson*, 58–59.

"The Undertaker's Story"
Rhodes, H. Whitney. *Frank Sargeson*, 68–69.

"White Man's Burden"
Rhodes, H. Whitney. *Frank Sargeson*, 90–91.

WILLIAM SAROYAN

"The Circus"
Shear, Walter. "Saroyan's Study of Ethnicity," *MELUS*, 13, i–ii (1986), 52–53.

"The Journey to Hanford"
Shear, Walter. "Saroyan's Study . . . ," 50–51.

"A Nice Old-Fashioned Romance with Love Lyrics and Everything"
Shear, Walter. "Saroyan's Study . . . ," 53–54.

"Old Country Advice to the American Traveler"
Shear, Walter. "Saroyan's Study . . . ," 49–50.

"The Pomegranate Trees"
Shear, Walter. "Saroyan's Study . . . ," 51–52.

"The Summer of the Beautiful White Horse"
Shear, Walter. "Saroyan's Study . . . ," 46–47.

JEAN-PAUL SARTRE

"Dépaysement"
Van den Hoven, Adrian. "The Truth of Falsehood: An Analysis of Sartre's
Short Story 'Dépaysement,'" *Univ Windsor R*, 20, i (1987), 71–79.

"Intimacy"
Barnes, Hazel E. *Humanistic Existentialism . . .* , 302–303.

"The Room"
Barnes, Hazel E. *Humanistic Existentialism . . .* , 302.

"The Wall"
Barnes, Hazel E. *Humanistic Existentialism . . .* , 222–223.

CHARLES SATTERWHITE [FREDERIK POHL]

"With Redfern on Capella XII"
Clareson, Thomas. *Frederik Pohl*, 45–46.

MARY M. SCHIDELER

"Mother and the Flying Saucer"
Sammons, Martha C. *"A Better Country" . . .* , 56–57.

ARNO SCHMIDT

"Alexander oder was ist Wahrheit"
Olma, Walter. "Arno Schmidts frühe Erzählung 'Alexander oder was ist Wahr-
heit': Tagebuch einer desillusionierenden Bildungsreise," in Schardt,
Michael M., Ed. *Arno Schmidt . . .* , 98–130.

"Caliban upon Setebos"
Gietema, Erika. "Narrenfreiheit oder Subversion? Versuch einer Funktionali-
sierung des Intertextualitätsbegriffs bei Arno Schmidt in Richtung auf die
humoristische Subjektivität," *Neophilologus*, 72 (1988), 418–433.

"Great Cain"
Steinwenker, Ernst-Dieter. "'And back. And forth': Arno Schmidt's Story 'Great
Cain' as a Dream-Text," trans. F. P. Ott, *R Contemp Fiction*, 8, i (1988), 111–
117.

JAMES SCHMITZ

"Grandpa"
McGregor, Gaile. *The Noble Savage . . .* , 250–251.

MARK SCHORER

"The Face Within the Face"
Petite, Joseph. "Schorer's 'The Face Within the Face,'" *Explicator*, 47, i (1988),
    43–46.

MARCEL SCHWOB

"La Croisade des enfants"
Büssing, Sabine. *Aliens in the Home . . . ,* 50–53.

DUNCAN CAMPBELL SCOTT

"The Bobolink"
New, W. H. *Dreams of Speech . . . ,* 183–184.

"Paul Farlette"
MacCulloch, Clare. *The Neglected Genre . . . ,* 37–39.

WALTER SCOTT

"Wandering Willie's Tale"
Doubleday, Neal F. *Variety of Attempt . . . ,* 49–60.

SEGUNDO SERRANO PONCELA

"El faro"
Brandenberger, Erna. *Estudios . . . ,* 169–170.

"La raya oscura"
Brandenberger, Erna. *Estudios . . . ,* 167–169.

SETOUCHI HARUMI

"Lingering Affection"
Tanaka, Yukiko. "Introduction," in Tanaka, Yukiko, and Elizabeth Hanson,
    Eds. *This Kind of Woman . . . ,* xvii–xix.

EFRAIM SEVELA

"The Sabbath Candleholders"
Milbauer, Asher Z. "Eastern Europe in American-Jewish Writing," in Fried,
    Lewis, Ed. *Handbook of American-Jewish Literature . . . ,* 357–360.

DAVID SHAHAR

"First Lesson"
Sokoloff, Naomi. "Discoveries of Reading: Stories of Childhood by Bialik, Sha-
    har, and Roth," *Hebrew Annual R,* 9 (1985), 333–336.

SHAHNON AHMAD

"Jungle Boar"
Johns, Anthony H. *Cultural Options . . . ,* 112–113.

JANET BEELER SHAW

"No Place To Be on Christmas"
Cassill, R. V. . . . *Instructor's Handbook,* 67–68.

ROBERT SHAW

"Light on Other Days"
Silverberg, Robert. "Three Worlds of Wonder," *Foundation,* 38 (1987), 16–20.

ROBERT SHECKLEY

"Love, Incorporated"
Broege, Valerie. "Technology and Sexuality in Science Fiction: Creating New
    Erotic Interfaces," in Palumbo, Donald, Ed. *Erotic Universe . . . ,* 118–119.

"A Ticket to Tranai"
Broege, Valerie. "Technology and Sexuality . . . ," 127–128.

SHEN CONGWEN

"Aboard and on Shore"
Kinkley, Jeffrey C. *The Odyssey . . . ,* 131–132.

"After Rain"
Kinkley, Jeffrey C. *The Odyssey . . . ,* 144–145.

"Chill"
Kinkley, Jeffrey C. *The Odyssey . . . ,* 216–217.

"Cotton Shoes"
Kinkley, Jeffrey C. *The Odyssey . . . ,* 73–74, 88–91.

"The Day Before He Deserted"
Kinkley, Jeffrey C. *The Odyssey . . . ,* 49–50.

"Dr. Ruomo"
Kinkley, Jeffrey C. *The Odyssey* . . . , 216–219.

"Fishing"
Kinkley, Jeffrey C. *The Odyssey* . . . , 169–170.

"Gazing at a Rainbow"
Kinkley, Jeffrey C. *The Odyssey* . . . , 254–256.

"Holiday Fruit Congee"
Kinkley, Jeffrey C. *The Odyssey* . . . , 115–116.

"Housewife"
Kinkley, Jeffrey C. *The Odyssey* . . . , 219–221.

"In a Private School"
Kinkley, Jeffrey C. *The Odyssey* . . . , 31–32.

"Long Zhu"
Kinkley, Jeffrey C. *The Odyssey* . . . , 152–153.

"The Lovers"
Kinkley, Jeffrey C. *The Odyssey* . . . , 183.

"Meijin, Baozi, and the White Kid"
Kinkley, Jeffrey C. *The Odyssey* . . . , 155–158.

"Mountain Spirit"
Kinkley, Jeffrey C. *The Odyssey* . . . , 163–164.

"My Primary School Education"
Kinkley, Jeffrey C. *The Odyssey* . . . , 25–27.

"The New and the Old"
Kinkley, Jeffrey C. *The Odyssey* . . . , 208–209.

"No. 4"
Kinkley, Jeffrey C. *The Odyssey* . . . , 217.

"Ox"
Kinkley, Jeffrey C. *The Odyssey* . . . , 180–181.

"Portrait of Eight Steeds"
Kinkley, Jeffrey C. *The Odyssey* . . . , 211–216.

"Sansan"
Kinkley, Jeffrey C. *The Odyssey* . . . , 161–163.

"Snow"
Kinkley, Jeffrey C. *The Odyssey* . . . , 131–133.

"Spring"
Kinkley, Jeffrey C. *The Odyssey* . . . , 217.

"Three Women"
Kinkley, Jeffrey C. *The Odyssey* . . . , 214–215.

"Under Moonlight"
Kinkley, Jeffrey C. *The Odyssey* . . . , 152–155.

"Water and Clouds"
Kinkley, Jeffrey C. *The Odyssey* . . . , 256–257.

PAVEL SHESTAKOV

"Fear of Heights"
Woeller, Waltraud, and Bruce Cassiday. *The Literature of Crime* . . . , 161.

"Three Days in Dagerstan"
Woeller, Waltraud, and Bruce Cassiday. *The Literature of Crime* . . . , 161–162.

SHIGA NAOYA

"At Kinosaki"
Fowler, Edward. *The Rhetoric of Confession* . . . , 222–223.
Kohl, Stephen W. "Shiga Naoya," in Swann, Thomas E., and Kinya Tsuruta, Eds. . . . *Modern Japanese Short Story*, 299–307.

"The Bonfire"
Kohl, Stephen W. "Shiga Naoya," 303–315.

"Han's Crime"
Kohl, Stephen W. "Shiga Naoya," 289–298.

"Late Autumn"
Fowler, Edward. *The Rhetoric of Confession* . . . , 200.

"Memories of Yamashina"
Fowler, Edward. *The Rhetoric of Confession* . . . , 199–200.

"Nayao's Younger Sister"
Okazaki, Yoshie. *Japanese Literature* . . . , 315.

"The Old Man"
Okazaki, Yoshie. *Japanese Literature* . . . , 314–315.

"The Shop Boy's Patron Saint"
Fowler, Edward. *The Rhetoric of Confession* . . . , 195–198.

SHIMAZAKI TŌSON

"From Shinkatamachi"
Okazaki, Yoshie. *Japanese Literature* . . . , 240.

"The Water-Color Painter"
Okazaki, Yoshie. *Japanese Literature* . . . , 240–241.

MIKHAIL SHOLOKHOV

"The Fate of a Man"
Lowe, David. *Russian Writing Since 1953* . . . , 66.
Luker, Nicholas, Ed. *From Furmanov to Sholokhov* . . . , 33–34.

LESLIE MARMON SILKO

"Coyote and the Stro'ro'ka Dancers"
Danielson, Linda L. *"Storyteller*: Grandmother Spider's Web," *J Southwest*, 30
   (1988), 348.

"A Geronimo Story"
Danielson, Linda L. *"Storyteller* . . . ," 348–349.

"Lullaby"
Danielson, Linda L. *"Storyteller* . . . ," 335–336.
McBride, Mary. "Shelter of Refuge: The Art of Mimesis in Leslie Marmon
   Silko's 'Lullaby,'" *Wicazo SA R*, 3, ii (1987), 15–17.

"The Man to Send Rainclouds"
Danielson, Linda L. *"Storyteller* . . . ," 343–344.

"Storyteller"
Danielson, Linda L. *"Storyteller* . . . ," 334–335.
Hirsch, Bernard A. "'The telling which continues': Oral Tradition and the
   Written Word in Leslie Marmon Silko's *Storyteller*," *Am Imago*, 12 (1988),
   4–8.

"Tony's Story"
Danielson, Linda L. *"Storyteller* . . . ," 341.
Evers, Lawrence J. "The Killing of a New Mexican State Trooper: Ways of
   Telling a Historical Event," *Wicazo SA R*, 1, i (1985), 17–25.
Jaskoski, Helen. "From the Time Immemorial: Native American Traditions in
   Contemporary Short Fiction," in Logsdon, Loren, and Charles W. Mayes,
   Eds. *Since Flannery O'Connor* . . . , 66.

"Yellow Woman"
Jaskoski, Helen. "From the Time Immemorial . . . ," 65–66.

ALAN SILLITOE

"The Loneliness of the Long-Distance Runner"
Hutchings, William. "The Work of Play: Anger and the Expropriated Athletes
   of Alan Sillitoe and David Storey," *Mod Fiction Stud*, 33 (1987), 35–47.

ROBERT SILVERBERG

"In the Group"
Broege, Valerie. "Technology and Sexuality in Science Fiction: Creating New
   Erotic Interfaces," in Palumbo, Donald, Ed. *Erotic Universe* . . . , 120–121.

WILLIAM GILMORE SIMMS

"Bald-Headed Bill Bauldy"
Meats, Stephen E. "Bald-Headed Bill Bauldy: Simms' Unredeemed Captive,"
    Stud Am Humor, 3 (1984–1985), 321–329.
Wimsatt, Mary A. "The Evolution of Simms's Backwoods Humor," in Guilds,
    John C., Ed. *"Long Years of Neglect"* . . . , 161–163.

ROGELIO SINÁN

"La boina roja"
Menton, Seymour. *El Cuento Hispanoamericano,* II, 189–190; 2nd ed., 189–190;
    3rd ed., 83–84.

ISAAC BASHEVIS SINGER

"Alone"
Farrell Lee, Grace. *From Exile* . . . , 29–30.
Friedman, Lawrence S. *Understanding* . . . , 206–208.

"The Black Wedding"
Farrell Lee, Grace. *From Exile* . . . , 42–43.

"A Crown of Feathers"
Friedman, Lawrence S. *Understanding* . . . , 220–222.
Sheidley, William E., and Ann Charters. *Instructor's Manual* . . . , 126–127;
    Charters, Ann, William E. Sheidley, and Martha Ramsey. *Instructor's Man-
    ual* . . . , 2nd ed., 125–126.

"The Destruction of Kreshev"
Friedman, Lawrence S. *Understanding* . . . , 223–226.

"The Gentleman from Cracow"
Farrell Lee, Grace. *From Exile* . . . , 57–59.
Friedman, Lawrence S. *Understanding* . . . , 226–230.

"Gimpel the Fool"
Farrell Lee, Grace. *From Exile* . . . , 15–24.
Friedman, Lawrence S. *Understanding* . . . , 89–92.

"Guests on a Winter Night"
Friedman, Lawrence S. *Understanding* . . . , 192–194.

"Jachid and Jechidah"
Farrell Lee, Grace. *From Exile* . . . , 27.

"Joy"
Friedman, Lawrence S. *Understanding* . . . , 199–201.

"The Key"
Friedman, Lawrence S. *Understanding . . .* , 208–210.

"The Last Demon"
Farrell Lee, Grace. *From Exile . . .* , 25–26.

"The Letter Writer"
Farrell Lee, Grace. *From Exile . . .* , 101–102.
Friedman, Lawrence S. *Understanding . . .* , 210–212.

"The Little Shoemaker"
Friedman, Lawrence S. *Understanding . . .* , 193–199.

"Lost"
Farrell Lee, Grace. *From Exile . . .* , 47–48.

"Old Love"
Farrell Lee, Grace. *From Exile . . .* , 4–11.

"The Old Man"
Friedman, Lawrence S. *Understanding . . .* , 194–196.

"On a Wagon"
Farrell Lee, Grace. *From Exile . . .* , 48–53.

"The Shadow of a Crib"
Farrell Lee, Grace. *From Exile . . .* , 100–101.
Friedman, Lawrence S. *Understanding . . .* , 215–218.

"Shiddah and Kuziba"
Farrell Lee, Grace. *From Exile . . .* , 54–55.

"Short Friday"
Farrell Lee, Grace. *From Exile . . .* , 104–105.

"Something Is There"
Farrell Lee, Grace. *From Exile . . .* , 96–97.

"The Son from America"
Perrine, Laurence, and Thomas R. Arp. *Instructor's Manual . . .* , 7th ed., 13–
    14.

"The Spinoza of Market Street"
Farrell Lee, Grace. *From Exile . . .* , 102–103.
Friedman, Lawrence S. *Understanding . . .* , 212–215.

"Stories from Behind the Stove"
Farrell Lee, Grace. *From Exile . . .* , 45–47.

"Taibele and Her Demon"
Farrell Lee, Grace. *From Exile . . .* , 43–45.

"The Warehouse"
Farrell Lee, Grace. *From Exile* . . . , 26–27.

"A Wedding in Brownsville"
Farrell Lee, Grace. *From Exile* . . . , 20–21.
Friedman, Lawrence S. *Understanding* . . . , 200–203.

"Yentl the Yeshiva Boy"
Schanfield, Lillian. "Singer's 'Yentl': The Fantastic Case of a Perplexed Soul,"
    in Palumbo, Donald, Ed. *Spectrum of the Fantastic,* 185–192.

"Zeidlus the First"
Friedman, Lawrence S. *Understanding* . . . , 218–220.

KHUSHWANT SINGH

"Karma"
Shahane, Vasant A. *Khushwant Singh,* 35–37.

ANNIE TRUMBULL SLOSSON

"Anna Malann"
Johns, Barbara A. "'Love-Cracked': Spinsters as Subversives in 'Anna Malann,'
    'Christmas Jenny,' and 'An Object of Love,'" *Colby Lib Q,* 23, i (1987), 5–
    10.

AGNES SMEDLEY

"Cell Mates"
Scheffler, Judith A. "Agnes Smedley's 'Cell Mates': A Writer's Discovery of
    Voice, Form, and Subject in Prison," in Kessler-Harris, Alice, and William
    McBrien, Eds. *Faith of a (Woman) Writer,* 199–207.

CORDWAINER SMITH [PAUL MYRON ANTHONY LINEBARGER] and GENEVIEVE LINEBARGER

"The Lady Who Sailed *The Soul*"
Suvin, Darko. *Positions and Presuppositions* . . . , 206–211.

RAY SMITH

"Break-up: From the Journals of Ti-Paulo"
MacKendrick, Louis K. "A Voice Within the Tavern Cried: Crossing the Bar
    with Raymond Fraser and Ray Smith," in Struthers, J. R. (Tim), Ed. *The
    Montreal Story Tellers* . . . , 118–120.

"Cape Breton Is the Thought-Control Centre of Canada"
Garber, Lawrence. "Ray Smith's *Cape Breton Is the Thought-Control Centre of Can-*

ada: The Diagnostics of the Absurd," in Struthers, J. R. (Tim), Ed. *The Montreal Story Tellers . . .* , 95–97.

"Colours"
Garber, Lawrence. ". . . Diagnostics of the Absurd," 86–94.

"A Cynical Tale"
Garber, Lawrence. ". . . Diagnostics of the Absurd," 99–100.

"The Dwarf in His Valley Ate Codfish"
Garber, Lawrence. ". . . Diagnostics of the Absurd," 97–98.

"Family Lives"
MacKendrick, Louis K. "A Voice Within the Tavern . . . ," 123–125.

"The Galoshes"
Garber, Lawrence. ". . . Diagnostics of the Absurd," 101–102.

"Nora Noon"
Barbour, Douglas. "Ray Smith: Some Approaches to the Entrances of *Lord Nelson's Tavern*," *Open Letter*, 5, Series 3 (Summer, 1976), 55.
MacKendrick, Louis K. "A Voice Within the Tavern . . . ," 117–118.

"Passion"
Garber, Lawrence. ". . . Diagnostics of the Absurd," 98–99.

"Peril"
Garber, Lawrence. ". . . Diagnostics of the Absurd," 102–104.

"Raphael Anachronic"
Garber, Lawrence. ". . . Diagnostics of the Absurd," 100.

"Sarah's Summer Holiday"
Barbour, Douglas. "Ray Smith . . . ," 53.
MacKendrick, Louis K. "A Voice Within the Tavern . . . ," 122–123.

"Smoke"
Barbour, Douglas. "Ray Smith . . . ," 55.
Garber, Lawrence. ". . . Diagnostics of the Absurd," 101.

"Symbols in Agony"
Garebian, Keith. "In the End, a Beginning: The Montreal Story Tellers," in Struthers, J. R. (Tim), Ed. *The Montreal Story Tellers . . .* , 189.

"Two Loves"
Barbour, Douglas. "Ray Smith . . . ," 54.
MacKendrick, Louis K. "A Voice Within the Tavern . . . ," 115–117.

"Were There Flowers in the Hair of the Girls Who Danced on His Grave in the Morning?"
Barbour, Douglas. "Ray Smith . . . ," 57–62.
MacKendrick, Louis K. "A Voice Within the Tavern . . . ," 120–122.

ISABELO SOBREVEGA

"Pinkaw"
Lucero, Rosario Cruz. "Notes on the Contemporary Hiligaynon Short Story," *Solitary*, 108–109 (1986), 168–169.

ALEXANDER SOLZHENITSYN

"Matryona's House"
Porter, Robert. "Animal Magic in Solzhenitsyn, Rasputin, and Voynovich," *Mod Lang R*, 82 (1987), 676–680.

"The Right Hand"
Charters, Ann, William E. Sheidley, and Martha Ramsey. *Instructor's Manual* . . . , 2nd ed., 152–153.

EDITH SOMERVILLE and MARTIN ROSS [VIOLET MARTIN]

"Lisheen"
Zimmermann, Georges-Denis. "Conflicting Contexts: Traditional Storytelling Performance in Irish Short Stories," in Forsyth, Neil, Ed. *Reading Contexts*, 112.

OREST MIKHAILOVICH SOMOV

"The Bandit"
Mersereau, John. "Orest Somov: An Introduction," *Slavonic & East European R*, 43 (1965), 362–365.

"The Holy Fool"
Mersereau, John. "Orest Somov . . . ," 358–362.

"Matchmaking"
Mersereau, John. "Orest Somov . . . ," 367–369.

"Monster"
Mersereau, John. "Orest Somov . . . ," 365–367.

SON CH'ANG-SŎP

"The Rainy Season"
Kim, Chong-un. "Postwar Korean Society and the Short Story: The Case of Son Ch'ang-sŏp," *Korean J*, 26, iv (1986), 26–27.

"The Surplus Human Being"
Kim, Chong-un. "Postwar Korean Society . . . ," 30–31.

"The Victim"
Kim, Chong-un. "Postwar Korean Society . . . ," 28.

"Walking in the Snow"
Kim, Chong-un. "Postwar Korean Society . . . ," 29–30.

"A Washed-Out Dream"
Kim, Chong-un. "Postwar Korean Society . . . ," 28–29.

"Writing in Blood"
Kim, Chong-un. "Postwar Korean Society . . . ," 27–28.

PEDRO JUAN SOTO

"Campeones"
Menton, Seymour. *El Cuento Hispanoamericano*, II, 302–303; 2nd ed., 302–303; 3rd ed., 197–198.

"Garabatos"
Melendez, Concha. *El arte del cuento . . .* , 352–353.

"Los inocentes"
Melendez, Concha. *El arte del cuento . . .* , 353–354.

ADRIAN SPIES

"Miri"
Büssing, Sabine. *Aliens in the Home . . .* , 41–43.

NORMAN SPINRAD

"The Big Flash"
Franklin, H. Bruce. *War Stars . . .* , 197–198.

CARL SPOHR

"The Final War"
Bartter, Martha A. *The Way to Ground Zero . . .* , 80–81.

JEAN STAFFORD

"And Lots of Solid Color"
Ryan, Maureen. *Innocence . . .* , 91–92.

"Bad Characters"
Ryan, Maureen. *Innocence . . .* , 139–141.

"Beatrice Trueblood's Story"
Ryan, Maureen. *Innocence* . . . , 105–106.

"The Captain's Gift"
Ryan, Maureen. *Innocence* . . . , 84–85.

"Children Are Bored on Sunday"
Leary, William. "Pictures at an Exhibit: Jean Stafford's 'Children Are Bored
    on Sunday,'" *Kenyon R,* 9 N.S. (Spring, 1987), 1–8.
Ryan, Maureen. *Innocence* . . . , 109–111.

"The Children's Game"
Ryan, Maureen. *Innocence* . . . , 92–94.

"The Connoisseurs"
Ryan, Maureen. *Innocence* . . . , 94–96.

"Cops and Robbers"
Ryan, Maureen. *Innocence* . . . , 134–136.

"A Country Love Story"
Oates, Joyce C. "The Interior Castle: The Art of Jean Stafford's Short Stories,"
    Shenandoah, 30, iii (1979), 62.
Ryan, Maureen. *Innocence* . . . , 99–101.

"The Darkening Moon"
Ryan, Maureen. *Innocence* . . . , 119–121.

"The Echo and the Nemesis"
Ryan, Maureen. *Innocence* . . . , 111–114.

"The End of a Career"
Ryan, Maureen. *Innocence* . . . , 86–88.

"The Hope Chest"
Ryan, Maureen. *Innocence* . . . , 83.

"I Love Someone"
Ryan, Maureen. *Innocence* . . . , 88–90.

"In the Zoo"
Ryan, Maureen. *Innocence* . . . , 132–134.

"An Influx of Poets"
Ryan, Maureen. *Innocence* . . . , 96–98.

"The Interior Castle"
Roberts, David. *Jean Stafford* . . . , 161–162.

"The Liberation"
Ryan, Maureen. *Innocence* . . . , 90–91.

"Life Is No Abyss"
Ryan, Maureen. *Innocence . . .* , 85–86.

"The Lippia Lawn"
Oates, Joyce C. "The Interior Castle . . . ," 61–62.

"Maggie Meriwether's Rich Experience"
Ryan, Maureen. *Innocence . . .* , 115–116.

"A Modest Proposal"
Ryan, Maureen. *Innocence . . .* , 131–132.

"The Mountain Day"
Ryan, Maureen. *Innocence . . .* , 116–119.

"The Philosophy Lesson"
Leary, William. "The Suicidal Thirties: Jean Stafford's 'The Philosophy Lesson,'" *Southwest R,* 72 (1987), 387–403.

"A Reading Problem"
Ryan, Maureen. *Innocence . . .* , 136–137.

"The Scarlet Letter"
Ryan, Maureen. *Innocence . . .* , 137–138.

"A Slight Maneuver"
Ryan, Maureen. *Innocence . . .* , 123–124.

"The Warlock"
Ryan, Maureen. *Innocence . . .* , 107–109.

"A Winter's Tale"
Ryan, Maureen. *Innocence . . .* , 121–123.

"Woden's Day"
Leary, William. "Grafting Onto Her Roots: Jean Stafford's 'Woden's Day,'" *Western Am Lit,* 23 (1988), 129–139.
Ryan, Maureen. *Innocence . . .* , 146–147.

CHRISTINA STEAD

"Day of Wrath"
Geering, R. G. *Christina Stead,* 50–51.

"The Dianas"
Geering, R. G. *Christina Stead,* 155–156.

"A Household"
Geering, R. G. *Christina Stead,* 152–153.

"In Doulcemer"
Geering, R. G. *Christina Stead,* 51–52.

"The Prodigy"
Lidoff, Joan. *Christina Stead,* 121–122.

"The Puzzleheaded Girl"
Geering, R. G. *Christina Stead,* 154–155.
Lidoff, Joan. *Christina Stead,* 167–169.

"The Rightangled Creek"
Lidoff, Joan. *Christina Stead,* 166–167.

"The Sensitive Goldfish"
Geering, R. G. *Christina Stead,* 49–50.

"Speculation in Lost Causes"
Geering, R. G. *Christina Stead,* 54–55.

"The Triskelion"
Geering, R. G. *Christina Stead,* 51.

"U.N.O. 1945"
Geering, R. G. *Christina Stead,* 153.

WALLACE STEGNER

"Genesis"
Gamble, David E. "Wallace Stegner and the Gift of Wallace Stegner," *No Dakota Q,* 56, iv (1988), 102–105.

GERTRUDE STEIN

"Melanctha"
Knight, Christopher J. "Gertrude Stein's 'Melanctha' and Radical Heterosexuality," *Stud Short Fiction,* 25 (1988), 295–300.

JOHN STEINBECK

"Adventures in Arcademy"
Hughes, R. S. *Beyond the Red Pony . . . ,* 7–8.

"The Affair at 7, Rue de M——"
Hughes, Robert S. "Steinbeck's Uncollected Stories," *Steinbeck Q,* 18 (1985), 86–87; rpt. in his *Beyond the Red Pony . . . ,* 118–120.

"Breakfast"
Hughes, R. S. *Beyond the Red Pony . . . ,* 70–72.

"Case History"
Hughes, R. S. *Beyond the Red Pony . . . ,* 79–80.

"The Case of the Hotel Ghost . . ." [same as "A Reunion at the Quiet Hotel"]
Hughes, Robert S. ". . . Uncollected Stories," 90–91; rpt. in his *Beyond the Red Pony* . . . , 124–125.

"The Chrysanthemums"
Charters, Ann, William E. Sheidley, and Martha Ramsey. *Instructor's Manual* . . . , 2nd ed., 120–121.
Ditsky, John. "A Kind of Play: Dramatic Elements in John Steinbeck's 'The Chrysanthemums,'" *Wascana R*, 21, i (1986), 62–72.
Hughes, R. S. *Beyond the Red Pony* . . . , 58–62.
Thomas, Leroy. "Steinbeck's 'The Chrysanthemums,'" *Explicator*, 45, iii (1987), 50–51.

"The Cottage That Wasn't There"
Hughes, R. S. *Beyond the Red Pony* . . . , 110–111.

"The Days of Long Marsh"
Hughes, R. S. *Beyond the Red Pony* . . . , 21–23.

"East Third Street"
Hughes, R. S. *Beyond the Red Pony* . . . , 14–16.

"The Elf of Algiers" [originally titled "The Story of an Elf"]
Hughes, R. S. *Beyond the Red Pony* . . . , 110.

"Fingers of Cloud"
Hughes, R. S. *Beyond the Red Pony* . . . , 4–6.

"Flight"
Hughes, R. S. *Beyond the Red Pony* . . . , 64–67.

"The Gift"
Hughes, R. S. *Beyond the Red Pony* . . . , 92–94.

"The Gifts of Iban"
Hughes, R. S. *Beyond the Red Pony* . . . , 25–28.

"The Great Mountains"
Hughes, R. S. *Beyond the Red Pony* . . . , 94–96.

"The Great Roque War"
Hughes, R. S. *Beyond the Red Pony* . . . , 117–118.

"The Harness"
Hughes, R. S. *Beyond the Red Pony* . . . , 75–77.

"Helen Van Deventer"
Hughes, R. S. *Beyond the Red Pony* . . . , 35–38.

"His Father"
Hughes, Robert S. ". . . Uncollected Stories," 85; rpt. in his *Beyond the Red Pony* . . . , 116–117.

"How Edith McGillcutty Met R. L. Stevenson"
Hughes, Robert S. ". . . Uncollected Stories," 80–82; rpt. in his *Beyond the Red Pony . . .* , 106–108.

"How Mr. Hogan Robbed a Bank"
Hughes, Robert S. ". . . Uncollected Stories," 89–90; rpt. in his *Beyond the Red Pony . . .* , 122–124.

"Johnny Bear"
Hughes, R. S. *Beyond the Red Pony . . .* , 80–85.

"Junius Maltby"
Hughes, R. S. *Beyond the Red Pony . . .* , 38–40.

"The Leader of the People"
Hughes, R. S. *Beyond the Red Pony . . .* , 99–103.

"The Lopez Sisters"
Hughes, R. S. *Beyond the Red Pony . . .* , 41–43.

"The Miracle of Tepayac"
Hughes, Robert S. ". . . Uncollected Stories," 83–84; rpt. in his *Beyond the Red Pony . . .* , 115–116.

"Molly Morgan"
Hughes, R. S. *Beyond the Red Pony . . .* , 43–45.

"The Murder"
Hughes, R. S. *Beyond the Red Pony . . .* , 85–87.

"The Nail"
Hughes, R. S. *Beyond the Red Pony . . .* , 23–25.

"The Nymph and Isobel"
Hughes, R. S. *Beyond the Red Pony . . .* , 20–21.

"The Pacific Grove Butterfly Festival"
Hughes, R. S. *Beyond the Red Pony . . .* , 117–118.

"Pat Humbert"
Hughes, R. S. *Beyond the Red Pony . . .* , 47–49.

"The Promise"
Hughes, R. S. *Beyond the Red Pony . . .* , 97–99.

"The Raid"
Hughes, R. S. *Beyond the Red Pony . . .* , 72–75.

"Raymond Banks"
Hughes, R. S. *Beyond the Red Pony . . .* , 45–47.

"St. Katy the Virgin"
Hughes, R. S. *Beyond the Red Pony* . . . , 88–90.

"The Short-Short Story of Mankind" [same as "We're Holding Our Own"]
Hughes, Robert S. ". . . Uncollected Stories," 88–89; rpt. in his *Beyond the Red Pony* . . . , 121–122.

"The Snake"
Hughes, R. S. *Beyond the Red Pony* . . . , 67–70.

"The Summer Before"
Hughes, Robert S. ". . . Uncollected Stories," 87–88; rpt. in his *Beyond the Red Pony* . . . , 120–121.

"The Time the Wolves Ate the Vice-Principal"
Hughes, Robert S. ". . . Uncollected Stories," 82–83; rpt. in his *Beyond the Red Pony* . . . , 112–113.

"Tularecito"
Hughes, R. S. *Beyond the Red Pony* . . . , 33–35.

"The Vigilante"
Hughes, R. S. *Beyond the Red Pony* . . . , 77–80.

"The White Quail"
Hughes, R. S. *Beyond the Red Pony* . . . , 62–64.

"The White Sisters of Fourteenth Street"
Hughes, R. S. *Beyond the Red Pony* . . . , 18–20.

"The Whiteside Family" [same as "The Whitesides"]
Hughes, R. S. *Beyond the Red Pony* . . . , 49–51.

"The Wicks Family" [same as "Shark Wicks"]
Hughes, R. S. *Beyond the Red Pony* . . . , 31–33.

ROBERT LOUIS STEVENSON

"The Merry Men"
Letley, Emma. *From Galt to Douglas Brown* . . . , 189–192.

"The Strange Case of Dr. Jekyll and Mr. Hyde"
Baldick, Chris. *In Frankenstein's Shadow* . . . , 144–146.
Brantlinger, Patrick, and Richard Boyle. "The Education of Edward Hyde: Stevenson's 'Gothic Gnome' and the Mass Readership of Late Victorian England," in Veeder, William, and Gordon Hirsch, Eds. *Dr. Jekyll and Mr. Hyde* . . . , 265–282.
Garrett, Peter K. "Cries and Voices: Reading 'Jekyll and Hyde,'" in Veeder, William, and Gordon Hirsch, Eds. *Dr. Jekyll and Mr. Hyde* . . . , 59–72.
Gaughan, Richard T. "Mr. Hyde and Mr. Seek: Utterson's Antidote," *J Narrative Technique*, 17 (1987), 184–197.

Hogle, Jerrold E. "The Struggle for a Dichotomy: Abjection in Jekyll and His Interpreters," in Veeder, William, and Gordon Hirsch, Eds. *Dr. Jekyll and Mr. Hyde* . . . , 161–207.

Lawler, Donald. "Reframing 'Jekyll and Hyde': Robert Louis Stevenson and the Strange Case of Gothic Science Fiction," in Veeder, William, and Gordon Hirsch, Eds. *Dr. Jekyll and Mr. Hyde* . . . , 247–261.

Letley, Emma, Ed. *"The Strange Case* . . . , *"* viii–xiv.

Meckier, Jerome. *Hidden Rivalries* . . . , 164–169.

Oates, Joyce C. *(Woman) Writer* . . . , 198–204.

Thomas, Ronald R. "The Strange Voices in the Strange Case: Dr. Jekyll, Mr. Hyde, and the Voices of Modern Fiction," in Veeder, William, and Gordon Hirsch, Eds. *Dr. Jekyll and Mr. Hyde* . . . , 73–93.

Veeder, William. "Children of the Night: Stevenson and Patriarchy," in Veeder, William, and Gordon Hirsch, Eds. *Dr. Jekyll and Mr. Hyde* . . . , 107–160.

"Weir of Hermiston"
Letley, Emma, Ed. *"The Strange Case* . . . ,*"* xvii–xxv.

ADALBERT STIFTER

"Mica"
Sjögren, Christine O. "Myths and Metaphors in Stifter's 'Katzensilber,'" *J Engl & Germ Philol*, 86 (1987), 358–371.

BRAM STOKER [ABRAHAM STOKER]

"Dracula's Guest"
Senf, Carol A. *The Vampire* . . . , 57.

WILLIAM LEETE STONE

"The Grave of the Indian King"
Doubleday, Neal F. *Variety of Attempt* . . . , 161–162.

"Mercy Disborough: A Tale of the Witches"
Doubleday, Neal F. *Variety of Attempt* . . . , 164–167.

"The Skeleton Hand"
Doubleday, Neal F. *Variety of Attempt* . . . , 167–168.

"The Spectre Fire-Ship"
Doubleday, Neal F. *Variety of Attempt* . . . , 168–171.

TOM STOPPARD [TOMAS STRAUSSLER]

"Life, Times: Fragments"
Longré, Felicia H. *Tom Stoppard*, 95–98.
Rusinko, Susan. *Tom Stoppard*, 19–20.

"Reunion"
Longré, Felicia H. *Tom Stoppard,* 92–95.
Rusinko, Susan. *Tom Stoppard,* 17–19.

"The Story"
Longré, Felicia H. *Tom Stoppard,* 98–99.
Rusinko, Susan. *Tom Stoppard,* 21–22.

THEODOR STORM

"A Doppelgänger"
Alt, A. Tilo. "Escape and Transformation: An Inquiry into the Nature of
    Storm's Realism," in Phelps, Leland R., Ed. *Creative Encounter...,* 124–
    126.

"Hans und Heinz Kirch"
Alt, A. Tilo. "Escape and Transformation ...," 126.

"The Rider of the White Horse"
Alt, A. Tilo. "Escape and Transformation ...," 127–130.

ARKADY STRUGATSKY and BORIS STRUGATSKY

"Far Rainbow"
Suvin, Darko. *Positions and Presuppositions...,* 206–211.

DON A. STUART [JOHN W. CAMPBELL]

"The Machine"
Berger, Albert I. "Theories of History and Social Order in *Astounding Science
    Fiction,* 1934–1955," *Sci-Fiction Stud,* 15 (1988), 15–16.

"Night"
Berger, Albert I. "Theories of History ...," 15.

"Twilight"
Berger, Albert I. "Theories of History ...," 15.

JESSE STUART

"Another April"
Herndon, Jerry A. "Jesse Stuart's World," *J Kentucky Stud,* 1 (July, 1984), 119–
    120; rpt. Herndon, Jerry A., and George Brosi, Eds. *Jesse Stuart...,* 106–
    107.

"As Ye Sow, So Shall Ye Reap"
Herndon, Jerry A. "Jesse Stuart's World," 122–123; rpt. Herndon, Jerry A.,
    and George Brosi, Eds. *Jesse Stuart...,* 110–111.

"Hot-Collared Mule"
Herndon, Jerry A. "Jesse Stuart's World," 123; rpt. Herndon, Jerry A., and
    George Brosi, Eds. *Jesse Stuart . . .* , 111–112.

"Rain on Tanyard Hollow"
Herndon, Jerry A. "Jesse Stuart's World," 121–122; rpt. Herndon, Jerry A.,
    and George Brosi, Eds. *Jesse Stuart . . .* , 109–110.

"This Farm for Sale"
Herndon, Jerry A. "Jesse Stuart's World," 121; rpt. Herndon, Jerry A., and
    George Brosi, Eds. *Jesse Stuart . . .* , 108–109.

"Walk in the Moon Shadows"
Herndon, Jerry A. "Jesse Stuart's World," 121; rpt. Herndon, Jerry A., and
    George Brosi, Eds. *Jesse Stuart . . .* , 109.

THEODORE STURGEON

"Grammy Won't Knit"
Bartter, Martha A. *The Way to Ground Zero . . .* , 188–189.

"Killdozer"
Bartter, Martha A. *The Way to Ground Zero . . .* , 180.

"Memorial"
Bartter, Martha A. *The Way to Ground Zero . . .* , 186.
Franklin, H. Bruce. *War Stars . . .* , 158–159.

"Microcosmic God"
Bartter, Martha A. *The Way to Ground Zero . . .* , 179–180.

"Never Underestimate"
Bartter, Martha A. *The Way to Ground Zero . . .* , 189.

"The Skills of Xanadu"
Bartter, Martha A. *The Way to Ground Zero . . .* , 191–192.

"Thunder and Roses"
Bartter, Martha A. *The Way to Ground Zero . . .* , 186–188.
Franklin, H. Bruce. *War Stars . . .* , 170–172.

"The Wages of Synergy"
Bartter, Martha A. *The Way to Ground Zero . . .* , 189–191.

WILLIAM STYRON

"The Long March"
Ruderman, Judith. *William Styron*, 72–78.

AUSTOLIO SUAREZ

"Intimations of Redemption"
Baguio, Tiburcio. "Cebuano Short Stories in the Last Twenty Years," *Solidarity*, 108–109 (1986), 139.

RUTH SUCKOW

"Eltha"
Oehlschlager, Fritz. "A Book of Resolutions: Ruth Suckow's *Some Others and Myself*," *Western Am Lit*, 21 (1987), 117–120.

"Memorial Eve"
Oehlschlager, Fritz. "A Book of Resolutions . . . ," 116–117.

"Merrittville"
Oehlschlager, Fritz. "A Book of Resolutions . . . ," 116.

"Mrs. Vogel and Ollie"
Oehlschlager, Fritz. "A Book of Resolutions . . . ," 115.

"One of Three Others"
Oehlschlager, Fritz. "A Book of Resolutions . . . ," 113–115.

CÈLIA SUNYOL

"L'Homme de les fires"
Enriquez de Salamanca, Cristina. "Cotidianeidad y creación literaria en 'L'Homme de les fires' de Cèlia Sunyol," *Monographic R*, 4 (1988), 347–354.

GLADYS SWAN

"Black Hole"
Kennedy, Thomas E. "Imagination as a Way of Knowing in the Fiction of Gladys Swan," *Writers' Forum*, 12 (Fall, 1986), 16–17.

"Getting an Education"
Kennedy, Thomas E. "Imagination . . . ," 17–19.

GRAHAM SWIFT

"Learning to Swim"
Cassill, R. V. . . . *Instructor's Handbook*, 68–69.

TAKAHASHI MICHITSUNA

"Killing Time"
Sakurai, Emiko. "Japan's New Generation of Writers," *World Lit Today*, 61 (1988), 406.

"The Sky of September"
Sakurai, Emiko. "Japan's New Generation . . . ," 406.

TAKAHASHI TAKAKO

"Doll Love"
Tanaka, Yukiko. "Introduction," in Tanaka, Yukiko, and Elizabeth Hanson, Eds. *This Kind of Woman* . . . , xxi.

ZAKARIYA TAMIR

"The Face of the Moon"
Al-Khateeb, H. "A Modern Syrian Short Story," *J Arabic Lit*, 3 (1972), 100–101, 103, 104–105; rpt. Allen, Roger, Ed. *Modern Arabic Literature*, 314–315.

TANIZAKI JUN'ICHIRŌ

"The Bridge of Dreams"
Merken, Kathleen. "Tanizaki Jun'ichirō," in Swann, Thomas E., and Kinya Tsuruta, Eds. . . . *Modern Japanese Short Story*, 333–338.

"The Tale of Shunkin"
Merken, Kathleen. "Tanizaki Jun'ichirō," 327–332.

"Tattoo"
Merken, Kathleen. "Tanizaki Jun'ichirō," 319–325.
Okazaki, Yoshie. *Japanese Literature* . . . , 290–292.

BOOTH TARKINGTON

"The Veiled Feminists of Atlantis"
Gilbert, Sandra M., and Susan Gubar. *No Man's Land* . . . , 40–41.

PETER TAYLOR

"Bad Dreams"
Robinson, James C. *Peter Taylor* . . . , 37–38.

"The Captain's Son"
Gower, Herschel. "The Nashville Stories," *Shenandoah,* 28 (Winter, 1977), 45–47.
Hanson, Philip. "Regionalism in Peter Taylor's Fiction," *J Short Story Engl,* 9 (Autumn, 1987), 93–99.
Robinson, James C. *Peter Taylor . . .* , 82–85.

"Cookies"
Robinson, James C. *Peter Taylor . . .* , 32–35.

"Daphne's Lover"
Robinson, James C. *Peter Taylor . . .* , 73–76.
Williamson, Alan. "Identity and the Wider Eros: A Reading of Peter Taylor's Stories," *Shenandoah,* 30, i (1978), 80–82.

"Dean of Men"
Robinson, James C. *Peter Taylor . . .* , 78–82.
Williamson, Alan. "Identity and the Wider Eros . . . ," 74–78.

"The Fancy Woman"
Brown, Ashley. "The Early Fiction of Peter Taylor," *Sewanee R,* 70 (1962), 594–596.
Robinson, James C. *Peter Taylor . . .* , 23–26.

"First Heat"
Charters, Ann, William E. Sheidley, and Martha Ramsey. *Instructor's Manual . . .* , 2nd ed., 148–149.
Vauthier, Simone. "Trying to Ride the Tiger: A Reading of 'First Heat,' " *J Short Story Engl,* 9 (August, 1987), 73–91.

"A Friend and Protector"
Robinson, James C. *Peter Taylor . . .* , 41–43.

"The Gift of the Prodigal"
Robinson, James C. *Peter Taylor . . .* , 76–77.

"The Guest"
Robinson, James C. *Peter Taylor . . .* , 50–52.

"The Hand of Emmagene"
Robinson, James C. *Peter Taylor . . .* , 66–69.

"Her Need"
Robinson, James C. *Peter Taylor . . .* , 71–72.

"In the Miro District"
Bloom, Lynn Z. "Peter Taylor," in Flora, Joseph M., and Robert Bain, Eds. *Fifty Southern Writers After 1900,* 477.
Gower, Herschel. "The Nashville Stories," 41–42.
Robinson, James C. *Peter Taylor . . .* , 85–90.

"The Instruction of a Mistress"
Robinson, James C. *Peter Taylor . . .* , 64–66.

"Je Suis Perdu"
Robinson, James C. *Peter Taylor* . . . , 48–50.

"A Long Fourth"
Brown, Ashley. "The Early Fiction . . . ," 597–599.
Robinson, James C. *Peter Taylor* . . . , 29–31.

"Miss Lenore When Last Seen"
Robinson, James C. *Peter Taylor* . . . , 59–61.

"1939"
Robinson, James C. *Peter Taylor* . . . , 44–50.
Williamson, Alan. "Identity and the Wider Eros . . . ," 72–74.

"The Old Forest"
Robinson, James C. *Peter Taylor* . . . , 89–94.

"The Other Times"
Robinson, James C. *Peter Taylor* . . . , 56–59.

"Reservations"
Williamson, Alan. "Identity and the Wider Eros . . . ," 72.

"The Scoutmaster"
Robinson, James C. *Peter Taylor* . . . , 26–29.

"Sky Line"
Brown, Ashley. "The Early Fiction . . . ," 590–593.

"A Spinster's Tale"
Andrews, Maureen. "A Psychoanalytic Appreciation of Peter Taylor's 'A Spinster's Tale,'" *J Evolutionary Psych,* 9 (1988), 309–316.
Brown, Ashley. "The Early Fiction . . . ," 593–594.
Robinson, James C. *Peter Taylor* . . . , 19–23.
Sodowsky, Roland and Garci. "Determined Failure, Self-styled Success: Two Views of Betsy in Peter Taylor's 'Spinster's Tale,'" *Stud Short Fiction,* 25 (1988), 49–54.

"Three Heroines"
Robinson, James C. *Peter Taylor* . . . , 68–70.

"The Throughway"
Robinson, James C. *Peter Taylor* . . . , 72–73.

"Two Ladies in Retirement"
Robinson, James C. *Peter Taylor* . . . , 38–41.

"Two Pilgrims"
Baumbach, Jonathan. *Moderns and Contemporaries* . . . , 344.

"Venus, Cupid, Folly and Time"
Robinson, David. "Tennessee, Taylor, the Critics, and Time," *Southern R*, 23, ii
    (1987), 281–294.
Robinson, James C. *Peter Taylor . . .* , 52–56.
Williamson, Alan. "Identity and the Wider Eros . . . ," 78–80.

"What You Hear From 'Em?"
Gower, Herschel. "The Nashville Stories," 45.
Robinson, James C. *Peter Taylor . . .* , 32–37.

JODOCUS D. T. TEMME

"The Hallbauer Woman"
Woeller, Waltraud, and Bruce Cassiday. *The Literature of Crime . . .* , 61.

"Who Was the Murderer?"
Woeller, Waltraud, and Bruce Cassiday. *The Literature of Crime . . .* , 61–62.

WILLIAM TENN

"The Masculinist Revolt"
Gilbert, Sandra M., and Susan Gubar. *No Man's Land . . .* , 58–59.

WILLIAM MAKEPEACE THACKERAY

"Frank Berry's Wife"
Peters, Catherine. *Thackeray's Universe . . .* , 103.

"The Ravenswing"
Peters, Catherine. *Thackeray's Universe . . .* , 103–105.

DOUGLAS THAYER

"Opening Day"
Jorgenson, B. W. "Romantic Lyric Form and Western Mormon Experience in
    the Stories of Douglas Thayer," *Western Am Lit*, 22, i (1987), 43–47.

"Under the Cottonwoods"
Jorgenson, B. W. "Romantic Lyric Form . . . ," 35–43.

JIM THEIS

"The Eye of Argon"
Schweitzer, Darrel. "One Fine Day in the Stygian Haunts of Hell: Being the
    Whole Truth about the Fabled 'Eye of Argon,'" *Fantasy R*, 10, vi (1987),
    23–24.

AUDREY THOMAS

"Aquarius"
Bowering, George. *The Mask . . .* , 71–72.

"Aunt Hettie James and the Gates of the New Jerusalem"
Bowering, George. *The Mask . . .* , 66–67.

"Dead Man's Body"
Bowering, George. *The Mask . . .* , 66.

"Green Stakes for the Garden"
Bowering, George. *The Mask . . .* , 73–74.

"If One Green Bottle"
Bowering, George. *The Mask . . .* , 65–66.

"Kill Day on the Government Wharf"
Bowering, George. *The Mask . . .* , 74–76.

"A Monday Dream"
Bowering, George. *The Mask . . .* , 72.

"Munchmeyer"
Bowering, George. *Imaginary Hand . . .* , I, 111–119.

"One Is One and All Alone"
Bowering, George. *The Mask . . .* , 68–69.

"Rapunzel"
Bowering, George. *The Mask . . .* , 72–73.

"Salon des Refusés"
Bowering, George. *The Mask . . .* , 71.

"A Winter's Tale"
Bowering, George. *The Mask . . .* , 69–70.

"Xanadu"
Bowering, George. *The Mask . . .* , 68.

DYLAN THOMAS

"The Peach"
Peach, Linden. *The Prose Writing . . .* , 80–82.

THOMAS BANGS THORPE

"The Big Bear of Arkansas"
Brown, Carolyn S. *The Tall Tale . . .* , 65–70.

Estes, David C. "Thomas Bangs Thorpe's Backwoods Hunters: Culture Heroes and Humorous Failures," *Univ Mississippi Stud Engl,* 5 (1984–1987), 163–165.

"The Devil's Summer Retreat in Arkansaw"
Estes, David C. "Thomas Bangs Thorpe's Backwoods Hunters . . . ," 165–167.

JAMES THURBER

"Am Not I Your Rosalind?"
Long, Robert E. *James Thurber,* 82–83.

"The Black Magic of Barney Haller"
Long, Robert E. *James Thurber,* 80–82.

"A Box to Hide In"
Long, Robert E. *James Thurber,* 61–62.

"The Breaking Up of the Winships"
Long, Robert E. *James Thurber,* 54–56.

"The Case of Dimity Ann"
Long, Robert E. *James Thurber,* 102–103.

"The Catbird Seat"
Long, Robert E. *James Thurber,* 75–77.
Perrine, Laurence. *Instructor's Manual . . . ,* 5th ed., 29–30; Perrine, Laurence, and Thomas R. Arp. *Instructor's Manual . . . ,* 7th ed., 28–30.

"A Couple of Hamburgers"
Long, Robert E. *James Thurber,* 54.

"The Curb in the Sky"
Long, Robert E. *James Thurber,* 60–61.

"The Departure of Emma Inch"
Long, Robert E. *James Thurber,* 91–92.

"The Evening's at Seven"
Long, Robert E. *James Thurber,* 88–89.

"The Figgerin' of Aunt Wilma"
Long, Robert E. *James Thurber,* 79–80.

"A Final Note on Chanda Bell"
Long, Robert E. *James Thurber,* 103–104.

"A Friend to Alexander"
Long, Robert E. *James Thurber,* 96–98.

"The Greatest Man in the World"
Long, Robert E. *James Thurber*, 84–86.

"The Imperturbable Spirit"
Long, Robert E. *James Thurber*, 49–50.

"The Indian Sign"
Long, Robert E. *James Thurber*, 56–57.

"The Interview"
Long, Robert E. *James Thurber*, 105–106.

"The Lady on 142"
Long, Robert E. *James Thurber*, 77–79.

"The Luck of Jad Peters"
Long, Robert E. *James Thurber*, 99–100.

"The Man Who Hated Moonbaum"
Long, Robert E. *James Thurber*, 82–83.

"Menace in May"
Long, Robert E. *James Thurber*, 87.

"Mr. Preble Gets Rid of His Wife"
Long, Robert E. *James Thurber*, 57–58.

"One Is a Wanderer"
Long, Robert E. *James Thurber*, 89–90.

"The Other Room"
Long, Robert E. *James Thurber*, 90–91.

"The Private Life of Mr. Bidwell"
Long, Robert E. *James Thurber*, 62.

"The Secret Life of Walter Mitty"
Long, Robert E. *James Thurber*, 64–73.
Sheidley, William E., and Ann Charters. *Instructor's Manual . . .* , 97; Charters, Ann, William E. Sheidley, and Martha Ramsey. *Instructor's Manual . . .* , 2nd ed., 101–102.

"Smashup"
Long, Robert E. *James Thurber*, 52–54.

"Something To Say"
Long, Robert E. *James Thurber*, 104–105.

"Tea at Mrs. Armsby's"
Long, Robert E. *James Thurber*, 49.

"Teacher's Pet"
Long, Robert E. *James Thurber*, 93–94.

"The Unicorn in the Garden"
Long, Robert E. *James Thurber,* 58–60.

"The Whip-Poor-Will"
Long, Robert E. *James Thurber,* 94–96.

"You Could Look It Up"
Long, Robert E. *James Thurber,* 86–87.

JOHANN LUDWIG TIECK

"Love Magic"
Birrell, Gordon. *The Boundless Present . . . ,* 133–134.

"Der Runenberg"
Arntzen, Helmut. "Tieck's Märchenerzählungen oder die Ambiguität der ro-
    manischen Poesie: Ein Vortrag," *Mod Lang Notes,* 103 (1988), 641–645.
Birrell, Gordon. *The Boundless Present . . . ,* 103–115.

ROSEMARY TIMPERLEY

"Street of the Blind Donkey"
Büssing, Sabine. *Aliens in the Home . . . ,* 134–135.

JAMES TIPTREE, JR. [ALICE HASTINGS SHELDON]

"All the Kinds of Yes"
Heldreth, Leonard G. "Close Encounters of the Carnal Kind: Sex with Aliens
    in Science Fiction," in Palumbo, Donald, Ed. *Erotic Universe . . . ,* 139–140.
Lefanu, Sarah. *Feminism and Science Fiction,* 113–115.

"And I Awoke and Found Me Here on the Cold Hill's Side"
Heldreth, Leonard G. "Close Encounters . . . ," 132–133.
Lefanu, Sarah. *Feminism and Science Fiction,* 107–108.

"Houston, Houston, Do You Read?"
Barr, Marleen S. *Alien to Femininity . . . ,* 9–12.
Hayley, Barbara J. "The Feminist Fiction of James Tiptree, Jr.: Women and
    Men as Aliens," in Palumbo, Donald, Ed. *Spectrum of the Fantastic,* 129–130.
Lefanu, Sarah. *Feminism and Science Fiction,* 107–108.

"Love Is the Plan, the Plan Is Death"
Barr, Marleen S. *Alien to Femininity . . . ,* 32–34.
Slusser, George E. "The *And* in Fantasy and Science Fiction," in Slusser,
    George E., and Eric S. Rabkin, Eds. *Intersections . . . ,* 157.

"On the Last Afternoon"
Lefanu, Sarah. *Feminism and Science Fiction,* 119.

"Painwise"
Lefanu, Sarah. *Feminism and Science Fiction,* 119–120.

"The Psychologist Who Wouldn't Do Awful Things to Rats"
McGregor, Gaile. *The Noble Savage . . . ,* 280–282.

"The Screwfly Solution"
Allen, Virginia, and Terri Paul. "Science and Fiction: Ways of Theorizing about
    Women," in Palumbo, Donald, Ed. *Erotic Universe . . . ,* 177–178.
Barr, Marleen S. *Alien to Femininity . . . ,* 27–30.
Gilbert, Sandra M., and Susan Gubar. *No Man's Land . . . ,* 119–120.
Hayley, Barbara J. "The Feminist Fiction . . . ," 131.
Lefanu, Sarah. *Feminism and Science Fiction,* 110–112.

"Slow Music"
Lefanu, Sarah. *Feminism and Science Fiction,* 119–120.

"Time Sharing Angel"
Lefanu, Sarah. *Feminism and Science Fiction,* 115–116.

"We Who Stole the Dream"
Baggesen, Sørgen. "Utopian and Dystopian Pessimism: Le Guin's *The Word for
    World Is Forest* and Tiptree's 'We Who Stole the Dream,'" *Sci-Fiction Stud,*
    14, i (1987), 34–43.
Lefanu, Sarah. *Feminism and Science Fiction,* 121–122.

"With Delicate Mad Hands"
Lefanu, Sarah. *Feminism and Science Fiction,* 127–129.

"The Women Men Don't See"
Allen, Virginia, and Terri Paul. "Science and Fiction: Ways of Theorizing about
    Women," in Palumbo, Donald, Ed. *Erotic Universe . . . ,* 165–167.
Hayley, Barbara J. "The Feminist Fiction . . . ," 129.
Lefanu, Sarah. *Feminism and Science Fiction,* 122–127.

"Your Haploid Heart"
Barr, Marleen S. *Alien to Femininity . . . ,* 34–36.
Hayley, Barbara J. "The Feminist Fiction . . . ," 128.

LEO TOLSTOY

"The Cossacks"
Bagby, Lewis, and Pavel Sigalov. "The Semiotics of Names and Naming in
    Tolstoj's 'The Cossacks,'" *Slavic & East European J,* 31 (1987), 473–489.

"The Death of Ivan Ilych"
Boyers, Robert. *After the Avant-Garde . . . ,* 86–89.
Cain, T. G. S. *Tolstoy,* 159–164.
Perrine, Laurence, and Thomas R. Arp. *Instructor's Manual . . . ,* 6th ed., 73–
    75; 7th ed., 75–78.
Sheidley, William E., and Ann Charters. *Instructor's Manual . . . ,* 16–18; Char-

ters, Ann, William E. Sheidley, and Martha Ramsey. *Instructor's Manual . . .* , 2nd ed., 17–18.
Wilson, A. N. *Tolstoy,* 366–367.

"Family Happiness"
Cain, T. G. S. *Tolstoy,* 57–61.
Heldt, Barbara. *Terrible Perfection . . .* , 39–41.
Monter, Barbara H. "Tolstoj's Path Towards Feminism," in Terras, Victor, Ed. *American Contributions . . .* , II, 524–527.

"Father Sergii"
Ziolkowski, Margaret. *Hagiography . . .* , 229–245.

"God Sees the Truth but Waits"
Wilson, A. N. *Tolstoy,* 256–257.

"Hadji Murat"
Cain, T. G. S. *Tolstoy,* 185–200.
Wilson, A. N. *Tolstoy,* 497–498.

"The Kreutzer Sonata"
Cain, T. G. S. *Tolstoy,* 148–154.
Heldt, Barbara. *Terrible Perfection . . .* , 41–42.
Knapp, Bettina L. *Music, Archetype . . .* , 58–74.
Monter, Barbara H. "Tolstoj's Path . . . ," 530–534.
Wilson, A. N. *Tolstoy,* 379–381.

"A Landowner's Morning"
Lee, Nicholas. "Ecological Ethics in the Fiction of L. N. Tolstoj," in Terras, Victor, Ed. *American Contributions . . .* , II, 423–426.

"Master and Man"
Heim, Michael H. "'Master and Man': 'Three Deaths' Redivivus," in Terras, Victor, Ed. *American Contributions . . .* , II, 260–271.
Wilson, A. N. *Tolstoy,* 422–428.

"Polikuska"
Lee, Nicholas. "Ecological Ethics . . . ," 426–427.

"The Posthumous Notes of the Elder Fedor Kuzmich"
Ziolkowski, Margaret. *Hagiography . . .* , 224–229.

"The Snowstorm"
Schultze, Sydney. "Meaning in 'The Snowstorm,'" *Mod Lang Stud,* 17, i (1987), 67–74.

"Three Deaths"
Heim, Michael H. "'Master and Man' . . . ," 260–271.

"Two Old Men"
Ziolkowski, Margaret. *Hagiography . . .* , 116–117.

TOMIOKA TAEKO

"Family in Hell"
Tanaka, Yukiko. "Introduction," in Tanaka, Yukiko, and Elizabeth Hanson, Eds. *This Kind of Woman* . . . , xxiii–xxiv.

JEAN TOOMER

"Avey"
*Blake, Susan L. "The Spectatorial Artist and the Structure of *Cane*," in O'Daniel, Therman B., Ed. *Jean Toomer* . . . , 203–204.
Callahan, John F. *In the African-American Grain* . . . , 85–86.
Hollis, Burney. "Control Conflict Between Rural Thesis and Urban Antithesis in Jean Toomer's 'Avey,'" in O'Daniel, Therman B., Ed. *Jean Toomer* . . . , 277–286.
Rice, Herbert W. "An Incomplete Circle: Repeated Images in Part Two of *Cane*," *Coll Lang Assoc J*, 29 (1986), 445–446.

"Becky"
*Blake, Susan L. "The Spectatorial Artist . . . ," 198–199.
Clark, J. Michael. "Frustrated Redemption: Jean Toomer's Women in *Cane*," *Coll Lang Assoc J*, 22 (1979), 325–326; rpt. O'Daniel, Therman B., Ed. *Jean Toomer* . . . , 408–409.
Dutch, William L. "Three Enigmas: Karintha, Becky, Carma," in O'Daniel, Therman B., Ed. *Jean Toomer* . . . , 267.
Eldridge, Richard. "The Unifying Images in Part I of Jean Toomer's *Cane*," *Coll Lang Assoc J*, 22 (1979), 207–209; rpt. O'Daniel, Therman B., Ed. *Jean Toomer* . . . , 230–232.

"Blood-Burning Moon"
Blackwell, Louise. "Jean Toomer's *Cane* and Biblical Myth," *Coll Lang Assoc J*, 17 (1974), 538–539; rpt. O'Daniel, Therman B., Ed. *Jean Toomer* . . . , 440–441.
*Blake, Susan L. "The Spectatorial Artist . . . ," 201–202.
Brannan, Tim. "Up from the Dusk: Interpretations of 'Blood-Burning Moon,'" *Pembroke Mag*, 8 (1977), 167–172.
Callahan, John F. *In the African-American Grain* . . . , 77–84.
Clark, J. Michael. "Frustrated Redemption . . . ," 329; rpt. O'Daniel, Therman B., Ed. *Jean Toomer* . . . , 411.
Dathorne, O. R. *Dark Ancestor* . . . , 96–97.
Eldridge, Richard. "The Unifying Images . . . ," 212–214; rpt. O'Daniel, Therman B., Ed. *Jean Toomer* . . . , 234–236.

"Bona and Paul"
*Blake, Susan L. "The Spectatorial Artist . . . ," 205–207.
Callahan, John F. *In the African-American Grain* . . . , 92–95.
Rice, Herbert W. "An Incomplete Circle . . . ," 456–461.

"Box Seat"
*Blake, Susan L. "The Spectatorial Artist . . . ," 204–205.

Bus, Heiner. "Jean Toomer and the Black Heritage," in Lenz, Günter H., Ed. *History and Tradition* . . . , 66–67.

Callahan, John F. *In the African-American Grain* . . . , 88–92.

Flowers, Sandra H. "Solving the Critical Conundrum of Jean Toomer's 'Box Seat,'" *Stud Short Fiction*, 25 (1988), 301–305.

Rice, Herbert W. "An Incomplete Circle . . . ," 451–455.

Schultz, Elizabeth. "Jean Toomer's 'Box Seat': The Possibility for 'Constructive Crises,'" *Black Am Lit Forum*, 13 (Spring, 1979), 7–12; rpt. O'Daniel, Therman B., Ed. *Jean Toomer* . . . , 297–310.

"Calling Jesus"

Jung, Udo O. H. "'Nora' Is 'Calling Jesus': A Nineteenth-Century European Dilemma in an Afro-American Garb," *Coll Lang Assoc J*, 21 (1977), 251–255; rpt. O'Daniel, Therman B., Ed. *Jean Toomer* . . . , 293–296.

Rice, Herbert W. "An Incomplete Circle . . . ," 450–451.

"Carma"

Blackwell, Louise. "Jean Toomer's *Cane* . . . ," 537–538; rpt. O'Daniel, Therman B., Ed. *Jean Toomer* . . . , 439–440.

*Blake, Susan L. "The Spectatorial Artist . . . ," 199–200.

Bus, Heiner. "Jean Toomer . . . ," 59.

Dutch, William L. "Three Enigmas . . . ," 267–268.

"Esther"

*Blake, Susan L. "The Spectatorial Artist . . . ," 201.

Bus, Heiner. "Jean Toomer . . . ," 62–63.

Clark, J. Michael. "Frustrated Redemption . . . ," 326–327; rpt. O'Daniel, Therman B., Ed. *Jean Toomer* . . . , 409–410.

Eldridge, Richard. "The Unifying Images . . . ," 203–206; rpt. O'Daniel, Therman B., Ed. *Jean Toomer* . . . , 227–230.

*Waldron, Edward E. "The Search for Identity in Jean Toomer's 'Esther,'" in O'Daniel, Therman B., Ed. *Jean Toomer* . . . , 273–276.

"Fern"

*Blake, Susan L. "The Spectatorial Artist . . . ," 200–201.

Bus, Heiner. "Jean Toomer . . . ," 61–62.

Clark, J. Michael. "Frustrated Redemption . . . ," 330–333; rpt. O'Daniel, Therman B., Ed. *Jean Toomer* . . . , 412–414.

Eldridge, Richard. "The Unifying Images . . . ," 209–211; rpt. O'Daniel, Therman B., Ed. *Jean Toomer* . . . , 232–234.

*Westerfield, Hargis. "Jean Toomer's 'Fern': A Mythical Dimension," in O'Daniel, Therman B., Ed. *Jean Toomer* . . . , 269–271.

"Kabnis"

Bus, Heiner. "Jean Toomer . . . ," 68–70.

Callahan, John F. *In the African-American Grain* . . . , 95–111.

"Karintha"

*Blake, Susan L. "The Spectatorial Artist . . . ," 217–219.

Callahan, John F. *In the African-American Grain* . . . , 66–69.

Clark, J. Michael. "Frustrated Redemption . . . ," 323–325; rpt. O'Daniel, Therman B., Ed. *Jean Toomer* . . . , 406–408.

Dutch, William L. "Three Enigmas . . . ," 265–267.
Eldridge, Richard. "The Unifying Images . . . ," 193–195; rpt. O'Daniel,
    Therman B., Ed. *Jean Toomer* . . . , 217–219.

"Theater"
*Blake, Susan L. "The Spectatorial Artist . . . ," 204.
Callahan, John F. *In the African-American Grain* . . . , 86–87.
*Kopf, George. "The Tensions in Jean Toomer's 'Theater,'" in O'Daniel,
    Therman B., Ed. *Jean Toomer* . . . , 287–292.
Rice, Herbert W. "An Incomplete Circle . . . ," 447–450.

MICHEL TOURNIER

"Le Coq de bruyère"
Davis, Colin. *Michel Tournier* . . . , 149–152.

"La Famille Adam"
Davis, Colin. *Michel Tournier* . . . , 192–193.

"La Jeune Fille et la mort"
Davis, Colin. *Michel Tournier* . . . , 71.

"La Reine blonde"
Davis, Colin. *Michel Tournier* . . . , 155–156.

CATHERINE PARR TRAILL

"The Settlers Settled; or, Pat Connor and His Two Masters"
Ballstadt, Carl P. "Catherine Parr Traill (1802–1899)," in Lecker, Robert, Jack
    David, and Ellen Quigley, Eds. *Canadian Writers* . . . , 175–177.

BRUNO TRAVEN [RET MARUT?]

"Death Songs of Hyotamore of Kyoena"
Küpfer, Peter. "Love and Death in the Early Works of B. Traven," in Schürer,
    Ernst, and Philip Jenkins, Eds. *B. Traven* . . . , 188–189.

"Khundar"
Küpfer, Peter. "Love and Death . . . ," 190–191.

WILLIAM TREVOR [TREVOR COX]

"Beyond the Pale"
Cassill, R. V. . . . *Instructor's Handbook,* 70–71.

"A Complicated Nature"
Perrine, Laurence, and Thomas R. Arp. *Instructor's Manual* . . . , 7th ed., 82–
    84.

LIONEL TRILLING

"Impediments"
Tanner, Stephen L. *Lionel Trilling*, 50–52.

"The Lesson and the Secret"
Tanner, Stephen L. *Lionel Trilling*, 59–60.

"Notes on Departure"
Tanner, Stephen L. *Lionel Trilling*, 52–54.

"Of This Time, Of That Place"
Cowan, S. A. "Parrington, Woolley, and Reality: A Note on Trilling's 'Of This
    Time, Of That Place,'" *Engl Lang Notes*, 26, ii (1988), 56–59.
O'Hara, Daniel T. *Lionel Trilling* . . . , 82–86.
Tanner, Stephen L. *Lionel Trilling*, 55–59.

"The Other Margaret"
Tanner, Stephen L. *Lionel Trilling*, 60–63.

CARLOS ARTURO TRUQUE

"Because People Were This Way"
Lewis, Marvin A. *Treading the Ebony Path* . . . , 43–44.

"Blood on the Plains"
Lewis, Marvin A. *Treading the Ebony Path* . . . , 47–48.

"The Dark Sunglasses"
Lewis, Marvin A. *Treading the Ebony Path* . . . , 44.

"The Day Summer Ended"
Lewis, Marvin A. *Treading the Ebony Path* . . . , 51–54.

"Death Had a Face and Seal"
Lewis, Marvin A. *Treading the Ebony Path* . . . , 46.

"The Encounter"
Lewis, Marvin A. *Treading the Ebony Path* . . . , 56.

"Flight"
Lewis, Marvin A. *Treading the Ebony Path* . . . , 48.

"Fucú"
Lewis, Marvin A. *Treading the Ebony Path* . . . , 56–57.

"Hailstorm"
Lewis, Marvin A. *Treading the Ebony Path* . . . , 46–47.

"Martin Finds Two Reasons"
Lewis, Marvin A. *Treading the Ebony Path* . . . , 44–45.

"Mumu"
Frost, Edgar L. "Turgenev's 'Mumu' and the Absence of Love," *Slavic & East European J*, 31 (1987), 171–186.

ESTHER TUSQUETS

"La casa oscura"
Lecumberri, María E. *"Siete miradas en un mismo paisaje* de Esther Tusquets: Una novela o siete relatos?" *Monographic R*, 4 (1988), 92–93.
Vosburg, Nancy B. *"Siete miradas en un mismo paisaje* de Esther Tusquets: Hacia un proceso de individuación," *Monographic R*, 4 (1988), 103–104.

"En la ciudad sin mar"
Lecumberri, María E. *"Siete miradas . . . ,"* 95.
Vosburg, Nancy B. *"Siete miradas . . . ,"* 101–102.

"Exiliados"
Lecumberri, María E. *"Siete miradas . . . ,"* 90–91.
Vosburg, Nancy B. *"Siete miradas . . . ,"* 102.

"Giselle"
Lecumberri, María E. *"Siete miradas . . . ,"* 93–94.
Vosburg, Nancy B. *"Siete miradas . . . ,"* 100.

"He besado tu boca, Yokanaán"
Lecumberri, María E. *"Siete miradas . . . ,"* 94.
Vosburg, Nancy B. *"Siete miradas . . . ,"* 102–103.

"Orquesta de verano"
Lecumberri, María E. *"Siete miradas . . . ,"* 91–92.
Vosburg, Nancy B. *"Siete miradas . . . ,"* 104.

"Los primos"
Lecumberri, María E. *"Siete miradas . . . ,"* 89–90.
Vosburg, Nancy B. *"Siete miradas . . . ,"* 100–101.

LISA TUTTLE

"The Hollow Man"
Barr, Marleen S. *Alien to Femininity . . . ,* 112–113.

"The Horse Lord"
Büssing, Sabine. *Aliens in the Home . . . ,* 69–70.

"Wives"
Barr, Marleen S. *Alien to Femininity . . . ,* 108.

MARK TWAIN [SAMUEL L. CLEMENS]

"Baker's Blue-Jay Yarn"
Cummings, Sherwood. *Mark Twain and Science* . . . , 97–99.
Wade, Clyde. "Twain's Psychic Force," *Pubs Arkansas Philol Assoc,* 13, i (1987),
    62–63.

"The Belated Russian Passport"
Wilson, James D. *A Reader's Guide* . . . , 8–9.

"Buck Fanshaw's Funeral"
Wilson, James D. *A Reader's Guide* . . . , 124–126.

"The Burning Brand"
Wilson, James D. *A Reader's Guide* . . . , 65–66.

"The California Tale"
Wilson, James D. *A Reader's Guide* . . . , 13–14.

"Cannibalism in the Cars"
Wilson, James D. *A Reader's Guide* . . . , 18–19.

"The Canvasser's Tale"
Wilson, James D. *A Reader's Guide* . . . , 23–24.

"Captain Stormfield's Visit to Heaven"
Wilson, James D. *A Reader's Guide* . . . , 88–90.

"Cecil Rhodes and the Shark"
Wilson, James D. *A Reader's Guide* . . . , 27–28.

"The Celebrated Jumping Frog of Calaveras County"
Wade, Clyde. "Twain's Psychic Force," 63–65.

"A Curious Dream"
Wilson, James D. *A Reader's Guide* . . . , 39.

"A Curious Experience"
Wilson, James D. *A Reader's Guide* . . . , 33.

"A Day at Niagara"
Wilson, James D. *A Reader's Guide* . . . , 37–38.

"The Death Disk"
Wilson, James D. *A Reader's Guide* . . . , 42–43.

"A Dog's Tale"
Wilson, James D. *A Reader's Guide* . . . , 49–50.

"A Double-Barreled Detective Story"
Wilson, James D. *A Reader's Guide* . . . , 56–59.

"A Dying Man's Confession"
Wilson, James D. *A Reader's Guide* . . . , 63.

"Edward Mills and George Benton: A Tale"
Wilson, James D. *A Reader's Guide* . . . , 67–70.

"The Esquimau Maiden's Romance"
Wilson, James D. *A Reader's Guide* . . . , 72–73.

"Extracts from Adam's Diary"
Wilson, James D. *A Reader's Guide* . . . , 96–97.

"A Fable"
Wilson, James D. *A Reader's Guide* . . . , 136–137.

"Facts Concerning the Recent Carnival of Crime in Connecticut"
Wilson, James D. *A Reader's Guide* . . . , 105–106.

"Facts in the Great Beef Contract"
Wilson, James D. *A Reader's Guide* . . . , 110–112.

"Facts in the Great Landslide Case"
Wilson, James D. *A Reader's Guide* . . . , 118–119.

"The Five Boons of Life"
Wilson, James D. *A Reader's Guide* . . . , 135–137.

"A Ghost Story"
Wilson, James D. *A Reader's Guide* . . . , 38–39.

"The Great Dark"
Walsh, Kathleen. "Rude Awakenings and Swift Recoveries: The Problem of Reality in Mark Twain's 'The Great Dark' and 'Three Thousand Years Among the Microbes,'" *Am Lit Realism*, 21, i (1988), 20–23.

"A Horse's Tale"
Wilson, James D. *A Reader's Guide* . . . , 50.

"How I Edited an Agricultural Paper Once"
Wilson, James D. *A Reader's Guide* . . . , 111–112.

"The International Lightning Trust"
Wilson, James D. *A Reader's Guide* . . . , 238–239.

"The Invalid's Story
Wilson, James D. *A Reader's Guide* . . . , 150–151.

"Is He Living or Is He Dead?"
Wilson, James D. *A Reader's Guide* . . . , 181–182.

"The Joke That Made Ed's Fortune"
Wilson, James D. *A Reader's Guide* . . . , 28.

"Journalism in Tennessee"
Wilson, James D. *A Reader's Guide* . . . , 38.

"The Legend of Dilsberg Castle"
Cummings, Sherwood. *Mark Twain and Science* . . . , 99–101.

"The Legend of the Capitoline Venus"
Wilson, James D. *A Reader's Guide* . . . , 180–181.

"Luck"
Wilson, James D. *A Reader's Guide* . . . , 190–191.

"The McWilliamses and the Burglar Alarm"
Wilson, James D. *A Reader's Guide* . . . , 78–80.

"The Man That Corrupted Hadleyburg"
Tabei, Koji. "Irony in 'The Man That Corrupted Hadleyburg,'" *Kyushu Am Lit*,
    29 (1988), 67–69.

"Mrs. McWilliams and the Lightning"
Wilson, James D. *A Reader's Guide* . . . , 78.

"The Mysterious Stranger"
Cummings, Sherwood. *Mark Twain and Science* . . . , 213–216.
Egashira, Rie. "Twain's Later Years of Thought in 'The Mysterious Stranger,'"
    Kyushu Am Lit, 29 (1988), 57–66.
———. "The Unity of 'The Mysterious Stranger': The Coordination of the Last
    Chapter," *Kyushu Am Lit*, 29 (1988), 71–72.

"The £1,000,000 Bank Note"
Wilson, James D. *A Reader's Guide* . . . , 226–227.

"Political Economy"
Wilson, James D. *A Reader's Guide* . . . , 230–231.

"Randall's Jew Story"
Wilson, James D. *A Reader's Guide* . . . , 239.

"The Second Advent"
Wilson, James D. *A Reader's Guide* . . . , 237–238.

"Some Learned Fables for Good Old Boys and Girls"
Wilson, James D. *A Reader's Guide* . . . , 244.

"The Stolen White Elephant"
Wilson, James D. *A Reader's Guide* . . . , 248–249.

"A Story Without End"
Wilson, James D. *A Reader's Guide* . . . , 28–29.

"The $30,000 Bequest"
Wilson, James D. *A Reader's Guide* . . . , 262–266.

"Three Thousand Years Among the Microbes"
Walsh, Kathleen. "Rude Awakenings . . . ," 23–26.

"A True Story"
Cummings, Sherwood. *Mark Twain and Science* . . . , 126–129.
Wilson, James D. *A Reader's Guide* . . . , 270–272.

"Two Little Tales"
Wilson, James D. *A Reader's Guide* . . . , 191–192.

MIGUEL DE UNAMUNO

"Abel Sánchez"
West, Paul. *The Modern Novel*, II, 418–419.

"Aunt Tula"
Navajas, Gonzalo. "The Self and the Symbolic in Unamuno's 'La tía Tula,'"
    Revista de Estudios Hispánicos (Univ. Alabama), 19, iii (1985), 117–132.
Ontañón de Lope, Paciencia. "En torno a 'La tía Tula,'" in Kossoff, A. David,
    et al. [3], Eds. *Actas del VIII Congreso* . . . , II, 383–389.
Ribbans, Geoffrey. "A New Look at 'La tía Tula,'" *Revista Canadienses*, 11 (1987),
    403–420.

"Nothing Less Than a Man"
Spires, Robert C. *Transparent Simulacra* . . . , 49–57.

"Saint Manuel the Good, Martyr"
Glannon, Walter. "Unamuno's 'San Manuel Bueno, mártir': Ethics Through
    Fiction," *Mod Lang Notes*, 102 (1987), 316–333.
Marcone, Rose M. "Unamuno's Impostors: An Approach to the 'Nivolas,'" *Neo-
    philologus*, 71 (1987), 66–71.
———. "Self and Self-Creation: Conflict in the *nivolas*," *Lang Q*, 26, iii–iv
    (1988), 35, 39.
Nepaulsingh, Colbert I. "In Search of a Tradition, Not a Source, for 'San
    Manuel Bueno, mártir,'" *Revista Canadienses*, 11 (1987), 315–330.

JOHN UPDIKE

"A & P"
Dessner, Lawrence J. "Irony and Innocence in John Updike's 'A & P,'" *Stud
    Short Fiction*, 25 (1988), 315–317.

"The Blessed Man of Boston, My Grandmother's Thimble, Fanning Island"
Luscher, Robert M. "John Updike's *Olinger Stories*: New Light among the Shad-
    ows," *J Short Story Engl*, 11 (Autumn, 1988), 111.

"Flight"
Sheidley, William E., and Ann Charters. *Instructor's Manual* . . . , 174–175;
    Charters, Ann, William E. Sheidley, and Martha Ramsey. *Instructor's Man-
    ual* . . . , 2nd ed., 194.

VICTORIA URBANO

ARTURO USLAR PIETRI

"El fuego fato"
Parra, Teresita J. "Perspectiva mítica de la realidad histórica en dos cuentos de
    Arturo Uslar Pietri," *Revista Iberoamericana*, 52 (1986), 948–950.

"Rain"
Menton, Seymour. *El Cuento Hispanoamericano*, II, 218–220; 2nd ed., 218–220;
    3rd ed., 112–114.

GLEB USPENSKY

"The Blind Singer"
Ziolkowski, Margaret. *Hagiography . . .* , 185–186.

"Paramon the Holy Fool"
Ziolkowski, Margaret. *Hagiography . . .* , 136–137.

"Rodion the Concerned"
Ziolkowski, Margaret. *Hagiography . . .* , 184–185.

"A Sensitive Heart"
Ziolkowski, Margaret. *Hagiography . . .* , 186–187.

BORIS BORISOVICH VAKHTIN

"The Sheepskin Coat"
Connolly, Julian W. "Boris Vakhtin's 'The Sheepskin Coat' and Gogol's 'The
    Overcoat,'" in Connolly, Julian W., and Sonia I. Ketchian, Eds. *Studies in
    Russian Literature . . .* , 74–85.

LUISA VALENZUELA

"Change of Guard"
Brunton, Rosanne. "A Note on Contemporary Argentine Women's Writing: A
    Discussion of *The Web*," *Int'l Fiction R*, 15 (1988), 12–13.

"The Verb To Kill"
Fulks, Barbara P. "A Reading of Luisa Valenzuela's Short Story 'La palabra
    asesino,'" *Monographic R*, 4 (1988), 179–188.

RIMA VALLBONA

"Chumico Tree"
Aldaya, Alicia G. R. "Three Short Stories by Rima Vallbona," trans. Eduardo C.
    Bejar, in Urbano, Victoria, Ed. *Five Women Writers . . .* , 124–125.

"Parable of the Impossible Eden"
Aldaya, Alicia G. R. "Three Short Stories . . . ," 126–127.

"Penelope"
Aldaya, Alicia G. R. "Three Short Stories . . . ," 125–126.

RAMÓN DEL VALLE-INCLÁN

"Eulalia"
Nickel, Catherine. "Recasting the Image of the Fallen Woman in Valle-Inclán's 'Eulalia,'" *Stud Short Fiction,* 24 (1987), 289–294.

"La generala"
González-del-Valle, Luis T. "La parodia del honor castizo en 'La generala': Un caso de prolepsis ideológica," *Anales de la Literatura Española,* 11 (1986), 279–293.
Nickel, Catherine. "Valle-Inclán's 'La generala': Woman as Birdbrain," *Hispania,* 71 (1988), 228–234.

"Rosarito"
Bieder, Maryellen. "La narración como arte visual: Focalización en 'Rosarito,'" in Gabriele, John P., Ed. *Genio y virtuosismo . . . ,* 89–100.
Rivas Domínguez, M. José. "Valle-Inclán entre el decadente y el nuevo siglo: 'Rosarito' de la esperpentización al esperpento," *Letras de Deusto,* 18 (September–December, 1988), 127–144.

JACK VANCE [JOHN HOLBROOK VANCE]

"The Moon Moth"
Blish, James. "The Arts of Science Fiction," in Chauvin, Cy, Ed. *A Multitude . . . ,* 60.

C. M. VAN DEN HEEVER

"Daiel's Farewell"
Coetzee, J. M. *White Writing . . . ,* 107–108.

GUY VANDERHAEGHE

"Going to Russia"
Cassill, R. V. . . . *Instructor's Handbook,* 74–75.

A. E. VAN VOGT

"Black Destroyer"
Berger, Albert I. "Theories of History and Social Order in *Astounding Science Fiction,* 1934–1955," *Sci-Fiction Stud,* 15 (1988), 18–19.

"The World of Null-A"
Berger, Albert I. "Theories of History . . . ," 21–22.

MARIO VARGAS LLOSA

"The Cubs"
Higgins, James. . . . *Peruvian Literature*, 228–229.

ANA LYDIA VEGA

"Letra para salsa y tres soneos por encargo"
Handelsman, Michael H. "Desnudando al macho: Un análisis de 'Letra para salsa y tres soneos por encargo,'" *Revista/Review Interamericana*, 12, iv (1982–1983), 559–564.

ENDRE VÉSZI

"Chapter from the Life of Vera Angi"
László, János. "Readers' Historical-Social Knowledge and Their Interpretation and Evaluation of a Short Story," *Poetics*, 17 (1988), 467–481.

JAVIER DE VIANA

"Los amores de Bentos Sagrera"
Menton, Seymour. *El Cuento Hispanoamericano*, I, 138–139; 2nd ed., 139–140; 3rd ed., 139–140.

"The Rustic"
Zum Felde, Alberto. *Critica de la literatura uruguaya*, 264–266.

[COUNT] VILLIERS DE L'ISLE-ADAM
[JEAN MARIE MATTHIAS PHILIPPE AUGUSTE]

"Les Demoiselles de Bienfilâtre"
Zielonska, Anthony. "Irony and Satire in 'Les Demoiselles de Bienfilâtre' by Villiers de l'Isle-Adam," *French Lit Series*, 14 (1987), 157–161.

"L'Intersigne"
Chambers, Ross. "Changing Overcoats: Villiers' 'L'Intersigne' and the Authority of Fiction," *L'Esprit Créateur*, 28, iii (1988), 63–77.

"Sombre récit, conteur plus sombre"
Cogman, P. W. M. "Subversion of the Reader in Villiers's 'Sombre récit, conteur plus sombre,'" *Mod Lang R*, 83, i (1988), 30–39.

JOAN D. VINGE

"Eyes of Amber"
Shreve, Gregory M. "A Lesson in Xenolinguistics: Congruence, Empathy, and
    Computers in Joan Vinge's 'Eyes of Amber,'" in Morse, Donald E., Ed. *The
    Fantastic* . . . , 25–27.

"Tin Soldier"
Barr, Marleen S. *Alien to Femininity* . . . , 110–112.

HELENA MARÍA VIRAMONTES

"Growing"
Alarcón, Norma. "Making *Familia* from Scratch: Subjectivities in the Work of
    Helena María Viramontes and Cherríe Moraga," *Chicano Creativity and Crit-
    icism,* 15, iii–iv (1987), 148–150.

"Snapshots"
Alarcón, Norma. "Making *Familia* from Scratch . . . ," 150–154.

JOSÉ LUIS VIVAS MALDONADO

"El de los cabos blancos"
Melendez, Concha. *El arte del cuento* . . . , 313–315.

"El héroe"
Melendez, Concha. *El arte del cuento* . . . , 311–312.

"Interludio"
Melendez, Concha. *El arte del cuento* . . . , 312–313.

RENÉE VIVIEN [PAULINE MARY TARN]

"The Crocodile Lady"
Jay, Karla. *The Amazon* . . . , 47–48.

"The Death of Psappha"
Jay, Karla. *The Amazon* . . . , 69–70.

"Mute Siren"
Jay, Karla. *The Amazon* . . . , 69.

"The Nut-Brown Maid"
Jay, Karla. *The Amazon* . . . , 44–45.

"Prince Charming"
Jay, Karla. *The Amazon* . . . , 96–99.

"The Veil of Vashti"
Jay, Karla. *The Amazon* . . . , 40–42.

"White as Foam"
Jay, Karla. *The Amazon* . . . , 49–50.

"The Woman of the West"
Jay, Karla. *The Amazon* . . . , 43–44.

GERALD VIZENOR

"Episode in Mystic Verism from Monsignor Missalwait's Interstate"
Ruoff, A. L. Brown. "Woodland Word Warrior: An Introduction to the Works
    of Gerald Vizenor," *MELUS*, 13, i–ii (1986), 30–31.

"Marleen American Horse"
Jaskoski, Helen. "From the Time Immemorial: Native American Traditions in
    Contemporary Short Fiction," in Logsdon, Loren, and Charles W. Mayes,
    Eds. *Since Flannery O'Connor* . . . , 61–64.

GEORGE VIZYINOS

"The Consequences of an Old Story"
Beaton, Roderick. "Realism and Folklore in Nineteenth-Century Greek Fic-
    tion," *Byzantine & Mod Greek Stud*, 8 (1983), 115–116.

"Moskóv-Selím"
Chryssanthopoulos, Michalis. "Reality and Imagination: The Use of History in
    the Short Stories of Yeóryios Viziinós," in Beaton, Roderick. *The Greek
    Novel* . . . , 11–22.

"The Only Journey of His Life"
Beaton, Roderick. "Realism and Folklore . . . ," 114–115.

GEORGIĬ NIKOLAEVICH VLADIMOV

"Pay No Attention, Maestro"
Mozur, Joseph. "Georgiĭ Vladimov: Literary Path into Exile," *World Lit Today*,
    59 (1985), 24–25.

KURT VONNEGUT

"Deer in the Works"
Orendain, Margarita R. "Confronting the Gods of Science: Kurt Vonnegut, Jr.
    in 'Welcome to the Monkey House,'" *St. Louis Univ Research J*, 18, i (1987),
    157, 158, 161.

"EPICAC"
Orendain, Margarita R. "Confronting the Gods . . . ," 157, 158–159, 162.

"The Euphio Question"
Orendain, Margarita R. "Confronting the Gods . . . ," 155, 156.

"Harrison Bergeron"
Orendain, Margarita R. "Confronting the Gods . . . ," 155, 159–160.

"The Manned Missiles"
Orendain, Margarita R. "Confronting the Gods . . . ," 156, 158, 160–161.

"Report on the Barnhouse Effect"
Franklin, H. Bruce. *War Stars . . .* , 119.
Orendain, Margarita R. "Confronting the Gods . . . ," 157–158, 161, 162.

"Tomorrow and Tomorrow and Tomorrow"
Orendain, Margarita R. "Confronting the Gods . . . ," 156.

"Welcome to the Monkey House"
Orendain, Margarita R. "Confronting the Gods . . . ," 155, 159.

M. S. WADDELL

"The Pale Boy"
Büssing, Sabine. *Aliens in the Home . . .* , 110–111.

ALICE WALKER

"Everyday Use"
Cassill, R. V. . . . *Instructor's Handbook,* 76.
Perrine, Laurence, and Thomas R. Arp. *Instructor's Manual . . .* , 7th ed., 71–73.

"Really, Doesn't Crime Pay?"
Bizet, Jean-Michel. "Alice Walker: 'Really, Doesn't Crime Pay?' ou 'les memoires d'une jeune femme rangée'?" *Revue Française,* 13 (April, 1987), 183–192.

"Roselily"
Charters, Ann, William E. Sheidley, and Martha Ramsey. *Instructor's Manual . . .* , 2nd ed., 222–223.

"The Welcome Table"
Ficken, Carl. *God's Story . . .* , 141–150.

MARTIN WALSER

"Die Gallistl'sche Krankheit"
Acker, Robert. "The Role of Film in 'Die Gallistl'sche Krankheit,'" in Schlunk, Jürgen E., and Armand E. Singer, Eds. *Martin Walser . . .* , 37–46.

"A Runaway Horse"

Clark, Jonathan P. "A Subjective Confrontation with the German Past in 'Ein fliehendes Pferd,'" in Schlunk, Jürgen E., and Armand E. Singer, Eds. *Martin Walser . . .*, 47–58.

Haase, Donald P. "Martin Walser's 'Ein fliehendes Pferd' and the Tradition of Repetitive Confession," in Martín, Gregorio, Ed. *Selected Proceedings . . .*, 137–144.

Hillman, R. "'Ein fliehendes Pferd': A Reconsideration," *J Australian Univs Lang & Lit Assoc,* 65 (May, 1986), 48–55.

Wiethölder, Waltraud. "'Otto': Oder sind Goethes *Wahlverwandschaften* auf den Hund gekommen? Anmerkungen zu Martin Walsers Novelle 'Ein fliehendes Pferd,'" *Zeitschrift für Deutsche Philologie,* 102 (1983), 240–259.

SYLVIA TOWNSEND WARNER

"A Dressmaker"

Baldwin, Dean. "The Stories of Sylvia Townsend Warner," *Crazyhorse,* 31 (Fall, 1986), 75–76.

"The Mother"

Baldwin, Dean. "The Stories . . . ," 73–74.

"The Mother Tongue"

Baldwin, Dean. "The Stories . . . ," 77–78.

"On Living for Others"

Baldwin, Dean. "The Stories . . . ," 74–75.

"The Three Cats"

Baldwin, Dean. "The Stories . . . ," 78–79.

"Total Loss"

Baldwin, Dean. "The Stories . . . ," 72–73.

"Winter in the Air"

Baldwin, Dean. "The Stories . . . ," 76–77.

SHEILA WATSON

"Antigone"

Miller, Judith. "Rummaging in the Sewing Basket of the Gods: Sheila Watson's 'Antigone,'" *Stud Canadian Lit,* 12 (1987), 212–221.

EVELYN WAUGH

"Incident in Azamia"

McCartney, George. *Confused Roaring . . .*, 124–125.

"Out of Depth"

McDonnell, Jacqueline. *Evelyn Waugh,* 66–67.

GORDON WEAVER

"The Parts of Speech"
Kennedy, Thomas E. "Fiction as Its Own Subject: An Essay and Two Examples: Anderson's 'Death in the Woods' and Weaver's 'The Parts of Speech,'" *Kenyon R,* 9, iii (1987), 67–70.

STANLEY G. WEINBAUM

"The Black Flame"
Chapman, Edgar L. "Weinbaum's Fire from the Ashes: The Postdisaster Civilization of *The Black Flame,*" in Yoke, Carl B., Ed. *Phoenix from the Ashes* . . . , 89–90.

"Dawn of Flame"
Chapman, Edgar L. "Weinbaum's Fire . . . ," 87–89.

H. G. WELLS

"The Door in the Wall"
Hammond, J. R. *H. G. Wells* . . . , 94–95.

"In the Abyss"
Scheick, William J. "The In-Struction of Wells's 'In the Abyss,'" *Stud Short Fiction,* 24 (1987), 155–159.

"The Rajah's Treasure"
Hammond, J. R. *H. G. Wells* . . . , 121.

"The Spoils of Mr. Blandish"
Hammond, J. R. *H. G. Wells* . . . , 120–122.

"A Story of the Days to Come"
Philmus, Robert M. "'A Story of the Days to Come' and *News from Nowhere:* H. G. Wells as a Writer of Anti-Utopian Fiction," *Engl Lit Transition,* 30 (1987), 450–455.
Pierce, John J. *Foundations* . . . , 94–96.

"The Story of the Last Trump"
Hammond, J. R. *H. G. Wells* . . . , 123–124.

"Through a Window"
Hammond, J. R. *H. G. Wells* . . . , 50–51.

"The Time Machine"
Baldick, Chris. *In Frankenstein's Shadow* . . . , 158–160.
Hammond, J. R. *H. G. Wells* . . . , 73–84.
Leiby, David A. "The Tooth That Gnaws: Reflections on Time Travel," in Slusser, George E., and Eric S. Rabkin, Eds. *Intersections* . . . , 109–110.
Pierce, John J. *Foundations* . . . , 85–88.

"The Wild Asses of the Devil"
Hammond, J. R. *H. G. Wells* . . . , 122.

EUDORA WELTY

"Asphodel"
Donaldson, Susan V. "Meditations on Nonpresence: Revisioning the Short Story in Eudora Welty's *The Wide Net*," *J Short Story Engl*, 11 (Autumn, 1988), 81–82.

"At the Landing"
Donaldson, Susan V. "Meditations . . . ," 86–88.

"The Burning"
Howell, Elmo. "Eudora Welty and the City of Man," *Georgia R*, 33 (1979), 776–777.

"The Death of a Traveling Salesman"
Dessner, Lawrence J. "Vision and Revision in Eudora Welty's 'Death of a Traveling Salesman,'" *Stud Am Fiction*, 15, ii (1987), 145–159.

"First Love"
Donaldson, Susan V. "Meditations . . . ," 82–83.

"June Recital"
Howell, Elmo. "Eudora Welty . . . ," 772–774.

"Kin"
Belsches, Alan T. "A Treasury Most Dear: The Use of Memory in Eudora Welty's Early Short Stories," *Notes Mississippi Writers*, 20, i (1988), 12–14.
Pitavy-Souques, Danièle. "A Blazing Butterfly: The Modernity of Eudora Welty," in Devlin, Albert J., Ed. *Welty* . . . , 133–135.

"Lily Daw and the Three Ladies"
Charters, Ann, William E. Sheidley, and Martha Ramsey. *Instructor's Manual* . . . , 2nd ed., 130–131.

"Livvie"
Donaldson, Susan V. "Meditations . . . ," 80–81.

"Moon Lake"
Pitavy-Souques, Danièle. "A Blazing Butterfly . . . ," 126–127.
Yaeger, Patricia S. "The Case of the Dangling Signifier: Phallic Imagery in Eudora Welty's 'Moon Lake,'" in Kessler-Harris, Alice, and William McBrien, Eds. *Faith of a (Woman) Writer*, 253–271.

"Old Mr. Marblehall"
Pitavy-Souques, Danièle. "A Blazing Butterfly . . . ," 130–133.

"Powerhouse"

Albert, Richard N. "Eudora Welty's Fats Waller: 'Powerhouse,'" *Notes Mississippi Writers*, 19, ii (1987), 63–71.

Pollack, Harriet. "Words Between Strangers: On Welty, Her Style, and Her Audience," in Devlin, Albert J., Ed. *Welty . . .* , 60–69.

"The Purple Hat"

Donaldson, Susan V. "Meditations . . . ," 80.

"Sir Rabbit"

Yaeger, Patricia S. "'Because a Fire Was in My Head': Eudora Welty and the Dialogic Imagination," in Devlin, Albert J., Ed. *Welty . . .* , 146–148.

"A Sketching Trip"

Belsches, Alan T. "A Treasury Most Dear . . . ," 10–12.

"A Still Moment"

Donaldson, Susan V. "Meditations . . . ," 83–85.

Pitavy-Souques, Danièle. "A Blazing Butterfly . . . ," 125–126.

"The Wide Net"

Donaldson, Susan V. "Meditations . . . ," 79.

Rouberol, Jean. "Aspects du mythe dans 'The Wide Net' de Eudora Welty," in Santraud, Jeanne-Marie, Ed. *Le Sud . . .* , 51–55.

"The Winds"

Donaldson, Susan V. "Meditations . . . ," 79–80.

"A Worn Path"

Perrine, Laurence, and Thomas R. Arp. *Instructor's Manual . . .* , 7th ed., 73–74.

Sheidley, William E., and Ann Charters. *Instructor's Manual . . .* , 133–134; Charters, Ann, William E. Sheidley, and Martha Ramsey. *Instructor's Manual . . .* , 2nd ed., 133–134.

Walter, James. "Love's Habit of Vision in Welty's Phoenix Jackson," *J Short Story Engl*, 7 (Autumn, 1986), 77–85.

GLENWAY WESCOTT

"The Pilgrim Hawk"

Bawer, Bruce. *Diminishing Fiction . . .* , 151–154.

NATHANAEL WEST

"A Cool Million"

Gorak, Jan. *God the Artist . . .* , 49–53.

West, Paul. *The Modern Novel*, II, 275.

Widmer, Kingsley. "Twisting American Comedy: Henry Miller and Nathanael West, Among Others," *Arizona Q*, 43 (1987), 224–226.

"The Dream Life of Balso Snell"
Gorak, Jan. *God the Artist . . .* , 41–45.
West, Paul. *The Modern Novel,* II, 274.
Widmer, Kingsley. "Twisting American Comedy . . . ," 226–227.

"Miss Lonelyhearts"
Gorak, Jan. *God the Artist . . .* , 45–50.
Keyes, John. "'Inarticulate Expressions of Genuine Suffering'? A Reply to the
    Correspondence in 'Miss Lonelyhearts,'" *Univ Windsor R,* 20, i (1987), 11–
    25.
Poznar, Walter. "The Apocalyptic Vision in Nathanael West's 'Miss Lonely-
    hearts,'" in James, JoAnn, and William J. Cleenan, Eds. *Apocalyptic Vi-
    sion . . .* , 111–119.
Prasad, Suman Prabha. "The Sympathetic Misogynist: A Consideration of the
    Treatment of Women in N. West's 'Miss Lonelyhearts,'" in Prasad, R. C.,
    and A. K. Sharma, Eds. *Modern Studies . . .* , 72–79.
West, Paul. *The Modern Novel,* II, 274–275.

EDITH WHARTON

"The Angel at the Grave"
Gilbert, Sandra M., and Susan Gubar. *No Man's Land . . .* , 173–174.

"Roman Fever"
Petry, Alice H. "A Twist of Crimson Silk: Edith Wharton's 'Roman Fever,'"
    Stud Short Fiction, 24 (1987), 163–166.
Sheidley, William E., and Ann Charters. *Instructor's Manual . . .* , 43–44; Char-
    ters, Ann, William E. Sheidley, and Martha Ramsey. *Instructor's Man-
    ual . . .* , 2nd ed., 52–53.

"Twilight Sleep"
Schriber, Mary S. *Gender . . .* , 167–170.

PATRICK WHITE

"Clay"
Pathak, Suraj. "Treatment of Love in Patrick's Short Stories," *Lit Endeavour,* 7,
    i–iv (1985), 155–156.

"The Dead Roses"
Pathak, Suraj. "Treatment of Love . . . ," 150–155.

"A Woman's Hand"
Dev, Jai. "Nature in 'A Woman's Hand,'" *Lit Endeavour,* 7, i–iv (1985), 136–
    148.

RUDY WIEBE

"Where Is the Voice Coming From?"
Bowering, George. *Imaginary Hand . . .* , I, 53–60.

OSCAR WILDE

"The Birthday of the Infanta"
Raby, Peter. *Oscar Wilde,* 61–63.

"The Canterville Ghost"
Raby, Peter. *Oscar Wilde,* 54–56.

"The Devoted Friend"
Raby, Peter. *Oscar Wilde,* 59–60.

"The Happy Prince"
Raby, Peter. *Oscar Wilde,* 57–58.

"Lord Arthur Savile's Crime"
Raby, Peter. *Oscar Wilde,* 52–54.

"The Portrait of Mr. W. H."
Bashford, Bruce. "Hermeneutics in Oscar Wilde's 'The Portrait of Mr. W. H.,'"
    Papers Lang & Lit, 24 (1988), 412–422.
Raby, Peter. *Oscar Wilde,* 64–65.

"The Star-Child"
Raby, Peter. *Oscar Wilde,* 63–64.

CHARLES WILLARD

"The Power and the Glory"
Bartter, Martha A. *The Way to Ground Zero . . . ,* 97.

JESSE LYNCH WILLIAMS

"The New Reporter"
Good, Howard. *Acquainted with the Night . . . ,* 29–30.

"The Old Reporter"
Good, Howard. *Acquainted with the Night . . . ,* 37–38.

JOY WILLIAMS

"Taking Care"
Cassill, R. V. . . . *Instructor's Handbook,* 77.

TENNESSEE WILLIAMS

"The Accent of a Coming Foot"
Vannatta, Dennis. *Tennessee Williams . . . ,* 10–13.

"Portrait of a Girl in Glass"
Vannatta, Dennis. *Tennessee Williams* . . . , 27–32.

"The Resemblance Between a Violin Case and a Coffin"
Vannatta, Dennis. *Tennessee Williams* . . . , 55–58.

"Sabbatha and Solitude"
Vannatta, Dennis. *Tennessee Williams* . . . , 72–73.

"Something by Tolstoi"
Vannatta, Dennis. *Tennessee Williams* . . . , 8–9.

"Ten Minute Stop"
Vannatta, Dennis. *Tennessee Williams* . . . , 16–17.

"Three Players of a Summer Game"
Vannatta, Dennis. *Tennessee Williams* . . . , 61–64.

"Twenty-Seven Wagons Full of Cotton"
Vannatta, Dennis. *Tennessee Williams* . . . , 13–15.

"Two on a Party"
Vannatta, Dennis. *Tennessee Williams* . . . , 58–61.

"The Vengeance of Nitocris"
Vannatta, Dennis. *Tennessee Williams* . . . , 5–7.

"The Vine"
Vannatta, Dennis. *Tennessee Williams* . . . , 39–41.

WILLIAM CARLOS WILLIAMS

"Jean Beicke"
Cowan, James C. "The *Pharmakos* Figure in Modern American Stories of Physicians and Patients," *Lit & Med,* 6 (1987), 105–107.

"A Night in June"
Charters, Ann, William E. Sheidley, and Martha Ramsey. *Instructor's Manual* . . . , 2nd ed., 84–85.

"The Use of Force"
Bell, Barbara C. "Williams' 'The Use of Force' and First Principles of Medical Ethics," *Lit & Med,* 3 (1985), 143–151.
Terry, James S., and Peter C. Williams. "Literature and Bioethics: The Tension in Goals and Styles," *Lit & Med,* 7 (1988), 6–8.

JACK WILLIAMSON

"Backlash"
Bartter, Martha A. *The Way to Ground Zero* . . . , 86–87.

ANGUS WILSON

"Raspberry Jam"
Büssing, Sabine. *Aliens in the Home . . .* , 94–95.

ETHEL WILSON

"Haply the Soul of My Grandmother"
Dahlie, Hallvard. *Varieties of Exile . . .* , 70–71.

"Lilly's Story"
Keith, W. J. "Overview: Ethel Wilson, Providence, and the Vocabulary of Vision," in McMullen, Lorraine, Ed. *The Ethel Wilson Symposium*, 109–110.

"Reflections in a Pool"
Keith, W. J. "Overview . . . ," 116.

"Tuesday and Wednesday"
Keith, W. J. "Overview . . . ," 108–109.

"We Have to Sit Opposite"
Dahlie, Hallvard. *Varieties of Exile . . .* , 71.

"Winter"
Keith, W. J. "Overview . . . ," 113–115.

THOMAS WILSON

"The Face of the Enemy"
Blish, James. "The Arts in Science Fiction," in Chauvin, Cy, Ed. *A Multitude . . .* , 60.

CHRISTA WOLF

"Change of Perspective"
Kuhn, Anna K. *Christa Wolf's Utopian Vision . . .* , 99–100.

"New Memoirs of a Tomcat"
Kuhn, Anna K. *Christa Wolf's Utopian Vision . . .* , 172.

"Unter den Linden"
Kuhn, Anna K. *Christa Wolf's Utopian Vision . . .* , 172–173.

GENE WOLFE

"A Story"
McGregor, Gaile. *The Noble Savage . . .* , 278–279.

THOMAS WOLFE

"Child by Tiger"
*Perrine, Laurence, and Thomas R. Arp. *Instructor's Manual . . .* , 7th ed., 2–4.

TOBIAS WOLFF

"In the Garden of the North American Martyrs"
Cassill, R. V. . . . . *Instructor's Handbook,* 78–79.

DOUGLAS WOOLF

"Bang Day"
Bowering, George. *The Mask . . .* , 151–154.

VIRGINIA WOOLF

"Kew Gardens"
Oakland, John. "Virginia Woolf's 'Kew Gardens,'" *Engl Stud,* 68 (1987), 264–273.

"The Lady in the Looking Glass"
Minow-Pinkney, Makiko. *Virginia Woolf . . .* , 36–37.

"The Mark on the Wall"
Minow-Pinkney, Makiko. *Virginia Woolf . . .* , 154–155.

"Moments of Being"
Sheidley, William E., and Ann Charters. *Instructor's Manual . . .* , 76; Charters, Ann, William E. Sheidley, and Martha Ramsey. *Instructor's Manual . . .* , 2nd ed., 71–72.

"A Society"
Dick, Susan. "'What Fools We Were!' Virginia Woolf's 'A Society,'" *Twentieth Century Lit,* 33 (1987), 51–66.

"An Unwritten Novel"
Engler, Bernd. "Virginia Woolfs 'An Unwritten Novel': Realistische Erzälkonventionen und innovative Ästhetik," *Anglia,* 105 (1987), 390–413.
Minow-Pinkney, Makiko. *Virginia Woolf . . .* , 25–26.

CONSTANCE FENIMORE WOOLSON

"At the Château of Corinne"
Weimer, Joan M. "Women Artists and Exile in the Fiction of Constance Fenimore Woolson," *Legacy,* 3, ii (1986), 9–11.
———, Ed. "Introduction," . . . *"Miss Grief" and Other Stories* [by Constance Fenimore Woolson], xxxvi–xxxvii.

"Bro"
Dean, Sharon L. "Constance Woolson's Southern Sketches," *Southern Stud,* 25
    (1986), 282–283.

"Castle Nowhere"
Weimer, Joan M., Ed. "Introduction," xxvii–xxx.

"Felipa"
Weimer, Joan M. "Women Artists . . . ," 7–8.
———, Ed. "Introduction," xxxiii–xxxiv.

"In the Cotton Country"
Weimer, Joan M. "Women Artists . . . ," 5–6.
———, Ed. "Introduction," xxxii–xxxiii.

"Jeannette"
Weimer, Joan M. "Women Artists . . . ," 5.

"The Lady of Little Fishing"
Weimer, Joan M. "Women Artists . . . ," 6–7.
———, Ed. "Introduction," xxvi–xxvii.

"Miss Elisabeth"
Dean, Sharon L. ". . . Southern Sketches," 278–279.
Weimer, Joan M., Ed. "Introduction," xxxi–xxxii.

"Miss Grief"
Gilbert, Sandra M., and Susan Gubar. *No Man's Land . . . ,* 178–179.
Torsney, Cheryl B., Ed. "'Miss Grief' by Constance Fenimore Woolson," *Legacy,*
    4, i (1987), 11–13.
Weimer, Joan M. "Women Artists . . . ," 11–12.

"Old Gardiston"
Dean, Sharon L. ". . . Southern Sketches," 278.

"St. Clair Flats"
Weimer, Joan M., Ed. "Introduction," xxx–xxxi.

"Sister St. Luke"
Dean, Sharon L. ". . . Southern Sketches," 280–281.

"The Street of the Hyacinth"
Weimer, Joan M. "Women Artists . . . ," 8–9.
———, Ed. "Introduction," xxxvi.

"Up in Blue Ridge"
Dean, Sharon L. ". . . Southern Sketches," 282.

EVERIL WORRELL

"The Canal"
Senf, Carol A. *The Vampire . . . ,* 7.

RICHARD WRIGHT

"Big Boy Leaves Home"
Atkinson, Michael. "Richard Wright's 'Big Boy Leaves Home' and a Tale from
    Ovid: A Metamorphosis Transformed," *Stud Short Fiction*, 24 (1987), 251–
    261; rpt. Trotman, C. James, Ed. *Richard Wright . . . ,* 43–57.
Douglas, Robert L. "Religious Orthodoxy and Skepticism in Richard Wright's
    Uncle Tom's Children and *Native Son*," *Griot*, 6, iii (1987), 49.
Walker, Margaret. *Richard Wright . . . ,* 82–84, 116–117.
Webb, Tracy. "The Role of Water Imagery in *Uncle Tom's Children*," *Mod Fiction
    Stud*, 34 (1988), 7–8.

"Bright and Morning Star"
Douglas, Robert L. "Religious Orthodoxy . . . ," 50–51.
Larson, Thomas. "A Political Vision of Afro-American Culture: Richard
    Wright's 'Bright and Morning Star,'" in Trotman, C. James, Ed. *Richard
    Wright . . . ,* 147–159.
Webb, Tracy. "The Role of Water . . . ," 13–14.

"Down by the Riverside"
Douglas, Robert L. "Religious Orthodoxy . . . ," 49.
Webb, Tracy. "The Role of Water . . . ," 8–10.

"Fire and Cloud"
Webb, Tracy. "The Role of Water . . . ," 12–13.

"Long Black Song"
Douglas, Robert L. "Religious Orthodoxy . . . ," 49–50.
Webb, Tracy. "The Role of Water . . . ," 10–12.

"The Man Who Lived Underground"
Dixon, Melvin. *Ride Out the Wilderness . . . ,* 64–69.
Lesser, Wendy. *The Life Below the Ground . . . ,* 102–125.
Walker, Margaret. *Richard Wright . . . ,* 173–176.

"The Man Who Was Almost a Man"
Sheidley, William E., and Ann Charters. *Instructor's Manual . . . ,* 129; Charters,
    Ann, William E. Sheidley, and Martha Ramsey. *Instructor's Manual . . . ,* 2nd
    ed., 129.

IDA A. WYLIE

"Witches' Sabbath"
Büssing, Sabine. *Aliens in the Home . . . ,* 54–56.

XI RONG

"An Unexceptional Post"
Kubin, Wolfgang. "Sexuality and Literature in the People's Republic of China:
    Problems of Chinese Women Prior to and Since 1949 as Seen in Ding

Ling's *Diary of Sophia* (1922) and Xi Rong's Story 'An Unexceptional Post' (1926)," in Kubin, Wolfgang, and Rudolf G. Wagner, Eds. *Essays in Modern Chinese Literature . . .* , 178–186.

YAMADA BIMYŌ

"Butterfly"
Okazaki, Yoshie. *Japanese Literature . . .* , 156–157.

HISAYE YAMAMOTO

"The Legend of Miss Sasagawara"
Cheung, King-Kok. "Introduction," *"Seventeen Syllables" and Other Stories* [by Hisaye Yamamoto], xxi–xxii.

"Seventeen Syllables"
Cheung, King-Kok. "Introduction," xv–xvi, xviii–xxi.

YAMAMOTO MICHIKO

"The Man Who Cut the Grass"
Tanaka, Yukiko. "Introduction," in Tanaka, Yukiko, and Elizabeth Hanson, Eds. *This Kind of Woman . . .* , xxi–xxii.

AUGUSTÍN YAÑEZ

"Aserrín de muñecos"
Giacoman, Helmy F., Ed. *Homenaje a Augustín Yañez*, 339.

"Las avispas"
Giacoman, Helmy F., Ed. *Homenaje a Augustín Yañez*, 338.

"Gota serena"
Giacoman, Helmy F., Ed. *Homenaje a Augustín Yañez*, 340–341.

"Música celestial"
Giacoman, Helmy F., Ed. *Homenaje a Augustín Yañez*, 338–339.

"Pasión y convalecencia"
Giacoman, Helmy F., Ed. *Homenaje a Augustín Yañez*, 339–340.

YAO XUEYIN

"Fuss over Forts"
Lyell, William A. "The Early Fiction of Yao Xueyin," in Kubin, Wolfgang, and Rudolf G. Wagner, Eds. *Essays in Modern Chinese Literature . . .* , 39–40.

"Story of the Red Lantern"
Lyell, William A. "The Early Fiction . . . ," 41.

ALEKSANDR YASHIN

"Levers"
Lowe, David. *Russian Writing Since 1953* . . . , 80.

ABRAHAM B. YEHOSHUA

"The Day's Sleep"
Fuchs, Esther. *Israeli Mythologies* . . . , 38.

"The Evening Voyage of Yatir"
Fuchs, Esther. *Israeli Mythologies* . . . , 39–40.

"Galia's Wedding"
Fuchs, Esther. *Israeli Mythologies* . . . , 39.

"Long Summer Day, His Despair, His Wife and His Daughter"
Fuchs, Esther. *Israeli Mythologies* . . . , 47–49.

"Missile Base 612"
Fuchs, Esther. *Israeli Mythologies* . . . , 49–50.

S. YIZHAR

"Habakuk"
Knapp, Bettina L. "Yizhar's 'Habakuk'—Archetypal Violin Music and the Prophetic Experience," *Mod Lang Stud,* 17, iii (1987), 41–53; rpt. in her *Music, Archetype* . . . , 144–157.

YOKOMITSU RIICHI

"After Picking Up a Blue Stone"
Keene, Dennis. *Yokomitsu Riichi* . . . , 119–123.

"The Bird"
Keene, Dennis. *Yokomitsu Riichi* . . . , 169–171.

"The Child Who Was Laughed At"
Keene, Dennis. *Yokomitsu Riichi* . . . , 200–201.

"The Defeated Husband" [originally "The Scroll of Love"]
Keene, Dennis. *Yokomitsu Riichi* . . . , 53–57.

"The Expressionist Actor"
Keene, Dennis. *Yokomitsu Riichi* . . . , 99–107.

"A Face to Sorrow Over"
Keene, Dennis. *Yokomitsu Riichi* . . . , 199–200.

"Ginseng and Sky"
Keene, Dennis. *Yokomitsu Riichi* . . . , 118–119.

"Heads and Bellies"
Keene, Dennis. *Yokomitsu Riichi* . . . , 71–73.

"Ideas of a Flower Garden"
Keene, Dennis. *Yokomitsu Riichi* . . . , 146–153.

"The Machine"
Keene, Dennis. *Yokomitsu Riichi* . . . , 167–169.

"The Pale Captain"
Keene, Dennis. *Yokomitsu Riichi* . . . , 123–126.

"Smile"
Keene, Dennis. *Yokomitsu Riichi* . . . , 211–212.

"Spring Riding in a Carriage"
Keene, Dennis. *Yokomitsu Riichi* . . . , 142–145.
Rimer, J. Thomas. *A Reader's Guide* . . . , 150–151.

"Time"
Keene, Dennis. *Yokomitsu Riichi* . . . , 211–212.
Rimer, J. Thomas. *A Reader's Guide* . . . , 150.
Viglielmo, Valdo H. "Yokomitsu Riichi's 'Jikan' ('Time'): An Allegorical Inter-
pretation," in Takeda, Katsuhiko, Ed. . . . *Japanese Literature*, 105–117.

AMADO YUZON

"Riddle"
Zapanta-Manlapaz, Edna. *Kampampangan Literature* . . . , 51.

ERACLIO ZEPEDA

"Benzulul"
Dorward, Frances R. "'Benzulul': El cuento indigenista y apoteosis," *Texto Crítico*, 12 (1986), 93–104.

MIKHAIL MIKHAĬLOVICH ZOSHCHENKO

"The Bathhouse"
Polley, J. Patrick. "When Cleanliness Was Next to Godliness: The Proletarian
Bathhouse," in Hartigan, Karelisa V., Ed. *From the Bard to Broadway*, 167–
176.

A CHECKLIST OF BOOKS USED

Aaron, Daniel. *The Unwritten War: American Writers and the Civil War.* New York: Knopf, 1973.

Abel, Darrell. *The Moral Picturesque: Studies in Hawthorne's Fiction.* West Lafayette: Purdue Univ. Press, 1988.

Achugar, Hugo. *Ideología y estructuras narrativas en José Donoso (1950–1970).* Caracas: Centre de Estudios Latinoamericanos Rómulo Gallegos, 1979.

Adam, Wolfgang, Ed. *Das achtzehnte Jahrhundert: Facetten einer Epoche.* Heidelberg: Carl Winter Univ. Press, 1988.

Adams, Edward C. L. *Tales of the Congaree,* ed. Robert G. O'Meally. Chapel Hill: Univ. of North Carolina Press, 1987.

Adelman, Gary. *Heart of Darkness: Search for the Unconscious.* Boston: Twayne, 1987.

Alazraki, Jaime. *Borges and the Kaballah.* Cambridge: Cambridge Univ. Press, 1988.

———, Ed. *Critical Essays on Jorge Luis Borges.* Boston: Hall, 1987.

Alexander, Anne. *Thomas Hardy: The "Dream Country" of His Fiction.* London: Vision, 1987; Am. ed. Totowa, N.J.: Barnes & Noble, 1987.

Allen, Roger, Ed. *In the Eye of the Beholder: Tales of Egyptian Life from the Writings of Yusuf Idris.* Chicago: Bibliotheca Islamica, 1978.

———. *Modern Arabic Literature.* New York: Ungar, 1987.

Alsen, Eberhard. *Salinger's Glass Stories as Composite Novel.* Troy, N.Y.: Whitston, 1983.

Ambrose, Jamie. *Willa Cather: Writing at the Frontier.* Oxford: Berg, 1988.

Amur, G. S., V. R. N. Prasad, B. V. Nemade, and N. K. Nihalani, Eds. *Indian Readings in Commonwealth Literature.* New Delhi: Sterling, 1985.

Anderson, Linda R. *Bennett, Wells, and Conrad: Narrative in Transition.* New York: St. Martin's Press, 1988.

Andrews, Joe. *Women in Russian Literature, 1780–1863.* New York: St. Martin's Press, 1988.

Antúnez, Rocío. *Felisberto Hernández: El Discurso inundado.* Mexico City: Katún, 1985.

Anyidoho, Kofi, Abioseh M. Porter, Daniel Racine, and Janice Spleth, Eds. *Interdisciplinary Dimensions of African Literature.* Washington: Three Continents Press, 1985.

Axthelm, Peter M. *The Modern Confessional Novel.* New Haven: Yale Univ. Press, 1967.

Bain, Robert, and Joseph M. Flora, Eds. *Fifty Southern Writers Before 1900.* Westport: Greenwood, 1987.

Baker, Houston A. *Modernism and the Harlem Renaissance.* Chicago: Univ. of Chicago Press, 1987.

Bakker, J., J. A. Verleun, and J. van der Vriesenaerde, Eds. *Essays on English and American Literature and a Sheaf of Poems.* Amsterdam: Rodopi, 1987.

Baldwin, Dean R. *V. S. Pritchett.* Boston: Twayne, 1987.

Bangerter, Lowell A. *Robert Musil.* New York: Continuum, 1988.

Bardeleben, Renate von, Dietrich Briesemeister, and Juan Bruce-Nocoa, Eds.

Missions in Conflict: Essays on U.S.-Mexican Relations and Chicano Culture. Tübingen: Narr, 1986.

Barnes, Hazel E. *Humanistic Existentialism: The Literature of Possibility.* Lincoln: Univ. of Nebraska Press, 1956.

Barr, Marleen S. *Alien to Femininity: Speculative Fiction and Feminist Theory.* Westport: Greenwood, 1987.

Bartter, Martha A. *The Way to Ground Zero: The Atomic Bomb in American Science Fiction.* Westport: Greenwood, 1988.

Bassein, Beth A. *Women and Death: Linkages in Western Thought and Literature.* Westport: Greenwood, 1984.

Batts, Michael S., Anthony W. Riley, and Heinz Wetzel, Eds. *Echoes and Influences of German Romanticism: Essays in Honor of Hans Eichner.* New York: Lang, 1987.

Baumbach, Jonathan. *Moderns and Contemporaries: Nine Masters of the Short Story.* New York: Random House, 1968.

Baumgaertner, Jill P. *Flannery O'Connor: A Proper Scaring.* Wheaton, Ill.: Harold Shaw, 1988.

Bawer, Bruce. *Diminishing Fiction: Essays on the Modern American Novel and Its Critics.* St. Paul, Minn.: Graywolf Press, 1988.

Bayley, John. *The Short Story: Henry James to Elizabeth Bowen.* New York: St. Martin's Press, 1988.

Baynton, Barbara. *The Portable Barbara Baynton,* ed. Sally Krimmer and Alan Lawson. St. Lucia: Univ. of Queensland Press, 1980.

Beaton, Roderick. *The Greek Novel AD 1–1985.* London: Croom Helm, 1988.

Bell, Ian F. A., Ed. *Henry James: Fiction as History.* Totowa, N.J.: Barnes & Noble, 1984.

Bellringer, Alan W. *Henry James.* New York: St. Martin's Press, 1988.

Bell-Villada, Gene H., Antonio Giménez, and George Pistorius, Eds. *From Dante to García Márquez: Studies in Romance Literatures and Linguistics.* Williamstown, Mass.: Williams College, 1987.

Bender, Eileen T. *Joyce Carol Oates, Artist in Residence.* Bloomington: Indiana Univ. Press, 1987.

Bennett, Benjamin, Anton Kaes, and William J. Lillyman, Eds. *Probleme der Moderne: Studien zur deutschen Literatur von Nietzsche bis Brecht.* Tübingen: Niemeyer, 1983.

Benstock, Bernard, Ed. *James Joyce: The Augmented Ninth.* Syracuse: Syracuse Univ. Press, 1988.

Benstock, Shari, Ed. *Feminist Issues in Literary Scholarship.* Bloomington: Indiana Univ. Press, 1987.

Beranger, Jean, Jean Cazemajou, Jean-Michel Lacroix, and Pierre Spriet, Eds. *Multilinguisme et multiculturalisme en Amérique du Nord: Survivances, transfert, métamorphoses.* Bordeaux: Univ. of Bordeaux Press, 1988.

Bernd, Clifford A., Ed. *Grillparzer's "Der arme Spielmann": New Directions in Criticism.* Columbia, S.C.: Camden House, 1988.

Besner, Neil K. *The Light of Imagination: Mavis Gallant's Fiction.* Vancouver: Univ. of British Columbia Press, 1988.

Bessière, Jean, Ed. *L'Ordre du descriptif.* Paris: Univ. de France Press, 1988.

Bhalla, Alok, Ed. *García Márquez and Latin America.* New York: Envoy Press, 1987.

Billy, Ted, Ed. *Critical Essays on Joseph Conrad.* Boston: Hall, 1987.

Binder, Hartmut, Ed. *Franz Kafka und die Prager deutsche Literatur: Deutungen und Wirkungen.* Bonn: Kulturstiftung der Deutschen Vertriebenen, 1988.

Birkerts, Sven. *An Artificial Wilderness: Essays on Twentieth-Century Literature.* New York: Morrow, 1987.

Birrell, Gordon. *The Boundless Present: Space and Time in the Literary Fairy Tales of Novalis and Tieck.* Chapel Hill: Univ. of North Carolina Press, 1979.

Bishop, George. *When the Master Relents: The Neglected Short Fictions of Henry James.* Ann Arbor: UMI Research Press, 1988.

Blansfield, Karen C. *Cheap Rooms and Restless Hearts: A Study of Formula in the Urban Tales of William Sydney Porter.* Bowling Green: Bowling Green State Univ. Popular Press, 1988.

Blodgett, E. D. *Configuration: Essays in the Canadian Literatures.* Downsview, Ont.: ECW Press, 1972.

———. *Alice Munro.* Boston: Twayne, 1988.

Bloom, Clive. *The Occult Experience and New Criticism.* Brighton, Sussex: Harvester, 1986; Am. ed. Totowa, N.J.: Barnes & Noble, 1987.

Bloom, Harold, Ed. *Joseph Conrad's "Heart of Darkness."* New York: Chelsea House, 1987.

———. *Stephen Crane.* New York: Chelsea House, 1987.

———. *J. D. Salinger.* New York: Chelsea House, 1987.

———. *Joyce Carol Oates.* New York: Chelsea House, 1987.

———. *Isaac Babel.* New York: Chelsea House, 1987.

———. *Rudyard Kipling.* New York: Chelsea House, 1987.

Blum, Joanne. *Transcending Gender: The Male/Female Double in Women's Fiction.* Ann Arbor: UMI Research Press, 1988.

Boelhower, William. *Through a Glass Darkly: Ethnic Semiosis in American Literature.* Venice: Edizione Helvetia, 1984; 2nd ed. New York: Oxford Univ. Press, 1987.

Bold, Alan. *MacDiarmid—Christopher Murray Grieve—A Critical Biography.* London: Murray, 1988.

Bonaccorso, Richard. *Sean O'Faolain's Irish Vision.* Albany: State Univ. of New York Press, 1987.

Boone, Joseph A. *Tradition Counter Tradition: Love and the Form of Fiction.* Chicago: Univ. of Chicago Press, 1987.

Bowering, George. *The Mask in Place: Essays on Fiction in North America.* Winnipeg: Turnstone, 1982.

———. *Imaginary Hand: Essays by George Bowering,* I. Edmonton, Alberta: NeWest Press, 1988.

Boyers, Robert. *After the Avant-Garde: Essays in Art and Culture.* University Park: Pennsylvania State Univ. Press, 1988.

Braendlin, Hans P., Ed. *Ambiguities in Literature and Film.* Tallahassee: Florida State Univ. Press, 1988.

Brancafore, Benito, Edward R. Mulvihill, and Roberto G. Sánchez, Eds. *Homenaje a Antonio Sánchez Barbudo: Ensayos de literatura española moderna.* Madison: Univ. of Wisconsin, 1981.

Brandenberger, Erna. *Estudios sobre el cuento español actual.* Madrid: Editora Nacional, 1973.

Brienza, Susan D. *Samuel Beckett's New Worlds: Style in Metafiction.* Norman: Univ. of Oklahoma Press, 1987.

Briosi, Sandro, and Jaap Lintvelt, Eds. *L'Homme et l'animal.* Groningen: Rijksuniv. Groningen, 1988.

Brown, Carolyn S. *The Tall Tale in American Folklore and Literature.* Knoxville: Univ. of Tennessee Press, 1987.

Buckley, William E. *Walter Pater: The Critic as Artist of Ideas.* New York: New York Univ. Press, 1987.

Budd, Louis J., and Edwin H. Cady, Eds. *On Melville: The Best from American Literature.* Durham: Duke Univ. Press, 1988.

Budhos, Shirley. *The Theme of Enclosure in Selected Works of Doris Lessing.* Troy, N.Y.: Whitston, 1987.

Bunin, Ivan. *In a Far Country: Selected Stories,* ed. and trans. Robert Bowie. Ann Arbor: Hermitage, 1983.

Burgos, Fernando, Ed. *Los ochenta mundos de Cortázar: Ensayos.* Madrid: EDI-6, 1987.

———. *Las voces del karaí: Estudios sobre Augusto Roa Bastos.* Madrid: Edelsa-Edi, 1988.

Burns, Robert A. *The Theme of Non-Conformism in the Works of Henrich Böll.* Warwick: Univ. of Warwick, 1973.

Buss, Helen M. *Mother and Daughter Relationships in the Manawaka Works of Margaret Laurence.* Victoria: Univ. of Victoria Press, 1985.

Büssing, Sabine. *Aliens in the Home: The Child in Horror Fiction.* Westport: Greenwood, 1987.

Cain, T. G. S. *Tolstoy.* New York: Barnes & Noble, 1977.

Call, Michael J. *Back to the Garden: Chateaubriand, Senancour and Constant.* Stanford: Anma Libri, 1988.

Callahan, John F. *In the African-American Grain: The Pursuit of Voice in Twentieth-Century Black Fiction.* Urbana: Univ. of Illinois Press, 1988.

Cantrell, Leon, Ed. *Bards, Bohemians, and Bookmen.* St. Lucia: Univ. of Queensland Press, 1976.

Caputi, Anthony. *Pirandello and the Crisis of Modern Consciousness.* Urbana: Univ. of Illinois Press, 1988.

Carpenter, William. *Death and Marriage: Structural Metaphors for the Work of Art in Joyce and Mallarmé.* New York: Garland, 1988.

Carter, Albert H. *Italo Calvino: Metamorphoses of Fantasy.* Ann Arbor: UMI Research Press, 1987.

Carter, Margaret L. *Specter or Delusion? The Supernatural in Gothic Fiction.* Ann Arbor: UMI Research Press, 1987.

Cassill, R. V. *The Norton Anthology of Contemporary Fiction: Instructor's Handbook.* New York: Norton, 1988.

Castellanos, Rosario. *A Rosario Castellanos Reader,* ed. Maureen Ahern. Austin: Univ. of Texas Press, 1988.

Cave, Terence. *Recognitions: A Study in Poetics.* Oxford: Oxford Univ. Press, 1988.

Cerasini, Marc A., and Charles Hoffman. *Robert E. Howard.* Mercer Island, Wash.: Starmont, 1987.

Chai, Leon. *The Romantic Foundations of the American Renaissance.* Ithaca: Cornell Univ. Press, 1987.

Charters, Ann, William E. Sheidley, and Martha Ramsey. *Instructor's Manual to Accompany "The Story and Its Writer: An Introduction to Short Fiction, Second Edition."* New York: St. Martin's Press, 1987.

Chauvin, Cy, Ed. *A Multitude of Visions.* Baltimore: T-K Graphics, 1975.

Chekhov, Anton. *"The Kiss" and Other Stories,* ed. Ronald Wilks. London: Penguin, 1982.

Clareson, Thomas. *Frederik Pohl.* Mercer Island, Wash.: Starmont, 1987.

Clark, Michael. *Dos Passos's Early Fiction, 1912–1938.* Cranbury, N.J.: Associated Univ. Presses [for Susquehanna Univ. Press], 1987.

Clingman, Stephen. *The Novels of Nadine Gordimer: History from the Inside.* London: Allen & Unwin, 1986.

Clowes, Edith W. *The Revolution of Moral Consciousness: Nietzsche in Russian Literature, 1890–1914.* DeKalb: Northern Illinois Univ. Press, 1988.

Coates, Paul. *The Double and the Other: Identity as Ideology in Post-Romantic Fiction.* New York: St. Martin's Press, 1988.

Coetzee, J. M. *White Writing: On the Culture of Letters in South Africa.* New Haven: Yale Univ. Press, 1988.

Collazos, Oscar. *García Márquez: La soledad y la gloria.* Barcelona: Plaza & Janes, 1983.

Collings, Michael R., Ed. *Reflections on the Fantastic: Selected Essays from the Fourth International Conference on the Fantastic in the Arts.* Westport: Greenwood, 1986.

Coloquio internacional: Lo lúdico y lo fantástico en la obra de Cortázar, 2 vols. Madrid: Fundamentos, 1986.

Columbus, Claudette K. *Mythological Consciousness and the Future: José María Arguedas.* New York: Lang, 1986.

Connolly, Julian W., and Sonia I. Ketchian, Eds. *Studies in Russian Literature in Honor of Vsevolod Setchkarev.* Columbus: Slavica, 1986.

Conradi, Peter. *Fyodor Dostoevsky.* New York: St. Martin's Press, 1988.

Cooper, Wayne F. *Claude McKay: Rebel Sojourner in the Harlem Renaissance.* Baton Rouge: Louisiana State Univ. Press, 1987.

Cornell, Louis L., Ed. *"The Man Who Would Be King" and Other Stories.* New York: Oxford Univ. Press, 1987.

Corngold, Stanley. *Franz Kafka: The Necessity of Form.* Ithaca: Cornell Univ. Press, 1988.

Cottrell, Robert. *Simone de Beauvoir.* New York: Ungar, 1975.

Coy, Juan José. *J. D. Salinger.* Barcelona: Fontanella, 1968.

Crawford, Gary W. *Ramsey Campbell.* Mercer Island, Wash.: Starmont, 1988.

Cudjoe, Selwyn R. *V. S. Naipaul: A Materialistic Reading.* Amherst: Univ. of Massachusetts Press, 1988.

Cummings, Sherwood. *Mark Twain and Science: Adventures of a Mind.* Baton Rouge: Louisiana State Univ. Press, 1988.

Dahlie, Hallvard. *Alice Munro and Her Works.* Toronto: ECW Press, 1984.

———. *Varieties of Exile: The Canadian Experience.* Vancouver: Univ. of British Columbia Press, 1986.

Dathorne, O. R. *Dark Ancestor: The Literature of the Black Man in the Caribbean.* Baton Rouge: Louisiana State Univ. Press, 1981.

Davey, Frank. *Margaret Atwood: A Feminist Poetics.* Vancouver: Talonbooks, 1984.

Daviau, Donald G., Ed. *Major Figures of Contemporary Austrian Literature.* New York: Lang, 1987.

———. *Major Figures in Modern Austrian Literature.* Riverside, Calif.: Ariadne Press, 1988.

Davidson, Arnold E., and Cathy N. Davidson, Eds. *The Art of Margaret Atwood: Essays in Criticism.* Toronto: Anansi, 1981.

Davis, Colin. *Michel Tournier: Philosophy and Fiction.* Oxford: Oxford Univ. Press, 1988.

Day, Leroy T. *Narrative Transgression and the Foregrounding of Language in Selected Prose Works of Poe, Valéry, and Hofmannsthal.* New York: Garland, 1988.

Dayan, Joan. *Fables of Mind: An Inquiry into Poe's Fiction.* New York: Oxford Univ. Press, 1987.

Debusscher, Gilbert, and Marc Maufort, Eds. *American Literature in Belgium.* Amsterdam: Rodopi, 1988.

Dekker, George. *The American Historical Romance.* Cambridge: Cambridge Univ. Press, 1987.

De Maegd-Soëp, Caroline. *Chekhov and Women: Women in the Life and Works of Chekhov.* Columbus: Slavica, 1987.

Desmond, John. *Risen Sons: Flannery O'Connor's Vision of History.* Athens: Univ. of Georgia Press, 1987.

Devlin, Albert J. *Welty: A Life in Writing.* Jackson: Univ. Press of Mississippi, 1987.

Díaz, Nancy G. *The Radical Self: Metamorphosis to Animal Form in Latin American Narrative.* Columbia: Univ. of Missouri Press, 1988.

Díez Huélamo, Beguña, Ed. *"Relato de un Naufrago" de Gabriel García Márquez.* Mexico City: Daimon, 1986.

Dixon, Melvin. *Ride Out the Wilderness: Geography and Identity in Afro-American Literature.* Urbana: Univ. of Illinois Press, 1987.

Docherty, Brian, Ed. *American Crime Fiction: Studies in the Genre.* New York: St. Martin's Press, 1988.

Doderer, Klaus, Brigitte Görk, Angela Krödel, Albrecht Weber, Theo Webert, and Elfriede Kitzing. *Interpretationen zu Heinrich Böll,* I. Munich: Oldenbourg, 1965.

Donaldson, Scott. *John Cheever: A Biography.* New York: Random House, 1988.

Donovan, Katie. *Irish Women Writers—Marginalised by Whom?* Dublin: Raven Arts Press, 1988.

Doubleday, Neal F. *Variety of Attempt: British and American Fiction in the Early Nineteenth Century.* Lincoln: Univ. of Nebraska Press, 1976.

Doyle, Pj, and E. W. McDiarmid, Eds. *The Baker Street Dozen.* New York: Congdon & Weed, 1987.

Druce, Robert, Ed. *A Centre of Excellence: Essays Presented to Seymour Betsky.* Amsterdam: Rodopi, 1987.

Dryden, Edgar A. *The Form of American Romance.* Baltimore: Johns Hopkins Univ. Press, 1988.

Dussère, Carolyn T. *The Image of the Primitive Giant in the Works of Gerhart Hauptmann.* Stuttgart: Heinz, 1979.

Eaden, P. R., and F. H. Mares, Eds. *Mapped But Unknown—The Australian Landscape of the Imagination: Essays and Poems Presented to Brian Elliott.* Netley, South Australia: Wakefield, 1986.

Early, Eileen. *Joy in Exile: Ciro Alegría's Narrative Art.* Washington: Univ. Press of America, 1980.

Echavarren, Roberto. *El espacio de la verdad: Práctica del texto en Felisberto Hernández.* Buenos Aires: Sudamericana, 1981.

Edwards, P. D. *Idyllic Realism from Mary Russell Mitford to Hardy.* New York: St. Martin's Press, 1988.

Elbert, Sarah. *A Hunger for Home: Louisa May Alcott's Place in American Culture.* New Brunswick: Rutgers Univ. Press, 1987.

Ellis, John M. *Heinrich von Kleist: Studies in the Character and Meaning of His Writings.* Chapel Hill: Univ. of North Carolina Press, 1979.

Erisman, Fred, and Richard W. Etulain, Eds. *Fifty Western Writers.* Westport: Greenwood, 1982.

Etulian, Richard W. *Ernest Haycock.* Boise: Boise State Univ. Press, 1988.

Eyler, Audrey, and Robert F. Garratt, Eds. *The Uses of the Past.* Cranbury, N.J.: Associated Univ. Presses [for Univ. of Delaware Press], 1988.

Ezergaillis, Inta, Ed. *Critical Essays on Thomas Mann.* Boston: Hall, 1988.

Fallaize, Elizabeth. *Simone de Beauvoir.* London: Routledge, 1988.

Falls, Cyril B. *Rudyard Kipling: A Critical Study.* London: Secker, 1915.

Farrell Lee, Grace. *From Exile to Redemption: The Fiction of Isaac Bashevis Singer.* Carbondale: Southern Illinois Univ. Press, 1987.

Ferré, Rosario. *"El acomodador": Una lectura fantastica de Felisberto Hernández.* Mexico City: Fondo de Cultura Economica, 1986.

Ficken, Carl. *God's Story and Modern Literature: Reading Fiction in Community.* Philadelphia: Fortress, 1985.

Fisher, Rudolph. *The Short Fiction of Rudolph Fisher,* ed. Margaret Perry. Westport: Greenwood, 1987.

Fleenor, Julian E., Ed. *The Female Gothic.* Montreal: Eden, 1983.

Flier, Michael S., and Simon Karlinsky, Eds. *Language, Literature, Linguistics: In Honor of Francis J. Whitfield on His Seventieth Birthday, March 25, 1986.* Berkeley: Berkeley Slavic Specialties, 1987.

Flora, Joseph M., and Robert Bain, Eds. *Fifty Southern Writers After 1900.* Westport: Greenwood, 1987.

Fogel, Aaron. *Coercion to Speak: Conrad's Poetics of Dialogue.* Cambridge: Harvard Univ. Press, 1985.

Ford, Dan, Ed. *Heir and Prototype: Original and Derived Characterizations in Faulkner.* Conway: Univ. of Central Arkansas Press, 1987.

Forsyth, Neil, Ed. *Reading Contexts.* Tübingen: Gunter Narr, 1988.

Foster, John W. *Fictions of the Irish Literary Revival: A Changeling Art.* Syracuse: Syracuse Univ. Press, 1987.

Foster, Thomas C. *Form and Society in Modern Literature.* De Kalb: Northern Illinois Univ. Press, 1988.

Fowler, Doreen, and Ann J. Abadie, Eds. *Faulkner and Race: Faulkner and Yoknapatawpha, 1986.* Jackson: Univ. Press of Mississippi, 1987.

Fowler, Edward. *The Rhetoric of Confession: "Shishōsetsu" in Early Twentieth-Century Japanese Fiction.* Berkeley: Univ. of California Press, 1988.

Fox, Robert E. *Conscientious Sorcerers: The Black Postmodernist Fiction of LeRoi Jones/ Amiri Baraka, Ishmael Reed, and Samuel R. Delany.* Westport: Greenwood, 1987.

Frances Vidal, Sorkunde. *La narrativa de Mujica Lainez.* Bilbao: Universidad del País Vasco, 1986.

Franklin, H. Bruce. *War Stars: The Superweapon and the American Imagination.* New York: Oxford Univ. Press, 1988.

Fraser, Gail. *Interweaving Patterns in the Works of Joseph Conrad.* Ann Arbor: UMI Research Press, 1988.

Freadman, Richard. *Eliot, James and the Fictional Self: A Study in Character and Narration.* New York: St. Martin's Press, 1986.

Freese, Peter. *Die amerikanische Kurzgeschichte nach 1945: Salinger, Malamud, Baldwin, Purdy, Barth.* Frankfurt: Athenäum, 1974.

French, Warren. *J. D. Salinger, Revisited.* Boston: Twayne, 1988.

Freund, Winfried. *Adelbert von Chamisso: Peter Schlemihl—Geld und Geist.* Paderborn: Schöningh, 1980.

Fried, Lewis, Ed. *Handbook of American-Jewish Literature: An Analytical Guide to Topics, Themes, and Sources.* Westport: Greenwood, 1988.

Fried, Michael. *Realism, Writing, Disfiguration.* Chicago: Univ. of Chicago Press, 1987.

Friedman, Ellen G., and Miriam Fuchs, Eds. *Breaking the Sequence: Women's Experimental Fiction.* Princeton: Princeton Univ. Press, 1989.

Friedman, Lawrence S. *Understanding Isaac Bashevis Singer.* Columbia: Univ. of South Carolina Press, 1988.

Friedman, Mary L. *The Emperor's Kites: A Mythology of Borges' Tales.* Durham: Duke Univ. Press, 1987.

Fuchs, Esther. *Israeli Mythologies: Women in Contemporary Hebrew Fiction.* Albany: State Univ. of New York Press, 1987.

Gage, Richard P. *Order and Design: Henry James' Titled Story Sequences.* New York: Lang, 1988.

Gaggin, John. *Hemingway and Nineteenth-Century Aestheticism.* Ann Arbor: UMI Research Press, 1988.

Gale, Steven H. *S. J. Perelman: A Critical Study.* Westport: Greenwood, 1987.

Gamache, Lawrence B., and Ian S. MacNiven, Eds. *The Modernists: Studies in Literary Phenomenology—Essays in Honor of Harry T. Moore.* Cranbury, N.J.: Associated Univ. Presses [for Fairleigh Dickinson Univ. Press], 1987.

García, John A., Theresa Córdova, and Juan R. García, Eds. *The Chicano Struggle: Analyses of Past and Present Efforts.* Binghamton: Bilingual Press, 1984.

Gardner, Burdett. *The Lesbian Imagination (Victorian Style): A Psychological and Critical Study of "Vernon Lee."* New York: Garland, 1987.

Gargano, James W., Ed. *Critical Essays on Henry James: The Early Novels.* Boston: Hall, 1987.

Gates, Barbara T. *Victorian Suicide: Mad Crimes and Sad Histories.* Princeton: Princeton Univ. Press, 1988.

Geering, R. G. *Christina Stead.* New York: Twayne, 1969.

Gekoski, R. A. *Conrad: The Moral World of the Novel.* London: Elek, 1978.

Gelber, Mark H., Ed. *Identity and Ethos: A Festschrift for Sol Liptzin on the Occasion of His 85th Birthday.* New York: Lang, 1986.

Gelley, Alexander. *Narrative Crossings: Theory and Pragmatics of Prose Fiction.* Baltimore: Johns Hopkins Univ. Press, 1987.

Giacoman, Helmy F., Ed. *Homenaje a Alejo Carpentier: Variaciones interpretativas en torno a su obra.* New York: Las Americas, 1970.

———. *Homenaje a G. García Márquez: Variaciones interpretativas en torno a su obra.* New York: Las Americas, 1972.

———. *Homenaje a Augustín Yañez: Variaciones interpretativas en torno a su obra.* New York: Las Americas, 1973.

———. *Homenaje a Augusto Roa Bastos: Variaciones interpretativas en torno a su obra.* New York: Las Americas, 1973.

Gibian, George, Ed. *The Man in the Black Coat: Russia's Literature of the Absurd* [selected works of Daniil Kharmas and Alexander Vvedensky]. Evanston: Northwestern Univ. Press, 1987.

Gilbert, Sandra M., and Susan Gubar. *No Man's Land: The Place of the Woman Writer in the Twentieth Century.* New Haven: Yale Univ. Press, 1988.

Gillespie, Bruce, Ed. *Philip K. Dick: Electric Shepherd.* Melbourne: Norstrilia, 1975.

Gilmore, Thomas B. *Equivocal Spirits: Alcoholism and Drinking in Twentieth-Century Literature.* Chapel Hill: Univ. of North Carolina Press, 1987.

Gindin, James. *John Galsworthy's Life and Art: An Alien Fortress.* Ann Arbor: Univ. of Michigan Press, 1987.

———. *William Golding.* New York: St. Martin's Press, 1988.

Glenny, Robert E. *The Manipulation of Reality in Works by Heinrich von Kleist.* New York: Lang, 1987.

Gobineau, Arthur de. *"Mademoiselle Irnois" and Other Stories,* trans. and ed. Annette Smith and David Smith. Berkeley: Univ. of California Press, 1988.

Goldberger, Avriel H., Ed. *Woman as Mediatrix: Essays on Nineteenth-Century European Women Writers.* Westport: Greenwood, 1987.

Gontarski, S. E., Ed. *On Beckett: Essays and Criticism*. New York: Grove, 1986.

González, Mirza L. *La novela y el cuento psicológicos de Miguel de Carrón*. Miami: Ediciones Universal, 1979.

Good, Howard. *Acquainted with the Night: The Image of Journalists in American Fiction, 1890–1930*. Metuchen, N.J.: Scarecrow, 1986.

Goonetilleke, D. C. R. *Images of the Raj: South Asia in the Literature of Empire*. New York: St. Martin's Press, 1988.

Gorak, Jan. *God the Artist: American Novelists in a Post-Realist Age*. Urbana: Univ. of Illinois Press, 1987.

Gottesman, Ronald, and Moshe Lazar, Eds. *The Dove and the Mole: Kafka's Journey into Darkness and Creativity*. Malibu, Calif.: Undena, 1987.

Graham, Kenneth. *Indirections of the Novel: James, Conrad, and Forster*. Cambridge: Cambridge Univ. Press, 1988.

Green, Geoffrey. *Freud and Nabokov*. Lincoln: Univ. of Nebraska Press, 1988.

Griffin, Constance M. *Henry Blake Fuller: A Critical Biography*. Philadelphia: Univ. of Pennsylvania Press, 1939.

Guggenheim, Michel, Ed. *Women in French Literature*. Saratoga, Calif.: Anma Libri, 1988.

Guilds, John C., Ed. *"Long Years of Neglect": The World and Reputation of William Gilmore Simms*. Fayetteville: Univ. of Arkansas Press, 1988.

Gunn, Daniel. *Psychoanalysis and Fiction: An Exploration of Literary and Psychoanalytic Borders*. Cambridge: Cambridge Univ. Press, 1988.

Gutierrez, Donald. *The Dark and the Light Gods: Essays on the Self in Modern Literature*. Troy, N.Y.: Whitston, 1987.

Gutiérrez Mouat, Ricardo. *José Donoso: Impostura e impostación: La modelización lúdica y carnavalesca de una producción literaria*. Gaithersburg, Md.: Ediciones Hispamérica, 1983.

Hadlich, Roger L., and J. D. Ellsworthy, Eds. *East Meets West*. Honolulu: Univ. of Hawaii, 1988.

Haig, Stirling. *Flaubert and the Gift of Speech: Dialogue and Discourse in Four "Modern" Novels*. London: Cambridge Univ. Press, 1987.

———. *The Madame Bovary Blues: The Pursuit of Illusion in Nineteenth-Century French Fiction*. Baton Rouge: Louisiana State Univ. Press, 1987.

Hale, Jane A. *The Broken Window: Beckett's Dramatic Perspective*. West Lafayette, Ind.: Purdue Univ. Press, 1987.

Halemann, Ulrich, Kurt Müller, and Klaus Weiss, Eds. *Wirklichkeit und Dichtung: Studien zur englischen und amerikanischen Literatur*. Berlin: Duncker & Humblot, 1984.

Hallissy, Margaret. *Venomous Woman: Fear of the Female in Literature*. Westport: Greenwood, 1987.

Hammond, J. R. *H. G. Wells and the Modern Novel*. New York: St. Martin's Press, 1988.

Harap, Louis. *In the Mainstream: The Jewish Presence in Twentieth-Century American Literature, 1950s–1980s*. Westport: Greenwood, 1987.

Harland, Catherine R. *Mark Rutherford: The Mind and Art of William Hale White*. Columbus: Ohio State Univ. Press, 1988.

Harris, Kenneth M. *Hypocrisy and Self-Deception in Hawthorne's Fiction*. Charlottesville: Univ. Press of Virginia, 1988.

Hart, Patricia. *The Spanish Sleuth: The Detective in Spanish Fiction*. Cranbury, N.J.: Associated Univ. Presses [for Fairleigh Dickinson Univ. Press], 1987.

Hartigan, Karelisa V., Ed. *From Bard to Broadway*. Lanham, Md.: Univ. Press of America, 1987.

Hayman, David. *Re-Forming the Narrative: Toward a Mechanics of Modernist Fiction.* Ithaca: Cornell Univ. Press, 1987.

Heldt, Barbara. *Terrible Perfection: Women and Russian Literature.* Bloomington: Indiana Univ. Press, 1987.

Helftrich, Eckhard, and Hans Wysling, Eds. *Internationales Thomas-Mann-Kolloquium 1986 in Lübeck.* Bern: Francke, 1987.

Heller, Terry. *The Delights of Terror: An Aesthetics of the Tale of Terror.* Urbana: Univ. of Illinois Press, 1987.

Hernández de López, Ana M., Ed. *En el punto de mira: Gabriel García Márquez.* Madrid: Editorial Pliegos, 1985.

Herndon, Jerry A., and George Brosi, Eds. *Jesse Stuart: The Man and His Books.* Ashland, Ky.: Jesse Stuart Foundation, 1988.

Herring, Phillip F. *Joyce's Uncertainty Principle.* Princeton: Princeton Univ. Press, 1987.

Herz, Judith S. *The Short Narratives of E. M. Forster.* New York: St. Martin's Press, 1988.

Hewitt, Douglas. *English Fiction of the Early Modern Period.* London: Longman, 1988.

Higgins, James. *A History of Peruvian Literature.* Liverpool: Francis Cairns, 1987.

Hijive, James A. *J. W. DeForest and the Rise of American Gentility.* Hanover, N.H.: Univ. Press of New England [for Brown Univ. Press], 1988.

Hodgson, Amanda. *The Romances of William Morris.* Cambridge: Cambridge Univ. Press, 1987.

Hogg, James, Ed. *Essays in Honour of Erwin Stürzl on His Sixtieth Birthday,* I. Salzburg: Univ. of Salzburg, 1980.

Höller, Hans, Ed. *Der dunkle Schatten, dem ich schon seit Anfang folge.* Vienna: Löcker, 1928.

Honig, Edith L. *Breaking the Angelic Image: Woman Power in Victorian Children's Fantasy.* Westport: Greenwood, 1988.

Hughes, R. S. *Beyond the Red Pony: A Reader's Companion to Steinbeck's Complete Short Stories.* Metuchen, N.J.: Scarecrow, 1987.

Irvine, Lorna. *Sub-version: Canadian Fiction by Women.* Toronto: ECW Press, 1986.

Jaffe, Jacqueline A. *Arthur Conan Doyle.* Boston: Twayne, 1987.

James, JoAnn, and William J. Cleenan, Eds. *Apocalyptic Vision Past and Present.* Tallahassee: Florida State Univ. Press, 1988.

Jay, Karla. *The Amazon and the Page: Natalie Clifford Barney and Renée Vivien.* Bloomington: Indiana Univ. Press, 1988.

Jiménez, José O., Ed. *Estudios críticos sobre la prosa modernista hispanoamericana.* New York: Eliseo Torres, 1975.

Jiménez de Báez, Yvette, Diana Morán, and Edith Negrín. *Ficción e historia: La narrativa de José Emilio Pacheco.* Mexico City: El Colegio de México, 1979.

Jofen, Jean. *The Jewish Mystic in Kafka.* New York: Lang, 1987.

Johns, Anthony H. *Cultural Options and the Role of Tradition: A Collection of Modern Indonesian and Malaysian Literature.* Canberra: Australian National Univ. Press, 1979.

Johnson, Charles. *Being & Race: Black Writers Since 1970.* Bloomington: Indiana Univ. Press, 1988.

Johnson, Greg. *Understanding Joyce Carol Oates.* Columbia: Univ. of South Carolina Press, 1987.

Johnston, Kenneth G. *The Tip of the Iceberg: Hemingway and the Short Story.* Greenwood, Fla.: Penkevill, 1987.

Joiner, Lawrence D. *Studies of Azorín,* ed. Joseph W. Zdenek. [n.p.]: Spanish Literature Publications, 1982.

Jurak, Mirko, Ed. *Cross-Cultural Studies: American, Canadian, and European Literatures.* Ljubljana: Edvard Kardelj Univ., 1988.

Kadish, Doris Y. *The Literature of Images: Narrative Landscape from "Julie" to "Jane Eyre."* New Brunswick: Rutgers Univ. Press, 1987.

Kaplan, Carey, and Ellen C. Rose, Eds. *Doris Lessing: The Alchemy of Survival.* Athens: Ohio Univ. Press, 1988.

Kason, Nancy M. *Breaking Traditions: The Fiction of Clemente Palma.* Cranbury, N.J.: Associated Univ. Presses [for Bucknell Univ. Press], 1988.

Keefe, Robert and Janice A. *Walter Pater and the Gods of Disorder.* Athens: Ohio Univ. Press, 1988.

Keefe, Terry. *Simone de Beauvoir: A Study of Her Writings.* Totowa, N.J.: Barnes & Noble, 1983.

Keene, Dennis. *Yokomitsu Riichi: Modernist.* New York: Columbia Univ. Press, 1980.

Keith, W. J. *Regions of the Imagination: The Development of British Rural Fiction.* Toronto: Univ. of Toronto Press, 1988.

Keller, Luzius, and André Oeschger, Eds. *Marcel Proust: Bezüge und Strukturen: Studien zur "Les Plaisirs et les jours."* Frankfurt: Insel, 1987.

Kemp, Sandra. *Kipling's Hidden Narratives.* Oxford: Blackwell, 1988.

Kennedy, J. Gerald. *Poe, Death, and the Life of Writing.* New Haven: Yale Univ. Press, 1987.

Kenner, Hugh. *A Sinking Island: The Modern English Writers.* New York: Knopf, 1988.

Kessler-Harris, Alice, and William McBrien, Eds. *Faith of a (Woman) Writer.* Westport: Greenwood, 1988.

Ketterer, David. *Imprisoned in Tesseract: The Life and Work of James Blish.* Kent: Kent State Univ. Press, 1987.

Kilroy, James F., Ed. *The Irish Short Story: A Critical History.* Boston: Twayne, 1984.

Kincaid, Paul, and Geoff Rippington, Eds. *Keith Roberts.* Kent: British Science Fiction Writers Association, 1983.

King, John, Ed. *On Modern Latin American Fiction.* New York: Hill & Wang, 1987.

Kinkley, Jeffrey C. *The Odyssey of Shen Congwen.* Stanford: Stanford Univ. Press, 1987.

Kipling, Rudyard. *Traffics and Discoveries,* ed. Hermione Lee. 1904; Hammondsworth: Penguin, 1987.

Knapp, Bettina L. *Stephen Crane.* New York: Ungar, 1987.

———. *Women in Twentieth-Century Literature: A Jungian Viewpoint.* University Park: Pennsylvania State Univ. Press, 1987.

———. *Music, Archetype, and the Writer: A Jungian View.* University Park: Pennsylvania State Univ. Press, 1988.

———, Ed. *Critical Essays on Albert Camus.* Boston: Hall, 1988.

Knister, Raymond. *The First Day of Spring: Stories and Other Prose,* ed. Peter Stevens. Toronto: Univ. of Toronto Press, 1976.

Koelb, Clayton. *Invention of Reading: Rhetoric and Literary Imagination.* Ithaca: Cornell Univ. Press, 1988.

———, and Susan Noakes, Eds. *The Comparative Perspective on Literature: Approaches to Theory and Practice.* Ithaca: Cornell Univ. Press, 1988.

Kort, Wesley A. *Modern Fiction and Human Time.* Tampa: Univ. of Southern Florida Press, 1985.

Kossoff, A. David, José Amor y Vázquez, Ruth H. Kossoff, and Geoffrey W. Ribbans, Eds. *Actas del VIII Congreso de la Asociación Internacional de Hispanistas,* 2 vols. Madrid: Istmo, 1986.

Kramer, Victor, Ed. *The Harlem Renaissance: A Re-Examination.* New York: AMS, 1987.

Krans, Horatio S. *Irish Life in Irish Fiction.* New York: Macmillan, 1903.

Kroeber, Karl. *Romantic Fantasy.* New Haven: Yale Univ. Press, 1988.

Kubin, Wolfgang, and Rudolf G. Wagner, Eds. *Essays in Modern Chinese Literature and Literary Criticism.* Bochum: Brockmeyer, 1982.

Kuhn, Anna K. *Christa Wolf's Utopian Vision: From Marxism to Feminism.* Cambridge: Cambridge Univ. Press, 1988.

Lacan, Jacques. *Écrits.* Paris: Éditions du Seuil, 1966.

Lambropoulos, Vassilis. *Literature as National Institution: Studies in the Politics of Modern Greek Culture.* Princeton: Princeton Univ. Press, 1988.

Lasarte, Francisco. *Felisberto Hernández y la escritura de "lo otro."* Madrid: Insula, 1981.

Laski, Marghanita. *From Palm to Pine: Rudyard Kipling Abroad and at Home.* New York: Facts on File, 1987.

Lavrin, Janko, Ed. *Russian Stories: Pushkin to Gorky.* London: Westhouse, 1946; rpt. Westport: Greenwood, 1975.

Lawson, Henry. *The Portable Henry Lawson,* ed. Brian Kiernan. St. Lucia: Univ. of Queensland Press, 1976.

Lawson, Richard H. *Franz Kafka.* New York: Ungar, 1987.

Lecker, Robert, Jack David, and Ellen Quigley, Eds. *Canadian Writers and Their Works.* Downsview, Ont.: ECW Press, 1983.

Lee, A. Robert, Ed. *Edgar Allan Poe: The Design of Order.* London: Vision, 1987; Am. ed. Totowa, N.J.: Barnes & Noble, 1987.

Lee, Leo Ou-fan. *Voices from the Iron House: A Study of Lu Xun.* Bloomington: Indiana Univ. Press, 1987.

Lefanu, Sarah. *Feminism and Science Fiction.* Bloomington: Indiana Univ. Press, 1988.

Lenz, Günter H., Ed. *History and Tradition in Afro-American Culture.* Frankfurt: Campus Verlag, 1984.

Lerner, Laurence. *The Frontiers of Literature.* Oxford: Blackwell, 1988.

Leskov, Nikolai. *"Lady Macbeth of Mtsensk" and Other Stories,* ed. David McDuff. London: Penguin, 1987.

Lesser, Wendy. *The Life Below the Ground: A Study of the Subterranean in Literature and History.* Winchester, Mass.: Faber & Faber, 1987.

Lester, John. *Conrad and Religion.* New York: St. Martin's Press, 1988.

Letley, Emma. *"The Strange Case of Dr. Jekyll and Mr. Hyde" and "Weir of Hermiston."* New York: Oxford Univ. Press, 1987.

———. *From Galt to Douglas Brown: Nineteenth-Century Fiction and the Scots Language.* Edinburgh: Scottish Academic Press, 1988.

Levine, George. *The Realistic Imagination: English Fiction from Frankenstein to Lady Chatterley.* Chicago: Univ. of Chicago Press, 1981.

Levine, Paul. *E. L. Doctorow.* London: Methuen, 1985.

Levitt, Morton P. *Modernist Survivors: The Contemporary Novel in England, the United States, France, and Latin America.* Columbus: Ohio State Univ. Press, 1987.

Lévy, Maurice. *Lovecraft: A Study in the Fantastic,* trans. S. T. Joshi. Detroit: Wayne State Univ. Press, 1988.

Lewis, Marvin A. *Treading the Ebony Path: Ideology and Violence in Contemporary Afro-Colombian Prose Fiction.* Columbia: Univ. of Missouri Press, 1987.

Lidoff, Joan. *Christina Stead.* New York: Ungar, 1982.

Lingeman, Richard. *Theodore Dreiser: At the Gates of the City, 1871–1907.* New York: Putnam, 1986.

Locklin, Gerald. *Gerald Haslam.* Boise: Boise State Univ., 1987.

Logsdon, Loren, and Charles W. Mayes, Eds. *Since Flannery O'Connor: Essays on the Contemporary American Short Story.* Macomb: Western Illinois Univ. Press, 1987.

Long, Robert E. *James Thurber.* New York: Continuum, 1988.

Longré, Felicia H. *Tom Stoppard.* New York: Ungar, 1981.

Loss, Archie K. *W. Somerset Maugham.* New York: Continuum, 1988.

Lowe, David. *Russian Writing Since 1953: A Critical Survey.* New York: Ungar, 1987.

Lowin, Joseph. *Cynthia Ozick.* Boston: Twayne, 1988.

Luker, Nicholas, Ed. *From Furmanov to Sholokhov: An Anthology of the Classics of Socialist Realism.* Ann Arbor: Ardis, 1988.

Lundquist, James. *Jack London: Adventures, Ideas, and Fiction.* New York: Ungar, 1987.

Luplow, Carol. *Isaac Babel's Red Cavalry.* Ann Arbor: Ardis, 1982.

Lutwack, Leonard. *The Role of Place in Literature.* Syracuse: Syracuse Univ. Press, 1984.

Lynch, Gerald. *Stephen Leacock: Humour and Humanity.* Montreal: McGill-Queens Univ. Press, 1988.

Lynn, Kenneth S. *Hemingway.* New York: Simon & Schuster, 1987.

MacAdam, Alfred J. *Textual Confrontations: Comparative Readings in Latin American Literature.* Chicago: Univ. of Chicago Press, 1987.

McCadden, Joseph F. *The Flight from Women in the Fiction of Saul Bellow.* Lanham, Md.: Univ. Press of America, 1980.

McCarthy, Albert. *Albert Camus: "The Stranger."* Cambridge: Cambridge Univ. Press, 1988.

McCartney, George. *Confused Roaring: Evelyn Waugh and the Modernist Tradition.* Bloomington: Indiana Univ. Press, 1987.

McCluskey, John, Ed. *The City of Refuge: The Stories of Rudolph Fisher.* Columbia: Univ. of Missouri Press, 1987.

McCombs, Judith, Ed. *Critical Essays on Margaret Atwood.* Boston: Hall, 1988.

McCort, Dennis. *States of Unconsciousness in Three Tales of C. F. Meyer.* Cranbury, N.J.: Associated Univ. Presses [for Bucknell Univ. Press], 1988.

MacCulloch, Clare. *The Neglected Genre: The Short Story in Canada.* Guelph, Ont.: Alive Press, 1973.

McDonnell, Jacqueline. *Evelyn Waugh.* New York: St. Martin's Press, 1988.

McDuffie, Keith, and Alfredo Roggiano, Eds. *Texto/Contexto en la Literatura Iberoamericana.* Madrid: Instituto Internacional de Literatura Iberoamericana, 1980.

McGregor, Gaile. *The Noble Savage in the New World Garden: Notes Toward a Syntactics of Place.* Toronto: Univ. of Toronto Press, 1988.

McGuirk, Bernard, and Richard Cardwell, Eds. *Gabriel García Márquez: New Readings.* Cambridge: Cambridge Univ. Press, 1987.

McHale, Brian. *Postmodern Fiction.* New York: Methuen, 1987.

Machor, James L. *Pastoral Cities: Urban Ideals and the Symbolic Landscape of America.* Madison: Univ. of Wisconsin Press, 1987.

Mackey, Douglas A. *Philip K. Dick.* Boston: Twayne, 1988.

McMullen, Lorraine, Ed. *The Ethel Wilson Symposium.* Ottawa: Ottawa Univ. Press, 1982.

McMurray, George R. *Gabriel García Márquez.* Fredericton, N.B.: York Press, 1987.

———. *Spanish American Writing Since 1914: A Critical Survey.* New York: Ungar, 1987.

Macpherson, Enid. *A Student's Guide to Böll.* London: Heinemann, 1972.

Mahaffey, Vicki. *Reauthorizing Joyce.* Cambridge: Cambridge Univ. Press, 1988.

Marks, Elaine. *Simone de Beauvoir: Encounters with Death.* New Brunswick: Rutgers Univ. Press, 1973.

Martín, Gregorio, Ed. *Selected Proceedings: 32nd Mountain Interstate Foreign Language Conference.* Winston-Salem, N.C.: Wake Forest Univ., 1984.

Martin, W. R. *Alice Munro: Paradox and Parallel.* Edmonton: Univ. of Alberta Press, 1987.

Martini, Fritz. *Das Wagnis der Sprache: Interpretationen deutscher Prosa von Nietzsche bis Benn.* Stuttgart: Klett, 1954.

Marucci, Franco, and Adriano Bruttini, Eds. *La performance del testo.* Siena: Ticci, 1986.

Marx, Leo. *The Pilot and the Passenger: Essays on Literature, Technology, and Culture in the United States.* New York: Oxford Univ. Press, 1988.

Massie, Allan. *Colette.* Hammondsworth: Penguin, 1986.

Mathé, Sylvie. *Morales et moralités aux Etats-Unis.* Aix-en-Provence: Univ. of Provence Press, 1988.

Maturo, Graciela. *Claves simbólicas de García Márquez.* Buenos Aires: Fernando García Cambiero, 1972.

Mazzioti, Nora, Ed. *Historia y Mito en la obra de Alejo Carpentier.* Buenos Aires: Fernando García Cambiero, 1972.

Meckier, Jerome. *Hidden Rivalries in Victorian Fiction: Dickens, Realism, and Revaluation.* Lexington: Univ. Press of Kentucky, 1987.

Meisel, Perry. *The Myth of the Modern: A Study in British Literature and Criticism after 1850.* New Haven: Yale Univ. Press, 1987.

Melendez, Concha. *El arte del cuento en Puerto Rico.* New York: Las Americas, 1961.

Mendelson, Danuta. *Metaphor in Babel's Short Stories.* Ann Arbor: Ardis, 1982.

Menton, Seymour. *El Cuento Hispanoamericano,* I. Mexico City: Fondo de Cultura Económica, 1964; 2nd ed., 1965; 3rd ed., 1970.

———. *El Cuento Hispanoamericano,* II. Mexico City: Fondo de Cultura Económica, 1964; 2nd ed., 1966; 3rd ed., 1970.

———. *El Cuento Costarricense.* Mexico City: Ediciones de Andrea, 1964; Am. ed. Lawrence: Univ. of Kansas Press, 1964.

Meyers, Jeffrey, Ed. *The Legacy of D. H. Lawrence.* New York: St. Martin's Press, 1987.

Michaels, Walter B. *The Gold Standard and the Logic of Naturalism: American Literature at the Turn of the Century.* Berkeley: Univ. of California Press, 1987.

Milbauer, Asher, and Donald G. Watson, Eds. *Reading Philip Roth.* New York: St. Martin's Press, 1988.

Miller, John, Ed. *Hot Type: America's Most Celebrated Writers Introducing the Next Word in Contemporary Fiction.* New York: Macmillan, 1988.

Minow-Pinkney, Makiko. *Virginia Woolf and the Problems of the Subject.* New Brunswick: Rutgers Univ. Press, 1987.

Minta, Stephen. *García Márquez: Writer of Colombia.* New York: Harper & Row, 1987.

Mizruchi, Susan L. *The Power of Historical Knowledge: Narrating the Past in Hawthorne, James, and Dreiser.* Princeton: Princeton Univ. Press, 1987.

Mocega-González, Esther P. *La narrativa de Alejo Carpentier: El concepto del tiempo como tema fundamental.* New York: Eliseo Torres, 1975.

———. *Alejo Carpentier: Estudios sobre su narrativa.* Madrid: Playor, 1980.

Modiano, Marko. *Domestic Disharmony and Industrialization in D. H. Lawrence's Early Fiction.* Uppsala: Almqvist & Wiksell, 1987.

Mohr, Eugene V. *The Nuyorican Experience: Literature of the Puerto Rican Minority.* Westport: Greenwood, 1982.

Moore, Thomas. *The Style of Connectedness: "Gravity's Rainbow" and Thomas Pynchon.* Columbia: Univ. of Missouri Press, 1987.

Mora Valcárcel, Carmen de. *Teoría y Práctica del Cuento en Los Relatos de Cortázar.* Seville: Escuela de Estudios Hispano-Americanos, 1982.

Morse, David. *American Romanticism, I: From Cooper to Hawthorne.* Totowa, N.J.: Barnes & Noble, 1987.

Morse, Donald E., Ed. *The Fantastic in World Literature and Art.* Westport: Greenwood, 1987.

Muller, John P., and William J. Richardson, Eds. *The Purloined Poe: Lacan, Derrida, and Psychoanalytic Reading.* Baltimore: Johns Hopkins Univ. Press, 1988.

Müller-Bergh, Klaus, Ed. *Asedios a Carpentier: Once ensayos críticos sobre el novelista cubano.* Santiago, Chile: Editorial Universitaria, 1972.

Murphy, Daniel. *Imagination and Religion in Anglo-Irish Literature.* Dublin: Irish Academic Press, 1987.

Murray, Don. *The Fiction of W. P. Kinsella: Tall Tales in Various Voices.* Fredericton, N.B.: York, 1987.

Myers, Eunice, and Ginette Adamson, Eds. *Continental, Latin-American and Francophone Women Writers: Selected Papers from the Wichita University Conference on Foreign Literature, 1984–1985.* Lanham, Md.: Univ. Press of America, 1987.

Myers, Thomas. *Walking Point: American Narrative of Viet Nam.* New York: Oxford Univ. Press, 1988.

Naimy, Nadim. *Mikhail Naimy: An Introduction.* Beirut: American Univ. at Beirut, 1967.

Nathan, Rhoda B. *Katherine Mansfield.* New York: Continuum, 1988.

Neilson, Emmanuel S., Ed. *Connections: Essays on Black Literatures.* Canberra: Aboriginal Studies Press, 1988.

Nelson, Robert J. *Willa Cather and France: In Search of the Lost Language.* Urbana: Univ. of Illinois Press, 1988.

New, W. H. *Dreams of Speech and Violence: The Art of the Short Story in Canada and New Zealand.* Toronto: Univ. of Toronto Press, 1987.

Newberry, Frederick. *Hawthorne's Divided Loyalties: England and America in His Works.* Cranbury, N.J.: Associated Univ. Presses [for Fairleigh Dickinson Univ. Press], 1987.

Newman, Benjamin. *Searching for the Figure in the Carpet in the Tales of Henry James: Reflections of an Ordinary Reader.* New York: Lang, 1987.

Nightingale, Peggy. *Journey Through Darkness: The Writing of V. S. Naipaul.* St. Lucia: Univ. of Queensland Press, 1987.

Nowakowski, Jan, Ed. *Litterae et Lingua: In Honorem Premislavi Mroczkowski.* Wroclaw: Polish Academy, 1984.

Nudas, Alfeo G. *Telic Contemplation: A Study of Grace in Seven Philippine Writers.* Quezon City: Univ. of Philippines Press, 1979.

Nueve asedios a García Márquez. Santiago, Chile: Editorial Universitaria, 1971.

Oates, Joyce C. *(Woman) Writer: Occasions and Opportunities.* New York: Dutton, 1988.

O'Brien, Sharon. *Willa Cather: The Emerging Voice.* New York: Oxford Univ. Press, 1987.

O'Daniel, Therman B., Ed. *Jean Toomer: A Critical Evaluation.* Washington: Howard Univ. Press, 1988.

Oellers, Norbert, Ed. *Politische Aufgaben und soziale Funktionen von Germanistik und Deutschunterricht.* Tübingen: Niemeyer, 1988.

O'Hara, Daniel T. *Lionel Trilling: The Work of Liberation.* Madison: Univ. of Wisconsin Press, 1988.

Okazaki, Yoshie. *Japanese Literature in the Meiji Era,* trans. V. H. Viglielmo. Tokyo: Ōbunsha, 1955.

Olesch, Reinhold, and Hans Rothe, Eds. *Festschrift für Herbert Bräuer zum 65. Geburtstag am 14. April, 1986.* Cologne: Böhlau, 1986.

Olsen, Lance. *Ellipse of Uncertainty: An Introduction to Post-Modern Fantasy.* Westport: Greenwood, 1987.

O'Prey, Paul. *A Reader's Guide to Graham Greene.* New York: Thames & Hudson, 1988.

Orel, Harold. *The Unknown Hardy: Lesser-Known Aspects of Hardy's Life and Career.* New York: St. Martin's Press, 1987.

Orr, Elaine N. *Tillie Olsen and Feminist Spiritual Vision.* Jackson: Univ. Press of Mississippi, 1987.

Palencia-Roth, Michael. *Gabriel García Márquez: La línea, el círculo y la metamorfosis del mito.* Madrid: Editorial Gredos, 1983.

———. *Myth and the Modern Novel: García Márquez, Mann, and Joyce.* New York: Garland, 1987.

Palumbo, Donald, Ed. *Erotic Universe: Sexuality and Fantastic Literature.* Westport: Greenwood, 1986.

———. *Spectrum of the Fantastic.* Westport: Greenwood, 1988.

Paolini, Gilbert, Ed. *LA CHISPA '87: Selected Proceedings.* New Orleans: Tulane Univ., 1987.

Parfitt, George. *Fiction of the First World War.* London: Faber & Faber, 1988.

Parker, Stephen J. *Understanding Vladimir Nabokov.* Columbia: Univ. of South Carolina Press, 1987.

Parrinder, Patricia. *The Failure of Theory: Essays on Criticism and Contemporary Fiction.* Totowa, N.J.: Barnes & Noble, 1987.

Pasco, Allan H. *Novel Configurations: A Study of French Fiction.* Birmingham, Ala.: Summa, 1987.

Patterson, David. *The Affirming Flame: Religion, Language, and Literature.* Norman: Univ. of Oklahoma Press, 1988.

Patterson, Richard F. *A World Outside: The Fiction of Paul Bowles.* Austin: Univ. of Texas Press, 1987.

Paulson, Suzanne M. *Flannery O'Connor: A Study of the Short Fiction.* Boston: Twayne, 1988.

Peach, Linden. *The Prose Writing of Dylan Thomas.* Totowa, N.J.: Barnes & Noble, 1988.

Peacock, Thomas Love. *"Headlong Hall" and "Gryll Grange,"* ed. Michael Baron and Michael Slater. Oxford: Oxford Univ. Press, 1987.

Pearce, Roy H. *Gesta Humanorum: Studies in the Historical Mode.* Columbia: Univ. of Missouri Press, 1987.

Pease, Donald E. *Visionary Compacts: American Renaissance Writings in Cultural Context.* Madison: Univ. of Wisconsin Press, 1987.

Perrine, Laurence. *Instructor's Manual to Accompany "Story and Structure, Fifth Edition."* New York: Harcourt Brace Jovanovich, 1978.

———, and Thomas R. Arp. *Instructor's Manual to Accompany "Story and Structure, Sixth Edition."* New York: Harcourt Brace Jovanovich, 1983.

———. *Instructor's Manual to Accompany "Story and Structure, Seventh Edition."* San Diego: Harcourt Brace Jovanovich, 1988.

Person, Leland S. *Aesthetic Headaches: Women and a Masculine Poetics in Poe, Melville, and Hawthorne.* Athens: Univ. of Georgia Press, 1988.

Peters, Catherine. *Thackeray's Universe: Shifting Worlds of Imagination and Reality.* New York: Oxford Univ. Press, 1987.

Petry, Alice H. *A Genius in His Way: The Art of Cable's "Old Creole Days."* Cranbury, N.J.: Associated Univ. Presses [for Fairleigh Dickinson Univ. Press], 1988.

Phelps, Leland R., Ed. *Creative Encounter: Festschrift for Herman Salinger.* Chapel Hill: Univ. of North Carolina Press, 1978.

Pierce, John J. *Foundations of Science Fiction: A Study in Imagination and Evolution.* Westport: Greenwood, 1987.

Pincus Sigele, Rizel, and Gonzalo Sobrejano, Eds. *Homenaje a Casalduero, Critica y Poesia.* Madrid: Editorial, Gredos, 1972.

Pinsker, Sanford. *The Uncompromising Fictions of Cynthia Ozick.* Columbia: Univ. of Missouri Press, 1987.

Ponomareff, Constantin V. *On the Dark Side of Russian Literature.* New York: Lang, 1987.

Portch, Stephen R. *Literature's Silent Language: Nonverbal Communication.* New York: Lang, 1985.

Prasad, R. C., and A. K. Sharma, Eds. *Modern Studies and Other Essays in Honour of Dr. R. K. Sinda.* New Delhi: Vikas, 1987.

Pritchett, V. S. *Chekhov: A Spirit Set Free.* New York: Random House, 1988.

Promis Ojeda, José, Cedomil Goic, Raúl Bueno Chávez, Fernando Moreno Turner, Antonio Cornejo Polar, Adriana Valdéz, and Edmundo Bendezü. *José Donoso: La destrucción de un mundo.* Buenos Aires: Fernando García Cambiero, 1975.

Raby, Peter. *Oscar Wilde.* Cambridge: Cambridge Univ. Press, 1988.

Raine, Craig, Ed. *A Choice of Kipling's Prose.* London: Faber & Faber, 1987.

Rauchbauer, Otto, Ed. *A Yearbook of Studies in English Language and Literature 1985/86.* Vienna: Braumüller, 1986.

Reid, J. H. *Heinrich Böll: A German for His Time.* Oxford: Berg, 1988.

Reilly, Patrick. *The Literature of Guilt: From "Gulliver" to Golding.* Iowa City: Univ. of Iowa Press, 1988.

Reino, Joseph. *Stephen King: The First Decade.* Boston: Twayne, 1988.

Ressler, Steve. *Joseph Conrad: Consciousness and Integrity.* New York: New York Univ. Press, 1988.

Reynolds, David S. *Beneath the American Renaissance: The Subversive Imagination in the Age of Emerson and Melville.* New York: Knopf, 1988.

Rhodes, H. Winston. *Frank Sargeson.* New York: Twayne, 1969.

Richardson, William D. *Melville's "Benito Cereno": An Interpretation with Annotated Text and Concordance.* Durham: Carolina Academic Press, 1987.

Rickels, Laurence A. *Aberrations of Mourning: Writings on German Crypts*. Detroit: Wayne State Univ. Press, 1988.

Ricks, Thomas M., Ed. *Critical Perspectives on Modern Persian Literature*. Washington: Three Continents Press, 1984.

Ricou, Laurie. *Everyday Magic: Child Languages in Canadian Literature*. Vancouver: Univ. of British Columbia Press, 1987.

Rigney, Barbara H. *Margaret Atwood*. Totowa, N.J.: Barnes & Noble, 1987.

Rimer, J. Thomas. *A Reader's Guide to Japanese Literature*. Tokyo: Kodansha International, 1988.

Rio, Carmen M. del. *Jorge Luis Borges y la ficción: El conocimiento como inverción*. Miami: Ediciones Universal, 1983.

Roberts, David. *Jean Stafford: A Biography*. Boston: Little, Brown, 1988.

Roberts, Edgar V., and Henry E. Jacobs. *Instructor's Manual [for] "Fiction: An Introduction to Reading."* Englewood Cliffs: Prentice-Hall, 1987.

Robinson, James C. *Peter Taylor: A Study of the Short Fiction*. Boston: Twayne, 1988.

Rodríguez-Alcalá, Hugo. *Narrativa Hispanoamericana*. Madrid: Editorial Gredos, 1973.

Rodríguez de Laguna, Asela, Ed. *Images and Identities: The Puerto Rican in Two World Contexts*. New Brunswick: Transaction, 1987.

Roellenbleck, Georg, Ed. *Le Discours polémiques: Aspects théoriques et interprétations*. Tübingen: Narr, 1985.

Rogers, Elizabeth S. and Timothy S., Eds. *In Retrospect: Essays on Latin American Literature (In Memory of Willis Knapp Jones)*. York, S.C.: Spanish Literature Publications, 1987.

Rosebury, Brian. *Art and Desire: A Study in the Aesthetics of Fiction*. New York: St. Martin's Press, 1988.

Rosensprung, Ingrid, Elisabeth Abela, Hannelore Beerheide, Rudolf H. Schäfer, Brigitte Frank, Ute Renken, Ulrike Seifried, Fritz Egger, and Albrecht Weber. *Interpretationen zu Heinrich Böll*, II. Munich: Oldenbourg, 1965.

Rosenthal, Bernard, and Paul E. Szarmach, Eds. *Medievalism in American Culture: Special Studies*. Binghamton: Center for Medieval and Early Renaissance Studies, 1987.

Ross, Janice. *The World of Barbara Pym*. New York: St. Martin's Press, 1987.

Rowe, Joyce A. *Equivocal Endings in Classic American Novels*. New York: Cambridge Univ. Press, 1988.

Roy, Ginette, Ed. *Études lawrenciennes*. Paris: Univ. of Paris, 1986.

Rubin-Dorsky, Jeffrey. *Adrift in the Old World: The Psychological Pilgrimage of Washington Irving*. Chicago: Univ. of Chicago Press, 1988.

Ruderman, Judith. *William Styron*. New York: Ungar, 1987.

Rusinko, Susan. *Tom Stoppard*. Boston: Twayne, 1986.

Ruzicka, William T. *Faulkner's Fictive Architecture: The Meaning of Place in the Yoknapatawpha Novels*. Ann Arbor: UMI Research Press, 1987.

Ryan, Maureen. *Innocence and Estrangement in the Fiction of Jean Stafford*. Baton Rouge: Louisiana State Univ. Press, 1987.

Sabin, Margery. *The Dialect of the Tribe: Speech and Community in Modern Fiction*. New York: Oxford Univ. Press, 1987.

Salgado, Gamini, and G. K. Das, Eds. *The Spirit of D. H. Lawrence*. Totowa, N.J.: Barnes & Noble, 1988.

Salmonson, Jessica A., Ed. *The Supernatural Tales of Fitz-James O'Brien*. New York: Doubleday, 1988.

Saltzman, Arthur M. *Understanding Raymond Carver.* Columbia: Univ. of South Carolina Press, 1988.

Sammons, Jeffrey L. *Wilhelm Raabe: The Fiction of the Alternative Community.* Princeton: Princeton Univ. Press, 1987.

Sammons, Martha C. *"A Better Country": The Worlds of Religious Fantasy and Science Fiction.* Westport: Greenwood, 1988.

Santraud, Jeanne-Marie, Ed. *Le Sud et autres points cardinaux.* Paris: Sorbonne, 1985.

Savolainen, Matti. *The Element of Stasis in William Faulkner: An Approach in Phenomenological Criticism.* Tampera, Finland: Univ. of Tampera, 1987.

Scambray, Kenneth. *A Varied Harvest: The Life and Works of Henry Blake Fuller.* Pittsburgh: Univ. of Pittsburgh Press, 1988.

Schardt, Michael M., Ed. *Arno Schmidt, Das Früwerk I: Erzählungen: Interpretationen von "Gadir" bis "Kosmas."* Aachen: Rader, 1987.

Schlunk, Jurgen E., and Armand E. Singer, Eds. *Martin Walser: International Perspectives.* New York: Lang, 1987.

Schriber, Mary S. *Gender and the Writer's Imagination: From Cooper to Wharton.* Lexington: Univ. Press of Kentucky, 1987.

Schürer, Ernst, and Philip Jenkins, Eds. *B. Traven: Life and Work.* University Park: Pennsylvania State Univ. Press, 1987.

Schwartz Lerner, Lía, and Isaías Lerner, Eds. *Homenaje a Ana María Barrenechea.* Madrid: Editorial Castalia, 1984.

Schweitzer, Darrell, Ed. *Discovering H. P. Lovecraft.* Mercer Island, Wash.: Starmont, 1987.

Scott, Bonnie K. *James Joyce.* Atlantic Highlands, N.J.: Humanities Press International, 1987.

See, Fred G. *Desire and the Sign: Nineteenth-Century American Fiction.* Baton Rouge: Louisiana State Univ. Press, 1987.

Seed, David. *The Fictional Labyrinths of Thomas Pynchon.* Iowa City: Univ. of Iowa Press, 1988.

Selous, Trista. *The Other Woman: Feminism and Femininity in the Work of Marguerite Duras.* New Haven: Yale Univ. Press, 1988.

Senf, Carol A. *The Vampire in Nineteenth Century English Literature.* Bowling Green: Bowling Green Univ. Popular Press, 1988.

Shahane, Vasant A. *Khushwant Singh.* New York: Twayne, 1972.

Shaked, Gershon. *The Shadow Within: Essays on Modern Jewish Writers.* Philadelphia: Jewish Publication Society, 1987.

Sharma, T. R., Ed. *Essays on D. H. Lawrence.* Meerut, India: Shalabh Book House, 1987.

Shaw, Bradley A., and Nora Vera-Godwin, Eds. *Critical Perspectives on Gabriel García Márquez.* Lincoln: Society of Spanish and Spanish-American Studies, 1986.

Shaw, Donald L. *Nueva narrativa hispanoamericana,* 2nd ed. Madrid: Cátedra, 1983.

Shechner, Mark. *After the Revolution: Studies in the Contemporary Jewish American Imagination.* Bloomington: Indiana Univ. Press, 1987.

Showalter, Elaine, Ed. *Speaking of Gender.* New York: Routledge, 1989.

Shulman, Robert. *Social Criticism and Nineteenth-Century American Fiction.* Columbia: Univ. of Missouri Press, 1987.

Sims, Robert L. *The Evolution of Myth in García Márquez from "La Hojarasca" to "Cien Años de Soledad."* Miami: Ediciones Universal, 1981.

Slusser, George E., and Eric S. Rabkin, Eds. *Aliens: The Anthropology of Science Fiction*. Carbondale: Southern Illinois Univ. Press, 1987.

———. *Intersections: Fantasy and Science Fiction*. Carbondale: Southern Illinois Univ. Press, 1987.

Smyer, Richard I. *Animal Farm: Pastoralism and Politics*. Boston: Twayne, 1988.

Somerwil-Ayrton, S. K. *Poverty and Power in the Early Works of Dostoevskij*. Amsterdam: Rodopi, 1988.

Spell, Jefferson R. *Contemporary Spanish-American Fiction*. Chapel Hill: Univ. of North Carolina Press, 1944.

Spencer, Sharon, Ed. *Anaïs, Art and Artist: A Collection of Essays*. Greenwood, Fla.: Penkevill, 1986.

Spires, Robert C. *Transparent Simulacra: Spanish Fiction, 1902–1926*. Columbia: Univ. of Missouri Press, 1988.

Spivak, Gayatri Chakravorty. *In Other Words: Essays in Cultural Politics*. New York: Methuen, 1987.

Srivastava, Ramesh K., Ed. *Perspectives on Anita Desai*. Ghaziabad: Vimal Prakashan, 1984.

Staines, David, Ed. *The Canadian Imagination: Dimensions of a Literary Culture*. Cambridge: Harvard Univ. Press, 1977.

Stambaugh, Sara. *The Witch and the Goddess in the Stories of Isak Dinesen: A Feminist Reading*. Ann Arbor: UMI Press, 1988.

Standley, Fred L., and Nancy V. Burt, Eds. *Critical Essays on James Baldwin*. Boston: Hall, 1988.

Stasz, Clarice. *American Dreamers: Charmian and Jack London*. New York: St. Martin's Press, 1988.

Stern, Madeleine B. *A Double Life: Newly Discovered Thrillers of Louisa May Alcott*. Boston: Little, Brown, 1988.

Stouck, David. *Major Canadian Authors*. Lincoln: Univ. of Nebraska Press, 1984.

Stout, Janis P. *Sodom in Eden: The City in American Fiction Before 1860*. Westport: Greenwood, 1976.

Struthers, J. R. (Tim), Ed. *The Montreal Story Tellers: Memoirs, Photographs, Critical Essays*. Montreal: Véhicule, 1985.

Strutz, Josef, Ed. *Kunst, Wissenschaft und Politik von Robert Musil bis Ingeborg Bachmann*. Munich: Fink, 1986.

———. *Robert Musils "Kakanien"—Subjekt und Geschichte*. Munich: Fink, 1987.

Suleiman, Susan R., and Inge Crossman, Eds. *The Reader in the Text: Essays on Audience and Interpretation*. Princeton: Princeton Univ. Press, 1980.

Sullivan, Walter. *A Requiem for the Renascence: The State of Fiction in the Modern South*. Athens: Univ. of Georgia Press, 1976.

Sundquist, Asebrit. *Pocahontas & Co.—The Fictional American Indian Woman in Nineteenth-Century Literature: A Study of Method*. Oslo: Solum, 1987.

Suvin, Darko. *Positions and Presuppositions in Science Fiction*. Kent: Kent State Univ. Press, 1988.

Swann, Thomas E., and Kinya Tsuruta, Eds. *Approaches to the Modern Japanese Short Story*. Tokyo: Waseda Univ. Press, 1982.

Takeda, Katsuhiko, Ed. *Essays on Japanese Literature*. Tokyo: Waseda Univ. Press, 1977.

Tanaka, Yukiko, and Elizabeth Hanson, Eds. *This Kind of Woman: Ten Stories by Japanese Women Writers, 1960–1976*. Stanford: Stanford Univ. Press, 1982.

Tanner, Stephen L. *Lionel Trilling*. Boston: Twayne, 1988.

Tanner, Tony. *Scenes of Nature, Signs of Men*. Cambridge: Cambridge Univ. Press, 1987.

Terras, Victor, Ed. *American Contributions to the Eighth International Congress of Slavists*, II. Columbus: Slavic Publishers, 1978.

Thieme, John. *The Web of Tradition: Uses of Allusion in V. S. Naipaul's Fiction.* Hertford: Hansib, 1987.

Thomas, Brian. *An Underground Fate: The Idiom of Romance in the Late Novels of Graham Greene.* Athens: Univ. of Georgia Press, 1988.

Thomas, Brook. *Cross-Examinations of Law and Literature: Cooper, Hawthorne, Stowe, and Melville.* New York: Cambridge Univ. Press, 1987.

Thomas, Kenneth E. *Andre Dubus: A Study of the Short Fiction.* Boston: Twayne, 1988.

Townsend, Kim. *Sherwood Anderson.* Boston: Houghton Mifflin, 1987.

Tracy, Laura. *"Catching the Drift": Authority, Gender, and Narrative Strategy.* New Brunswick: Rutgers Univ. Press, 1988.

Treat, John W. *Pools of Water, Pillars of Fire: The Literature of Ibuse Masuji.* Seattle: Univ. of Washington Press, 1988.

Trotman, C. James, Ed. *Richard Wright: Myths and Realities.* New York: Garland, 1988.

Twitchell, James B. *Forbidden Partners: The Incest Taboo in Modern Culture.* New York: Columbia Univ. Press, 1987.

Udoff, Alan, Ed. *Kafka and the Contemporary Critical Performance.* Bloomington: Indiana Univ. Press, 1987.

Unrue, Darlene H. *Understanding Katherine Anne Porter.* Columbia: Univ. of South Carolina Press, 1988.

Urbano, Victoria, Ed. *Five Women Writers of Costa Rica.* Beaumont: Asociación de Literatura Femenina Hispánica, 1978.

Vannatta, Dennis. *Tennessee Williams: A Study of the Short Fiction.* Boston: Twayne, 1988.

Vansant, Jacqueline. *Against the Horizon: Feminism and Postwar Austrian Women Writers.* Westport: Greenwood, 1988.

Vargas Llosa, Mario. *García Márquez: historia de un deicidio.* Barcelona: Barral Editores, 1971.

Varnado, S. L. *Haunted Presence: The Numinous in Gothic Fiction.* Tuscaloosa: Univ. of Alabama Press, 1987.

Veeder, William, and Gordon Hirsch, Eds. *Dr. Jekyll and Mr. Hyde After One Hundred Years.* Chicago: Univ. of Chicago Press, 1988.

Venugopal, C. V. *The Indian Short Story in English.* Bareilly: Prakash, 1976.

Verani, Hugo, Ed. *José Emilio Pacheco ante la critica.* Mexico City: Univ. Autónoma Metropolitana, 1987.

Vidal, Sorkunde F. *La narrativa de Mújica Láinez.* Bilbao: Universidad del Pais Vasco, 1986.

Vilanova, Antonio, Ed. *Clarín y su obra en el centenario de La Regenta* (Barcelona, 1884–1885). Barcelona: Univ. de Barcelona, 1985.

Vogt, Michael, Ed. *Die boshafte Heiterkeit des Wilhelm Busch.* Bielefeld: Aistheses, 1988.

Waegner, Cathy. *Recollection and Discovery: The Rhetoric of Character in William Faulkner's Novels.* Bern: Lang, 1983.

Wagenknecht, Edward. *The Tales of Henry James.* New York: Ungar, 1984.

Wagner, Linda W., Ed. *Critical Essays on Sylvia Plath.* Boston: Hall, 1984.

Wagoner, Mary S. *Agatha Christie.* Boston: Twayne, 1986.

Walker, Margaret. *Richard Wright: Demonic Genius.* New York: Warner, 1988.

Walker, Nancy A. *A Very Serious Thing: Women's Humor and American Culture.* Minneapolis: Univ. of Minnesota Press, 1988.

Walsh, Mary E. W. *Jean Stafford*. Boston: Twayne, 1985.

Ward, J. A. *American Silences: The Realism of James Agee, Walker Evans, and Edward Hopper*. Baton Rouge: Louisiana State Univ. Press, 1985.

Warren, Alan. *Roald Dahl*. Mercer Island, Wash.: Starmont, 1988.

Warrick, Patricia S. *Mind in Motion: The Fiction of Philip K. Dick*. Carbondale: Southern Illinois Univ. Press, 1987.

Waszink, P. M. *"Such Things Happen in the World": Deixis in Three Short Stories by N. V. Gogol*. Amsterdam: Rodopi, 1988.

Watson, Carole M. *Prologue: The Novels of Black American Women, 1891–1965*. Westport: Greenwood, 1985.

Watson, James G. *William Faulkner: Letters and Fiction*. Austin: Univ. of Texas Press, 1987.

Weinreich, Uriel, Ed. *The Field of Yiddish: Studies in Yiddish Language, Folklore, and Literature*. New York: Lexik House, 1954.

Weinstein, Arnold. *The Fiction of Relationship*. Princeton: Princeton Univ. Press, 1988.

Weiss, Daniel. *The Critical Agonistes: Psychology, Myth, and the Art of Fiction*, ed. Eric Solomon and Stephen Arkin. Seattle: Univ. of Washington Press, 1985.

Wellbery, David E., Ed. *Positionen der Literaturwissenschaft: Acht Modellanalysen am Beispiel von Kleists "Das Erdbeben in Chili."* Munich: Beck, 1985.

Welsh, Alexander. *George Eliot and Blackmail*. Cambridge: Harvard Univ. Press, 1985.

Welty, Eudora. *The Eye of the Storm*. New York: Random House, 1978.

Werner, Craig H. *Dubliners: A Pluralistic World*. Boston: Twayne, 1988.

West, Paul. *The Modern Novel*, II. 1963; London: Hutchinson, 1965.

Westarp, Karl-Heinz, Ed. *Joyce Centenary Offshoots: James Joyce, 1882–1892*. Aarhus, Denmark: Univ. of Aarhus, 1983.

Whiteley, Patrick J. *Knowledge and Experimental Realism in Conrad, Lawrence, and Woolf*. Baton Rouge: Louisiana State Univ. Press, 1987.

Widmer, Kingsley. *Countering Utopian Dialectics in Contemporary Contexts*. Ann Arbor: UMI Research Press, 1988.

Wilde, Alan. *Middle Grounds: Studies in Contemporary American Fiction*. Philadelphia: Univ. of Pennsylvania Press, 1987.

Wilding, Michael. *Marcus Clarke*. Melbourne: Oxford University Press, 1977.

Williams, Merryn. *Six Women Novelists*. New York: St. Martin's Press, 1988.

Williams, Michael J. S. *A World of Words: Language and Displacement in the Fiction of Edgar Allan Poe*. Durham: Duke Univ. Press, 1988.

Willis, Sharon. *Marguerite Duras: Writing on the Body*. Urbana: Univ. of Illinois Press, 1987.

Wilson, A. N. *Tolstoy*. New York: Norton, 1988.

Wilson, James D. *A Reader's Guide to the Short Stories of Mark Twain*. Boston: Hall, 1987.

Wilson, Jonathan. *On Bellow's Planet: Readings from the Dark Side*. Cranbury, N.J.: Associated Univ. Presses [for Fairleigh Dickinson Univ. Press], 1985.

Wilson, Michiko N. *The Marginal World of Ōe Kenzaburo: A Study in Themes and Techniques*. Armonk, N.Y.: Sharpe, 1986.

Wilson, Robert. *Conrad's Mythology*. Troy, N.Y.: Whitston, 1987.

Winchell, Mark R. *Leslie Fiedler*. Boston: Twayne, 1985.

Winners, Anthony. *Culture and Irony: Studies in Joseph Conrad's Major Novels*. Charlottesville: Univ. Press of Virginia, 1988.

Winter, Douglas E., Ed. *Shadowings: The Reader's Guide to Horror Fiction—1981–1982*. Mercer Island, Wash.: Starmont, 1983.

Witt, Mary A. F. *Existential Prisons: Captivity in Mid-Twentieth-Century French Literature*. Durham: Duke Univ. Press, 1985.

Wittkowski, Wolfgang, Ed. *Verantwortung und Utopie: Zur Literatur der Goethezeit*. Tübingen: Max Niemeyer, 1988.

Woeller, Waltraud, and Bruce Cassiday. *The Literature of Crime and Detection*. New York: Ungar, 1988.

Wolfe, Peter. *Something More Than Night: The Case of Raymond Chandler*. Bowling Green: Bowling Green State Univ. Popular Press, 1985.

Wolff, Rudolf, Ed. *Thomas Mann: Erzählungen und Novellen*. Bonn: Bouvier, 1984.

Wood, Dennis. *Benjamin Constant: "Adolphe."* Cambridge: Cambridge Univ. Press, 1987.

Woodress, James. *Willa Cather: A Literary Life*. Lincoln: Univ. of Nebraska Press, 1987.

Woolrich, Cornell. *The Fantastic Stories of Cornell Woolrich*. Carbondale: Southern Illinois Univ. Press, 1981.

Woolson, Constance Fenimore. *Women Artists, Women Exiles: "Miss Grief" and Other Stories*, ed. Joan M. Weimer. New Brunswick: Rutgers Univ. Press, 1988.

Wuletich-Brinberg, Sybil. *Poe: The Rationale of the Uncanny*. New York: Lang, 1988.

Wykes, David. *A Preface to Orwell*. London: Longman, 1987.

Yamamoto, Hisaye. *"Seventeen Syllables" and Other Stories*, introd. King-Kok Cheung. Latham, N.Y.: Kitchen Table—Women of Color Press, 1988.

Yeazell, Ruth B., Ed. *Sex, Politics, and Science in the Nineteenth-Century Novel*. Baltimore: Johns Hopkins Univ. Press, 1986.

Yoke, Carl B., Ed. *Phoenix from the Ashes: The Literature of the Remade World*. Westport, Conn.: Greenwood, 1987.

Yu, Beongcheon. *Natsume Soseki*. New York: Twayne, 1969.

———. *Akutagawa: An Introduction*. Detroit: Wayne State Univ. Press, 1972.

Zach, Wolfgang, and Heinz Kosak, Eds. *Literary Interrelations: Ireland, England, and the World*, II. Tübingen: Narr, 1987.

Zahorski, Kenneth J. *Peter Beagle*. Mercer Island, Wash.: Starmont, 1988.

Zapanta-Manlapaz, Edna. *Kapampangan Literature: A Historical Survey and Anthology*. Manila: Manila Univ. Press, 1981.

Zayas-Bazán, Eduardo, and M. Laurentino Suárez, Eds. *Selected Proceedings of the Twenty-Seventh Annual Mountain Interstate Foreign Language Conference*. Johnson City, Tenn.: Research Council of East Tennessee State Univ., 1978.

Ziegler, Heide. *John Barth*. London: Methuen, 1987.

Ziolkowski, Margaret. *Hagiography and Modern Russian Literature*. Princeton: Princeton Univ. Press, 1988.

Zum Felde, Alberto. *Critica de la literatura uruguaya*. Montevideo: Maximo García, 1921.

A CHECKLIST OF JOURNALS USED

	Acta Literaria
Am Imago	*American Imago: A Psychoanalytic Journal for Culture, Science, and the Arts*
Am Lit	*American Literature: A Journal of Literary History, Criticism, and Bibliography*
Am Lit Realism	*American Literary Realism, 1870–1910*
Am Notes & Queries	*American Notes and Queries*
Am Transcendental Q	*American Transcendental Quarterly: A Journal of New England Writers*
	Americas [formerly *Revista Chicano Riqueña*]
Analele Ştiinţifice ale Universităţii	*Analele Ştiinţifice ale Universităţii "Al.I. Cuza" din Iaşi*
Anales de la Literatura Española	*Anales de la Literatura Española Contemporánea*
Anales de la Universidad Complutense	*Anales de la Universidad Complutense* (Madrid)
	Anales de la Universidad de Chile
Analysis	*Analysis: Quaderni di Anglistica*
Anglia	*Anglia: Zeitschrift für Englische Philologie*
Antigonish R	*The Antigonish Review*
Ariel	*Ariel: A Review of International English Literature*
Arizona Q	*Arizona Quarterly*
Armchair Detective	*Armchair Detective: A Quarterly Journal Devoted to the Appreciation of Mystery, Detective, and Suspense Fiction*
Australian J French Stud	*Australian Journal of French Studies*
Baker Street J	*The Baker Street Journal: An Irregular Quarterly of Sherlockiana*
Ball State Univ Forum	*Ball State University Forum*
Belfagor	*Belfagor: Rassegna di Varia Umanità*
Black Am Lit Forum	*Black American Literature Forum* [formerly *Negro American Literature Forum*]

Boletin de la Academia Colombiana

Boletín del Instituto de Estudios Asturianos

Brahmavidya · *Brahmavidya: The Adyar Library Bulletin*

Bucknell R · *Bucknell Review: A Scholarly Journal of Letters, Arts and Sciences*

Bull des Amis · *Bulletin des Amis d'André Gide*

Bull Hispanique · *Bulletin Hispanique*

Cahiers Roumains · *Cahiers Roumains d'Études Littéraires: Revue Trimestrielle de Critique, d'Esthétiques et d'Histoire Littéraires*

Cahiers Victoriens et Edouardiens · *Cahiers Victoriens et Edouardiens: Revue du Centre d'Études et de Recherches Victoriennes et Edouardiennes de l'Université Paul Valéry, Montpellier*

Caliban

Canadian J Irish Stud · *Canadian Journal of Irish Studies*

Canadian Lit · *Canadian Literature*

Casa de las Americas

Centennial R · *Centennial Review*

Central Asian Survey

Chasqui · *Chasqui: Revista de Literatura Latinoamericana*

Chicano Creativity and Criticism · *Chicano Creativity and Criticism: Charting New Frontiers in Literature*

Christianity & Lit · *Christianity and Literature*

Círculo · *Círculo: Revista de Cultura*

Cithara · *Cithara: Essays in the Judaeo-Christian Tradition*

Classical & Mod Lit · *Classical and Modern Literature*

Colby Lib Q · *Colby Library Quarterly*

Coll Engl · *College English*

Coll Engl Assoc Critic · *CEA Critic: An Official Journal of the College English Association*

Coll Lang Assoc J · *College Language Association Journal*

Colloquia Germanica · *Colloquia Germanica, Internationale Zeitschrift für Germanische Sprach- und Literaturwissenschaft*

	Commentary
Commonwealth Essays	*Commonwealth Essays and Studies*
Comp Lit	*Comparative Literature*
Conference Coll Teachers Engl Stud	*Conference of College Teachers of English Studies* [formerly *Conference of College Teachers of English of Texas*]
Confluencia	*Confluencia: Revista Hispánica de Cultura y Literatura*
The Conradian	*The Conradian: Journal of the Joseph Conrad Society* [U.K.]
Conradiana	*Conradiana: A Journal of Joseph Conrad*
	Co-textes
	Crazyhorse
Cristallo	*Cristallo: Rassegna di Varia Umanità*
	Crítica Hispánica
	Critical Exchange
Criticism	*Criticism: A Quarterly for Literature and the Arts*
Critique S	*Critique: Studies in Modern Fiction*
	Cuadernos Americanos
	Cuadernos del Norte
Cuadernos Hispanoamericanos	*Cuadernos Hispanoamericanos: Revista Mensual de Cultura Hispanica*
D. H. Lawrence R	*The D. H. Lawrence Review*
Dalhousie R	*Dalhousie Review*
Denver Q	*Denver Quarterly*
Der Deutschunterricht	*Der Deutschunterricht: Beiträge zu seiner Praxis und wissenschaftlichen Grundlegung*
Dickensian	*The Dickensian*
Dieciocho	*Dieciocho: Hispanic Enlightenment, Aesthetics, and Literary Theory*
Dires	*Dires: Revue du Centre d'Études Freudiennes*
Discourse	*Discourse Processes: A Multidisciplinary Journal*
Duquesne Hispanic R	*Duquesne Hispanic Review*

Dutch Q R	*Dutch Quarterly Review of Anglo-American Letters*
	Eco
ESQ: J Am Renaissance	*Emerson Society Quarterly: Journal of the American Renaissance*
Edebiyat: J Middle Eastern Lit	*Edebiyat: A Journal of Middle Eastern Literatures*
Engl Africa	*English in Africa*
Engl Lang Notes	*English Language Notes*
Engl Lit Transition	*English Literature in Transition*
Engl Stud	*English Studies: A Journal of English Language and Literature*
Engl Stud Africa	*English Studies in Africa: A Journal of the Humanities*
Engl Stud Canada	*English Studies in Canada*
Epos	*Epos: Revista de Filología*
Escritura	*Escritura: Teoría y Crítica Literarias*
	L'Esprit Créateur
Essays Canadian Writing	*Essays on Canadian Writing*
Essays Crit	*Essays in Criticism: A Quarterly Journal of Literary Criticism*
Essays French Lit	*Essays in French Literature*
Essays Lit	*Essays in Literature* (Western Illinois)
	Estudios Anglo-Americanos
	Estudos Anglo-Americanos
	Études Germaniques
	Études Irlandaises
	Explicación de Textos Literarios
	Explicator
	Extrapolation
Fantasy R	*Fantasy Review*
Faulkner J	*Faulkner Journal*
Flannery O'Connor Bull	*Flannery O'Connor Bulletin*

	Foro Literario
Forum Mod Lang Stud	Forum for Modern Language Studies
Foundation	Foundation: Review of Science Fiction
Fourah Bay Stud	Fourah Bay Studies in Language and Literature
Fransiz Dili Edebiyati	Fransiz Dili Edebiyati Bölümü Dergisi
	French Forum
French Lit Series	French Literature Series
French R	French Review: Journal of the American Association of Teachers of French
	Genders
	Genre
George Eliot Fellowship R	The George Eliot Fellowship Review
Germ Life & Letters	German Life and Letters
Germ Notes	Germanic Notes
Germ Q	German Quarterly
Germ R	Germanic Review
Germano-Slavica	Germano-Slavica: A Canadian Journal of Germanic and Slavic Comparative Studies
Gettysburg R	Gettysburg Review
Gissing Newsletter	The Gissing Newsletter
Griot	Official Journal of the Southern Conference on Afro-American Studies
Hawthorne Soc Newsletter	Hawthorne Society Newsletter
Hebrew Annual R	Hebrew Annual Review
Hemingway R	Hemingway Review [formerly Hemingway Notes]
Henry James R	Henry James Review
Hiroshima Stud Engl Lang & Lit	Hiroshima Studies in English Language and Literature
Hispamerica	Hispamerica: Revista de Literatura
Hispania	Hispania: A Journal Devoted to the Interests of the Teaching of Spanish and Portuguese
Hispanic J	Hispanic Journal

Hispanic R	*Hispanic Review*
	Hispanófila
	Hollins Critic
Horen	*Die Horen: Zeitschrift für Literatur, Kunst und Kritik*
Iberoromania	*Iberoromania: Zeitschrift für Iberoromanischen Sprachen und Literaturen in Europa und Amerika*
Ilha do Desterro	*Ilha do Desterro: A Journal of Language and Literature*
Interpretation	*Interpretation: A Journal of Political Philosophy*
Inti	*Inti: Revista de literatura Hispánica*
Int'l Fiction R	*International Fiction Review*
Int'l J Middle East Stud	*International Journal of Middle East Studies*
Iowa J Lit Stud	*Iowa Journal of Literary Studies*
Irish Slavonic Stud	*Irish Slavonic Studies*
Italian Q	*Italian Quarterly*
	Italianist
J Am Research Center	*Journal of the American Research Center* (Cairo)
J Am Stud Assoc Texas	*Journal of the American Studies Association of Texas*
J Arabic Lit	*Journal of Arabic Literature*
J Assoc Teachers Japanese	*Journal of the Association of Teachers of Japanese*
J Australasian Univs Lang & Lit Assoc	*Journal of the Australasian Universities Language and Literature Association: A Journal of Literary Criticism, Philology & Linguistics*
J Commonwealth Lit	*The Journal of Commonwealth Literature*
J Engl & Germ Philol	*Journal of English and Germanic Philology*
J European Stud	*Journal of European Studies*
J Evolutionary Psych	*Journal of Evolutionary Psychology*
J Japanese Stud	*Journal of Japanese Studies*
J Kentucky Stud	*Journal of Kentucky Studies*
J Mental Imagery	*Journal of Mental Imagery*

J Narrative Technique	*Journal of Narrative Technique*
J Pop Culture	*Journal of Popular Culture*
J Ritual Stud	*Journal of Ritual Studies*
J Short Story Engl	*Journal of the Short Story in English*
J Southwest	*Journal of the Southwest*
J Spanish Stud	*Journal of Spanish Studies: Twentieth Century*
J William Morris Soc	*Journal of the William Morris Society*
Jean Rhys R	*Jean Rhys Review*
	Jewish Book Annual
Káñina	*Káñina: Revista de Artes y Letras de la Universidad de Costa Rica*
Kentucky Romance Q	*Kentucky Romance Quarterly*
Kenyon R	*Kenyon Review*
Kipling J	*The Kipling Journal*
Korean J	*Korean Journal*
	Kwartalnik Neofilologiczny
Kyushu Am Lit	*Kyushu American Literature*
Lamar J Humanities	*Lamar Journal of the Humanities*
Lang & Style	*Language and Style: An International Journal*
Lang Q	*The University of Southern Florida Language Quarterly*
Langs & Communications	*Languages & Communications: An Interdisciplinary Journal*
Les Langues Néo-Latines	*Les Langues Néo-Latines: Bulletin Trimestriel de la Sociéte de Langues Néo-Latines*
Latin Am Lit R	*Latin American Literary Review*
Latin Am Theatre R	*Latin American Theatre Review*
Legacy	*Legacy: A Journal of Nineteenth-Century American Women Writers*
Letras	*Letras* (Univ. Católica Argentina)
	Letras de Deusto
	Letras Femeninas

Lexis	*Lexis: Revista de Lingüística y Literatura*
Licorne	*La Licorne*
LiLi	*LiLi: Zeitschrift für Literaturwissenschaft und Linguistik*
Lit & Belief	*Literature and Belief*
Lit & Hist	*Literature and History*
Lit & Med	*Literature and Medicine*
Lit & Psych	*Literature and Psychology*
Lit Criterion	*Literary Criterion*
Lit Endeavour	*The Literary Endeavour: A Quarterly Journal Devoted to English Studies*
Lit/Film Q	*Literature/Film Quarterly*
Lit No Queensland	*Literature in North Queensland*
Literatur in Wissenschaft	*Literatur in Wissenschaft und Unterricht*
Littérature	*Littérature* (Paris)
Lovecraft Stud	*Lovecraft Studies*
Luso-Brazilian R	*Luso-Brazilian Review*
MELUS	*The Journal of the Society for the Study of the Multi-Ethnic Literature of the United States*
McNeese R	*McNeese Review*
Massachusetts R	*Massachusetts Review: A Quarterly of Literature, the Arts and Public Affairs*
Massachusetts Stud Engl	*Massachusetts Studies in English*
	Meanjin
Michigan Academician	*Michigan Academician: Papers of the Michigan Academy of Science, Arts, and Letters*
Mid-Hudson Lang Stud	*Mid-Hudson Language Studies* (Bulletin of the Mid-Hudson Modern Language Association)
	Midstream
Midwest Q	*Midwest Quarterly: A Journal of Contemporary Thought*
Mississippi Q	*Mississippi Quarterly: The Journal of Southern Culture*

Mitteilungen der E. T. A. Hoffmann	Mitteilungen der E. T. A. Hoffman-Gesellschaft-Bamberg
Mod Austrian Lit	Modern Austrian Literature: Journal of the International Arthur Schnitzler Research Association
Mod Chinese Lit	Modern Chinese Literature
Mod Fiction Stud	Modern Fiction Studies
Mod Lang Notes	MLN: Modern Language Notes
Mod Lang Q	Modern Language Quarterly
Mod Lang R	Modern Language Review
Mod Lang Stud	Modern Language Studies
Mod Langs	Modern Languages: Journal of the Modern Language Association (London)
Mod Philol	Modern Philology: A Journal Devoted to Research in Medieval and Modern Literature
Monatshefte	Monatshefte: Für Deutschen Unterricht, Deutsche Sprache und Literatur
Monographic R	Monographic Review/Revista Monográfia
Mosaic	Mosaic: A Journal for the Comparative Study of Literature and Ideas for the Interdisciplinary Study of Literature
Mount Olive R	Mount Olive Review
Nabokovian	The Nabokovian [formerly Vladimir Nabokov Research Newsletter]
La Nación (Lit Supp)	Suplemento Literario, La Nación
Names	Names: Journal of the American Name Society
Nathaniel Hawthorne R	Nathaniel Hawthorne Review
	Neophilologus
	Neue Germanistik
New Comparison	New Comparison: A Journal of Comparative and General Literature
	New Criterion
New Lit Hist	New Literary History
New Orleans R	New Orleans Review

New Q	*New Quarterly: New Directions in Canadian Writing*
	Nineteenth-Century Fiction
Nineteenth-Century French Stud	*Nineteenth-Century French Studies*
Nineteenth-Century Lit	*Nineteenth-Century Literature* [formerly *Nineteenth-Century Fiction*]
No Dakota Q	*North Dakota Quarterly*
Notes Contemp Lit	*Notes on Contemporary Literature*
Notes Mississippi Writers	*Notes on Mississippi Writers*
Notes Mod Am Lit	*NMAL: Notes on Modern American Literature*
Novel	*Novel: A Forum on Fiction*
	Nueva Revista de Filología Hispánica
	Oral Tradition
Orbis Litterarum	*Orbis Litterarum: International Review of Literary Studies*
PMLA	*PMLA: Publications of the Modern Language Association of America*
La Palabra y el Hombre	*La Palabra y el Hombre: Revista de la Universidad Veracruzana*
Panjab Univ Research Bull	*Panjab University Research Bulletin (Arts)*
Papers Lang & Lit	*Papers on Language and Literature: A Journal for Scholars and Critics of Language and Literature*
Partisan R	*Partisan Review*
Pembroke Mag	*The Pembroke Magazine*
Perspectives Contemp Lit	*Perspectives on Contemporary Literature*
Philippine Stud	*Philippine Studies* (Manila)
Philol Q	*Philological Quarterly*
Philosophical Stud	*Philosophical Studies: An International Journal for Philosophy in the Analytic Tradition*
Philosophy & Lit	*Philosophy and Literature*
Plural	*Plural: Revista Cultural de Excelsior*
Poe Stud	*Poe Studies*

Prooftexts	*Prooftexts: A Journal of Jewish Literary History*
	Le Psychanalyse
Pubs Arkansas Philol Assoc	*Publications of the Arkansas Philological Association*
Pubs Engl Goethe Soc	*Publications of the English Goethe Society*
	Pynchon Notes
Quaderni Ibero-Americani	*Quaderni Ibero-Americani: Attualità Culturale nella Penisola Iberica e America Latina*
Quimera	*Quimera: Revista de Literatura*
	La Quinzaine Litteraire
R Contemp Fiction	*Review of Contemporary Fiction*
R Engl Stud	*Review of English Studies*
R Lettres Modernes	*La Revue des Lettres Modernes: Histoire des Idées des Littératures*
	RE: Artes Liberales
Recherches et Études	*Recherches et Études Comparatistes Ibéro-Françaises de la Sorbonne*
Religion & Lit	*Religion and Literature*
Renascence	*Renascence: Essays on Value in Literature*
Rendezvous	*Rendezvous: Journal of Arts and Letters* (Pocatello, Idaho)
	Representations
Research African Lit	*Research in African Literature*
Resources Am Lit Stud	*Resources for American Literary Study*
Revista Canadiense	*Revista Canadiense de Estudios Hispánicos*
Revista Canaria	*Revista Canaria de Estudios Ingleses*
	Revista Chilena Literatura
	Revista de Estudios Hispánicos (Poughkeepsie)
	Revista de Occidente
	Revista Iberoamericana
	Revista Letras
	Revista/Review Interamericana

Revue d'Histoire Littéraire	*Revue d'Histoire Littéraire de la France*
	Revue de Littérature Comparée
	Revue des Sciences Humaines
Revue Française	*Revue Française d'Études Américaines*
Riverside Q	*Riverside Quarterly*
	Romance Notes
Romance Q	*Romance Quarterly* [formerly *Kentucky Romance Quarterly*]
Romanic R	*Romanic Review*
	Romanische Forschungen
Russian Lang J	*Russian Language Journal*
Russian Lit	*Russian Literature*
SPAN	*SPAN: Newsletter of the South Pacific Association for Comonwealth Literature and Language Studies*
St. Louis Univ Research J	*St. Louis University Research Journal of the Graduate School of Arts & Sciences*
Saul Bellow J	*Saul Bellow Journal* [formerly *Saul Bellow Newsletter*]
Sci & Soc	*Science & Society*
Sci Fiction	*Science Fiction: A Review of Speculative Literature*
Sci-Fiction Stud	*Science-Fiction Studies*
Seminar	*Seminar: A Journal of Germanic Studies*
Sewanee R	*Sewanee Review*
	Shenandoah
Shoin Lit R	*Shoin Literary Review*
Slavic & East European J	*Slavic and East European Journal*
Slavonic & East European R	*Slavonic & East European Review*
So Atlantic Q	*South Atlantic Quarterly*
So Atlantic R	*South Atlantic Review*
So Central R	*South Central Review*
So Dakota R	*South Dakota Review*

Solitary	*Solitary* (Manila)
Southern Hum R	*Southern Humanities Review*
Southern Lit J	*Southern Literary Journal*
Southern Q	*The Southern Quarterly: A Journal of the Arts in the South*
Southern R	*Southern Review* (Baton Rouge)
Southern R (Adelaide)	*Southern Review: Literary and Interdisciplinary Essays* (Adelaide)
Southern Stud	*Southern Studies: An Interdisciplinary Journal of the South*
Southwest R	*Southwest Review*
Steinbeck Q	*Steinbeck Quarterly*
Stud Am Fiction	*Studies in American Fiction*
Stud Am Humor	*Studies in American Humor*
Stud Am Jewish Lit	*Studies in American Jewish Literature*
Stud Canadian Lit	*Studies in Canadian Literature*
Stud Hum	*Studies in the Humanities*
Stud Lit Imagination	*Studies in Literary Imagination*
Stud Novel	*Studies in the Novel*
Stud Romanticism	*Studies in Romanticism*
Stud Short Fiction	*Studies in Short Fiction*
Stud Twentieth-Century Lit	*Studies in Twentieth-Century Literature*
	Studi di Letteratura Francese
Studia Anglica Posnaniensia	*Studia Anglica Posnaniensia: An International Review of English Studies*
Studia Neophilologica	*Studia Neophilologica: A Journal of Germanic and Romance Languages and Literature*
	Studien zum Indologie und Iranistik
Symposium	*Symposium: A Quarterly Journal of Modern Literatures*
	Temps Modernes
Texas Stud Lit & Lang	*Texas Studies in Literature and Language: A Journal of the Humanities*

	Text & Kontext
	Texto Crítico
Thought	*Thought: A Review of Culture and Ideas*
Torre	*La Torre: Revista de la Universidad de Puerto Rico*
Transcriptions/Zapiski	*Transcriptions/Zapiski of the Association of Russian-American Scholars in the U.S.A.*
	Tropos
	Turn-of-the-Century Women
Twentieth Century Lit	*Twentieth Century Literature: A Scholarly and Critical Journal*
ULULA	*ULULA: Graduate Studies in Romance Languages*
Univ Dayton R	*University of Dayton Review*
Univ Mississippi Stud Engl	*University of Mississippi Studies in English*
Univ Saga Stud Engl	*University of Saga Studies in English*
Univ Windsor R	*University of Windsor Review*
Virginia Q R	*Virginia Quarterly Review: A National Journal of Literature and Discussion*
Wascana R	*Wascana Review*
Weber Stud	*Weber Studies: An Interdisciplinary Humanities Journal*
Weimarer Beiträge	*Weimarer Beiträge: Zeitschrift für Literaturwissenschaft, Ästhetik und Kulturtheorie*
Die Welt der Slaven	*Die Welt der Slaven: Halbjahresschrift für Slavistik*
Western Am Lit	*Western American Literature*
Wicazo SA R	*The Wicazo SA Review: A Journal of Indian Studies*
Wilkie Collins Soc J	*Wilkie Collins Society Journal*
Wirkendes Wort	*Wirkendes Wort: Deutsche Sprache in Forschung und Lehre*
Women Germ Yearbook	*Women in German Yearbook: Feminist Studies and German Culture*
Women's Stud	*Women's Studies: An Interdisciplinary Journal*
World Lit Today	*World Literature Today: A Literary Quarterly of the University of Oklahoma*

World Lit Written Engl	*World Literature Written in English*
Writers' Forum	*Writers' Forum* (Colorado Springs)
Yale J Criticism	*Yale Journal of Criticism*
	Yiddish
	Zeitschrift für Deutsche Philologie

INDEX OF SHORT STORY WRITERS